The mini **Ro**

Pa

written and researched by

Ruth Blackmore and James McConnachie

with additional research by

Roger Norum

NEW YORK • LONDON • DELHI

www.roughguides.com

Contents

◀◀ Bofinger: a great Parisian brasserie ◀ The Eiffel Tower

Introduction to Paris

No visitor sees Paris for the first time – images of the city are endlessly reproduced on calendars and postcards around the world, and it has been the setting for countless films and novels. Yet Paris is still capable of taking your breath away. Nothing quite prepares you for the full impact of the Eiffel Tower up close, the splendour of the vista leading from the Louvre up the Champs Élysées to the Arc de Triomphe, or the grandeur of Notre Dame towering above the Seine. Paris excels in these great architectural set pieces. Just about every ruler has wanted to leave the stamp of their authority on the city – seen in the elegant royal squares of Place de la Concorde and Place des Vosges, Napoleon's imperial edifices and the bold *Grands Projets* of President Mitterrand, most famously his glass pyramid in the Louvre.

With all its monuments, Paris can seem inhumanly magnificent at times, yet it's also made up of numerous *quartiers*, operating on a human scale, where life revolves around the local boulangerie and café. In fact this is where much of the appeal of Paris lies. It can feel like a collection of little villages, full of atmospheric streets, charming architectural details, traditional cafés and independent shops.

Much of the allure and romance of the city stems from the days when it was the artistic and intellectual capital of the world. At the beginning of the twentieth century, artists such as Picasso and Modigliani flocked here, and writers Ernest Hemingway and Scott Fitzgerald made it their home for a while. Jazz musicians, such as Sidney Béchet, fleeing racism in America, found a haven in the city, as did political exiles – White Russians escaping communism and Jews seeking refuge from Hitler.

▼ Chic Paris shopping

Partly as a legacy of its years of artistic pre-eminence and partly as a result of Napoleon's acquisitive tendencies, Paris has an **art collection** that's second to none. The greatest works are spread among the Louvre, Musée d'Orsay and the Pompidou Centre, but some of the most satisfying places to visit are the numerous smaller museums, many of which are dedicated to individual artists. Some even incorporate the artist's original studio.

The city is equally well endowed with **restaurants and cafés**, ranging from ultra-modern fashion temples to traditional, mirrored palaces, and from tiny *bistrots* where the emphasis is all on the cooking to bustling Vietnamese diners. You could blow out on the meal of a liftetime in one of the city's famed gastronomic restaurants or sample any number of cheeses and *saucissons* from one of the many open-air markets.

After dark, Paris's theatres and concert halls host inventive and

▲ Fine chocolates, Debauve & Gallais

world-leading productions of **theatre** and **dance**, while many classical concerts take place in fine settings, such as churches and museums. **Jazz and world music** have a strong following, with many Malian and Algerian stars choosing to base themselves in the capital, reflecting France's strong links with these countries. Above all, Paris is a real **cinema** capital, with well over three hundred *salles*.

What to see

The city is divided into twenty arrondissements, or districts, which spiral out from the centre in a clockwise direction. The central arrondissements (1er–8e) contain the main sights and are the most alluring – you can easily explore this area on foot. Through the middle of the city flows the **Seine**, spanned by 36 bridges. The river encircles two islands at the heart of the capital: the **Ile de la Cité**, the kernel from which Paris grew, is the site of the Gothic cathedral of **Notre Dame** and the **Sainte-Chapelle**, renowned for its magnificent stained-glass windows, while the smaller **Ile Saint-Louis** is packed with handsome town houses and fringed with leafy *quais*.

North of the river, the Right Bank (*rive droite*) is characterized by broad avenues, lined with neoclassical buildings, radiating out from grand squares. The chief attraction here is the splendid **Louvre** palace and museum. Extending from the Louvre west is the city's longest and grandest vista – the Voie Triomphale – incorporating some of the capital's most famous landmarks: the **Tuileries** gardens, the Champs-Élysées, the **Arc de Triomphe** and the **Grande Arche de la Défense**. The area around the **Champs-Élysées** is currently one of the city's hottest spots, a hub of new and fashionable bars, cafés and shops.

North of the Louvre lies the commercial and financial quarter, bounded by the busy **Grands Boulevards**. Here you'll find the large department stores Galeries Lafayette and Printemps, as well as smaller and more unusual boutiques hidden away in the *passages*, nineteenth-century shopping arcades. More mainstream stores congregate in the 1970s **Les Halles** underground shopping complex, weathering badly compared to its neighbour the **Pompidou Centre**, which still wows visitors with its radical "inside-out" architecture and houses a superb collection of modern art. To the east of the Louvre, the **Marais** was the pres-

▲ View from Pont Alexandre III

▼ View from the Tour Montparnasse

tige address in the seventeenth century; along with the **Bastille** next door, it's now one of the most exciting areas of the city, alive with trendy shops, cafés and nightlife.

The south bank of the river, or Left Bank (*rive gauche*), is quite different in character from the Right Bank, quieter and more village-like. The **Quartier Latin** is the traditional domain of the intelligentsia, along with **St-Germain**, which becomes progressively snootier as you as you travel west towards the ministries, embassies and museums that surround the **Eiffel Tower**. Once you move towards glitzy **Montparnasse** and the southern swathe of the Left Bank, high-rise flats alternate with charming bourgeois neighbourhoods.

Back on the Right Bank, many of the outer or higher-number arrondissements were once outlying villages, and were gradually absorbed by the expanding city in the nineteenth century – some, such as **Montmartre** in the north, **Belleville** on the eastern edges, and **Passy** in the west, have succeeded in maintaining something of their village identity. The areas to the east were traditionally poor and working class, while those to the west were affluent – divisions that to some extent hold true today.

When to go

Spring is deservedly the classic time to visit Paris, when the weather is mild, with bright days balanced by rain showers. **Autumn**, similarly mild, and winter can be very rewarding, but on overcast days – all too common – the city can feel very melancholy; **winter** sun on the other hand is the city's most flattering light, and hotels and restaurants are relatively uncrowded in this season. By contrast, high **summer** is not the best time to go: large numbers of Parisians desert the capital between July 15 and the end of August for the beach or mountains and many restaurants and shops close down for much of this period.

Paris's climate

	F° Average daily		C° Average daily		Rainfall Average monthly	
	max	min	max	min	in	mm
Jan	43	34	6	1	2.2	56
Feb	45	34	7	1	1.8	46
March	54	39	12	4	1.4	35
April	60	43	16	6	1.7	42
May	68	49	20	10	2.2	57
June	73	55	23	13	2.1	54
July	76	58	25	15	2.3	59
Aug	75	58	24	14	2.5	64

13

things not to miss

It's not possible to see everything that Paris has to offer in one trip – and we don't suggest you try. What follows is a selective taste of the city's highlights: its best landmarks, most engaging museums, and liveliest neighbourhoods. They're arranged in five colour-coded categories, which you can browse through to find the very best things to see and experience. All highlights have a page reference to take you straight into the guide, where you can find out more.

01 Brasseries Page **192** • The combination of antique décor, the hum of conversation and classic dishes makes a meal at one of Paris's traditional brasseries a must.

02 Eiffel Tower Page **103** • So exhilarating, it's worth seeing during the day and at night-time, too.

03 Bastille bars Page **233** • After dark, the Bastille quarter comes alive with great bars and trendy clubs.

05 Markets Page **264** • Paris's street-markets are living testimony to the city's love of food, and great places for people-watching.

07 Sainte-Chapelle Page **30** • The soaring walls of this Gothic chapel are one intense blaze of stained glass.

04 Jardin du Luxembourg Page **95** • A favourite with students, families and visitors alike, the Luxembourg gardens is the largest and loveliest of central Paris's parks.

06 Musée d'Orsay Page **99** • A brilliantly converted railway station makes a magnificent setting for the works of the French Impressionists and their contemporaries.

08 Pompidou Centre Page **66** • The inside-out, multi-coloured architecture of the Pompidou Centre is a superb advert for the museum of modern art inside.

09 Musée Rodin Page **108** • Rodin's most intimate and intense sculptures are housed in an exquisite eighteenth-century mansion.

11 Père Lachaise Page **137** • The last resting place of Paris's famous – and infamous – dead is a wonderful place for a wander.

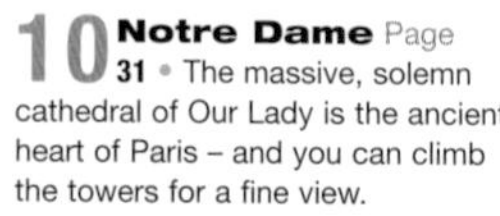

10 Notre Dame Page **31** • The massive, solemn cathedral of Our Lady is the ancient heart of Paris – and you can climb the towers for a fine view.

12 The Louvre Page **35** • More than the *Mona Lisa* and the glass pyramid: the Louvre is simply the greatest art gallery in the world, and a fine museum of antiquities to boot.

13 Place des Vosges Page **77** • A serene architectural gem from the seventeenth century: pink, arcaded townhouses surround a lovely garden square.

Basics

Basics

Arrival

It's easy to get from both of Paris's main airports to the city centre using the efficient public transport links. The budget-airline airport, Beauvais, is served by buses. If you're arriving by train, of course, it's easier still: just get on the métro.

By Air

The two main Paris **airports** dealing with international flights are Roissy-Charles de Gaulle and Orly. Information on them can be found on Ⓦwww.adp.fr. A third airport, Beauvais, is used by low-cost airline Ryanair.

Roissy-Charles de Gaulle Airport

Some 23km to the northeast of the city, **Roissy-Charles de Gaulle Airport** (24hr information in English ①01.48.62.22.80), usually referred to simply as Charles de Gaulle and abbreviated to CDG or Paris-CDG, has three terminals, CDG1, CDG2 and CDG3, linked by a shuttle bus; when you leave, make sure you check which terminal your flight departs from.

There are various ways of getting to the centre of Paris, but the simplest is on **RER line B**, part of the suburban train network (see p.19), which takes thirty minutes (every 12min 5am–midnight; €8 one-way). You can pick it up direct from CDG2 and CDG3, but from CDG1 you have to get a shuttle bus (*navette*) to the RER station first. The train stops at Gare du Nord, Châtelet-les-Halles, St-Michel and Denfert-Rochereau, all of which have métro stations for onward travel, which is included in the price of the ticket.

Various **bus companies** provide services to city-centre locations, but they're slightly more expensive than Roissyrail, and may take longer. A more useful alternative is the Blue Vans door-to-door, round-the-clock **minibus service** (from €14.50 per head if there are two or more people, from €22 for a single person; no extra charge for luggage; ①01.30.11.13.00,

Ⓦwww.bluvan.fr). Book at least a week in advance online to get the lowest fares.

Taxis into central Paris from CDG cost around €50 during the day and around €60 at night (7pm–7am), on Sundays and public holidays, with an extra charge of €1 for each item of heavy luggage. The journey to the city centre should take between fifty minutes and an hour. Note that if your flight gets in after midnight, a taxi or pre-booked Blue Van is your only means of transport.

Orly Airport

Orly Airport (information in English daily 6am–11.30pm; Ⓣ01.49.75.15.15), 14km south of Paris, has two terminals, Orly Sud (south; for international flights) and Orly Ouest (west; for domestic flights), linked by shuttle bus, but easily walkable.

The easiest way into the centre is the fast **Orlyval train shuttle** link to RER line B station Antony, followed by métro connection stops at Denfert-Rochereau, St-Michel and Châtelet-les-Halles. It runs every four to eight minutes from 6am to 11pm (€9.05 one-way; 35min to Châtelet). Another service connecting with the RER is the **Orlyrail** bus-rail link; a shuttle bus takes you to RER line C station Pont de Rungis, from where the Orlyrail train leaves every fifteen to thirty minutes from 5am to 11.30pm for the Gare d'Austerlitz and other métro connection stops (€5.65 one-way; train 35min, total journey around 50min). Leaving Paris, the train runs from Gare d'Austerlitz from 5am to 12.20am.

A **taxi** will take around 35 minutes to the centre of Paris and cost around €35, slightly more at night, on Sundays and public holidays.

Disneyland Paris is linked by bus from both Charles de Gaulle and Orly airports; for details of these services, plus train links from the centre to the purpose-built Marne-La-Vallée TGV, see p.164.

Beauvais airport

Beauvais airport (Ⓣ08.92.68.20.66, Ⓦwww.aeroportbeauvais.com), 65km northwest of Paris, is served by Ryanair from Dublin, Shannon and Glasgow (Prestwick). **Coaches** (€13 one-way) shuttle between the airport and Porte

Maillot in the 17e arrondissement, connected by métro line 1 with the centre, and take about an hour. The coach leaves approximately twenty minutes after the flight has arrived and three hours and fifteen minutes before the flight departs on the way back. Tickets can be bought online via the airport's web address (see above), at Arrivals or from the Beauvais shop at 1 boulevard Pershing, near the Porte Maillot métro/RER stop.

By rail

Eurostar trains (Ⓣ08.36.35.35.39, Ⓦwww.eurostar.com) terminate at **Gare du Nord**, rue Dunkerque, in the northeast of the city – a bustling convergence of international, long-distance and suburban trains, the métro, RER and several bus routes. Coming off the train, turn left for the métro and the RER, right for taxis (a sample price would be €10 to a hotel in the 4e) and the secure left luggage (daily 6.15am–11.15pm; €3.50–9.50 depending on the locker size), both down the escalators opposite the Avis car rental desk.

The Gare du Nord is also the arrival point for trains from Calais and other north-European countries. Paris has five other mainline train stations, part of the national SNCF network. On the Right Bank, the **Gare de l'Est** (place du 11-Novembre-1918, 10e) serves eastern France and central and eastern Europe; the **Gare St-Lazare** (place du Havre, 8e) is for trains to the Normandy coast and Dieppe; and the **Gare de Lyon** (place Louis-Armand, 12e) receives trains from Italy, Switzerland and southeast France. South of the river, the **Gare Montparnasse** on boulevard de Vaugirard, 15e, is the terminus for Chartres, Brittany, the Atlantic coast and TGV lines from southwest France. **Gare d'Austerlitz**, on boulevard de l'Hôpital, 13e, serves the Loire Valley and the Dordogne. The motorail station, **Gare de Paris-Bercy**, is down the tracks from the Gare de Lyon on boulevard de Bercy, 12e.

By road

If you're arriving by **bus** – international or domestic – you'll almost certainly arrive at the main **gare routière** at 28 avenue du Général-de-Gaulle, Bagnolet, on the eastern edge of the city; métro Gallieni (line 3) links it to the centre. If you're **driving** in yourself, don't try to go straight across the city to your destination. Use the ring road – the **boulevard périphérique** – to get to the *porte* nearest to your destination: it's much quicker, except at rush hour, and far easier to navigate.

City transport

Finding your way around Paris is remarkably easy, as the city proper, stripped of its suburbs, is compact and relatively small, with an integrated public transport system – the RATP (Régie Autonome des Transports Parisiens). The system is cheap, fast and meticulously signposted, comprising buses, underground métro and suburban express trains, known as RER (Réseau Express Régional) trains. Even the Batobus along the river comes under the same network. For information on all RATP services visit ⓦwww.ratp.fr.

At its widest point, Paris is only about 12km across, which, at a brisk pace, is not much more than a pleasant two-hour walk.

Tickets and Passes

The standard RATP ticket (€1.40) is valid for any one-way métro, bus or RER express rail ride anywhere within the city limits and immediate suburbs (zones 1 and 2). Only one ticket is ever needed on the métro system, but you can't switch between buses or between bus and métro/RER on the same ticket. For a short stay in the city consider buying a reduced-price carnet of ten tickets (€10.70). Tickets are available at stations and *tabacs* (newsagent/tobacconist). Children under 4 travel free, and kids aged 4 to 11 pay half price.

If you're travelling beyond the city limits (zones 3 to 5), to La

Défense, for example, you'll need to buy a separate RER ticket. **Mobilis** day passes (€5.40) give unlimited access to métro, buses and RER trains within the city limits (zones 1 and 2). If you've arrived early in the week and are staying more than three days, it might be more economical to buy the **Carte Orange** weekly coupon (€15.70 for zones 1 and 2), which is valid for an unlimited number of journeys from Monday morning to Sunday evening; you can buy it at all métro stations and *tabacs* up until the Wednesday – you'll need a passport photo. On the métro you put the coupon through the turnstile slot; on a bus you show the whole *carte* to the driver as you board – don't put it into the punching machine. Note that the Carte Orange is being slowly phased out in favour of the new **Navigo** swipe card, which you simply press against (or wave next to) the magnetic reader on the ticket barrier; see Ⓦwww.ratp.fr for the latest information.

Paris Visite cards can be good value if bought at the airport when you arrive, as they cover all travel within the city limits plus the airport rail links, Versailles and Disneyland Paris, as well as offering one or two minor reductions on a few more touristy attractions. They cost €8.35, €13.70, €18.25 and €26.65 for one, two, three and five days respectively, and can begin on any day. A half-price under-12s version is also available. You can buy these passes at métro stations and from tourist offices or, if you're travelling to Paris by Eurostar, the information point in the departure lounge area of Waterloo International.

The métro and RER

The **métro** (M°), combined with the **RER** suburban express lines, is the simplest way of moving around the city. Both run from around 5.30am to roughly 12.30am. Lines are colour-coded and designated by numbers for the métro and letters for the RER. Platforms are signposted using the name of the terminus station; travelling north from Montparnasse to Châtelet, for example, you need to follow the signs for "Direction Porte-de-Clignancourt", at the northernmost end of the line. For RER journeys beyond the city, make sure that the station you want is illuminated on the platform display board. **Stations** are evenly spaced and usually very close together, though interchanges can involve a lot of legwork.

Free **maps** of varying sizes and detail are available at most stations. The most useful is the *Grand Plan de Paris numéro 2*, which overlays the métro, RER and bus routes on a map of the city, so you can see exactly how transport lines and streets match up. If you just want a handy pocket-sized métro/bus map ask for the *Petit Plan de Paris* or the even smaller *Paris Plan de Poche*. In addition, there's a big map of the network displayed in every station.

A colour map of the Paris métro can be found at the back of the *Guide*.

Buses

Buses are often neglected in favour of the métro, but can be very useful where the métro journey doesn't quite work. Every bus stop displays the numbers of the buses that stop there and a map showing all the stops on the route. Free **route maps** are available from métro stations. Generally speaking, buses run from around 6.30am to 8.30pm, with some services continuing to 12.30am. Around half the lines do not operate on Sundays and holidays, or run a reduced service.

Night buses (Noctilien; ⓦwww.noctilien.fr) ply 35 routes at least every hour from 12.30am to 5.30am. On Fridays and Saturdays, the main routes are served every ten to fifteen minutes. Among the most useful are N01 and N02, which run a circular route linking the main nightlife areas (Champs-Elysées, Bastille, Pigalle, etc) and a number of train stations; they run every ten minutes on weekends (Fri night to Sun morning) and every twenty minutes during the rest of the week. Tickets (€1.40) are interchangeable with métro tickets, and can be bought from the driver; make sure you put your ticket in the little stamping machine at the entrance to validate it. All passes (Mobilis, Paris Visite and Carte Orange) are valid.

Some bus routes are particularly good for **sightseeing**, notably bus #29, which has an open platform at the back, and traverses the Right Bank from the Opéra to the Bastille; bus #24, along the Left Bank; and bus #73, down the Voie Triomphale. A number of bus routes are **wheelchair accessible**; for a full list visit ⓦwww.infomobi.com.

Taxis

The best place to get a **taxi** is at one of the taxi ranks (*arrêt taxi*) found at major junctions or railway stations – usually more effective than trying to hail one from the street. Taxis can be any colour but carry distinctive roof lights – the large white light signals the taxi is free; the orange light means it's in use. You can also call a taxi out for a fee of roughly €2 – phone numbers are shown at the taxi ranks, or try Taxis Bleus (ⓣ08.91.70.10.10) or Alpha Taxis (ⓣ01.45.85.85.85). That said, finding a taxi at lunch-time and any time after 7pm can be almost impossible.

Charges – always metered – are fairly reasonable: between €7 and €12 for a central daytime journey, though considerably more if you call one out. Different day/night and city/suburb rates apply per kilometre and the minimum fare for any journey is €5.20. One heavy piece of luggage is allowed free; €0.90 is levied per extra item. Taxi drivers do not have to take more than three passengers (they prefer not to have anyone sitting in the front); if a fourth passenger is accepted, an extra charge of €2.70 is added.

Batobus

A pleasant alternative to road and rail, the **Batobus** boat shuttle (ⓦwww.batobus.com) operates from early February to December, stopping at eight points along the Seine between Port de la Bourdonnais (M° Eiffel Tower/Trocadéro) and Port des Champs-Elysées (M° Champs-Elysées). Halts include the Louvre, Notre-Dame and Musée d'Orsay. Boats run every fifteen to twenty-five minutes from 10am to 10pm from May to September, from 10am to 7pm in March, April and October and from 10.30am to 4.30pm in November, December and February. The total journey time is around thirty minutes, and tickets (€7.50) are valid for one journey for a maximum of four stops. There is also an €11 day pass, a two-day pass for €13 and a five-day one at €16. Information on Bateaux-Mouches and other boat trips is given in "Activities" on p.279.

Information

The main Paris tourist office is at 25 rue des Pyramides, 1er (daily 9am–7pm; ⓣ08.92.68.31.12, ⓦwww.paris-info.com; M° Pyramides/RER Auber). There are branch offices at 11 rue Scribe, 9e (Mon–Sat 9am–6.30pm; M° Pyramides); at the Eiffel Tower (daily 11am–6.30pm); 21 place du Tertre, 18e (daily 10am–7pm; M° Abbesses); the Gare du Nord (daily 8am–6pm); and at the Gare de Lyon (Mon–Sat 8am–6pm) by the Grandes Lignes arrivals. They give out information on Paris and the suburbs, can book hotel accommodation and also sell the Carte Musées et Monuments (see opposite) and travel passes. It's also worth picking up a free map of Paris.

Alternative sources of information are the **Hôtel de Ville information office** – Bureau d'Accueil – at 29 rue de Rivoli (Mon–Sat 10am–6pm; ⓣ01.42.76.43.43, ⓦwww.paris.fr; M° Hôtel-de-Ville), and the **Espace du Tourisme d'Île de France**, within the Carrousel du Louvre, underground below the triumphal arch at the east end of the Tuileries (daily 10am–6pm; ⓣ01.44.50.19.98), which has information on the region around Paris.

For detailed what's-on information it's worth buying one of Paris's inexpensive weekly **listings magazines** from a newsagent or kiosk. The best and glossiest is *Zurban* (ⓦwww.zurban.com), though *Pariscope* has a comprehensive section on films. The free monthly magazine *Paris Voice* (ⓦwww.parisvoice.com), available online and from English-language bookshops, has good listings and reviews as well as ads for flats and courses.

The **maps** in this guide and the free *Paris Map* (see above) should be adequate for a short sightseeing stay, but for a more detailed map your best bet is one of the pocket-sized *L'indispensable* series booklets, sold everywhere in Paris.

Museums and monuments

Entrance tickets to **museums and monuments** can really add up, though the permanent collections at all municipal museums are **free** all year round, while all national museums (including the Louvre, Musée d'Orsay and Pompidou Centre) are free on the first Sunday of the month – see Ⓦwww.rmn.fr for a full list.

Each institution has its own policy for **children** and **teenagers**. In many museums under-18s go free, while all monuments are free for under-12s. Under-4s almost always get free admission. Half-price or reduced admission is normally available for 5- to 18-year-olds and students, though some commercial attractions charge adult rates from 12. The ISIC card (Ⓦwww.isiccard.com) is often the only card accepted for reduced-price **student** admission – often around a third off. For those **over 60 or 65**, depending on the institution (regardless of whether you are still working or not), reductions are sometimes available; you'll need to carry your passport around with you as proof of age.

If you are going to do a lot of museum duty, consider buying the **Carte Musées et Monuments** (€18 one-day, €36 three-day). Available from the tourist office, RER/métro stations and museums, as well as the Eurostar terminal at London Waterloo, it's valid for seventy museums and monuments in and around Paris, and allows you to bypass ticket queues.

Opening hours and holidays

Most shops and businesses in Paris are open from 8 or 9am through to 6.30 or 7.30pm. Bigger stores open Monday to Saturday, but smaller shops may close on Monday. Designer-type shops in trendier areas such as the Marais or Abbesses often open on Sundays but close on Monday and sometimes Tuesday as well. Note that smaller enterprises may close for lunch between roughly 12.30 and 2pm.

Restaurants, bars and cafés often close on Sunday or Monday, and quite a few restaurants also close on Saturdays. It's common for bars and cafés to stay open to 2am, and even extend hours on a Friday and Saturday night, closing earlier on Sunday. Restaurants won't usually serve after 10pm, though some brasseries cater for night owls and serve meals till the early hours. Many restaurants and shops take a holiday between the middle of July and the end of August.

Don't be caught out by museum closing days – usually Monday or Tuesday and sometimes both. France celebrates eleven national holidays: January 1; Easter Monday; May 1; May 8; Ascension Day; Whitsun; Whit Monday; July 14; August 15; November 11; December 25. Note that the opening hours we give for Sundays also apply to these public holidays, and that with three and sometimes four holidays, May is a particularly festive month.

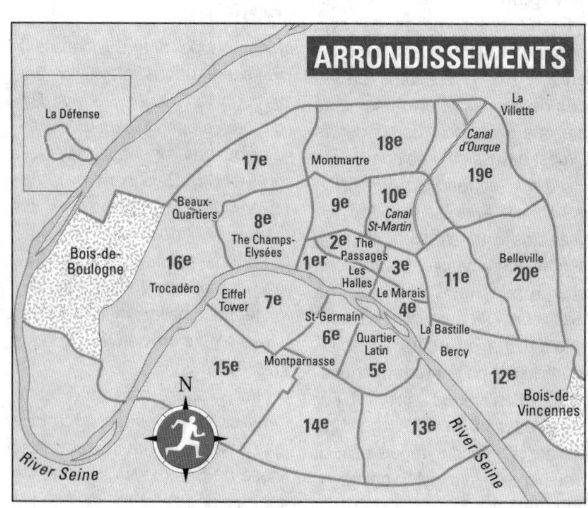

Guide

Guide

1

The Islands

There's no better place to start a tour of Paris than with its two river islands, the charming, village-like **Île St-Louis** and the **Île de la Cité**, the city's ancient core, harbouring the capital's most treasured monuments – the Gothic cathedral of Notre-Dame and the stunning Sainte-Chapelle.

Île de la Cité

Map 2, G8. M° Cité & M°/RER St-Michel.

The **Île de la Cité** is where Paris began. It was settled in around 300 BC by a Celtic tribe, the Parisii, and in 52 BC was overrun by Julius Caesar's troops. A natural defensive site commanding a major east–west river trade route, the island was an obvious candidate for a bright future – the Romans garrisoned it and laid out one of their standard military town plans. Lutetia Parisiorum, as the settlement was named by the Romans, developed into an important administrative centre and was endowed with a palace-fortress that served as the stronghold of the Merovingian kings, then of the counts of Paris, who in 987 became kings of France. The Frankish kings set about transforming the old Gallo-Roman fortress into a splendid palace, of which the Gothic **Sainte-Chapelle** and **Conciergerie** prison survive today. At the other end of the island, they erected the great cathedral of

Notre-Dame. By the early thirteenth century the tiny Île de la Cité teemed with life, somehow managing to accommodate twelve parishes, not to mention numerous chapels and monasteries.

Today it takes quite a stretch of the imagination to picture what this medieval city must have looked like, for most of it was erased in the nineteenth century by the over-zealous Baron Haussmann, Napoléon III's Préfet de la Seine (a post equivalent to mayor of Paris – for more on Haussmann see Contexts p.323). He demolished the homes of around 25,000 people, as well as churches, shops and ninety lanes – though it has to be said that these narrow, dark streets were notoriously squalid and dangerous at night. In their place Haussmann raised several vast Neoclassical edifices, including the Préfecture de Police, an extension to the Palais de Justice law courts and the Hôtel-Dieu hospital. He also cleared the space in front of the cathedral of **Notre-Dame**, creating an unnecessarily large square with shades of a military parade ground about it, but it does at least allow uncluttered views of the cathedral's facade. The few corners of the island that escaped Haussmann's attentions include the leafy **square du Vert-Galant** and charming **place Dauphine**.

The island's chief attractions, the cathedral, Conciergerie and Sainte-Chapelle, inevitably attract large crowds and it's not unusual to have to queue for entry. Things are generally a bit quieter if you visit in the early morning or late afternoon.

Pont-Neuf and square du Vert-Galant

Map 2, F7 & E6. M° Pont-Neuf.

A popular approach to the Île de la Cité is via the graceful, twelve-arched **Pont-Neuf**, linking the island's western tip with both the Left and Right banks. Built in 1607 by Henri

IV, it was the first in Paris not to have the usual medieval complement of houses built on it, hence the name "new bridge". This daring construction was, in its day, as potent a symbol of Paris as the Eiffel Tower is today. Henri is commemorated with a bronze equestrian statue halfway across and also lends his nickname to the **square du Vert-Galant**, enclosed within the triangular "stern" of the island and reached via steps leading down behind the statue. "Vert-Galant", meaning a "green" or "lusty gentleman", is a reference to Henri's legendary amorous exploits, and he would no doubt have approved of this tranquil, tree-lined garden, a popular haunt of lovers; the prime spot to make for is the knoll dotted with trees at the extreme point of the island, where you can watch the sun set over the Seine. At the other end of the garden is the dock for the river boats, the Bateaux-Vedettes du Pont-Neuf.

For more information on river boats, see p.279.

Place Dauphine

Map 2, F7. M° Cité.

On the eastern side of the bridge, across the street from the statue of Henri IV, seventeenth-century houses flank the entrance to **place Dauphine**, one of the city's most secluded and attractive squares. Here, the noise of traffic recedes and is replaced by nothing more intrusive than the gentle tap of boules being played in the shade of the giant chestnuts. At the far end of the square looms the hulking mass of the **Palais de Justice**, the site of the old palace lived in by the Frankish kings until Étienne Marcel's bloody revolt in 1358 frightened them off to the greater security of the Louvre.

1 Sainte-Chapelle

Map 2, F7. Daily: April–Sept 9.30am–6.30pm; Oct–March 10am–5pm; €6.10, combined ticket with Conciergerie €9; M° Cité.

Within the Palais de Justice complex and accessed from the boulevard du Palais, the only part of the old palace that remains in its entirety is Louis IX's chapel, the **Sainte-Chapelle**, its delicate spire soaring above the Palais buildings. It was built in 1242–48 to house a collection of holy relics, including the supposed Crown of Thorns and fragments of the True Cross, that Louis had bought for extortionate rates – far more than it cost to build the Sainte-Chapelle – from the bankrupt empire of Byzantium. Though damaged in the Revolution, the chapel was sensitively restored in the mid-nineteenth century and remains one of the finest achievements of French High Gothic. There are actually two chapels. The simple **lower chapel**, which would have been used by servants, gives no clue as to the splendour that lies ahead in the upper chapel, a truly dazzling sight, its walls made almost entirely of magnificent stained glass. The seemingly pencil-thin supports, made possible by the minimal use of structural masonry, coupled with the sheer vastness of the windows, combine to create what appears to be a huge uninterrupted expanse of glowing jewel-like blues, reds and emerald-greens. The windows tell the story of the Book of Genesis (on the left), followed by various other books of the Old Testament, continuing with the Passion of Christ (east end), the history of the relics (on the right) and ending with the Book of Revelation in the rose window. Each window panel is read from the bottom up and from left to right.

The Sainte-Chapelle is the splendid setting for regular evening classical music **concerts**. Tickets cost €10–25 and can be booked in advance from branches of FNAC (see pp.257 & 263) or Virgin Megastore (see p.263), though you stand a good chance of getting in on the door if you turn up half an hour or so beforehand.

The Conciergerie

Map 2, G7. Daily: March–Oct 9.30am–6pm; Nov–Feb 9am–5pm; €6.10, combined ticket with Ste-Chapelle €9; M° Cité.

Also in the Palais de Justice complex, at 2 boulevard du Palais, is the medieval **Conciergerie**, the oldest prison in Paris. One of its towers, on the corner of the quai de l'Horloge, bears Paris's first public clock, built in 1370 and now fully restored. The Conciergerie was where Marie-Antoinette and, in their turn, the leading figures of the Revolution were incarcerated before execution; you can see the queen's cell as well as various other reconstructed rooms, such as the innocent-sounding "salle de toilette", where the condemned had their hair cropped and shirt collars ripped in preparation for the guillotine. The other main point of interest is the enormous, vaulted, late-Gothic **Salle des Gens d'Armes**, canteen and recreation room of the royal household staff.

The Cathédrale de Notre-Dame

Map 2, H8. Cathedral daily 7.45am–6.45pm; free. Towers daily 9.30am–7.30pm, last entry 6.45pm; €5.50. ⓦwww.cathedraledeparis.com; M° Cité & M°/RER St-Michel.

The **Cathédrale de Notre-Dame** is one of the masterpieces of the Gothic age. The Romanesque influence is still visible, not least in its solid H-shaped west front, but the overriding impression is one of lightness and grace, created in part by the filigree work of the rose windows and galleries and the exuberant flying buttresses. Built on the site of the Merovingian cathedral of Saint-Étienne, Notre-Dame was begun in 1160 under the auspices of Bishop de Sully and completed around 1345. The cathedral's seminaries became an ecclesiastical powerhouse, churning out six popes in the course of the thirteenth and fourteenth centuries, though it subsequently lost some of its pre-eminence to other sees, such as Rheims and St-Denis. The building fell into decline over the centuries, suffering its worst depredations during the Revolution when the frieze of Old Testament kings on the facade was damaged by enthusiasts who mistook them for the kings of France.

It was only in the 1820s that the cathedral was at last given a much-needed **restoration**, a task entrusted to the great architect-restorer Viollet-le-Duc, who carried out a thorough – arguably too thorough – renovation, remaking much of the statuary on the facade (the originals can be seen in the Musée National du Moyen-Age, see p.84) and adding the steeple and baleful-looking gargoyles, which you can see close up if you brave the ascent of the **towers**.

The facade was given a thorough clean in the run-up to the millennium, removing years of accumulated grime and allowing the magnificent **carvings** over the portals to make their full impact. Over the central portal is the *Day of Judgement*: the lower frieze is a whirl of movement as the dead rise up from their graves, while above Christ presides, sending those on his right to heaven and those on his left to grisly torments in hell. The left portal shows Mary being crowned by Christ, with scenes of her life in the lower friezes, while the right portal depicts the Virgin enthroned and, below, episodes from the life of St Anne (Mary's mother) and the life of Christ.

Inside, you're immediately struck by the dramatic contrast between the darkness of the nave and the light falling on the first great clustered pillars of the choir, which emphasizes the sacred nature of the sanctuary. It is the end walls of the transepts that admit all this light, as they are nearly two-thirds glass, including two magnificent rose windows coloured in imperial purple. These windows, the vaulting and the soaring shafts reaching to the springs of the vaults, are all definite Gothic elements, though there remains a strong sense of Romanesque in the stout round pillars of the nave.

Free guided **tours** (1hr–1hr 30min) take place in English on Wednesday and Thursday at noon and on Saturday at 2.30pm; gather at the welcome desk near the entrance.

Kilomètre zéro and the crypte archéologique

Notre-Dame isn't only at the heart of Paris, it's also the symbolic centre of France – outside on the pavement by the west door is a spot, marked by a bronze star, known as **kilomètre zéro**, from which all main-road distances in France are calculated. At the other end of the square, steps lead down to the atmospherically lit **crypte archéologique** (Tues–Sun 10am–6pm; €3.30) a large excavated area revealing remains of the original cathedral, as well as vestiges of the streets and houses that once clustered around Notre-Dame: most are medieval, but some date as far back as Gallo-Roman times.

The Mémorial de la Déportation

Map 2, H9. Daily 10am–noon & 2–5pm; free; M° Cité.

At the eastern tip of the island is the **Mémorial de la Déportation**, the symbolic tomb of the 200,000 French who died in Nazi concentration camps during World War II – Resistance fighters, Jews and forced labourers. Their moving memorial, barely visible above ground, is a kind of bunker-crypt studded with thousands of points of light representing the dead. Above the exit are the words "Forgive. Do not forget …".

Île St-Louis

Map 2, I8 & I9. M° Pont-Marie/Sully-Morland.

Edged with attractive tree-lined quais, the compact **Île St-Louis** feels somewhat removed from the rest of Paris and has a village-like air about it. Unlike its larger neighbour, the Île de la Cité, it has no monuments or sights as such, save for a small **museum** at 6 quai d'Orléans, devoted to the Romantic Polish poet **Adam Mickiewicz** (Thurs 2–6pm or by appointment on ☎01.43.54.35.61; free). Instead you'll find austerely beautiful houses on single-lane streets, assorted restaurants and cafés, and interesting little shops.

For centuries, Île-St-Louis was nothing but swampy pastureland, owned by Notre-Dame, until Christopher Marie, the seventeenth-century version of a real-estate developer, had the bright idea of filling it with elegant mansions, so that by 1660 the island was transformed to what we see today. In the 1840s, the island became a popular Bohemian hang-out. The Club des Hachichins, whose members included Baudelaire, Dumas, Delacroix and Daumier, met every month and got high on hashish at the **Hôtel Lauzun**, 17 quai d'Anjou. Baudelaire, in fact, lived for a while in the attic where he wrote *Les Fleurs du Mal.* The *hôtel*, built in 1657, has an intact interior, complete with splendid trompe l'oeil decorations; prearranged group visits are possible (☎01.42.76.57.99).

2

The Louvre

The palace of the Louvre cuts a magnificent Classical swathe right through the centre of the city – a fitting setting for one of the world's grandest and most gracious art galleries. Originally little more than a feudal fortress, begun by Philippe-Auguste in the 1190s, the castle was enlarged by Charles V in the 1360s. However, it wasn't until 1546 that the first stones of the Louvre we see today were laid. Over the next century and a half, France's rulers continued to enlarge and aggrandize their palace without significantly altering its style, and the result is an architecturally harmonious building entirely suited to its role as the most historic of Parisian landmarks.

The origins of the Musée du Louvre lie in the personal art collection of François I. While the royal academy mounted exhibitions, known as salons, in the palace as early as 1725, the Louvre was only opened as an art gallery in 1793, the year of Louis XVI's execution. Within a decade, Napoleon's wagonloads of war booty transformed the Louvre's art collection into the world's largest – and not all the loot has been returned.

Napoleon's pink marble Arc du Carrousel has always looked a bit out of place at the end of the main courtyard, but the emperor's nephew, Napoléon III, returned to form in the late nineteenth century, with the conservative courtyard facades of the Richelieu and Denon wings. It was only in

1989, when I.M. Pei's controversial Pyramide erupted from the centre of the Cour Napoléon like a visitor from another architectural planet, that the Louvre received its first radical makeover. Since then, the museum has palpably basked in its status as a truly first-class art gallery.

Tickets and practicalities

The **main entrance** is via the Pyramide, but if it's raining or the queues look too long make for the **alternative entrances**: via the Porte des Lions, just east of the Pont Royal, or directly under the Arc du Carrousel; the latter can also be accessed from 99 rue de Rivoli and from the line #1 platform of the Palais Royal-Musée du Louvre métro stop. If you've already got a ticket or a museum pass (see p.23) you can also enter from the passage Richelieu. **Disabled access**

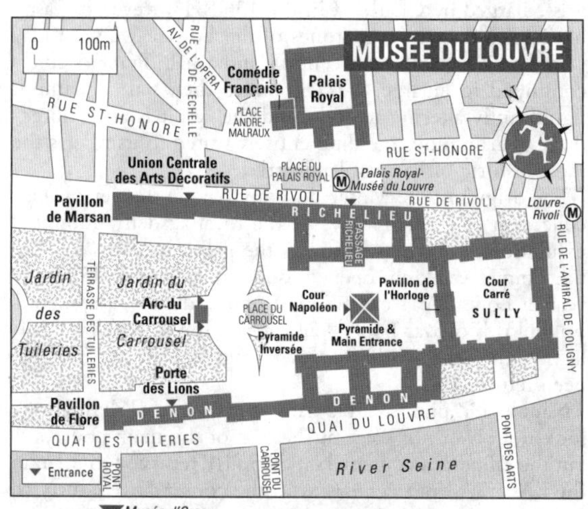

is via the futuristic rising and sinking column in the middle of the Pyramide.

Opening hours for the permanent collection are 9am to 6pm every day except Tuesday, when the museum is closed. On Wednesday and Friday the museum stays open till 9.45pm. Note that almost a quarter of the museum's rooms are closed one day a week on a rotating basis (see ⓦwww.louvre.fr for more details), though the most popular rooms are always open.

The **entry fee** is €8.50. Under-18s get in free at all times, and on the first Sunday of each month admission is free for everyone. **Tickets** can be bought in advance from branches of FNAC (see pp.257 & 263), Virgin Megastore (conveniently, there's one right outside the entrance under the Arc du Carrousel) and the big Parisian department stores. The ticket allows you to step outside for a break, though the museum itself has three good **cafés** – the relatively quiet *Café Richelieu* (first floor, Richelieu), the cosy *Café Denon* (lower ground floor, Denon) and the busier *Café Mollien* (first floor, Denon), which also has a summer terrace. The various cafés and restaurants directly under the Pyramide are less attractive.

Orientation and highlights

From the Hall Napoléon under the **Pyramide**, stairs lead into each of the three wings: Denon (south), Richelieu (north) and Sully (east, around the giant quadrangle of the Cour Carré). Few visitors will be able to resist the allure of the *Mona Lisa* (see pp.40–41), in the **Denon** wing, housed along with the rest of the Louvre's Italian paintings and sculptures and its large-scale French nineteenth-century canvases. A relatively peaceful alternative would be to focus on the grand chronologies of French painting and sculpture, in the **Richelieu** wing. For a complete change of scene, descend to the **Medieval Louvre** section on the lower ground floor of Sully where you'll find the dramatic stump of Philippe-Auguste's keep and vestiges of Charles V's medieval palace walls.

A **floor plan**, available free from the information booth in the Hall Napoléon, will help you find your way around. It's wise not to attempt to see too much – even if you spent the entire day here you'd only see a fraction of the collection. The museum's size does at least make it easy to get away from the crowds – beyond the Denon wing you can explore the Louvre in relative peace. For a really **quiet visit**, come for the evening opening on Wednesdays and Fridays.

Painting

The main chronological circuit of **French painting** begins on the second floor of the Richelieu wing. It traces the development of French painting from its edgy Pre-Renaissance beginnings through Classical bombast and on to ardent Romanticism, ending with Corot, whose airy landscapes anticipate the Impressionists. The preliminary Richelieu section is chiefly of interest for the portraits of French kings and the strange atmosphere of the two **Schools of Fontainebleau** (rooms 9 and 10). In a Second School piece from the 1590s, Gabrielle d'Estrées, the favourite of Henri IV, is shown sharing a bath with her sister, pinching her nipple as if plucking a cherry.

It's not until the seventeenth century, when Poussin breaks onto the scene (room 13), that the style known as **French Classicism** emerges. Poussin's *Arcadian Shepherds* shows four shepherds interpreting the inscription "et in arcadia ego" (I, too, in Arcadia) – meaning that death exists even in pastoral paradise. You'll need a healthy appetite for Classicism in the next suite of rooms, but there are some arresting portraits by Hyacinthe Rigaud and Philippe de Champaigne as well as some idiosyncratically-mystical works by Georges de la Tour.

Moving into the less severe **eighteenth century**, the more intimate paintings of Watteau come as a relief, as do Chardin's intense still lifes and the inspired, hasty rococo sketches by Fragonard known as the *Figures of Fantasy*. Immediately beyond, the chilly wind of **Neoclassicism** blows through the post-Revolution paintings of Gros, Gérard, Prud'hon, David and Ingres. This in turn contrasts with the more sentimental style launched by Greuze, which flows into the **Romanticism** of Géricault and Delacroix. The final set of rooms covers Millet, Corot and the **Barbizon school** of painting, the precursor of Impressionism. For anything later than 1848 you'll have to head over to the Musée d'Orsay (see p.99).

Northern European painting

The western end of Richelieu's second floor is given over to **German**, **Flemish** and **Dutch** paintings. Here you'll find no fewer than twelve paintings by Rembrandt – look out for *Bathsheba* and *The Supper at Emmaus* in room 31 – and two serene canvases from Vermeer, *The Astronomer* and *The Lacemaker*, in room 37. An awesome set of two-dozen works by Rubens can be found in the **Galerie Médicis** (room 18), the entire cycle dedicated to the glory of Queen Marie de Médicis.

The Grande Galerie

Over in the Denon wing, the first floor is dominated by the staggering **Italian collection**. The high-ceilinged **Salon Carré** (room 3) has been used to exhibit paintings since the first exhibition or "salon" of the Académie royale in 1725 and now displays thirteenth- to fifteenth-century works from Italian painters such as Giotto, Cimabue and Fra Angelico, as well as one of Uccello's panels depicting the *Battle of San Romano*.

To the west of the Salon, the famous **Grande Galerie**, originally built to link the palaces of the Louvre and the now-destroyed Tuileries, stretches into the distance. It begins with Mantegna's opulent *Madonna of Victory*, and continues through

Giovanni Bellini, Filippo Lippi, Raphael, Coreggio and Titian. Leonardo da Vinci's *Virgin of the Rocks*, *St John the Baptist* and *Virgin and Child with St Anne* are on display just after the first set of pillars, while the Mannerists make their entrance roughly halfway along.

The relatively small **Spanish Collection** is relegated to the far end of Denon but has a few gems, notably Murillo's tender *Beggar Boy*, and the *Marquise de Santa Cruz* amongst the Goya portraits.

Large-format French painting and the Mona Lisa

Running parallel to the Grande Galerie are two giant rooms labelled "large-format French paintings" on the plan. The

The Mona Lisa

The **Mona Lisa** receives some six million visitors a year, many of whom wonder how such a small, dark portrait acquired such amazing celebrity. The answer lies in the painting's story. It was probably brought to France by Leonardo himself, when he came to work for François I in 1516, but it remained largely neglected until the nineteenth-century poet and novelist Théophile Gautier turned his hand to a guidebook to the Louvre. Her "sinuous, serpentine mouth", he wrote, "turned up at the corners in a violet penumbra, mocks the viewer with such sweetness, grace and superiority that we feel timid, like schoolboys in the presence of a duchess".

In the Anglophone world the painting was made famous by the critic Walter Pater in 1869. According to Pater, her presence "is expressive of what in the ways of a thousand years men had come to desire". But the *Mona Lisa* only really hit the international big time when she was stolen by an Italian security guard in August 1911. By the time she was recovered, in December 1913, her face had graced the pages of endless books and newspapers. Then, in 1919, the Dadaist Marcel Duchamp bought a cheap postcard

Salle Mollien (room 75), dedicated to post-Revolution **French Nationalism**, boasts David's epic *Coronation of Napoleon I.* In the Salle Daru (room 77), early- to mid-nineteenth-century **Romanticism** is heralded by Géricault's dramatic *Raft of the Medusa*, showing shipwrecked survivors despairing as sails disappear over the horizon. The model for the dead figure lying face down with his arm extended was Delacroix, whose iconic *Liberty Leading the People* also hangs in this room.

After five years of restoration, the **Salle des Etats** (room 6) is once again the proud setting for Leonardo da Vinci's **Mona Lisa** (see box below). If you want to meet *la Joconde* without the usual flash-toting swarm for company, be the first to arrive, the last to leave, or schedule your visit for

reproduction, coloured in a goatee beard and scrawled underneath "L.H.O.O.Q.", which when pronounced in French translates as "she's got a hot ass". Since Duchamp, the Mona Lisa's celebrity has fed on itself, and critics have complained about the painting in vain. Bernard Berenson, for example, decided Lisa was "watchful, sly, secure, with a smile of anticipated satisfaction and a pervading air of hostile superiority", while Roberto Longhi claimed to prefer Renoir's women to this "wan fusspot".

In recent years, the *Mona Lisa*'s fame has only swelled as a result of her bit-part appearance in Dan Brown's conspiracy thriller, *The Da Vinci Code*, which suggests (among other wilder theories) that the *Mona Lisa* is a Leonardo self portrait in drag. (It is at least true that the artist was known for painting androgynous-looking figures.) Visitors today often find the painting surprisingly small – and very dark. Basically, it's filthy, and while the new, air-conditioned glass frame adds a corrective tint, no art restorer has yet dared to propose actually working on the picture. Eventually, time may force the museum's hand, as the thin poplar panel on which the image is painted is slowly warping.

one of the evening opening sessions. Elsewhere in the same room, you can't miss Paolo Veronese's huge *Marriage at Cana*.

Sculpture

French Sculpture is arranged on the lowest two levels of the Richelieu wing, with the more monumental pieces housed in two grand, glass-roofed courtyards. Many sculptures removed from the park at Marly grace the **Cour Marly**, notably the four triumphal equestrian statues known as the *Marly Horses*. The **Cour Puget** has Pierre Puget's dynamic *Milon de Crotone* as its centrepiece. The surrounding rooms trace the development of sculpture in France from painful Romanesque Crucifixions to smooth Neoclassicism. Among the startlingly realistic Gothic pieces, you can't miss the Burgundian *Tomb of Philippe Pot*. Towards the end of the course, however, you may find yourself crying out for an end to all the gracefully perfect nudes and grandiose busts of noblemen. The only real antidote is Rodin and you'll have to head west to the Musée d'Orsay (see p.99) or Musée Rodin (see p.108) to see any of his works, as he postdates the 1848 watershed.

Alternatively, make for the smaller, more intense **Italian sculpture** section in the long Galerie Mollien (room 4), on the ground and basement floors of Denon. Here you'll find two of Michelangelo's writhing *Slaves*, the anonymous *Veiled Woman* and Canova's irresistible *Cupid and Psyche*. In the old stables on the lower ground floor (room 1), you can admire early Italian sculpture, notably Duccio's virtuoso *Virgin and Child Surrounded by Angels*. For a more intimate approach, visit the **Tactile Gallery**, where you can run your hands over copies of some of the most important sculptures from the collection. In the small, adjacent rooms A–C you can seek out some severe but impressive **Gothic Virgins** from Flanders and Germany.

Objets d'art

The vast **Objets d'art** section, on the first floor of the Richelieu wing, presents the finest tapestries, ceramics, jewellery and furniture commissioned by France's wealthiest and most influential patrons. Walking through the entire 81-room chronology affords a powerful sense of the evolution of aesthetic taste at its most refined and opulent. The exception is the **Middle Ages** section, which is of a decidedly pious nature, while the apotheosis of the whole experience comes towards the end, as the circuit passes through the breathtakingly plush **apartments** of Napoléon III's Minister of State.

Antiquities

The enormous **Antiquities** collection practically forms a parallel museum of its own, taking up most of the Sully wing, aside from the top floor. **Oriental Antiquities** (Richelieu wing, ground floor) covers the sculptures, stone-carved writings, pottery and other relics of the Mesopotamian, Sumerian, Babylonian, Assyrian and Phoenician civilizations, plus the art of ancient Persia. Watch out for the black, two-metre-high *Code of Hammurabi*, a hugely important find from the Mesopotamian civilization, dating from around 1800 BC. The utterly refined **Arts of Islam** collection lies below, on the lower ground floor.

Egyptian antiquities

The Louvre's collection of **Egyptian Antiquities** is the most important in the world after that of the Egyptian Museum in Cairo. Starting on the ground floor of the Sully wing, the thematic circuit takes the visitor through the everyday life of pharaonic Egypt by way of cooking utensils, jewellery, musical instruments, sarcophagi and a host of mummified cats. Among the major exhibits of the first floor's chronological tour are: the *Great Sphinx*, carved from a single block of pink granite; the polychrome *Seated Scribe* statue; the striking, life-size wooden statue of Chancellor Nakhti; and a bust of Amenophis IV.

Greek and Roman antiquities

The lower ground ("*entresol*") floor of Denon contains the fascinating **Pre-Classical Greece** section, while on the ground-floor level, above, the handsomely vaulted room to the south of the main pyramid hall (room A) houses Italian Renaissance copies and restorations of antique sculptures. Immediately west of here, the Galerie Mollien begins the Italian sculpture section, while mirroring it to the east is the long **Galerie Daru** (room B). This kicks off the main Antiquities section with the poised energy of Lysippos's *Borghese Gladiator*. At the eastern end of the gallery, Lefuel's imperial **Escalier Daru**, or Daru staircase, rises triumphantly under the billowing, famous feathers of the *Winged Victory of Samothrace*.

Skirt this staircase to continue through the **Etruscan and Roman** collections and on into the Sully wing, where you enter Lescot's original sixteenth-century palace. In the **Salle des Caryatides** (room 17), which houses Roman copies of Greek works, the musicians' balcony is supported by four giant caryatids, sculpted in 1550 by Jean Goujon. The celebrated *Venus de Milo* is found in room 12, surrounded by hordes of less familiar Aphrodites.

Union Centrale des Arts Décoratifs

107 rue de Rivoli. Tues–Fri 11am–6pm, Sat & Sun 10am–6pm; €6; Ⓦwww.ucad.fr.

The other museums housed in the Palais du Louvre come under the umbrella organization **Union Centrale des Arts Décoratifs**.

The **Musée de la Mode et du Textile** holds high-quality temporary exhibitions drawn from the large permanent collection aimed at demonstrating the most brilliant and cutting-edge of Paris fashions from all eras. On the top floor, the **Musée de la Publicité** shows off its collection of advertising posters through cleverly themed, temporary exhibitions. The **Musée des Arts Décoratifs** is re-opening in May 2006 after an extensive renovation. Its eclectic collection of art and superbly crafted furnishing includes anything from medieval chairs to Renaissance tapestries, and the new design will include a contemporary set of rooms dedicated to works by French, Italian and Japanese designers.

3

The Champs-Élysées and around

Synonymous with Parisian glitz and glamour, the **Champs-Élysées** cuts through one of the city's most exclusive districts, studded with luxury hotels and top fashion boutiques. The avenue forms part of a grand, nine-kilometre axis that extends from the Louvre at the heart of the city to the Grande Arche de la Défense in the west. Often referred to as the Voie Triomphale, or Triumphal Way, it offers impressive vistas along its length and is punctuated with some of the city's most recognizable landmarks – including the **place de la Concorde**, **Tuileries gardens** and the **Arc de Triomphe** – erected over the centuries by kings and emperors, presidents and corporations, each a monumental gesture aimed at promoting French power and prestige.

The Champs-Élysées

Map 7, E2–L5.

Tree-lined and broad, the celebrated **avenue des Champs-Élysées** sweeps down from the Arc de Triomphe towards the place de la Concorde. Seen from a distance it's an impressive sight, but close up the avenue can be a little disappointing, with its constant stream of traffic and fast-food outlets, airline offices and chain stores. Over the last few years, however, the Champs has regained something of its former cachet as a chic address, enjoying a renaissance that started with a mid-1990s facelift, when the rows of trees that the Nazis removed during World War II were replanted and pavements were widened and repaved. Louis Vuitton and other designer outlets subsequently moved in and once-dowdy shops such as the Publicis drugstore and the Renault car flagship showroom underwent stylish makeovers and acquired cool bar-restaurants. Completing the transformation, an influx of new, fashionable cafés and restaurants in the streets around have injected the area with fresh buzz and glamour. Running south off the avenue, **rue Francois 1er** and **avenue Montaigne**, part of the *triangle d'or* (golden triangle), are home to the most exclusive names in fashion: Dior, Prada, Chanel and many others.

The Champs-Élysées began life as a leafy promenade, an extension of the Tuileries gardens. It was transformed into a fashionable thoroughfare during the Second Empire, when members of the *haute bourgeoisie* built themselves splendid mansions along its length and high society frequented its cafés and theatres. Most of the mansions finally gave way to office blocks and the *beau monde* moved elsewhere, but remnants of that particular glitzy heyday live on at the *Lido* cabaret, *Fouquet's* café-restaurant (see p.196), the perfumier Guerlain's shop, occupying an exquisite 1913 building, and the former *Claridges* hotel, now a swanky shopping arcade.

The less commercial stretch of the Champs-Élysées, between place de la Concorde and the Rond-Point roundabout, is bordered by chestnut trees and attractive flowerbeds. On the north side stand the guarded walls of the presidential **Élysée Palace**. The gigantic building with grandiose Neoclassical exteriors, glass roofs and exuberant flying statuary rising above the greenery to the south, is the Grand Palais, created with its neighbour, the Petit Palais, for the 1900 Exposition Universelle. Today, both the Grand Palais and Petit Palais contain permanent museums and host major exhibitions.

Petit Palais

Map 7, K5. Tues–Sun 10am–6pm; free; M° Champs-Élysées-Clemenceau.

The **Petit Palais** houses the Musée des Beaux-Arts, which, as we went to press, was about to come out of a major revamp intended to free up more gallery space for its extensive holdings. The collection, encompassing every period from the Renaissance to the 1920s, includes some real gems, such as Monet's *Sunset at Lavacourt* and Boudin's *Gust of Wind at Le Havre*. There's also fantasy jewellery from the Art Nouveau period, effete eighteenth-century furniture and vast canvases recording Paris's street battles during the 1830 and 1848 revolutions.

The Grand Palais

Map 7, J5. M° Champs-Élysées-Clemenceau/Franklin-D.-Roosevelt.

The 144-foot-high glass cupola of the **Grand Palais** can be seen from most of the city's viewpoints. Inside, the nave has just emerged from a lengthy restoration project – it was hastily closed in 1993 when a metal rivet fell 35m from the ceiling. The glass of the dome – covering some 15,000 square metres – has been entirely replaced and the steel supports given a fresh coat of sea-green paint. Extensive work has been done, too, to shore up the structure's rocky foundations. Renovation work on the exterior is ongoing, so the nave may be intermittently closed, but it's gradually resuming its role as a cultural centre, hosting music festivals and art exhibitions, as well as trade fairs and fashion shows.

Unaffected by the renovation work, in the west wing of the building the **Galeries Nationales** (Tues–Sun 10am–8pm, till 10pm on Wed; admission fee varies) is one of the city's major exhibition spaces and well known for its blockbuster shows, such as the Whistler-Turner-Monet one in 2004. The Grand Palais' east wing houses the **Palais de la Découverte** (Tues–Sat 9.30am–6pm, Sun & hols 10am–7pm; €6.50, combined ticket with planetarium €10), Paris's original science museum, which was opened in the late 1930s. Although it can't really compete, it's been brightened up considerably since the Cité des Sciences (see p.133) came on the scene and has plenty of interactive exhibits, some engaging temporary exhibitions on subjects such as climate change and the Brazilian rainforest, as well as an excellent **planetarium**.

The Arc de Triomphe

Map 7, E2. Daily: April–Sept 9.30am–11pm; Oct–March 10am–10.30pm; €7; M° Charles-de-Gaulle-Étoile.

The best views of the Champs-Élysées are to be had from the terrace at the top of the **Arc de Triomphe**, modelled on the ancient Roman triumphal arches and impressive in scale. It was begun by Napoleon in 1806 in homage to his Grande Armée, but wasn't actually finished until 1836 by Louis-Philippe, who dedicated it to the French army in general. Later, in 1871 and 1942, victorious German armies would make a point of marching through the arch to compound the humiliation of the French. After the Prussians' triumphal parade in 1871, the Parisians lit bonfires beneath the arch and down the Champs-Élysées to eradicate the "stain" of German boots. Still a potent symbol of the country's military might, the arch is the starting point for the annual Bastille Day procession, a bombastic march-past of tanks, guns and flags. A more poignant ceremony is conducted every evening at 6.30pm, when the continually burning flame on the tomb of an unknown soldier, killed in the Great War, is stoked up by war veterans. In the little museum, just below the viewing terrace, is a small collection of prints and photos depicting illustrious scenes from the history of the arch, as well as preliminary drawings for the glorious friezes and sculptures that adorn the pillars. The Champs-Élysées side in particular boasts a fine high-relief sculpture, *the Marseillaise* by François Rude.

Access to the Arc de Triomphe is gained from stairs on the north corner of the Champs-Élysées. Views from the top are at their best towards dusk on a sunny day when the marble of the Grande Arche de la Défense sparkles in the setting sun and the Louvre is bathed in warm light. Your attention is also likely to be caught by the mesmerizing traffic movements below in place Charles-de-Gaulle or the Étoile, the world's first roundabout, otherwise popularly known as place de la Traffic.

Étoile and around

Map 7, E2. M° Charles-de-Gaulle-Étoile.

Twelve avenues make up the star of the **Étoile**, with the Arc de Triomphe at its centre. The avenues sparring off into the northern 16e and eastern 17e arrondissements are for the most part cold and soulless, and the huge fortified apartments here are empty much of the time, as their owners – royal, exiled royal, ex-royal or just extremely rich – move between their other residences dotted about the globe. The 8e arrondissement, north of the Champs-Élysées, however, has more to offer commercially and culturally, with some of the *hôtels particuliers* (mansions) housing fine museums.

The Haussmannian Hôtel André, at 158 boulevard Haussmann, offers the highlight of the area, the magnificent art collection of the **Musée Jacquemart-André** (map 7, J1; daily 10am–6pm, Mon until 9.30pm; ⓦwww.musee-jacquemart-andre.com; €9.50; M° Miromesnil/St-Philippe-du-Roule), accumulated on the travels of the art-lover

Édouard André and his wife, former society portraitist Nélie Jacquemart. They loved Italian art above all, and a stunning collection of fifteenth- and sixteenth-century Italian genius, including the works of Tiepolo, Botticelli, Donatello, Mantegna and Uccello, forms the core of their collection. Almost as compelling as the splendid interior and art collection is the insight gleaned into an extraordinary marriage and grand nineteenth-century lifestyle.

The Musée Jacquemart-André has a fabulously elegant *salon de thé*. See p.197.

At 63 rue de Monceau, a grand mansion in the style of the Petit Trianon at Versailles is the fitting setting for an impressive collection of eighteenth-century decorative art and painting, the **Musée Nissim de Camondo** (map 7, I1; Wed–Sun 10am–5pm; €6; M° Monceau/Villiers), built up by Count Moïse de Camondo, son of a wealthy Sephardic Jewish banker who had emigrated from Istanbul to Paris in the late nineteenth century.

Further north at 7 avenue Velásquez, ancient Chinese art reigns at the **Musée Cernuschi** (map 7, I1; Tues–Sun 10am–5.40pm; free), bequeathed to the state by the banker Cernuschi, who nearly lost his life for giving money to the insurrectionary Commune of 1871. The ground floor hosts temporary exhibitions, while the first floor displays the permanent collection, among which are some exquisite pieces, including intricately worked bronze vases from the Shang era (1550–1050 BC) and some unique ceramics detailing everyday life in ancient China.

Place de la Concorde

Map 2, A3. M° Concorde.

Marking the beginning of the Champs-Élysées' graceful gradients is the grand **place de la Concorde**, marred only by the constant stream of traffic around its perimeter. At the centre of the *place* is an obelisk from the temple of Ramses at Luxor, offered to Louis-Philippe as a favour-currying gesture by the viceroy of Egypt in 1829. Despite the harmony implied in its name, the square's history is anything but peaceful: the equestrian statue of Louis XV that formerly stood at the centre of the square was toppled by revolutionaries in 1792 and, between 1793 and 1795, some 1300 people died here beneath the guillotine, among them Louis XVI, Marie-Antoinette, Danton and Robespierre. From the centre of the square there are magnificent views of the Champs-Élysées and Tuileries, and you can admire the alignment and symmetry of the Assemblée Nationale, on the far side of the Seine, with the church of the Madeleine at the end of rue Royale, to the north. The Neoclassical *Hôtel Crillon* – the ultimate luxury address for visitors to Paris – and its twin, the *Hôtel de la Marine*, housing the Ministry of the Navy, flank the entrance to rue Royale.

The Tuileries

Map 2, B4. M° Tuileries/Concorde.

With its splendid vistas, grand avenues, fountains and manicured lawns, the **Jardin des Tuileries**, extending from the place de la Concorde to the Louvre, is the formal French garden *par excellence*. It's especially popular on Sunday mornings when half the city seems to be in the park jogging; families come to promenade and children push toy boats around the central pond and get treated to pony rides. Named after the medieval warren of tilemakers (*tuileries*) that once occupied the site, the Tuileries gardens are all that survive of the palace and grounds commissioned by Catherine des Médicis in the mid-sixteenth century (the palace was burnt down during the Paris Commune in 1871). A hundred years after that, Le Nôtre, who landscaped the grounds at Versailles, created the current schema of the gardens, laying out a grand central alley, *terrasses* and pools both round and octagonal in shape. Later, sculptures were brought here from Versailles and Marly, including Coysevox's rearing horses *Fama* and *Mercury*. The originals are now housed in the Richelieu wing of the Louvre and have been replaced here by copies.

During the eighteenth century, fashionable Parisians came to the gardens to preen and party and, in 1783, the Montgolfier brothers, Joseph and Étienne, launched the first successful hot-air balloon here. The first serious replanting was carried out after the Revolution and, in the nineteenth century, rare species such as honey locusts and pagoda trees were added to the garden, at this time dominated by chestnut trees. Sadly, some of the oldest specimens were lost in the December 1999 storms: the centennial chestnuts around the two central oval ponds are now the most senior.

At the eastern end of the gardens in front of the Louvre is the **Jardin du Carrousel**, a raised terrace where the Palais des Tuileries was sited. It's now planted with trim yew hedges, between which stand oddly static bronzes of buxom female nudes by Maillol.

One of the best of the pleasant, shady cafés in the Jardin des Tuileries is *Café Véry* (see p.197).

The Orangerie

Map 2, A4. M° Concorde.

Situated at the west end of the Tuileries gardens is the **Orangerie**, undergoing renovation at the time of writing and due to re-open sometime in 2006. It houses eight of Monet's *Water Lilies* paintings, as well as a private art collection, weighted heavily in favour of the Impressionists and including paintings by Matisse, Cézanne, Utrillo, Modigliani, Renoir, Soutine and Sisley. The current work involves replacing many of the existing exterior walls with glass, in line with Monet's request that as much natural light as possible reach his masterpieces. After all the upheaval, much of the Orangerie's collection will be rearranged and, with any luck, extra room will be created for paintings from the museum's reserves.

Jeu de Paume

Map 2, A3. Tues noon–9.30pm, Wed–Fri noon–7pm, Sat & Sun 10am–7pm; €6; Ⓦwww.jeudepaume.org; M° Concorde.

Opposite the Orangerie stands the Neoclassical **Jeu de Paume**, built under Napoleon III as a royal tennis court; when lawn tennis replaced "real tennis" in the early twentieth century, the building became a gallery and was where French Impressionist paintings were displayed before their transfer to the Musée d'Orsay. The Centre National de la Photographie now resides here and mounts major photographic exhibitions.

4

The Grands Boulevards and around

Built in the eighteenth century on the site of the city's fourteenth-century ramparts, the **Grands Boulevards** extend in a long arc from the Église de la Madeleine in the west to the Bastille in the east. The streets off the Grands Boulevards are home to grandiose financial, cultural and state institutions and are associated with established commerce such as the clothing trade, plus well-heeled shopping. Crisscrossing the boulevards, attractive nineteenth-century shopping arcades or **passages** conceal chic boutiques, while the classy department stores Galeries Lafayette and Printemps (see p.245) congregate nearby in the 9e (neuvième) arrondissement, just north of the **Palais Garnier** opera house. Catering to the seriously rich, the boutiques at the western end of the 1er (premier), around the church of the **Madeleine** and **place Vendôme**, display the wares of top couturiers, jewellers and art dealers. The peaceful gardens of the **Palais Royal**, to the south, make for an ideal rest-stop and are a handy shortcut to the venerable **Bibliothèque Nationale**.

The Grands Boulevards

The **Grands Boulevards** is the collective name given to the eight streets that form one continuous, broad thoroughfare running from the Madeleine to République, then down to the Bastille. Lined with solid Haussmann-era mansion blocks, imposing banks, cinemas, theatres, brasseries and neon-lit fast-food outlets, these broad boulevards are busy and vibrant, if not the most alluring or glamorous parts of Paris – though this was not always so. The western section, from the Madeleine to Porte St-Denis, was especially fashionable in the nineteenth century. Parisians came in droves to stroll and sit out drinking lemonade or beer in the numerous cafés, and the chic café clientele of the **boulevard des Italiens** set the trends for all of Paris in terms of manners, dress and conversation. The eastern section, meanwhile, developed a more colourful reputation, derived from its association with street theatre, mime, juggling, puppets, waxworks and cafés of ill repute. This earned it the nickname the *boulevard du Crime* – much of which was swept away in the latter half of the nineteenth century by Baron Haussmann when he created the huge place de la République.

As recently as the 1950s, a visitor to Paris would, as a matter of course, have gone for a stroll along the Grands Boulevards to see *Paris vivant*. Still today theatres and cinemas (including the Max Linder and the Grand Rex – the latter an extraordinary building inside and out, see p.268), hold their ground amongst the burger joints and numerous brasseries and cafés, which uphold the tradition of the Grands Boulevards immortalized in the film *Les Enfants du Paradis*.

Musée Grévin

Map 3, H8. 10 bd Montmartre; Mon–Fri 10am–6.30pm, Sat & Sun 10am–7pm; last admission one hour beforehand; €17, children 6–14 €10; Ⓦwww.grevin.com; M° Grands Boulevards.

The waxworks in the **Musée Grévin** are a remnant from the fun-loving times of the Grands Boulevards. The collection comprises mainly French literary, media and political personalities as well as the usual bunch of Hollywood actors. Perhaps the best things about the museum are the original rooms: the magical Palais des Mirages (Hall of Mirrors), built for the World Fair in 1900; the theatre, with its sculptures by Bourdelle; and the 1882 Baroque-style Hall of Columns where, among other unlikely juxtapositions, Lara Croft prepares for action a few feet away from a dignified Charles de Gaulle, while Voltaire smiles across at the billowing skirts of Marilyn Monroe.

The Opéra (Palais Garnier)

Map 3, E8. Interior daily 10am–5pm; €6; Ⓦwww.opera-de paris.fr; M° Opéra.

Set back from the boulevard des Capucines is the dazzling nineteenth-century Opéra de Paris – now commonly referred to as the **Palais Garnier** to distinguish it from the new opera house at the Bastille. The architect, Charles Garnier, drew on a number of existing styles and succeeded in creating a magnificently ornate building the like of which Paris had never seen before. Its **exterior** is a fairy-tale concoction of white, pink and green marble, colonnades, rearing horses, winged angels and gleaming gold busts of composers. Four allegorical sculptures punctuate the facade, one of which, Carpeaux's *La Danse*, caused a scandal on its unveiling on account of its sensuous, naked figures, and even had ink thrown over it; the original is now in the Musée d'Orsay and has been replaced by a copy. The opera house took fourteen years to complete and was opened in 1875. Part of the reason construction took so long was the discovery of a water table that had to be drained and replaced by a huge concrete well, giving rise to the legend of an underground lake, popularized by Gaston Leroux's *Phantom of the Opera*. By day, you can visit the sumptuous gilt-marble **interior**, including the auditorium, as long as there are no rehearsals – your best chance is between 1 and 2pm. The colourful ceiling, depicting opera and ballet scenes, is easily recognized as the work of **Chagall**.

For information on booking tickets for the opera see p.306.

Paris-Story

Map 3, D8. Daily with shows on the hour 9am–7pm; €8; M° Opéra/Chaussée-d'Antin-La-Fayette & RER Auber.

West of the Opéra and next door to the main tourist office, at 11bis rue Scribe, the Paris-Story multimedia show is an enjoyable, if partial and highly romanticized, history of Paris "narrated" by Victor Hugo, with simultaneous translation in English. The 45-minute film uses a kaleidoscope of computer-generated images and archive footage, set against a luscious classical-music soundtrack.

Madeleine

Map 3, B9–C9. M° Madeleine.

South of boulevard Haussmann, occupying nearly the whole of the place de la Madeleine, is the huge, imperious-looking **Église de la Madeleine**, the parish church of Parisian high society. Modelled on the Parthenon, the church is surrounded by 52 Corinthian columns and fronted by a huge pediment depicting The Last Judgement. Originally intended as a monument to Napoleon's army, the building narrowly escaped being turned into a railway station before finally being consecrated to Mary Magdalene in 1845. Inside, the wide, single nave is decorated with Ionic columns and surmounted by three huge domes – the only source of natural light. A theatrical stone sculpture of the Magdalene being swept up to heaven by two angels draws your eye to the high altar. The half-dome above is decorated with a fresco by Jules-Claude Ziegler (1804–56), a student of Ingres; entitled *The History of Christianity*, it commemorates the concordat signed between the church and state after the end of the Revolution, and shows all the key figures in Christendom, with Napoleon centre-stage, naturally.

If the Madeleine caters to spiritual needs, the rest of the square is given over to nourishment of an earthier kind, for this is where Paris's top **gourmet food stores**, Fauchon and Hédiard (see p.259), are located. Their remarkable displays are a feast for the eyes, and both have *salons de thé* where you can sample some of their epicurean treats. On the east side of the church is one of the city's oldest flower markets, dating back to 1832 and open every day except Monday. Also nearby are some rather fine Art Nouveau public toilets, built in 1905, which are definitely worth inspecting.

Place Vendôme and around

Map 3, C2.

Built by Hardouin-Mansart, **Place Vendôme** is one of the city's most impressive set pieces. It's a pleasingly symmetrical, eight-sided *place*, enclosed by a harmonious ensemble of elegant mansions, graced with Corinthian pilasters, mascarons (decorative masks) and steeply pitched roofs. Once the grand residences of tax collectors and financiers, they now house such luxury establishments as the *Ritz*, one of the three original *Ritz* hotels, along with those in London and Madrid, established by César Ritz at the turn of the last century. Elsewhere in the square top-flight jewellers Cartier, Bulgari and others reinforce the air of exclusivity. Somewhat out of proportion with the rest of the *place*, the centrepiece is a towering triumphal **column**, surmounted by a statue of Napoleon dressed as Caesar. It was raised in 1806 to celebrate the Battle of Austerlitz – bronze reliefs of scenes of the battle, cast from 1200 recycled Austro-Russian cannons, spiral their way up the column.

An air of luxury also pervades the surrounding streets, especially ancient **rue St-Honoré**, a preserve of top fashion designers and art galleries; you can marvel at John Galliano's extravagant creations at no. 392 or join the style-conscious young Parisians perusing the latest designs at the Colette concept store at no. 213.

The passages

The 2e and 9e arrondissements are scattered with around twenty **passages**, or shopping arcades, that have survived from the early nineteenth century. Built at a time when pavements were unknown in Paris, they were places where people could shop, dine and drink, protected from mud and horse-drawn vehicles. Their popularity declined with the advent of department stores in the latter half of the nineteenth century and most were demolished by Haussmann to make way for his building projects. The remaining *passages* were left to crumble and decay, and it's only over the last decade or so that many have now been renovated and restored to something approaching their former glory; their tiled floors and glass roofs have been repaired and chic boutiques have moved in alongside the old-fashioned traders and secondhand dealers. Their entrances are easy to miss, and where you emerge at the other end can be quite a surprise. Most are closed at night and on Sundays.

Galerie Véro-Dodat

Map 2, E4.

Between rue Croix-des-Petits-Champs and rue Jean-Jacques Rousseau, **Galerie Véro-Dodat**, named after the two pork butchers who set it up in 1824, is the most homogeneous and aristocratic of the *passages*, with painted ceilings and mahogany-panelled shop fronts divided by faux-marble columns. It's been spruced up and fashionable new shops have begun to open up in place of the older businesses.

Galerie Colbert and Galerie Vivienne

Map 2, E2.

The flamboyant decor of Grecian and marine motifs of Galerie Vivienne, linking rue Vivienne with rue des Petits-Champs, establishes the perfect ambience in which to buy Jean-Paul Gaultier gear, or you can browse in the antiquarian bookshop, Librairie Jousseaume, which dates back to the *passage*'s earliest days. Neighbouring **Galerie Colbert** has recently been incorporated into a new national institute of art history, but you can still gain access to the 1830s-style brasserie, *Le Grand Colbert*, on the corner of the *passage* and rue Vivienne, to which senior librarians and academics retire for lunch.

Passage des Panoramas

Map 3, H8.

Slightly scruffier is the **passage des Panoramas**, the grid of arcades north of the Bibliothèque Nationale, beyond rue St-Marc. Most of the eateries here make no pretence at style, but one old brasserie, now a tea room, *L'Arbre à Cannelle* (see p.199), has fantastic carved wood panelling, and there are still bric-a-brac shops, stamp dealers and an old print shop with its original 1867 fittings. It was around the Panoramas, in 1817, that the first Parisian gas lamps were installed.

Passage Jouffroy and passage Verdeau

Map 3, H8/7.

Passage Jouffroy, across boulevard Montmartre, is full of the kind of stores that make shopping an adventure rather than a chore. One of them, M. Segas, sells walking canes and theatrical antiques opposite a shop displaying every conceivable fitting and furnishing for dolls' houses. Near the romantic *Hôtel Chopin*, Paul Vulin sets out his secondhand books along the passageway, and Ciné-Doc appeals to cinephiles with its collection of old film posters. Crossing rue de la Grange-Batelière, you enter **passage Verdeau**, where a few of the old postcard and camera dealers still trade alongside new art galleries and a designer Italian delicatessen.

Passage des Princes

Map 3, G8.
At the top of rue Richelieu, the tiny **passage des Princes**, with its beautiful glass ceiling, stained-glass decoration and twirly lamps, has been taken over by the toy emporium, JouéClub. Its erstwhile neighbour, the passage de l'Opéra, described in surreal detail by Louis Aragon in *Paris Peasant*, was eaten up with the completion of Haussmann's boulevards.

Passage du Grand-Cerf

Map 2, H3. M° Étienne-Marcel.
Back in the 2e arrondissement the three-storey **passage du Grand-Cerf**, between rue St-Denis and rue Dessoubs, is stylistically the most impressive of all the *passages*. The wrought-iron work, glass roof and plain-wood shop fronts have all been cleaned, attracting chic arts, crafts and design shops.

The Palais Royal

Map 2, E3–E4. M° Palais-Royal-Musée-du-Louvre.
At the heart of the 1er arrondissement stands the **Palais Royal**, a handsome, colonnaded palace built for Cardinal Richelieu in 1629, though little remains of the original edifice. It now houses various government and constitutional bodies, as well as the **Comédie Française**, longstanding venue for the classics of French theatre.

North of the palace lie sedate gardens surrounded by stately eighteenth-century buildings built over arcades, housing quirky antique and design shops. The gardens are an attractive and peaceful oasis, with avenues of clipped limes, fountains and flowerbeds. You'd hardly guess that for many years this was a site of gambling dens, brothels (it was to a prostitute here that Napoleon lost his virginity in 1787) and funfair attractions – there was even a *café mécanique*, where you sat at a table, sent your order down one of its legs, and were served via the other. The prohibition on public gambling in 1838, however, put an end to the fun. Folly, some might say, has returned – in the form of Daniel Buren's black-and-white striped pillars, rather like sticks of Brighton rock, all of varying heights, dotted about the main courtyard in front of the palace. Installed in 1986, they're a rather disconcerting sight, but seem popular with children and rollerbladers, who treat them as an adventure playground and obstacle course respectively.

The Bibliothèque Nationale

Map 2, E2. Library reading rooms Mon–Fri 9/10am–6pm, Sat 10am–5pm; exhibitions Tues–Sun 10am–7pm; €4.5–7. Cabinet des Monnaies, Médailles et Antiques Mon–Fri 1–5.45pm, Sat 1–4.45pm, Sun noon–6pm; free.

Cutting through the Palais Royal gardens brings you to the forbidding wall of the **Bibliothèque Nationale**, much of whose enormous collection has been transferred to the new François Mitterrand site in the 13e. The library's origins go back to the 1660s, when Louis XIV's finance minister Colbert deposited a collection of royal manuscripts here, and it was first opened to the public in 1692. There's no restriction on entering the library, nor on peering into the atmospheric reading rooms; the central room, with its slender iron columns supporting nine domes, is a fine example of the early use of iron-frame construction. Visiting the library's temporary exhibitions (closed Sun) will give you access to the beautiful **Galerie Mazarine**, with its panelled ceilings painted by Romanelli (1617–62). It's also worth calling into the **Cabinet des Monnaies, Médailles et Antiques**, a permanent display of coins, Etruscan bronzes, ancient Greek jewellery and some exquisite medieval cameos. One of the highlights is Charlemagne's ivory chess set, its pieces malevolent-looking characters astride elephants.

5

Beaubourg and Les Halles

Straddling the 3e (troisième) and 4e (quatrième) arrondissements, the quartier Beaubourg hums with lively cafés, shops and art galleries. At its heart stands the Pompidou Centre, one of the city's most popular attractions. The ground-breaking "inside-out" architecture of this huge arts centre provoked a storm of controversy on its opening in 1977, but since then it has won over critics and public alike. Now it is one of the city's most recognizable landmarks, drawing large numbers to its excellent modern art museum and high-profile exhibitions. By contrast, nearby Les Halles, a massive underground shopping complex built around the same time as the Pompidou Centre to replace a centuries-old food market, has never really endeared itself to the city's inhabitants and is probably the least inspired of all the urban developments undertaken in Paris in the last thirty years; the good news is that it's soon to undergo a major revamp.

The Pompidou Centre

Map 2, H5. Ⓦ www.centrepompidou.fr; M° Rambuteau/Hôtel-de-Ville.

The **Pompidou Centre**, also known locally as Beaubourg, is one of the twentieth century's most radical buildings. Wanting to move away from the traditional idea of galleries as closed treasure chests in order to create something more open and accessible, the architects Renzo Piano and Richard Rogers stripped the "skin" off the building and made all the "bones" visible. The infrastructure was put on the outside: escalator tubes and utility pipes, brightly colour-coded according to their function, climb around the exterior in snakes-and-ladders fashion.

The centre's main draw is the **Musée National d'Art Moderne**, and major retrospectives of modern and contemporary artists, but there's also a huge public library, two cinemas and performance spaces. One of the treats of visiting the museum is that you get to ascend the transparent **escalator** on the outside of the building, affording superb views over the city.

Musée National d'Art Moderne

Daily except Tues 11am–9pm; €7, joint ticket for museum and temporary exhibitions €11.40, free first Sun of the month.

The **Musée National d'Art Moderne** is spread over floors four and five of the Pompidou Centre, with the latter covering the period 1905 to 1960, and the former 1960 to the present day. Thanks to an astute acquisitions policy and some generous gifts, the collection is a near-complete visual essay on the history of twentieth-century art and is so large that only a fraction of the 50,000 works are on display at any one time (they're frequently rotated).

The collection on **floor five** starts with **Joan Miró**'s three huge, azure-blue canvases *Bleu I, Bleu II and Bleu III*, executed in just three months in 1961. A fascination with colour continues in **room 2** with the **Fauvists** – **Braque,**

Derain, Vlaminck and **Matisse**, among others. A fine example of the movement's desire to create form rather than imitate nature is Braque's *L'Estaque* (1906); colour becomes a way of composing and structuring a picture, with trees and sky reduced to blocks of vibrant reds and greens.

In **room 3**, shape is broken down even further in Picasso's and Braque's early **Cubist** paintings. One of the highlights here is **Picasso**'s portrait of his lover Fernande (*Femme assise dans un fauteuil;* 1910), in which different angles of the figure are shown all at once, giving rise to complex patterns and creating the effect of movement.

Room 7 is devoted to the nihilistic Dada movement; art students cluster round leading Dadaist **Marcel Duchamp**'s notorious *Fontaine* (1917), a urinal elevated to the rank of "art" simply by being taken out of its ordinary context and put on display.

Room 10 contains a particularly fine collection of **Kandinskys**. You can follow the artist's experiments with abstract art through his series "Impressions, Improvisations and Compositions". Fellow abstract-art pioneers, **Robert and Sonia Delaunay**, set the walls of **room 12** ablaze with a number of their characteristically colourful paintings.

Surrealist painters Magritte, Dalí and Ernst figure in later rooms. **Ernst**'s *Ubu Imperator* (1923; **room 20**), typical of the movement's exploration of the darker recesses of the mind, depicts a figure that is part man, part Tower of Pisa and part spinning top, apparently symbolizing the perversion of male authority.

Shying away from the figurative, American abstract expressionists **Jackson Pollock** and **Mark Rothko** make an appearance in **room 34**. In Pollock's splattery *No 26A, Black and white* (1948), the two colours seem to struggle for domination; the dark bands of colour in Rothko's large canvas *No. 14 (Browns over Dark)*, in contrast, draw the viewer in. **Matisse**'s later experiments with form and colour are on show in **room 41**. His cut-out gouache technique is perfected in his masterpiece *La Tristesse du Roi* (1952), a meditation on old age and memory.

The collection continues on the **fourth floor** with **Pop Art**. Easily recognizable is Andy Warhol's piece *Ten Lizes* (1963), which features the actress Elizabeth Taylor sporting a Mona Lisa-like smile. In room 3 **Yves Klein** prefigures performance art with his *Grande anthropophagie bleue; Hommage a Tennessee Williams* (1960), one in a series of "body prints" in which the artist turned female models into human paintbrushes by covering them in paint. Displays of more recent works are subject to change, but established artists you're likely to come across include Christian Boltanski and Daniel Buren. **Boltanski** is known for his large *mise-en-scène* installations, often containing veiled allusions to the Holocaust. **Buren**'s works are easy to spot: they all bear his trademark stripes, exactly 8.7cm in width.

Atelier Brancusi

Daily except Tues 2–6pm; combined ticket with the Musée.

Down some steps off the Pompidou Centre's piazza, in a small, separate building, is the **Atelier Brancusi**, the reconstructed studio of the sculptor **Constantin Brancusi**, who bequeathed the contents of his *atelier* to the state on condition that the rooms be arranged exactly as he left them. Studios one and two are crowded with fluid sculptures of highly polished brass and marble and his trademark abstract bird and column shapes. In studios three and four, Brancusi's private quarters, you get a real sense of how the artist lived and worked.

Quartier Beaubourg

Map 2, H5. M° Hôtel-de-Ville.

The lively **quartier Beaubourg** around the Pompidou Centre also offers much in the way of visual art. The colourful, moving sculptures and fountains in the pool in front of Église St-Merri on **place Igor Stravinsky**, on the south side of the Pompidou Centre, were created by Jean Tinguely and Niki de St-Phalle; this squirting waterworks pays homage to Stravinsky – each fountain corresponds to one of his compositions (*The Firebird*, *The Rite of Spring*, etc) – though shows scant respect for passers-by.

North of the Pompidou Centre, numerous commercial galleries take up the contemporary art theme on **rue Quincampoix**, the most attractive street in the area: narrow, pedestrianized and lined with handsome *hôtels particuliers*. Running east of here is **passage Molière**, an enchanting little alley with some quirky shops, such as Des Pieds et des Mains, where you can get a plaster cast made of your hand or foot.

Hôtel de Ville

Map 2, H7. M° Rambuteau/Hôtel-de-Ville.

South of the Pompidou Centre stands the **Hôtel de Ville**, the seat of the city's mayor. It's a mansion of gargantuan proportions in florid neo-Renaissance style, modelled almost entirely on the previous building, which was burned down during the Commune in 1871. A succession of conservative governments decided that Paris was too unruly to be allowed its own administration and it was only in 1977 that the office of mayor was restored – with Jacques Chirac winning the post. The huge square in front of the Hôtel de Ville, a notorious guillotine site during the Revolution, becomes the location of a popular **ice-skating rink** from December to March; it's free and you can hire skates for around €4.

Les Halles and around

Map 2, F4–G5. M° Les-Halles/RER Châtelet-Les-Halles.

Les Halles was the site of the city's main food market for over eight hundred years until it was moved out to the suburbs in 1969, despite widespread opposition. It was replaced by landscaped gardens and a large underground shopping and leisure complex, known as the Forum des Halles.

Unsightly, rundown, even unsavoury in parts, the complex is now widely acknowledged as an architectural disaster – so much so that steps are underway to give Les Halles a major facelift. The French architect, David Mangin, who won the competition to redevelop the site, plans to suspend a vast glass roof over the forum, allowing light to flood in, while also re-designing the gardens and creating a wide promenade on the model of Barcelona's Ramblas. Work is due to start in 2007 and should be complete by 2012.

For now, the Forum comprises a busy metro/RER station, some 180 shops spread over four levels, a swimming pool, cinemas and an exhibition space, the **Pavillon des Arts** (Tues–Sun 11.30am–6.30pm; €5.50). The shops, housed in aquarium-like arcades and arranged around a sunken patio, are mostly devoted to high-street fashion, though there's a decent FNAC bookshop and the Forum des Créateurs, an outlet for young fashion designers.

You can still catch a flavour of the old market atmosphere on pedestrianized **rue Montorgueil** to the north, where traditional grocers, horse butchers and fishmongers still ply their trade, jostling for space with the trendy cafés that have sprung up over the last few years.

It's impossible to avoid the temptation of the exquisite pastries at Stohrer's *pâtisserie,* 51 rue Montorgueil, in business since 1730; it seems her majesty Queen Elizabeth couldn't resist either – when she stopped off here during her Entente Cordiale centenary visit in April 2004 she was presented with a handmade chocolate Easter egg.

St-Eustache

Map 2, G4. M° Les-Halles/RER Châtelet-Les-Halles.

For an antidote to the steel and glass troglodytism of Les Halles head for the soaring vaults of the beautiful church of **St-Eustache**, on the north side of the gardens. Built between 1532 and 1637, it's Gothic in structure, with lofty naves and graceful flying buttresses, and Renaissance in decoration, with Corinthian columns, pilasters and arcades. Molière, Richelieu and Madame de Pompadour were baptized here, while Rameau and Marivaux were buried here. The church has a long musical tradition and is an atmospheric venue for concerts and organ recitals.

Fontaine des Innocents

Map 2, G5.

On the other side of Les Halles, you can join the throng around the **Fontaine des Innocents** to admire the way water cascades down its perfect Renaissance proportions. The fountain takes its name from the cemetery that used to occupy this site, the Cimetière des Innocents. Full to overflowing, the cemetery was closed down in 1786 and its contents transferred to the catacombs in Denfert-Rochereau (see p.115).

6

The Marais

Comprising most of the 3e (troisième) and 4e (quatrième) arrondissements, the **Marais** is one of the most seductive districts of Paris. Having largely escaped the heavy-handed attentions of Baron Haussmann and unspoiled by modern development, the quartier is full of handsome Renaissance *hôtels particuliers* (mansions), narrow lanes and inviting cafés and restaurants. Originally little more than a riverside swamp (*marais*), the area was drained and became a magnet for the aristocracy in the early 1600s after the construction of the **place des Vosges** – or place Royale, as it was then known. This golden age was relatively short-lived, however, for the king took his court to Versailles in the latter part of the seventeenth century. The mansions were left to the trading classes, who were in turn displaced during the Revolution. From then on, the buildings became multi-occupied slum tenements and the streets degenerated into unserviced squalor.

The area remained dilapidated and unfashionable right up until the 1960s, when the government started to renovate the district and clean up the old *hôtels*. Inevitably, much of the traditional population of artisans and small businesses began to move out, to be replaced by more affluent residents, though it's still a pretty diverse neighbourhood. There's a significant Jewish community here, established in the twelfth century and centred on **rue des Rosiers**. Known for its long tradition of tolerance of minorities, the area has also become popular with gay Parisians.

Prime streets for wandering are **rue des Francs-Bourgeois**, lined with fashion and interior design boutiques, **rue Vieille-du-Temple** and **rue des Archives**, their trendy cafés and bars abuzz at all times of day and night. The Marais' animated streets and atmospheric old buildings would be reason enough to visit, but the quartier also boasts a high concentration of excellent museums, not least among them the **Musée Picasso**, the **Carnavalet** history museum and the **Musée d'Art et d'Histoire du Judaïsme**, all set in fine *hôtels particuliers*.

Musée de l'Histoire de France and around

Map 4, B9. Mon–Fri 10am–12.30pm & 2–5.30pm; €3; M° Rambuteau/St-Paul.

The entire block from rue des Quatre Fils and rue des Archives, and from rue Vieille-du-Temple to rue des Francs-Bourgeois, was once filled by a magnificent early-eighteenth-century palace complex. Only half remains standing today, but what's left is utterly splendid, especially the grand colonnaded courtyard of the **Hôtel Soubise**, with its vestigial fourteenth-century towers on rue des Quatre Fils. The *hôtel* houses the **Musée de l'Histoire de France**, a collection of documents taken from the **Archives Nationales de France** – the museum was closed at the time of writing while the *hôtel*'s fabulous Rococo decor underwent restoration, but should be open again by the beginning of 2006. Its fascinating collection includes Joan of Arc's trial proceedings, with a doodled impression of her in the margin, and a Revolutionary calendar, where "J" stands for Jean-Jacques Rousseau and "L" for "labourer". More sumptuous interiors are on show at the adjacent **Hôtel de Rohan** (Mon–Fri 10am–12.30pm & 2–5.30pm; €3), notably the charming,

Chinese-inspired Cabinet des Singes, whose walls are painted with monkeys acting out various aristocratic scenes.

Chamber music recitals (€10) are held most Saturdays at 6.30pm in the Chambre du Prince, on the ground floor of the Hôtel Soubise.

Musée Carnavalet

Map 4, C10. 23 rue de Sévigné. Daily except Mon 10am–6pm; free; M° St-Paul.

Just off rue des Francs-Bourgeois is the fascinating **Musée Carnavalet**, charting the history of Paris from its origins up to the belle époque through an extraordinary collection of paintings, sculptures, decorative arts and archeological finds. The museum's setting, in two beautiful adjacent Renaissance mansions, Hôtel Carnavalet and Hôtel Le Peletier, surrounded by attractive gardens, in itself makes a visit worthwhile.

The **ground floor** displays nineteenth- and early-twentieth-century shop and inn signs and engrossing models of Paris through the ages, accompanied by maps and plans, showing how much Haussmann's boulevards changed the face of the city. The renovated **orangerie** houses a significant collection of Neolithic finds, including a number of wooden dug-out canoes unearthed during the redevelopment of the Bercy riverside area in the 1990s.

On the **first floor**, decorative arts feature strongly, with numerous re-created salons and boudoirs full of richly sculpted wood panelling and tapestries from the time of Louis XII to Louis XVI, rescued from buildings that had to be destroyed to make way for Haussmann's boulevards. Room 21 is devoted to the famous letter writer **Madame de Sévigné**, who lived in the Carnavalet mansion and corresponded almost on a daily basis with her daughter, vividly portraying high-society life during the reign of Louis XIV. You can see her Chinese lacquered writing desk, as well as portraits of her and various contemporaries, such as Molière and Corneille. Rooms 128 to 148 are largely devoted to the **belle époque**, evoked through numerous paintings from the period and some wonderful **Art Nouveau** interiors, among which is the sumptuous peacock-green interior designed by Alphonse Mucha for Fouquet's jewellery shop in the Rue Royale. Also well preserved is José-Maria Sert's **Art Deco** ballroom, with its extravagant gold-leaf decor and grand-scale paintings, including one of the Queen of Sheba with a train of elephants. Nearby is a section on literary life at the beginning of the twentieth century. You can see a reconstruction of **Proust's bedroom** (room 147), with its cork-lined walls, designed to muffle external noise and allow the writer to work in peace – he spent most of his last three years closeted away here, penning his great novel.

The **second floor** rooms are full of mementos of the **French Revolution**: models of the Bastille, original declarations of the Rights of Man and the Citizen, sculpted allegories of Reason, crockery with revolutionary slogans, glorious models of the guillotine and execution orders to make you shed a tear for the royalists as well.

Musée Cognacq-Jay

Map 4, C10. Daily except Mon 10am–5.40pm; free; M° St-Paul/Chemin-Vert.

The **Musée Cognacq-Jay**, occupying the fine Hôtel Donon at 8 rue Elzévir, houses artworks collected by the family who built up the Samaritaine department store – you can see a history of the Cognacq-Jays and their charitable works in a series of dioramas on the tenth-floor terrace of the store. As well as being noted philanthropists, the Cognacq-Jays were lovers of European art. Their small collection of eighteenth-century pieces includes works by Canaletto, Fragonard, Greuze, Tiepolo and Rembrandt, displayed in beautifully carved wood-panelled rooms.

Musée Picasso

Map 4, C9. 5 rue de Thorigny. Daily except Tues: April–Sept 9.30am–6pm; Oct–March 9.30am–5.30pm; €5.50, free on the first Sun of the month; ⓦwww.musee-picasso.fr; M° Chemin Vert/St-Paul.

On the northern side of rue des Francs-Bourgeois, rue Payenne leads up to the lovely gardens and houses of rue du Parc-Royal and on to rue de Thorigny. At no. 5, a magnificent classical seventeenth-century mansion, the Hôtel Salé, houses the **Musée Picasso**, the world's largest collection of the artist's works, representing most periods of his life from 1905 onwards, though there are some gaps, notably the early Blue and Rose periods. Many of the paintings were owned by Picasso and on his death in 1973 were offered by the family to the state in lieu of taxes owed. The result is an unedited body of work, which, though not containing the most recognizable masterpieces, nevertheless provides a sense of the artist's development and an insight into the person behind the myth.

The **exhibition** unfolds chronologically, with a handful of paintings from the Blue period, studies for the *Demoiselles d'Avignon*, and experiments with Cubism and Surrealism. It then moves on to larger-scale works on themes of war and peace (such as *Massacre in Korea*, 1951) and the artist's later preoccupations with love and death, reflected in the Minotaur and bullfighting paintings. Perhaps some of the most engaging works are Picasso's more personal ones – those of his children, wives and lovers – such as *Olga pensive* (1923), in which his first wife is shown lost in thought, the deep blue of her dress reflecting her mood. Two portraits of later lovers, Dora Maar and Marie-Thérèse (both painted in 1937), exhibited side by side in room 13, show how the two women inspired Picasso in very different ways: they strike the same pose, but Dora Maar is painted with strong lines and vibrant colours, suggesting a passionate, vivacious personality, while Marie-Thérèse's muted colours and soft contours convey serenity and peace.

The museum also holds a substantial number of Picasso's **engravings**, **ceramics** and **sculpture**, reflecting the remarkable ease with which the artist moved from one medium to another. Some of the most arresting sculptures (room 17) are those he created from recycled household objects, such as the endearing *La Chèvre* (The Goat), whose stomach is made from a basket, and the *Tête de taureau* (Bull's head), an ingenious pairing of a bicycle seat and handlebars. Interspersed throughout the collection are paintings that Picasso bought or was given by his contemporaries, as well as his collection of African masks and sculptures, his Communist party membership cards and sketches of Stalin, and photographs of him in his studio taken by Brassaï.

Place des Vosges and around

Map 4, D11. M° Chemin-Vert/St-Paul/Bastille.

Arguably the city's most beautiful square, the **place des Vosges** is a masterpiece of aristocratic elegance. Bordered by arcaded pink-brick and stone mansions, with a formal garden at its centre, the *place* is the first example of planned development in the history of Paris. It was commissioned in 1605 by Henri IV and was inaugurated in 1612 for the wedding of Louis XIII and Anne of Austria; it is Louis' statue – or, rather, a replica of it – that stands hidden by chestnut trees in the middle of the grass and gravel gardens. The gardens' shady benches are ideal for a break from sightseeing or you can dine al fresco at one of the restaurants under the arcades while buskers fill the air with jazz or classical music. Children play in the sandpits or make the most of the fact that this is one of the few parks in Paris where the grass isn't out of bounds.

Through all the vicissitudes of history, the *place* has never lost its cachet as a smart address. Among the many celebrities who made their homes here was Victor Hugo; his house, at no. 6, where he wrote much of his novel *Les Misérables*, is now a museum, the **Maison de Victor Hugo** (Tues–Sun

10am–6pm; closed public hols; free). Hugo's life, including his nineteen years of exile in Jersey and Guernsey, is evoked through a somewhat sparse collection of memorabilia, portraits, photographs and first editions of his works. What you do get, though, is an idea of his prodigious creativity: as well as being a prolific writer he drew – a number of his ink drawings are exhibited – and designed his own furniture; he even put together a Chinese-style dining room, re-created in its entirety here.

From the southwest corner of the *place*, a door leads through to the formal château garden, *orangerie* and exquisite Renaissance facade of the **Hôtel de Sully**. The garden, with its benches, makes for a peaceful rest-stop. Temporary photographic exhibitions, usually with social, historical or anthropological themes, are mounted in the *hôtel* by the **Mission du Patrimoine Photographique** (Tues–Sun 10am–6.30pm; €4).

Rue des Rosiers and the Jewish Quarter

Map 4, B10–C11. M° St-Paul.

Crammed with kosher food shops, delicatessens, restaurants and Hebrew bookshops, the narrow **rue des Rosiers**, one block south of the rue des Francs-Bourgeois, has been the heart of the city's **Jewish quarter** ever since the twelfth century, despite incursions by trendy bars and clothes shops in recent times. There's also a distinctly Mediterranean flavour to the quartier, as seen in the many falafel stalls, testimony to the influence of the **North African Sephardim**, who, since the end of World War II, have sought refuge here from the uncertainties of life in the French ex-colonies. They have replenished Paris's Jewish population, depleted when its Ashkenazim, having escaped the pogroms of Eastern Europe, were rounded up by the Nazis and the French police and transported back east to concentration camps in 1942–44.

Musée d'Art et d'Histoire du Judaïsme

Map 4, A8. Mon–Fri 11am–6pm, Sun 10am–6pm; €6.80; Ⓦwww.mahj.org; M° Rambuteau.

Housed in the attractively restored Hôtel de Saint-Aignan, the **Musée d'Art et d'Histoire du Judaïsme**, at 71 rue du Temple, traces the culture and history mainly of the Jews in France, though there are also many artefacts from the rest of Europe and North Africa. The result is a comprehensive collection, as educational as it is beautiful. The free audioguides in English are well worth picking up if you want to get the most out of the museum.

Highlights include a Gothic-style Hanukkah lamp, one of the very few French Jewish artefacts to survive from the period before the expulsion of the Jews from France in 1394; an Italian gilded circumcision chair from the seventeenth century; and a completely intact late-nineteenth-century Austrian *Sukkah*, a temporary dwelling for the celebration of the Harvest, decorated with paintings of Jerusalem and the Mount of Olives. Among other artefacts are Moroccan wedding garments, highly decorated marriage contracts from eighteenth-century Modena and gorgeous, almost whimsical, spice containers.

The museum also holds the Dreyfus archives, a gift from his grandchildren, and appropriately enough, one room is devoted to the notorious **Dreyfus affair** of the 1890s, in which Alfred Dreyfus, who was a captain in the French army and a Jew, was wrongly convicted of spying for the Germans and only released after a high-profile campaign by prominent left-wing intellectuals and republicans. The affair is documented with photographs, press clippings and letters – including some from Dreyfus to his wife speaking of his terrible loneliness and suffering in the penal colony of Devil's Island in French Guyana.

The last few rooms contain a significant collection of paintings and sculpture by **Jewish artists** – Marc Chagall, Samuel Hirszenberg, Chaïm Soutine and Jacques Lipchitz

– who came to live in Paris at the beginning of the twentieth century.

More recent Jewish history is taken up by the Mémorial de la Shoah on the other side of the Marais (see below). Also here is an installation by contemporary artist Christian Boltanski: one of the exterior walls of a small courtyard is covered with black-bordered death announcements printed with the names of the Jewish artisans who once lived in the building, a number of whom were deported to concentration camps.

Mémorial de la Shoah

Map 4, B12. Mon–Fri & Sun 10am–6pm; free; ⓦ www.memorialdelashoah.org; M° St-Paul/Pont-Marie.

On the other side of rue de Rivoli, at 17 rue Geoffroy l'Asnier, the grim fate of French Jews in the last war is commemorated at the **Mémorial de la Shoah**. Since 1956 this has been the site of the Mémorial du Martyr Juif Inconnu (Memorial to an Unknown Jewish Martyr), a sombre crypt containing a large black marble star of David, with a candle at its centre. In January 2005, President Chirac opened a new museum here and unveiled a **Wall of Names**, four giant slabs of marble engraved with the names of the 76,000 French Jews – around a quarter of the war-time population – sent to death camps from 1942 to 1944; ten researchers spent two and a half years trawling Gestapo documents and interviewing French families to compile the list. The weight of all these names is overwhelming.

The new **museum** is absorbing and gives a very detailed account of the history of Jews in France, especially Paris, during the German occupation. There are numerous documents, last letters from deportees to their families, videotaped testimony from survivors, numerous ID cards and photos.

The Quartier St-Paul-St-Gervais

The **Quartier St-Paul-St-Gervais**, below rues de Rivoli and St-Antoine, harbours some of the city's most atmospheric streets: rue Cloche-Perce with its crooked steps and lanterns; rue François-Miron, lined with its tottering medieval timbered houses; and cobbled rue des Barres, perfumed by the scent of roses from nearby gardens and intermittent wafts of incense from the late-Gothic **church of St-Gervais-St-Protais** (map 4, A11). On the outside, the church is somewhat battered owing to a direct hit from a shell fired from Big Bertha in 1918. However, it's more pleasing inside, with some lovely stained glass, carved misericords and a seventeenth-century organ, Paris's oldest.

Between rues Fourcy and François-Miron (entrance at 4 rue de Fourcy), a gorgeous Marais mansion, the early eighteenth-century Hôtel Hénault de Cantobre, has been turned into the **Maison Européenne de la Photographie** (map 4, B11; Wed–Sun 11am–8pm; €6, free Wed after 5pm; Ⓦwww.mep-fr.org; M° St-Paul/Pont-Marie), dedicated to the art of contemporary photography. Temporary shows combine with a revolving exhibition of the Maison's permanent collection; young photographers and photo-journalists get a look in, as well as artists using photography in multimedia creations or installation art. A library and *videothèque* can be freely consulted, and there's a stylish café.

7

The Quartier Latin and the southeast

The traditional heartland of the **Quartier Latin** lies between the river and the Montagne-Ste-Geneviève, a hill once crowded with medieval colleges and now proudly crowned by the giant dome of the **Panthéon**. In medieval times, the quarter's name was a simple description of its Latin-speaking, scholarly inhabitants. Today, the name has stuck, often used – as here – to refer to the modern 5e (cinquième) arrondissement, an area defined by the boulevard St-Michel, to the west, and the river, to the north. It's still a deeply scholarly area: the northern half of the arrondissement alone boasts the famous **Sorbonne** and Jussieu campuses, plus a cluster of stellar academic institutes. While few students can afford the rents these days, they still maintain the quarter's traditions in its cheaper bars, cafés and *bistrots*, decamping to the Luxembourg gardens, over in St-Germain (see p.95) on sunny days.

The quarter's medieval heritage is superbly displayed in the **Musée National du Moyen Age**, which is worth visiting for the stunning tapestry series, the *Lady with the Unicorn*, alone. Out towards the eastern end of the 5e, the theme is more Arabic than Latin in the brilliantly designed **Institut du Monde Arabe** and **Paris Mosque**. Nearby, you'll find the flowerbeds, zoo and natural history museum of the leafy **Jardin des Plantes**.

The southern half of the 5e is less interesting, with the exception of the ancient, romantic thoroughfare of the **rue Mouffetard**, which still snakes its way south to the boundary of the 13e (treizième) arrondissement and the **Gobelins tapestry works**. Deep in the otherwise undistinguished southern swathe of Paris, **Chinatown** and the **Butte-aux-Cailles** are worth seeking out for their restaurants and bars, while east, on the riverfront, stand the dramatic library towers of the **Bibliothèque Nationale**.

Place St-Michel and around

The pivotal point of the Quartier Latin is **place St-Michel**, where the tree-lined boulevard St-Michel begins. The very name of this broad, leafy avenue evokes student chic, though these days dull commercial outlets have largely taken over the famous "boul' Mich". Nevertheless, the cafés and shops around the square are constantly jammed with people, mainly young and, in summer, largely foreign. A favourite meeting point is the pink-and-white fountain, which spills down from a statue of the archangel Michael stomping on the devil, at the back end of the *place*.

The touristy scrum is at its most ugly on and around **rue de la Huchette**, just east of the place St-Michel, which is largely given over to cheap bars and Greek seafood-and-disco tavernas. At the end of rue de la Huchette, **rue St-Jacques** follows the line of Roman Paris's main thoroughfare. Just west stands the largely fifteenth-century **church of St-Séverin**, with its entrance on rue des Prêtres

St-Séverin (Mon–Sat 11am–7.15pm, Sun 9am–8.30pm; M° St-Michel/Cluny-La Sorbonne). It's one of the city's most elegant churches, with splendidly virtuoso stonework in the Flamboyant (flame-like) Gothic style – notably in the choir and the window arch above the entrance.

The riverside

A short way east, the green **square Viviani** provides the most flattering of all views of Notre-Dame, and contains what is reputed to be Paris's oldest tree, a false acacia brought over from Guyana in 1680. The mutilated and disfigured church behind is **St-Julien-le-Pauvre** (daily 9.30am–12.30pm & 3–6.30pm; M° St-Michel/Maubert Mutualité), which dates from the same Gothic era as Notre-Dame.

A few steps along, rue de la Bûcherie brings you to the famous American-run bookshop **Shakespeare and Co**. The original shop – as owned by Sylvia Beach, long-suffering publisher of James Joyce's *Ulysses* – was on rue de l'Odéon. The modern successor is almost as writerly, staffed by would-be Hemingways who sleep upstairs and pay their rent by manning the tills. More books, postcards and prints are on sale from the **bouquinistes**, who display their wares in green, padlocked boxes hooked onto the parapet of the **riverside quais**. Upstream, the **Pont de l'Archevêche** – the archbishop's bridge – offers fine views of the Île-St-Louis.

The Musée du Moyen Age

Wed–Mon 9.15am–5.45pm; €5.50, €4 on Sun; Ⓦwww.musee-moyenage.fr; M° Cluny-La Sorbonne.

Heading south down boulevard St-Michel, away from the river, a couple of minutes' walk brings you to the remains of the third-century **Roman baths** and the **Hôtel de Cluny**, a sixteenth-century mansion built by the abbots of the powerful Cluny monastery in Burgundy as their Paris pied-à-terre. The *hôtel* now houses the richly rewarding **Musée National du Moyen Age**. Over and above the superb museum of medieval art, excellent **concerts** of medieval music are usually held on Friday lunchtimes (12.30pm) and Saturday afternoons (4pm).

On the ground floor, the highlight is the **Gallo-Roman bathhouse**. Displayed here are the twenty-one thirteenth-century heads of the **Kings of Judea**, lopped off the west front of Notre-Dame during the French Revolution. Arching over the *frigidarium*, or cold room, the vaults are preserved intact – though temporarily protected by corrugated sheets pending funds for restoration. They shelter two beautifully carved first- and second-century capitals, the *Seine Boatmen's Pillar* and the *Pillar of St-Landry*, which has animated-looking gods and musicians adorning three of its faces.

The undisputed star of the collection is the exquisitely executed **Lady with the Unicorn**, displayed in a specially darkened, chapel-like chamber on the first floor. Even if you don't like tapestries, it'll be hard not to be amazed by this one. The richly coloured, detailed and highly allegorical series, which was probably made in Brussels in the late fifteenth century, depicts the five senses. Each tapestry features a beautiful woman flanked by a lion and a unicorn, with a rich red background worked with myriad tiny flowers, birds, plants and animals. The meaning of the sixth and final panel, entitled *A Mon Seul Désir* ("To My Only Desire"), and depicting the woman putting away her necklace into a jewellery box held out by her servant, remains a mystery.

The rest of the first floor is an amazing ragbag of carved choir stalls, altarpieces, ivories, stained glass, illuminated Books of Hours, games, brassware and all manner of precious objets d'art. There's also the *hôtel*'s original Flamboyant **chapel**, its remarkable vault still splaying out from the central pillar.

The Sorbonne

In the heart of the Quartier Latin, on the south side of rue des Écoles, a cluster of grim-looking buildings belongs to a trio of élite institutions: the **Sorbonne**, Collège de France and Lycée Louis le Grand. Just like the medieval colleges that once huddled here, on the top of the Montagne-Ste-Geneviève, they attract some of the finest scholars from all over Europe.

At the head of narrow **rue Champollion**, with its huddle of arty cinemas, stands the traffic-free **place de la Sorbonne**. With its lime trees, fountains, cafés and book-toting students, it's a lovely spot for lingering. Overshadowing the graceful ensemble is the **Chapelle Ste-Ursule**, built in the 1640s by the great Cardinal Richelieu, whose tomb lies within. The chapel is certainly the most architecturally distinctive part of the modern-day Sorbonne, as the university buildings were entirely rebuilt in the 1880s. Sadly, in the era of anti-terrorism measures you're no longer able to go inside the Sorbonne's main **courtyard**, one of the flash-points of the historic student protests of May 1968.

The Panthéon

Daily: April–Sept 10am–6.30pm; Oct–March 10am–6pm; €7; RER Luxembourg/M° Cardinal-Lemoine.

The most visible of Paris's many domes graces the hulk of the **Panthéon**, the towering mausoleum that tops the Montagne-Ste-Geneviève. It was originally built as a church by Louis XV, on the site of the ruined Ste-Geneviève abbey, to thank the saint for curing him of illness and to emphasize the unity of church and state – not only had the original abbey church entombed Geneviève, Paris's patron saint, but it had been founded by Clovis, France's first Christian king. The building was only completed in 1789, whereupon the Revolution promptly transformed it into a mausoleum, adding the words *Aux grands hommes la patrie reconnaissante* ("The nation honours its great men") underneath the pediment of the giant portico. The remains of French heroes such as Voltaire, Rousseau, Hugo and Zola are now preserved in the vast, barrel-vaulted crypt below, along with more recent arrivals: Marie Curie (the only woman), with her husband Pierre (1995), writer and landmark culture minister André Malraux (1996), and the novelist Alexandre Dumas (2002).

The interior is well worth a visit for its unusual, secular decor. You can also see a working model of **Foucault's Pendulum** swinging from the dome. The original experiment, conducted here by the French physicist Léon Foucault in 1851, was the first to clearly demonstrate the rotation of the earth.

St-Étienne-du-Mont

Sloping downhill from the main portico of the Panthéon, broad rue Soufflot entices you west towards the Luxembourg gardens (see p.95). On the east side of the Panthéon, however, peeping over the walls of the **Lycée Henri IV**, a lone Gothic tower is all that remains of the earlier church of Ste-Geneviève. Geneviève's mortal remains, and those of two seventeenth-century literary greats who didn't make the Panthéon, Pascal and Racine, lie close at hand in the church of **St-Étienne-du-Mont**, on the corner of rue Clovis. The church's facade is a bit of an architectural hotch-potch, but it conceals a stunning interior, where the transition from Flamboyant Gothic choir to sixteenth-century nave is masked by an elaborate, catwalk-like rood screen, which arches across the width of the nave. This last feature is highly unusual in itself; most French rood screens fell victim to Protestant iconoclasts, reformers or revolutionaries.

Place de la Contrescarpe to Gobelins

East of the Panthéon, the villagey **rue de la Montagne-Ste-Geneviève**, with its cluster of café-bars and restaurants, descends towards place Maubert. Heading uphill, rue Descartes runs into the tiny and attractive **place de la Contrescarpe**, hub of the area's café life. On the sunnier, south-facing side of the square, the swanky *Café Delmas* was once the famous café *La Chope*, as described by Ernest Hemingway in *A Moveable Feast.*

Place de la Contrescarpe once stood at the edges of the medieval city. Leading south, the narrow, ancient incline of **rue Mouffetard** – or "La Mouffe", as it's known to locals – was for generations one of the great **market streets** of Paris. These days, its top half is given over to touristy eating places, but the market traditions still cling on at the southern end, and fascinating traces of the past can be seen adorning the older shop fronts – look out for nos. 6, 69 and 122. At no. 12, the old sign depicts a black man in stripey trousers waiting on his mistress, with the unconvincing legend, "*Au Nègre Joyeux*". Fruit and vegetable stalls do good business in the mornings, while the surrounding shops sell fine cheeses, wines and delicatessen foods. At 118bis is a great, old-fashioned market café (see p.207).

At the foot of rue Mouffetard, just beyond the beautiful, painted facade at no. 134, you'll find the church of **St-Médard** (Tues–Sun 8am–12.30pm & 2.30-7.30pm). Once a country parish church, with a simple Gothic nave, it now has a more elaborate, late-sixteenth-century choir. A short distance south of the church, across the wide boulevard St-Marcel, lies the **Gobelins tapestry works**, at 42 avenue des Gobelins, which has operated here for some four hundred years. On the fascinating, sixty-minute guided tour (in French only; Tues–Thurs 2pm & 2.45pm; €8; M° Gobelins), you can watch tapestries being made by painfully slow, traditional methods: each weaver completes between one and four square metres a year.

Val-de-Grâce

West of rue Mouffetard, you quickly leave other tourists behind as you penetrate the academic heart of the Quartier Latin. It's a closed world to outsiders, and there's little point in visiting this corner of the city unless it's to see the magnificent Baroque church of **Val-de-Grâce**, set just back from rue St-Jacques. Built by Anne of Austria as an act of pious gratitude following the birth of her first son in 1638, its skyward-thrusting dome and double-pedimented facade make it a suitably awesome monument to the young prince who went on to reign as Louis XIV.

You can only enter via the **Musée du Service de Santé des Armées** (Tues & Wed noon–5pm, Sat & Sun 1.30–5pm; closed Aug; €5), which occupies an old Benedictine convent that has now been converted into a wearyingly thorough history of military medicine. The church, properly known as the **Chapelle St-Louis**, isn't quite as large as you'd imagine after seeing the grandiose exterior, but it's still staggeringly impressive in the Roman Baroque manner. Inside the dome, Pierre Mignard's wonderful trompe l'oeil fresco of Paradise depicts Anne of Austria offering a model of the church up to the Virgin.

The Paris Mosque

Daily except Fri & Muslim holidays 9am–noon & 2–6pm; €3; ⓦwww.mosquee-de-paris.net.

East of rue Mouffetard, across rue Monge, lie some of the city's most agreeable surprises. Just beyond place du Puits de l'Ermite stand the gate and crenellated walls of the **Paris Mosque**, built in a Moroccan-influenced style in the early 1920s. You can wander among the sunken gardens and patios with their polychrome tiles and carved ceilings, but non-Muslims are asked not to enter the prayer room. The back gate, on the southeast corner of the complex, on rue Daubenton, leads into a lovely **tearoom** (see p.206), and an atmospheric **hammam** (see p.285).

Jardin des Plantes

Daily: April–Aug 8am–7.30pm; Sept–March 8am–dusk; free; ⓦwww.mnhn.fr; M° Gare d'Austerlitz/Jussieu/Place Monge. Natural History

Museum Wed–Mon 10am–6pm; €8. Ménagerie summer Mon–Sat 9am–6pm, Sun 9.30am–6.30pm; winter daily 9am–5pm; €7.

Behind the mosque, the **Jardin des Plantes** was founded as a medicinal herb garden in 1626 and gradually evolved into Paris's botanical gardens. With hothouses, shady avenues of trees, lawns to sprawl on, museums and a zoo, it's a pleasant oasis in which to while away a few hours. Magnificent, varied floral beds make a fine approach to the collection of buildings that form the **Muséum National d'Histoire Naturelle**, of which the most interesting part is the **Grande Galerie de l'Évolution**, housed in a dramatically restored nineteenth-century glass-domed building (the entrance is off rue Buffon). The story of evolution and the relations between human beings and nature is told with the aid of stuffed animals (rescued from the old zoology museum) and clever sound and light effects. Real, live animals can be seen in the unpleasantly cramped **ménagerie** across the park to the northeast near rue Cuvier. Founded just after the Revolution, this is France's oldest zoo – and it shows.

Institut du Monde Arabe

Tues–Sun 10am–6pm; free, museum €3; Ⓦwww.imarabe.org; M° Jussieu/Cardinal-Lemoine.

By the river, immediately to the north of the uncompromisingly modern and much-loathed Jussieu campus building stands the **Institut du Monde Arabe**. It is a stunning and radical piece of architecture, designed by the celebrated Jean Nouvel. The southern facade comprises thousands of tiny diaphragm-like shutters, which modulate the light levels inside while simultaneously mimicking a *moucharabiyah*, the traditional Arab latticework balcony.

The institute regularly puts on hit exhibitions and has an excellent concert programme. There's also a sleek permanent **museum**, which uses an array of exquisite artefacts to trace the evolution of the arts and sciences in the Islamic world. The most precious treasures are on the lowest floor, where you'll find exquisitely crafted ceramics, metalwork and carpets from all over the Muslim world.

Up on the ninth floor, the terrace offers brilliant **views** over the Seine towards the apse of Notre-Dame. At the adjacent café-restaurant you can drink mint tea and nibble on cakes.

Chinatown and the Butte aux Cailles

Much of the **13e arrondissement**, in the southeastern corner of Paris, was completely cleared in the 1960s, its crowded, tight-knit slums replaced by tower blocks. The overall architectural gloom is only alleviated by the culinary delights of the **Chinese quarter**. Avenues de Choisy and d'Ivry, in particular, are full of Vietnamese, Thai, Cambodian and Laotian restaurants and food shops, as is **Les Olympiades**, a pedestrian area bizarrely suspended between giant tower blocks, and accessed solely by escalator.

Where the prewar streets were left untouched, however, around the minor hillock of the **Butte-aux-Cailles**, a community-spirited neighbourhood flourishes, making this one of the most attractive areas of Paris for low-key nightlife. Alongside the old left-wing establishments – the bar *La Folie en Tête* at no. 33 and the restaurant *Le Temps des Cerises* at nos. 18–20 – are plenty of relaxed, youthful places to eat and drink till the small hours. The easiest way to arrive is via métro Corvisart, from which you cross the road and head straight through a passageway in the large apartment building opposite, then climb the steps that lead up through the small Brassaï gardens to rue des Cinq Diamants, in the heart of the Butte.

Bibliothèque Nationale

Tues–Sat 10am–8pm, Sun noon–7pm; €3 for a day pass; ⓦwww.bnf.fr; M° Quai de la Gare/Bibliothèque-François Mitterrand.

The easternmost edge of the 13e, between the river and the Austerlitz train tracks, has been utterly transformed in the last decade as part of the **Paris Rive Gauche** urban redevelopment scheme. The star architectural attraction is the **Bibliothèque Nationale de France**, its four enormous L-shaped towers intended to look like open books. They attracted widespread derision after shutters had to be added behind the glazing in order to protect the collections from sunlight. Once you mount the giant wooden steps surrounding the library, however, the perspective changes utterly. From here you can look down into a huge sunken pine grove, with glass walls that filter light into the floors below your feet. There are occasional small-scale exhibitions, and the **reading rooms** on the "haut-jardin" level – along with their unrivalled collection of foreign newspapers – are open to everyone over 16.

A short way upstream, the futuristic double-ribbon walkways of the brand new **Passerelle Bercy-Tolbiac** now span the Seine. Between the bridge and the Pont de Tolbiac, several **barges** have made the area a nightlife attraction in its own right (see p.236). The ex-lighthouse boat called *Batofar*, and the Chinese barge *La Guinguette Pirate,* in particular, make excellent venues for a drink, a gig, or a night's low-key clubbing.

8

St-Germain

Picturesque **St-Germain** has all the sophistication of the Right Bank mixed with a certain easy-going chic that makes it uniquely appealing. Encompassing the chichi 6e (sixième) arrondissement and the eastern fringe of the 7e (septième), it is one of the liveliest quarters of the city. Since the postwar era, when it was the natural home of arty trendsetters, the quartier has moved ever further upmarket. Luckily, despite gentrification it has retained some of its former offbeat charm.

That said, **shopping** is now king. The streets around the Carrefour de la Croix-Rouge and place St-Sulpice, in particular, swarm with designer boutiques, while towards the river, it's antique shops and art dealers that dominate. Meanwhile, well-heeled foodies now flock to celebrity chefs' gastronomic **restaurants**, and foreign visitors fill the simpler *bistrots* around Mabillon.

Chief among the quartier's many attractions are the **Musée d'Orsay**, loved as much for its stunning railway-station setting as its Impressionist collection, and the notoriously romantic **Jardin du Luxembourg**, one of the largest and loveliest green spaces in the city. There are some fine buildings to take in as you shop or stroll, notably the domed **Collège de France** and the churches of St-Germain-des-Prés and **St-Sulpice**. Two small, single-artist museums, the **Musée Maillol** and **Musée Delacroix**, make for an intimate visit, while the art exhibitions at the **Musée du Luxembourg** are regularly among the city's most exciting.

From the river to the Odéon

The most dramatic approach to St-Germain is across the river from the Louvre via the elegant footbridge, the **Pont des Arts**. From here you can take in the classic upstream view of the Île de la Cité and admire the graceful dome and pediment at the end of the bridge, which belong to the **Collège des Quatre-Nations**, seat of the arts and sciences academies of the **Institut de France**. Next door to the institute, at 11 quai de Conti, is the **Hôtel des Monnaies**, redesigned as the Mint in the late eighteenth century and now reduced to housing the **Musée de la Monnaie** (Tues–Fri 11am–5.30pm, Sat & Sun noon–5.30pm; €8), a dry collection of coins and coin-making tools.

The riverside chunk of the 6e is defined by **rue St-André-des-Arts** and **rue Jacob**, both lined with bookshops, commercial art galleries, antique shops, cafés and restaurants. If you're looking for lunch, you'll find numerous little *bistrots* on **place** and **rue St-André-des-Arts**. Alternatively, you could make for **rue de Buci**, up towards boulevard St-Germain, which was once a proper street market, but has now been almost completely gentrified.

Towards the end of rue St-André-des-Arts, just short of the main action on rue de Buci, look out for the intriguing little passage of the **Cour du Commerce St André**. Backing onto the street is *Le Procope* – Paris's first coffee house, which opened its doors in 1686 and was frequented by Voltaire and Robespierre. Sadly, the atmosphere is a bit stiff these days. At its southern end, the Cour du Commerce opens out at the **Carrefour de l'Odéon**, named after the recently restored **Théâtre de l'Odéon**, whose proud Doric facade fronts a handsome semi-circular plaza a few steps to the south.

Jardin du Luxembourg

The **Palais du Luxembourg**, immediately south of the Odéon theatre, stands proudly at the eastern end of rue de Vaugirard, Paris's longest street. Today, the palace belongs to the French Senate, but it was originally constructed for Marie de Médicis, Henri IV's widow, to remind her of the Palazzo Pitti, in her native Florence.

Behind lies the delightful **Jardin du Luxembourg** (open roughly dawn to dusk), the lovely gardens that are the chief lung of the Left Bank, with formal lawns, floral parterres and quieter wooded areas, all dotted with sculptures. The gardens get fantastically crowded with visitors on summer days, but they're busy pretty much year round with Parisian families and students. Children can rent toy yachts to sail on the central round pond, or head to the more active, western side of the park which boasts **tennis courts**, donkey rides, a marionette show, a large playground and the inevitable sandy area for boules. There's a pleasant tree-shaded **café** roughly 100m northeast of the pond.

At the northwestern end of the garden, entered via 19 rue de Vaugirard, the **Musée du Luxembourg** (hours and prices vary for each exhibition) puts on some of Paris's biggest and most exciting art exhibitions. Recent successes have included twentieth-century self portraits and "Veronèse profane". You can check what's showing, and when, at ⓦwww.museeduluxembourg.fr.

Place St-Sulpice

North of the Jardin du Luxembourg, the **church of St-Sulpice** (daily 7.30am–7.30pm) fronts onto the broad and enchanting place St-Sulpice, with its lion fountain and chestnut trees. The church itself is a muscular classical edifice erected either side of 1700. For decades, the gloomy **interior** was best known for three **Delacroix murals** which can be found in the first chapel on the right, but since the publication of a certain thriller (see box below), St-Sulpice's visitors have come for one thing alone: the **gnomon**. A lens in the south transept window, long since removed, once focused the sun's rays on a narrow strip of brass, which still runs right across the floor of the nave to an obelisk on the north side, marking the exact time of the winter and summer solstices. As a printed notice coldly points out, it is an astronomical device, and from it "no mystical notion can be derived".

On the sunny north side of the square, the outside tables at the *Café de la Mairie* hum with trendy chatter on fine

Da Vinci Paris

Ever since the publication of Dan Brown's multi-million-selling thriller, *The Da Vinci Code*, guides and security guards at the Louvre and the church of St-Sulpice have been fielding some unusual questions: Are Mary Magdalene's remains really buried at the foot of the Pyramide Inversée? Is the Mona Lisa a representation of an androgynous god/goddess? And does the Louvre pyramid have exactly 666 panes of glass?

Of course, there are no holy relics of Mary Magdalene, Mona Lisa's real story is very different – if just as fascinating (see p.40) – and the Louvre pyramid in fact has 673 panes, not 666. As for St-Sulpice, a notice in the church tersely proclaims, "contrary to fanciful allegations in a recent best-selling novel", it is "not a vestige of pagan temple". And neither does it stand on the meridian, let alone some mystical "Rose Line".

There is a real gnomon at St-Sulpice, and an Arago line beginning at the Paris observatory, but otherwise the book's woeful inaccuracies had Parisians wincing. Worst of all is the book's wayward geography: Dan Brown has a Citroën skimming south past the Opéra to Place Vendôme, when it should be skimming north, and ploughing west from the Tuileries towards the Louvre, when it should be ploughing east. Most heinously, the heroine buys two tickets to Lille at the Gare St-Lazare when, as any self-respecting Parisian knows, she should have been at the Gare du Nord...

days. However, the main attractions here are the fashion boutiques, such as the very elegant **Yves Saint Laurent Rive Gauche**, on the corner of the ancient rue des Canettes.

Mabillon and St-Germain-des-Prés

North of St-Sulpice, pretty rue Mabillon passes the **Marché St-Germain**, a 1990s reconstruction of an ancient covered market. The area around the Marché, on rues Princess, Lobineau, Guisarde and des Canettes, is a favoured dining destination.

The **boulevard St-Germain** was bulldozed right through the Left Bank under Baron Haussmann (see p.323). For the greater part of its length, it looks much the same as any of Paris's great avenues, but a short stretch around **place St-Germain-des-Prés** forms the very heart of the quarter. The famous **Deux Magots** café stands on one corner of the square, while the equally celebrated **Flore** lies a few steps further along the boulevard. Both cafés are renowned for the number of *philosophes*, politicos and literary greats whose backsides have shined their seats.

The robust tower opposite the *Deux Magots* belongs to the **church of St-Germain-des-Prés**, which is all that remains of an enormous Benedictine monastery whose lands once stretched right across the Left Bank. The church itself is one of twenty-first-century Paris's oldest surviving buildings, parts of it dating back to the late tenth and early eleventh centuries. The choir, however, was rebuilt in the fashionable Gothic style in the mid-twelfth century – work that's just about visible under the heavy greens and golds of nineteenth-century paintwork.

Place de Furstenberg and the Musée Delacroix

Hidden away around the back of St-Germain-des-Prés, off rue Jacob, **place de Furstenberg** is one of Paris's prettiest and quietest squares. Tucked into its northwest corner is the **Musée Delacroix**, 6 rue de Furstenberg (daily except Tues 9.30am–5pm; €5), a charming miniature museum displaying sketches by the artist and various personal effects. Delacroix lived and worked in the house here from 1857 until his death in 1863, watched over by Jenny Le Guillou, who'd been his servant since 1835. You can visit the bedroom where he died, now graced by Jenny's portrait, while the little sitting room houses the museum's only really notable work, the intense *Madeleine au désert* of 1845.

Around Sèvres-Babylone

The area around Sèvres-Babylone métro station, at the western end of the 6ᵉ arrondissement and the eastern fringe of the 7ᵉ, is one of the best for **shopping**. You might not find the most exclusive Right Bank designers or the more alternative-minded Marais and Montmartre boutiques, but rues Bonaparte, Madame, de Sèvres, de Grenelle, du Vieux-Colombier, du Dragon, du Four and des Saints-Pères are lined with well-known names, from Agnès B on rue du Vieux-Colombier to Zara on rue de Rennes.

On Sunday mornings, the celebrated Raspail **Marché Bio**, or organic food market, lines the boulevard Raspail between the Sèvres-Babylone and Rennes métro stations. Just over the boundary with the 7ᵉ arrondissement, at the far side of the green Square Boucicaut, stands the city's oldest department store, **Le Bon Marché** (see p.245), now one of Paris's best and most upmarket.

Musée Maillol and Deyrolle

Museum: 61 rue de Grenelle; Wed–Mon 11am–6pm; €8; Ⓦwww.museemaillol.com; M° Rue-du-Bac.

The **Musée Maillol** overstuffs its tiny building with post-Impressionist sculptor Aristide Maillol's endlessly buxom nudes. Maillol's most famous work, the dumpily curvacious *Mediterranean*, sits on the first floor at the top of the stairs. The exhibits all belong to Dina Vierny, Maillol's former model and inspiration. Works by other contemporaries are also collected here, including drawings by Bonnard (for whom Dina also modelled), Dufy and Matisse, and a room full of Poliakoff's jaggedy abstracts on the second floor. The museum also organizes excellent exhibitions of twentieth-century art.

You might not normally go out of your way to visit a taxidermist's, but **Deyrolle**, 46 rue du Bac (Mon–Sat 10am–7pm; free), just north of the Rue-du-Bac métro, should be an exception. On the first floor above an upscale gardening shop is a deeply old-fashioned room packed with scores of stuffed rabbits, ducks, sheep, deer, boars, bears – and even big cats and a polar bear. Children, in particular, tend to be fascinated by the place.

The Musée d'Orsay

1 rue de la Légion d'Honneur; Tues, Wed, Fri & Sat 10am–6pm, Thurs 10am–9.45pm, Sun 9am-6pm; €7.50, free to under-18s and on first Sun of the month; Ⓦwww.musee-orsay.fr; M° Solférino/RER Musée-d'Orsay.

Facing the Tuileries gardens across the river is one of Paris's most-visited sites, the **Musée d'Orsay**, with its entrance on rue de la Légion de l'Honneur. Housing painting and sculpture from the period spanning 1848 to 1914, the gallery's highlights are the electrifying works of the **Impressionists** and **Post-Impressionists**.

The **building** itself was inaugurated as a railway station for the 1900 World Fair and continued to serve the stations of southwest France until 1939. It stood disused until 1986, when the job of redesigning the interior as a museum was given to the fashionable Milanese architect Gae Aulenti. The **café** on the upper level of the museum – with its summer terrace and wonderful view of Montmartre through the giant railway clock – and the resplendently gilded restaurant and tea room on the middle level, are great spots to recuperate.

The collection

The **ground floor**, under the great glass arch, is devoted to pre-1870 work, with a double row of sculptures running down the central aisle like railway tracks. On the south side of this level, towards rue de Lille, the first set of rooms is dedicated to **Ingres**, **Delacroix** and the serious-minded, Classically-influenced works of the painters acceptable to the mid-nineteenth-century salons; just beyond are the relatively wacky works of Puvis de Chavannes, Gustave Moreau and the younger Degas.

The influential **Barbizon school** and the **Realists** are showcased on the Seine side, with canvases by Daumier, Corot, Millet and Courbet; these were some of the first to break with the established norms of moralism and idealization of the past. Just a few steps away, room 14 explodes with the early controversies of **Monet**'s violently light-filled *Femmes au Jardin* (1867) and **Manet**'s provocative *Olympia* (1863), which heralded the arrival of Impressionism.

To continue chronologically, make for the **upper level**, which has been done up like a suite of attic studios. Many visitors experience electrifying feelings of familiarity and recognition as they encounter paintings such as Monet's *Poppies*, Manet's *Déjeuner sur l'Herbe*, Degas' *L'Absinthe* and Renoir's *Bal du Moulin de la Galette*. Beyond lie the heavyweight masterpieces of **Monet** and **Renoir** in their middle and late periods, and the experimental, fervid works of **Van Gogh** and **Cézanne**.

Passing the café, the final suites are devoted to pastels and the various offspring of Impressionism, from **Rousseau**'s dream-like *La Charmeuse de Serpent* (1907) to **Gauguin**'s Tahitian paintings and **Pointillist** works by Seurat, Signac and others. The upper level ends with **Toulouse-Lautrec** at his caricaturial, nightclubbing best.

Down on the middle level, the flow of the painting section's chronology continues with **Vuillard** and **Bonnard**. On the far side of this level, overlooking the Seine, you can see a less familiar side of late-nineteenth-century painting, featuring large-scale, epic, naturalist works. The painting collection ends with a troubling handful of international **Symbolist** paintings, including **Klimt**'s *Rosiers sous les Arbres* and some of **Munch**'s lesser-known works.

On the parallel sculpture terraces, nineteenth-century marbles on the Seine side face early-twentieth-century pieces across the divide, but the **Rodin terrace** bridging the two puts almost everything else to shame.

9

The Eiffel Tower quarter

Standing sentinel over a great bend in the Seine as it flows southwest out of Paris, the monumental flagpole that is the **Eiffel Tower** surveys the most splendid of all Paris's districts, embracing the palatial heights of the Trocadéro, on the Right Bank, and the wealthy, western swathe of the 7e (septième) arrondissement, on the Left. Sparsely populated by members of the old and new aristocracies, the area is home to some compelling **museums**. Newest on the block in the 7e is the museum of primitive art at **Quai Branly**. At the other end of the scale, though close at hand, the city's museum of the sewer system is actually found down in the **sewers**. A little further east, the huge military complex of **Les Invalides** is home to a gigantic war museum, while nearby the sculptor **Rodin** has a beautiful private house entirely devoted to his works. Across the river, in the Trocadéro quarter of the 16e arrondissement, the **Musée Guimet** displays a sumptuous collection of Asian Buddhist art, while the landmark Neo-classical palaces of **Tokyo**, **Chaillot** and **Galliera**, on the elevated north bank of the Seine, house museums devoted to modern and contemporary art, fashion and architecture. But for all the pomp and history, corners of neighbourhood life do exist in this quarter – along **rue de Babylone**, for example, and in the wedge of homely streets between the Invalides and the Champ de Mars, centred on the **rue Cler** market.

The Eiffel Tower and around

Daily: mid-June to Aug 9am–midnight; Sept to mid-June 9.30am–11pm; €10.70 (for the top; access until 10.30pm), €7.50 (second level) or €4.10 (first level). Stairs to second level €3.80 (access closes 6pm Sept to mid-June). RER Champ-de-Mars–Tour Eiffel.

It's hard to believe that the **Eiffel Tower**, the quintessential symbol both of Paris and the brilliance of industrial engineering, was designed to be a temporary structure for a world fair – the 1889 Exposition Universelle, to be precise. When completed, the tower was, at 300m, the tallest building in the world. Outraged critics protested against this "grimy factory chimney" while Eiffel took a more romantic view, claiming that his tower "was formed by the wind itself".

Outside daylight hours, distinctive sodium lights illuminate the structure, while a double searchlight has swept the city's skies since the millennium celebrations. For the first ten minutes of every hour thousands of effervescent lights scramble and fizz about the structure, defining the famous silhouette in luminescent champagne.

It's well worth going all the way up: Paris looks surreally microscopic from the top, even if the views are arguably better from the second level, especially on hazier days.

Stretching out from the legs of the Eiffel Tower, the **Champs de Mars** have been open fields ever since they were used as a parading area for royal troops – hence their name "the Martial Fields". At the far southern end lie the eighteenth-century buildings of the **École Militaire**, originally founded in 1751 by Louis XV for the training of aristocratic army officers – including the "little corporal", Napoleon Bonaparte. Behind lies the uninspiring headquarters of **UNESCO**, built in 1958.

The riverbank south of the Eiffel Tower

Heading south along the left bank of the Seine, you can watch the métro trains trundling across to Passy on the top level of the two-decker **Pont de Bir-Hakeim**. Up on the adjacent, raised walkway, at the beginning of boulevard de Grenelle, a bronze sculptural group commemorates the notorious **rafle du Vel d'Hiv**, the Nazi and French-aided round up of 13,152 Parisian Jews in July 1942. Leading down from the very middle of the Pont de Bir-Hakeim is the **Allée des Cygnes**, or "swan walk"; a narrow, midstream island built up on raised concrete embankments, it offers one of Paris's most curious and satisfying walks. At the downstream end is a scaled-down version of the **Statue of Liberty** – a reminder that the statue, rather like the idea of liberty itself, was originally France's gift to America.

Further south still, on the fringe of the city limits, lies the delightful **Parc André-Citroën** (daily dawn–dusk; M° Javel/Balard). It's as much a sight to visit in its own right as a place to lounge around or throw a Frisbee. The central grassy area is straightforward enough, but around it you'll find futuristic terraces, concrete-walled gardens with abstract themes, a massive electronically controlled dancing fountain – a favourite children's play area on hot days – and a **tethered balloon**, which rises and sinks regularly on calm days, taking small groups 150m above the ground (daily 9.30am to 45min before the park closes; call to check weather conditions on the day ⓣ01.44.26.20.00; Mon–Fri €10, Sat & Sun €12, children aged 3–12 €5/7).

Musée du Quai Branly

See Ⓦwww.quaibranly.fr for opening hours and ticket prices; RER Pont de l'Alma.

The sparkling new **Musée du Quai Branly** stands just a short distance upstream of the Eiffel Tower. One of Jacques Chirac's pet projects (the president has a passion for non-European art), it brings together the Musée des Arts d'Afrique et d'Océanie and the ethnography department from the Musée de l'Homme, while also providing space for temporary exhibitions, plays and contemporary non-European dance. Even if the rather specialized collections of exotic, folky art-objects aren't your thing, the museum is worth visiting for its bold architecture and spectacular, open-air roof terrace, complete with restaurant, designer ponds and views of the Eiffel Tower.

The sewers

May–Sept Mon–Wed, Sat & Sun 11am–5pm; Oct–April Mon–Wed, Sat & Sun 11am–4pm; €3.80; RER Pont de l'Alma.

A little way east of the quai Branly site, on the northeast side of the busy junction of place de la Résistance, is the entrance to the **sewers**, or **les égouts**. It's dark, damp and noisy with gushing water down there, but thankfully not all that smelly. The main part of the visit runs along a gantry walk perched alarmingly above a main sewer. Here, bilingual displays of photographs, engravings, dredging tools, lamps and other flotsam and jetsam turn the history of the city's water supply and waste management into a surprisingly fascinating topic. What the exhibit doesn't tell you is that around thirty times a year parts of the system become overloaded with rainwater, and the sewer workers have to empty the excess – waste and all – straight into the Seine.

Quai d'Orsay and rue Cler

A little further upstream from the sewers, the **American Church** on the quai d'Orsay, together with the American College nearby at 31 avenue Bosquet, is a nodal point in the well-organized life of Paris's large American community.

Just to the south, and in stark contrast with the austerity of much of the rest of the 7^{e} arrondissement, is the attractive, village-like wedge of early-nineteenth-century streets between avenue Bosquet and the Invalides. The heart of this miniature *quartier* is the lively market street **rue Cler**, whose cross-streets, rue de Grenelle and rue St-Dominique, are full of neighbourhood shops, posh *bistrots* and little hotels.

The **Pont Alexandre III** is surely the most extravagant bridge in the city, its single-span metal arch stretching 109m across the river. It was unveiled in 1900, just in time for the world fair. The nymph stretching out downstream represents the Seine, matched by a nymph symbolizing St Petersburg's River Neva facing upstream.

On the Left Bank, the green **Esplanade des Invalides** parades down towards the resplendently gilded dome of the **Hôtel des Invalides**. Built as a home for wounded soldiers on the orders of Louis XIV, whose equestrian statue tops the building's giant central arch, it's a kind of barracks version of Versailles, stripped of finer flourishes but crushingly grand nonetheless. The 12kg of gold added to the dome for the bicentennial of the Revolution only accentuates its splendour. A short way further east sits the Palais Bourbon, whose riverfront facade was added by Napoleon to match the pseudo-Greek of the Madeleine. It is now the home of the **Assemblée Nationale**, or French parliament.

The Musée de l'Armée and the Église du Dôme

Daily: April–Sept 10am–5.30pm; Oct–March 10am–4.30pm; €7, ticket also valid for Napoleon's tomb, see below; Ⓦwww.invalides.org; M° Invalides/Varenne/La Tour-Maubourg.

The Hôtel des Invalides, formerly a hospice for wounded or infirm soldiers, today houses the vast **Musée de l'Armée**, the national war museum, whose most interesting wing, reached via the south entrance beside the Église du Dôme, is devoted to Général de Gaulle and World War II. By comparison, the vast collection of armour, uniforms and weapons that makes up the main part of the museum, on either side of the front court, is probably best left to tin-soldier fanatics or military-history buffs. That said, a complete refit of these sections (scheduled to finish in 2007) will do much to shake off the collection's long-gathered dust.

Up in the attics of the east wing, the super-scale models of French ports and fortified cities in the **Musée des Plans-Reliefs** (same hours and ticket as Musée de l'Armée above) are crying out for a few miniature armies. Giant three-dimensional maps, they were created to plan defences or plot potential artillery positions. With the eerie green glow of their landscapes only just illuminating the long, tunnel-like attic, the effect is rather chilling.

At the core of the complex is a double church, built in the 1670s by Jules Hardouin-Mansart. The spartan northern section, known as the **Église des Soldats**, is reached via the main northern courtyard of Les Invalides (no ticket required). It is lined with almost a hundred banners, captured by the French army over the centuries. The **Église du Dôme** (same hours and ticket as Musée de l'Armée, above) has a separate entrance on the south side of the complex. It was intended for the private worship of Louis XIV and the royal family and is a supreme example of architectural pomp. Today, it centres around Napoleon's massive sarcophagus, grandiosely carved in deep red quartzite.

The Musée Rodin

Tues–Sun: April–Sept 9.30am–5.45pm, garden closes at 6.45pm; Oct–March 9.30am–4.45pm, garden closes at 5pm; €5, or €3 on Sun, garden only €1; M° Varenne.

Immediately east of Les Invalides, the **Musée Rodin** stands at the corner of handsome rue de Varenne. The museum's setting is superbly elegant, a beautiful eighteenth-century mansion that the sculptor leased from the state in return for the gift of all his work upon his death. Bronze versions of major projects like *The Burghers of Calais*, *The Thinker*, *The Gates of Hell* and *Ugolino and His Sons* are exhibited in the garden – the latter forming the centrepiece of the ornamental pond.

Inside, the vigorous energy of the sculptures contrasts with the elegantly worn wooden panelling (or "*boisieries*") and the tarnished mirrors and chandeliers. Crowds gather round the marble and bronze versions of Rodin's most famous works, including *The Kiss*, but it's well worth lingering over the museum's smaller, more impressionistic clay works as well, studies that Rodin took from life. *The Kiss* actually portrays Paolo and Francesca da Rimini, from Dante's *Divine Comedy*, in the moment before they are discovered and murdered by Francesca's husband. It is one of only four marble versions of the work.

The Palais de Chaillot

Facing the Eiffel Tower across the river is the bastardized Modernist-Neoclassical monster that is the **Palais de Chaillot** (M° Trocadéro). Built for the 1937 world fair on the proud, elevated site of the old Trocadéro palace, it has acquired a forlorn air since a major fire in 1996. The northern wing, however, is being transformed into the **Cité de l'Architecture et du Patrimoine**, a combined institute, library and museum of architecture which is due to open in 2007. On the ground floor, giant plaster casts of sections of great French buildings will tell the story of French architecture from the Middle Ages through to the nineteenth century; upstairs will be the nineteenth- and twentieth-century galleries, with photographs, designs and original architectural models.

The broad *terrasse* extending between the two wings is a popular hang-out for in-line skaters and souvenir vendors – and the ideal place to plant yourself for a fine view across to the Eiffel Tower and the École Militaire.

The Musée Guimet and Musée de la Mode

Musée Guimet: Wed–Mon 10am–6pm; €6; ⓦwww.museeguimet.fr; M° Iéna. Musée de la Mode: Tues–Sun 10am–6pm; €7; M° Iéna/Alma-Marceau.

The **Musée National des Arts Asiatiques – Guimet**, overlooking busy place d'Iéna, houses a world-renowned collection of **Khmer sculpture** – from the civilization that produced Cambodia's Angkor Wat. The museum winds round four floors, groaning under the weight of statues of Buddhas and gods, some fierce, some meditative, all of them dramatically lit and imaginatively displayed on plinths or in sometimes surprising niches and cabinets.

A little further to the east, opposite the Palais de Tokyo, set in small gardens at 10 avenue Pierre 1er de Serbie, stands the grandiose Palais Galliera, home to the **Musée de la Mode et du Costume**. The museum's magnificent collection of clothes and fashion accessories from the eighteenth century to the present day is exhibited in temporary, themed shows of which there are two or three a year – during changeovers the museum is closed for weeks at a time, so be sure to check what's on and when.

The Palais de Tokyo

Tues–Fri 10am–5.45pm, Sat & Sun 10am–6.45pm; closed Mon & public hols; free; ⓦ www.palaisdetokyo.com; M° Iéna/Alma-Marceau.

Nearby, with its entrance on avenue du Président-Wilson, the **Palais de Tokyo** houses the **Musée d'Art Moderne de la Ville de Paris**. The museum can't rival the Pompidou Centre, but it has two marvellous centrepieces. Facing the stairs as you descend, the chapel-like **salle Matisse** is devoted to Matisse's *La Danse de Paris*, its sinuous figures seemingly leaping through colour. Further on, Dufy's enormous mural *La Fée Electricité* ("The Electricity Fairy") fills an entire, curved room with 250 lyrical, colourful panels recounting the story of electricity from Aristotle to the then-modern power station. The main collection is chronologically themed, starting with Fauvism and Cubism, and progressing through to Dada and the École de Paris and beyond. Most artists working in France – Braque, Chagall, Delaunay, Derain, Dufy, Léger, Modigliani, Picasso and many others – are represented and there is a strong Parisian theme to many of the works.

In the western wing of the palace, the **Site de Création Contemporaine** (Tues–Sun noon–midnight; €6) has staged a number of avant-garde exhibitions and endless events, talks, installations and projections since it opened in 2002, including a show of works by Paris-born Louise Bourgeois and a temporary occupation by squatter-artists. The interior has been deliberately left semi-derelict and the young French artists working and hanging out in the bar-restaurant, bookshop and library add to the arty, informal ambience.

Just beyond the Palais de Tokyo, in **place de l'Alma**, you'll find a full-scale replica of the Statue of Liberty's flame which was given to France in 1987 as a symbol of Franco-American relations. It's now an unofficial memorial to **Princess Diana**, whose car crashed in the adjacent underpass.

10

Montparnasse

The swathe of cafés, brasseries and cinemas that runs through the heart of modern **Montparnasse** has long been a honeypot for pleasure-seekers, as well as a kind of border town dividing the lands of well-heeled St-Germain from the amorphous populations of the three arrondissements of **southern Paris**. In the nineteenth century, Bohemians and left-leaning intellectuals abandoned the staid city centre for Montparnasse's inexpensive cafés and nightspots, but the *quartier*'s lasting fame rests on the patronage of artists in the 1920s, following the exodus from Montmartre. Picasso, Matisse, Kandinsky, Man Ray, Modigliani, Giacometti and Chagall were all habitués of the celebrated **cafés** around Place Vavin, and many were buried in **Montparnasse cemetery**. Still more bones lie nearby in the grim **catacombs**. The area is now dominated by the looming **Tour Montparnasse**, which you can ascend for a superb view of the city. In the tower's shadow, a handful of **museums** recall the quarter's artistic traditions.

The Tour Montparnasse

Daily: April–Sept 9.30am–10.30pm; Oct–March 9.30am–10pm; €8.50; Ⓦ www.tourmontparnasse56.com.

Montparnasse's most prominent and least-loved landmark is the brown, glass blade of the **Tour Montparnasse**. At the time of its construction, this was one of Paris's first skyscrapers, and few Parisians have a good word to say for it now. The **view** from the top, however, is arguably better than the one from the Eiffel Tower – it has the Eiffel Tower in it, after all, plus there are no queues and it costs less to ascend. Sunset is the best time to visit.

The station and Jardin Atlantique

The interior of the **Gare Montparnasse** is a modernist confusion of concrete and glass built over one of the city's largest métro interchanges. Down below ground, the uniquely high-speed **tapis roulant**, or "rolling carpet" has become a rather surprising tourist attraction, speeding along at 9km per hour, or three times the speed of a normal travelator, between the two main junctions of lines 4 and 12, and lines 6 and 13. Children love it, but note that it's often closed for lack of supervision in quieter periods, including weekends.

Behind the station lies the **Jardin Atlantique**, a public park actually suspended above the tracks. Completed in 1994, between cliff-like glass walls of high-rise blocks, it's a remarkable piece of engineering – and imagination. The lawns rise and fall in waves to better distribute their weight over hidden concrete struts below. Access is via lifts on rue Cdt. R. Mouchotte and boulevard Vaugirard, or by the stairs alongside platform #1.

Musée de Montparnasse and Musée Bourdelle

Just north of Montparnasse station are two little-visited yet beguiling **museums**. At 21 avenue du Maine, a half-hidden, ivy-clad alley leads to what was once the Russian painter Marie Vassilieff's studio, now converted into the **Musée de Montparnasse** (Tues–Sun 12.30pm–7pm; €5; M° Montparnasse-Bienvenüe/Falguière), hosting temporary exhibitions based on Montparnasse artists past and present.

A few steps north of the station, on rue Antoine-Bourdelle, a garden of sculptures invites you into the **Musée Bourdelle** (Tues–Sun 10am–6pm; free; M° Montparnasse-Bienvenüe/Falguière), a museum built around the artist's former studio. As Rodin's pupil and Giacometti's teacher, Bourdelle bridged the period between naturalism and a more geometrically conceived style. His monumental sculptures get pride of place in the chapel-like, modernist grand hall, while the sculptor's atmospheric old **studio** is littered with half-complete works.

Boulevard du Montparnasse

Most of the bustle in Montparnasse is concentrated on **boulevard du Montparnasse**, particularly the section between the station and Vavin métro. The *quartier*'s most famous cafés are clustered around the Vavin crossroads. If the *Select*, *Coupole*, *Dôme*, *Rotonde* and *Closerie des Lilas* are no longer the wildly social venues they were during the inter-war artistic and literary boom, they remain proud Parisian classics. This stretch of the boulevard still stays up late and the relatively simple *Le Select* (best for a coffee; see p.217) and the sumptuous *La Coupole* (best for a meal; see p.217) preserve much of the flavour of the old days, and are as worthy of a visit as any museum.

The Musée Zadkine and Fondation Cartier

Just north of the boulevard du Montparnasse, and within a few minutes' walk of the Jardin du Luxembourg (see p.95), is the tiny **Musée Zadkine**, at 100bis rue d'Assas (Tues–Sun 10am–6pm; free; M° Vavin & RER Port-Royal). The museum occupies the Russian-born sculptor **Ossip Zadkine**'s studio-house, where he lived and worked from 1928 until his death in 1967. In the garden, enclosed by ivy-covered studios and dwarfed by tall buildings, his angular Cubist bronzes seem to struggle for light. Inside is a collection of his gentler wooden torsos, along with smaller-scale bronze and stone works, notably *Femme à l'éventail*.

Taking a shortcut down rue Campagne-Première leads through to boulevard Raspail and the **Fondation Cartier pour l'Art Contemporain**, at no. 261 (Tues–Sun noon–8pm; €6.50; ⓦwww.fondation.cartier.fr; M° Raspail). The stunning glass-and-steel building was designed by the fashionable French architect Jean Nouvel. It has a glass wall following the line of the street, like a false start to the building proper. Inside, temporary exhibitions showcase all kinds of contemporary art – installations, videos, multi-media – often by foreign artists little known in France.

Montparnasse cemetery and Fondation Cartier-Bresson

Cemetery: March 16–Nov 5 Mon–Fri 8am–6pm, Sat 8.30am–6pm, Sun 9am–6pm; Nov 6–March 15 closes 5.30pm; free; M° Raspail/Gaîté/Edgar Quinet. Fondation Cartier-Bresson: Wed 1–8.30pm, Thurs & Fri 1–6.30pm, Sat 11am–6.45pm; €4; ⓦwww.henricartierbresson.org; M° Gaîté.

Just east of the station, along boulevard Edgar Quinet, is the main entrance to **Montparnasse cemetery**. It is home to plenty of the illustrious dead, from Baudelaire to Beckett and Sainte-Beuve to Saint-Saëns – you can pick up a leaflet and map from the guardhouse by each entrance. The joint grave of Jean-Paul Sartre and Simone de Beauvoir lies immediately right of the entrance on boulevard Edgar-Quinet. The eastern angle of the cemetery lies across a road; in its far northern corner is a tomb crowned with a version of Brancusi's sculpture *The Kiss* – an utterly poignant statement of grief.

Hidden away a couple of minutes' walk south of the cemetery – walk south down rue Raymond Losserand, then turn right on rue Lebouis and right again up the tiny Impasse Lebouis – is the **Fondation Henri Cartier-Bresson**. Fascinating shows of the work of the grand old photographer of Paris and his contemporaries alternate with exhibitions promoting younger photographers.

The catacombs

Tues–Sun 10am–4pm; €5.50.

The **catacombs**, whose entrance is near the cemetery on place Denfert-Rochereau, were originally part of the gigantic quarry network underlying southern Paris – there are still some 300km of tunnels. Between 1785 and 1871, some of these quarried-out spaces were stacked with millions of bones cleared from the over crowded public charnel houses and cemeteries. Today, it's estimated that the remains of six million Parisians are interred here. Lining the passageways, the long thighbones are stacked end-on, forming a bizarre wall behind which the smaller bones can just be seen heaped higgledy-piggledy. Older children often love the whole experience, but be forewarned that there are a good two or three often claustrophobic kilometres to walk, and it can be surprisingly cold, not to mention damp and gungy underfoot.

11

Montmartre and around

Huddled on a hilltop in the northern part of Paris, the buildings of **Montmartre** stand apart from the city at their feet. The area's chief landmark, visible from all over the city, is the all-white church of **Sacré-Cœur**, which crowns the Butte like fairytale icing. The slopes below preserve something of the spirit of the little village that once basked here but, unlike most villages, Montmartre has a very diverse and dynamic population, by turns lefty, trendy, arty and sleazy. Some of the city's hippest and most individualistic clothes shops, cafés and restaurants are hidden away in the streets around **Abbesses** métro.

East of Montmartre, you can explore the poor, ethnically mixed **Goutte d'Or** quartier; to the south stretch the twin arrondissements of the **9e** (neuvième) and **10e** (dixième). Where the 10e is rough, boisterous and shabby, the 9e is largely genteel and well-groomed – though the area around **Blanche** and **Pigalle**, just below the Butte Montmartre, is famous for its cabarets and sex shows.

Abbesses

Place des Abbesses is postcard-pretty, centred on one of Guimard's rare, canopied Art Nouveau métro entrances. For **shopping** and **eating**, the area around Abbesses is one of the most satisfying in Paris. A few peeling, shuttered-up old shops survive from the old Montmartre, but these days most have been turned into restaurants or jazzy little boutiques. Some of the best addresses are listed in the Shopping chapter (see pp.247–249), but you can let your eye for fashion guide you round rue des Martyrs, rue des Trois-Frères, rue de la Vieuville, rue Houdon and rue Durantin. Heading west from the métro, **rue des Abbesses** is best for cafés, especially the popular suntrap of *Le Sancerre* (see p.219). On the downhill side of place des Abbesses, the red-brick church of **St-Jean de Montmartre** is worth putting your nose inside for its radical reinforced concrete construction, dating from the early 1900s.

The Butte Montmartre

At 130m, the "Mound", or **Butte Montmartre** is the highest point in Paris. The name is probably a corruption of *Mons Martyrum* – "the Martyrs' hill" – the martyrs being St Denis and his companions, or possibly of *Mons Martis*, after a Roman shrine to Mars. If you're in any doubt about finding your way **up the Butte**, just keep heading uphill – the area is so charming that there's no such thing as a wrong turn.

Two of the quietest and most attractive paths begin at place des Abbesses. You can climb rue de la Vieuville and the stairs in rue Drevet to the minuscule **place du Calvaire**, which has a lovely view back over the city; alternatively, go up rue Durantin, then right on rue Tholozé and right again on rue Lepic into rue des Norvins. Along rue Lepic, you'll pass the **Moulin de la Galette**, a lone survivor of Montmartre's forty-odd windmills whose famous dances were immortalized by Renoir in his *Bal du Moulin de la Galette*.

Artistic and literary associations abound hereabouts. In 1904, Picasso took up a studio in an old piano factory known as the **Bateau-Lavoir**, on the tiny place Emile-Goudeau. He stayed for the best part of a decade, painting *Les Demoiselles d'Avignon* and sharing loves, quarrels and opium trips with Braque, Juan Gris, Modigliani, Max Jacob, Apollinaire and others. Although the original building burnt down some years ago, the modern reconstruction still provides studio space for artists, and you wouldn't notice any change on the square itself. Even the graceful, green **Wallace fountain** is still in place – one of the last of the fifty famous drinking fountains donated to the city in 1872 to survive. Rue Poulbot, at the beginning of rue des Norvins, leads round to the depressing, underground **Espace Montmartre – Salvador Dalí**, at no. 9–11 (daily 10am–6pm; €8; M° Abbesses), which is more of a giant souvenir shop than a gallery.

If you don't want to walk, you can take the diminutive and determinedly ecological **Montmartrobus** (normal métro/bus tickets are valid), which makes a useful circular route from place Pigalle up to the Sacré-Cœur and back.

Sacré-Cœur and around

Church: daily 6am–10.15pm; M° Abbesses/Anvers. Tower daily: April–Sept 8.30am–7pm; Oct–March 9am–6pm; €5.

The core of Montmartre, the photogenic but bogus **place du Tertre**, is jammed with tourists, overpriced restaurants and "artists" knocking up lurid oils of Paris landmarks. Between the square and the Sacré-Cœur stands the **church of St-Pierre**, one of the oldest in Paris. Though much altered, with modern stained glass throughout, it still retains its Romanesque and early Gothic feel.

Crowning the Butte is the **Sacré-Cœur**, a weird pastiche of a Byzantine church whose pimply tower and white ice-cream dome have somehow become an essential part of the Paris skyline. Construction was started in the 1870s on the initiative of the Catholic Church to atone for the "crimes" of the Commune. The interior is more neo-Byzantine nonsense, and the best thing about the Sacré-Cœur is the **view from the top**.

Rue des Saules tips steeply down the north side of the Butte past the terraces of the tiny **Montmartre vineyard**, which produces some 1500 bottles of pretty foul wine every year. To the right, rue Cortot cuts through to the water tower, whose distinctive, white, lighthouse-like form is another landmark of the city's skyline.

At 12 rue Cortot, a pretty old house with a grassy courtyard was occupied at different times by Renoir, Dufy, Suzanne Valadon and her mad son, Utrillo. It's now the **Musée de Montmartre** (Tues–Sun 10am–6pm; €5.50; M° Lamarck-Caulaincourt), which attempts to recreate the atmosphere of Montmartre's pioneering heyday via a selection of Toulouse-Lautrec posters, mock-ups of various period rooms – including a bar complete with original *zinc*, or pewter top – and various painted impressions of how the Butte once looked.

The Halle St-Pierre and around

To the south and east of the Sacré-Cœur, the slopes of the Butte drop steeply down towards boulevard Barbès and the Goutte d'Or. Directly below are the gardens of square Willette, overrun with tourists. To avoid the crowds, head down the steeply stepped rue Utrillo, turning right at the pleasant café, *L'Eté en Pente Douce* (see p.218), which has outdoor tables on the corner of rue Paul Albert. From here, more steps lead down along the edge of the gardens to rue Ronsard, where overhanging greenery masks the now-sealed entrances to the quarries. The original plaster of Paris was extracted from here.

The circular **Halle St-Pierre** (daily 10am–6pm; €7; M° Anvers), at the bottom of rue Ronsard, was once a market building but is now an exhibition space dedicated to Art Brut, or works by artists that mainstream galleries won't touch. The biannual exhibitions encompass anything from naïve paintings to sci-fi sculptures.

Montmartre cemetery

March 16–Nov 5 Mon–Fri 8am–6pm, Sat from 8.30am, Sun from 9am; Nov 6–March 15 closes 5.30pm; M° Blanche/Place-de-Clichy.

West of the Butte, near the beginning of rue Caulaincourt, **Montmartre cemetery** is an atmospheric tangle of trees and funerary pomposity. Tucked down below street level in the hollow of an old quarry, it's more intimate and somehow less melancholy than Père-Lachaise or Montparnasse. The entrance is on avenue Rachel, underneath the bridge section of rue Caulaincourt. The illustrious dead at rest here include Stendhal, Berlioz, Degas, Feydeau, Offenbach, Nijinsky and François Truffaut, as well as La Goulue, the Moulin Rouge dancer immortalized by Toulouse-Lautrec.

The Goutte d'Or

Immediately north of the wide, grotty boulevard de la Chapelle, the poetically named quartier of the **Goutte d'Or** stretches between **boulevard Barbès** and the **Gare du Nord** rail lines. The setting for Zola's *L'Assommoir*, a classic novel of gritty realism, its name – "Drop of Gold" – is derived from the vineyard that occupied this site in medieval times. For much of the post war period, this was *the* North African quarter, but it is now home to a host of vibrant mini-communities, predominantly – and colourfully – West African and Congolese, with pockets of South Asian, Haitian, Turkish and other ethnicities.

On the rue de la Goutte d'Or itself you'll find one of the city's green ironwork **Wallace fountains** on the corner with the rue de Chartres, but the main sight is a few steps north on rue Dejean, where the **Marché Dejean** (closed

Sun afternoon and all day Mon; M° Château-Rouge) heaves with African groceries and thrums with shoppers. Most of the quartier's cafés and bars tend to be very local in flavour, but there are a couple of friendly cafés and restaurants on the **rue Léon**.

Blanche and Pigalle

From place Clichy in the west to Barbès-Rochechouart in the east, the hill of Montmartre is underlined by the sleazy **boulevards de Clichy** and **de Rochechouart**. Between **place Blanche** and **place Pigalle**, sex shows, sex shops and prostitutes – both male and female – vie for the custom of *solitaires* and couples alike. Perfectly placed amongst all the sex shops and shows is the **Musée de l'Erotisme** (daily 10am–2am; €7), testament to its owner's fascination with sex as expressed in folk art. The ground floor and first floor are awash with model phalluses, fertility symbols and intertwined figurines from all over Asia, Africa and pre-Colombian Latin America. A few steps west, the photogenic **Moulin Rouge** (Ⓣ01.53.09.82.82, Ⓦwww.moulinrouge.fr) still thrives on place Blanche. Once Toulouse-Lautrec's inspiration, it trades on its traditional, bare-breasted, can-canning "Doriss Girls", albeit now with a flashy accompanying sound-and-light show and an expensive price tag, at €97, or €140 and upwards with dinner.

The 9e (neuvième)

The heart of the 9e arrondissement was first developed in the early nineteenth century as a fashionable suburb. It was soon dubbed the **Nouvelle Athènes**, or New Athens, after the Romantic artists and writers who moved in made it the centre of a minor artistic boom. The handsome centrepiece of the quartier is the circular **place St-Georges**. To get the full flavour of the *neuvième*'s nineteenth-century heyday, make for the **Musée de la Vie Romantique**, at 16 rue Chaptal (daily except Mon 10am–6pm, closed public hols; €7 during exhibitions, otherwise free; M° St-Georges/ Blanche/Pigalle), which sets out to evoke the Romantic period in a shuttered building at the end of a private alley. The interior preserves the rich colours of a typical bourgeois home of the nineteenth century.

A short way south down rue de la Rochefoucauld, you'll find the curious and little-visited **Musée Moreau** (daily except Tues 10am–12.45pm & 2–5.15pm; €4; M° St-Georges/Blanche/Pigalle), dedicated to the fantastical, Symbolist paintings of **Gustave Moreau**. The museum's design was conceived by Moreau himself, to be created in the house he shared with his parents for many years; you can visit their tiny, stuffy apartment rooms. The paintings get more room – two huge, studio-like spaces where Moreau's canvases hang cheek-by-jowl, every surface crawling with decadent and weirdly symbolic figures and decorative swirls.

The 10e (dixième)

The gritty life of the 10e is coloured by the presence of the big **northern railway stations**. The southern end of the arrondissement is its liveliest, a poor but vibrant quarter that has become home to Indian, black African, and Near Eastern communities as well as, in recent years, a small vanguard of bourgeois-bohemians – what Parisians call "*les bo-bos*". At its lower end, the **rue du Faubourg St-Denis** is full of charcuteries, butchers, greengrocers and ethnic delicatessens, as well as a number of restaurants, including the historic brasseries *Julien* and *Flo* (see p.220).

On boulevard St-Denis, at the border with the 2^{e} arrondissement, you get a powerful sense of the old city limits; two triumphal arches stand at either end of the street, now looking oddly out of place in the midst of motor traffic and shop hoardings. The **Porte St-Denis** was erected in 1672 to celebrate Louis XIV's victories on the Rhine. With France's northern frontier secured, Louis ordered Charles V's city walls to be demolished and replaced by leafy promenades; these became known as the *boulevards* after the Germanic word for an earth rampart, a *bulwark*. Two hundred metres east, the more graceful **Porte St-Martin** was built two years after its sibling, in celebration of further victories.

12

The Bastille and around

Indissolubly linked with events that triggered the French Revolution of 1789, the **Bastille quarter** traditionally belongs in spirit and in style to the working-class districts of eastern Paris. Since the 1990s, with the construction of the new opera house, the **Opéra-Bastille**, however, it's become a magnet for artists, fashion folk and young people who have brought with them trendy shops and an energetic nightlife, making this one of Paris's central hotspots. Much of the action takes place on **rue de Lappe**, continuing a tradition that goes back to the nineteenth century when migrant workers from the Auvergne colonized this street and opened dancehalls and music clubs. Cocktail haunts and theme bars now dominate the street and the surrounding area, edging out the old tool shops, cobblers and ironmongers. Some of the working-class flavour lingers on, though, especially in the furniture workshops off **rue Faubourg St-Antoine**, east of the Bastille, testimony to a long history of cabinet-making and woodworking in the district.

South of the Bastille, the relatively unsung **12e (douzième)** arrondissement offers an authentic slice of Paris, traditionally working class and full of neighbourhood shops and bars. Much is changing here too, though, and a fashionable crowd is moving in, attracted by new developments, such as the landscaping of a large park in the **Bercy** riverside area and the conversion of the old Bercy wine warehouses into attractive cafés and shops. One of the most imaginative projects has been the creation of the **Promenade Plantée**, an ex-railway line turned into an elevated garden walkway, running from the Bastille right across the twelfth arrondissement to the green expanse of the **Bois de Vincennes** in the east.

Place de la Bastille

Map 4, E12. M° Bastille.

The huge **place de la Bastille** is where Parisians congregate to celebrate Bastille Day, France's most important national holiday, marking the storming of the Bastille prison on July 14, 1789, which kicked off the French Revolution. Hardly anything survives now of the prison – the few remains have been transferred to square Henri-Galli at the end of boulevard Henri-IV. A Société Générale bank is situated on the former site of the prison and the square is where the fortress's ramparts originally were. A gleaming, gold, winged figure of Liberty stands atop a bronze column at the centre of the square, erected to commemorate not, as you might expect, the surrender of the prison, but the July Revolution of 1830, that replaced the autocratic Charles X with the "Citizen King" Louis-Philippe. When Louis-Philippe fled in the more significant 1848 Revolution, his throne was burnt beside the column. The victims – some seven hundred – of both conflicts are buried in vaults underneath the monument and their names inscribed around the shaft of the column. The square is still an important rallying point for political protest; massive demonstrations against far-right presidential candidate Jean-Marie Le Pen took place here in 2002 and it's an obligatory halt on the route of any left-wing march.

The Bicentennial of the Revolution in 1989 was marked by the inauguration of the **Opéra Bastille**, one of François Mitterrand's pet projects. Filling almost the entire block between rues de Lyon, Charenton and Moreau, it has shifted the focus of place de la Bastille, so that the column is no longer the pivotal point; in fact, it's easy to miss it altogether when dazzled by the night-time glare of lights emanating from the Opéra. One critic described it as a "hippopotamus in a bathtub", and you can see his point. The architect, Uruguyan Carlos Ott, was concerned that his design should not bring an overbearing monumentalism to place de la Bastille. The different depths and layers of the semicircular facade do give a certain sense of the building stepping back, but self-effacing it is not. With time, use and familiarity, Parisians seem to have become reconciled to the new opera house, and people happily sit on its steps, wander into its shops and libraries, and camp out all night for the free performance on July 14.

For information on tickets and performances given at the Opéra Bastille, see p.306.

Rue de Lappe and around

Map 4, F12. M° Bastille.

Northeast of place de la Bastille, off rue de la Roquette, narrow, cobbled **rue de Lappe** is one of the liveliest nightspots in Paris, crammed with animated bars, catering to a young crowd and full to bursting on the weekends. At number 32, *Balajo* is one remnant of a very Parisian tradition: the *bals musettes*, or music halls of 1930s *gai Paris* established by the area's large Auvergnat population and frequented between the wars by Piaf, Jean Gabin and Rita Hayworth. It was founded by one Jo de France, who introduced glitter and spectacle into what were then seedy gangster dives, enticing Parisians from the other side of the city to drink absinthe and savour the rue de Lappe low-life. Parisians are still drawn to the area and frequent the hip bars and restaurants of the nearby section of **rue de Charonne**, also home to trendy fashion boutiques and wacky interior designers; and **rue Keller**, clustered with alternative, hippy outfits, indie record stores and young fashion designers.

The Promenade Plantée

Map 4, F14. M° Bastille/Ledru-Rollin.

The **Promenade Plantée**, also known as the Coulée Verte, is an excellent way to see a little-visited part of the city – and from an unusual angle. This stretch of disused railway line, much of it along a viaduct, has been ingeniously converted into an elevated garden walk and planted with a profusion of trees and flowers – cherry trees, maples, limes, roses and lavender. The walkway starts near the beginning of **avenue Daumesnil**, just south of the Bastille opera house, and is reached via a flight of stone steps – or lifts – with a number of similar access points all the way along. From there it extends to the Parc de Reuilly, then descends to ground level and continues nearly as far as the *périphérique*, from where you can follow signs to the Bois de Vincennes. The whole walk is around 4.5km long, but if you don't feel like doing the entire thing you could just walk the first part – along the viaduct – which also happens to be the most attractive stretch, running past venerable old mansion blocks and giving you a bird's-eye view of the street below.

The arches of the viaduct itself, collectively known as the **Viaduc des Arts**, have had their red brickwork scrubbed clean and have been converted into attractive spaces for artisans' studios and craft shops. The workshops house a wealth of creativity: furniture and tapestry restorers, interior designers, cabinet-makers, violin- and flute-makers, embroiderers and fashion and jewellery designers; a full list and map is available from no. 23 avenue Daumesnil.

Bercy

Map 1, G6 & map 5, N5. M° Bercy/Cour St Emilion.

Over the last decade or so, the former warehouse district of **Bercy**, where for centuries the capital's wine supplies were unloaded from river barges, has been transformed by a series of ambitious, ultramodern developments designed to complement the grand-scale Seine Rive Gauche project on the opposite bank. The heart of this development is **Bercy village**, a complex of old wine warehouses stylishly converted into shops, restaurants and, appropriately enough, wine bars – popular places to come before or after a film at the giant Bercy multiplex cinema at the eastern end of Cour Saint Emilion.

West of here extends the **Parc de Bercy**, which incorporates elements of the old warehouse site such as disused railway tracks and cobbled lanes. The western section of the park is a fairly unexciting expanse of grass with a huge stepped fountain (popular with children) set into one of the grassy banks, but the area east has arbours, rose gardens, lily ponds, an orangerie and a **Maison du Jardinage** (March–Oct Tues–Sun 1–5.30pm; Nov–Feb Tues–Sat 1–5.30pm), which provides information on all aspects of gardening.

Of the new buildings surrounding the park, the most striking, at 51 rue de Bercy, on the north side, is the building housing the **Cinémathèque** (Ⓦwww.cinematheque.fr), with its four cinema screens and a museum, designed by the architect Frank O. Gehry. Constructed from zinc, glass and limestone, it resembles a falling pack of cards – according to Gehry, the inspiration was Matisse's collages, done "with a simple pair of scissors".

Bois de Vincennes

Map 1, I6.

The **Bois de Vincennes** is one of the largest parks that the city has to offer. Unfortunately, it's so crisscrossed with roads that countryside sensations don't stand much of a chance, but it has some pleasant corners, including Paris's best garden, the **Parc Floral** (daily: summer 9.30am–8pm; winter 9.30am–dusk; €1.50; ⓦwww.parcfloraldeparis.com; M° Château de Vincennes, then bus #112 or a short walk) – flowers are always in bloom in the Jardin des Quatre Saisons, and you can picnic beneath pines, then wander through concentrations of camellias, rhododendrons, cacti, ferns, irises and bonsai trees. Between April and September there are art and horticultural exhibitions in several pavilions, free jazz and

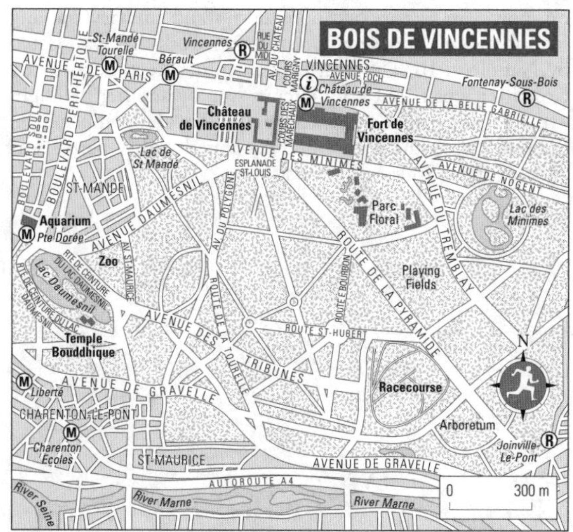

classical music concerts, and numerous activities for children, including a mini-golf of Parisian monuments.

If you feel like a lazy day out in the park, you can go boating on the **Lac Daumesnil** (M° Porte-Dorée), near the Porte Dorée entrance. North of the Lac Daumesnil, at 53 avenue de St-Maurice, the city's largest **zoo** has been closed indefinitely since 2004 for restoration and many of the animals have been transferred to other zoos; its fake rocks, now some seventy years old, started falling apart and posed a danger to animals and visitors alike.

Château de Vincennes

Map 1, I5. Daily 10am–noon & 1.15–6pm. Guided tours daily: 1hr 15min €6.10; 40min €4.60; M° Château-de-Vincennes.

On the northern edge of the *bois*, the **Château de Vincennes** – erstwhile royal medieval residence, then state prison, porcelain factory, weapons dump and military training school – is still undergoing restoration work that was started by Napoleon III. The fourteenth-century keep is currently closed for repairs but both circuits stop by another highlight – the Flamboyant-Gothic **Chapelle Royale**, completed in the mid-sixteenth century and decorated with superb Renaissance stained-glass windows.

13

Eastern Paris

Traditionally home to the working classes, eastern Paris is nowadays one of the most diverse and vibrant parts of the city, colonized over recent years by sizeable ethnic populations, as well as students and artists, attracted by the area's low rents. The main quartiers, **Belleville** and **Ménilmontant**, were once villages on the fringes of the city, which drew migrants from the countryside in the nineteenth century. During this time, the area developed a reputation as a revolutionary hotbed, with the impoverished inhabitants regularly taking to the barricades. Much of the district these days is characterized by high-rise housing developments, though some charming old villagey streets do remain. Of chief interest to visitors are the **Parc de La Villette**, containing a state-of-the-art science museum and a superb music museum, and the **Père-Lachaise cemetery**, the burial place of numerous well-known artists and writers. The area's current arty, bohemian denizens ensure a cutting-edge arts and nightlife scene, especially around the **Canal St-Martin** and **Ménilmontant**. Ascending the hilly heights of the **Parc de Belleville** and the **Parc des Buttes-Chaumont** reveals the east's other chief asset – fine views of the city below.

The Canal St-Martin

Map 4, D1–D14.

Effectively marking the boundary between central Paris and the eastern districts, the **Canal St-Martin** was built in 1825 so that river traffic could shortcut the great western loop of the Seine around Paris. As it happened, it also turned out to be a splendid natural defence for the rebellious quarters of eastern Paris: the canal was spanned by six swing bridges, which could easily be drawn up to halt the advance of government troops. Napoleon III simply got round this by covering over the lower stretch in the latter half of the nineteenth century; the canal now runs underground at the Bastille, emerging after a mile and a half near the rue du Faubourg-du-Temple, and continuing north to the **place de la Bataille de Stalingrad**.

The northern reaches of the exposed canal still have a slightly industrial feel, but the southern part, along the **quai de Jemmapes** and **quai de Valmy** (M° Jacques-Bonsergent), has a

Canal cruises

A leisurely way of seeing the Canal St-Martin is to take one of the boat trips operated by **Canauxrama** (reservations ⓣ01.42.39.15.00, ⓦwww.canauxrama.com) between the Port de l'Arsenal, opposite 50 boulevard de la Bastille, 12e (M° Bastille), and the Bassin de la Villette, 13 quai de la Loire, 19e (M° Jaurès), north of the Canal St-Martin. Daily departures are at 9.45am and 2.45pm from La Villette and at 9.45am and 2.30pm from the Port de l'Arsenal. At the Bastille end there's a long, spooky tunnel from which you don't surface till the 10e arrondissement. The ride lasts two and a half hours and costs €9 for morning cruises, €10 on weekday afternoons and €14 on weekend afternoons. **Paris Canal** (ⓣ01.42.40.96.97, ⓦwww.pariscanal.com) also runs trips, usually from November to March, between the Musée d'Orsay, quai Anatole-France, 7e (RER Musée d'Orsay), and the Parc de la Villette (La Folie des Visites du Parc; M° Porte-de-Pantin). Prices are €16 for adults, €9 for children aged 4 to 11, and you'll need to book by phone or online.

great deal of charm, with plane trees lining the cobbled quais, and elegant high-arched footbridges punctuating the spaces between the locks, from where you can still watch the odd barge slowly rising or sinking to the next level. At 102 quai de Jemmapes is the **Hôtel du Nord**, made famous by Marcel Carné's eponymous film, starring Arletty and Jean Gabin; it's had its facade restored and now thrives as a bar and bistro. In the last decade or so the district has been colonized by the new art and media intelligentsia who are catered to by trendy bars, cafés and boutiques. The area is particularly lively on Sundays when the quais are closed to traffic, and pedestrians, cyclists and rollerbladers take over the streets, while students hang out along the canal's edge, drinking beer or strumming guitars.

Parc de la Villette

Map 1, G1. ⓣ01.40.03.75.75, ⓦwww.lavillette.com. M° Porte-de-Pantin/Porte-de-la-Villette.

Built in 1986 on the site of what was once Paris's largest abattoir and meat market, the Parc de la Villette is a postmodern arts and science park. The landscaped grounds include a huge science museum, a music museum, various satellite attractions, a series of themed gardens and a number of jarring, bright-red "follies". The effect of these numerous, disparate elements can be quite disorienting – all in line with the creators' aim of eschewing meaning and deconstructing the whole into its parts. All very well, but on a practical level you'll probably want to pick up a plan at the information centre at the southern entrance near M° Porte-de-Pantin, and our map should also help you get your bearings.

Cité des Sciences et de l'Industrie

Tues–Sat 10am–6pm, Sun 10am–7pm; €7.50; ⓦwww.cite-sciences.fr; M° Porte-de-la-Villette.

The park's main attraction is the enormous **Cité des Sciences et de l'Industrie**. This is the science museum to

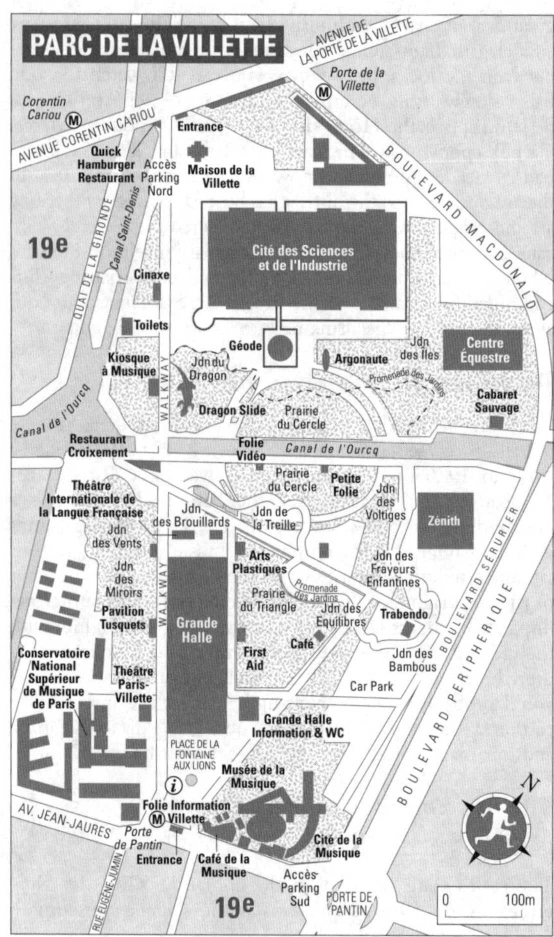

13 EASTERN PARIS | Parc de la Villette

end all science museums and worth visiting for the building alone: all glass and stainless steel, crow's nests and cantilevered platforms, bridges and suspended walkways, the different levels linked by lifts and escalators around a huge central space open to the full 40m height of the roof. An excellent programme of temporary exhibitions complements the permanent exhibition, called **Explora**, covering subjects such as sound, robotics, energy, light, ecology, maths, medicine, space and language. As the name suggests, the emphasis is on exploring, and there are plenty of interactive computers, videos, holograms, animated models and games. Many of the exhibits are accompanied by English-language translation.

In Les Sons (sounds), you can watch a video of an x-rayed jaw and throat talking or sit in a cubicle and feel your body tingle as a rainstorm crashes around you. Videos in L'homme et les gènes trace the development of an embryo from fertilization to birth, while in Images you can use computer simulation to manipulate Mona Lisa's smile. In Etoiles et Galaxies, there are large-scale models of space rockets and space stations and a real Mirage jet fighter. Especially popular with children, the Jeux de Lumière is a whole series of experiments to do with colour, optical illusions, refraction and the like. Best of all for children, though, is the Cité des Enfants (see below). You can have your head spun further by a session in the planetarium (around six shows daily; €3 supplement).

Cité des Enfants

90min sessions: Tues, Thurs & Fri 9.30am, 11.30am, 1.30 & 3.30pm; Wed, Sat, Sun & public hols 10.30am, 12.30, 2.30 & 4.30pm; €5; advance reservations at the Cité des Sciences ticket office on ⓣ08.92.69.70.72 are advised to avoid disappointment.

The museum's special section for children, the **Cité des Enfants**, with areas for 3- to 5-year-olds and 6- to 12-year-olds, is totally engaging. Children can play about with water, construct buildings on a miniature construction site (complete with cranes, hard hats and barrows), experiment with sound and light, manipulate robots, race their own shadows, and superimpose their image on a landscape. They can listen to different languages by inserting telephones into the appropriate country on a globe, and put together their own television news. The whole area is beautifully organized and managed. If you haven't got a child, it's worth borrowing one to get in here.

Musée de la Musique

Tues–Sat noon–6pm, Sun 10am–6pm; €6.50; M° Porte-de-Pantin.

The **Musée de la Musique**, within the **Cité de la Musique** complex, near the Porte-de-Pantin entrance, presents the history of music from the end of the Renaissance to the present day, both visually, exhibiting some 4500 instruments, and aurally, via headsets (available in English; free). Glass case after glass case hold gleaming, beautiful instruments: jewel-inlaid crystal flutes and a fabulous lyre-guitar are some impressive examples. The instruments are presented in the context of a key work in the history of Western music: as you step past each case, the headphones are programmed to emit a short scholarly narration, followed by a delightful concert.

The park grounds

Daily 6am–1am; entry to park free; M° Porte-de-Pantin & M° Porte-de-la-Villette.

The extensive **park grounds** contain ten landscaped **themed gardens**, featuring mirrors, trampolines, water jets and spooky music. All are linked by a walkway called the Promenade des Jardins. The most popular with children is the Jardin du Dragon with its eighty-metre-long **Dragon Slide**.

In front of the Cité des Sciences floats the **Géode** (hourly shows daily; €9; Ⓦwww.lageode.fr), a bubble of reflecting steel, which looks as though it's been dropped from an intergalactic boules game into a pool of water. Inside the bubble, half the sphere is a screen for Omnimax 180° films, not noted for their plots but a great visual experience. Or there's the **Cinaxe**, between the Cité and the Canal St-Denis (screenings every 15min daily; €4.80 with Explora ticket), combining 70mm film shot at thirty frames a second with seats that move. Next to the Géode, you can clamber around a decommissioned 1957 French **submarine**, the **Argonaute** (Mon–Fri 10.30am–5.30pm, Sat & Sun 11am–6.30pm; €3), and view the park through its periscope.

Père-Lachaise cemetery

Map 1, H4. Mon–Fri 8am–5.30pm, Sat 8.30am–5.30pm, Sun 9am–5.30pm; free; M° Père-Lachaise/Philippe Auguste.

Final resting place of a host of French and foreign luminaries, **Père-Lachaise** draws around two million visitors a year. Located on a hill commanding grand views of Paris, it extends across some 116 acres, making it one of the world's largest cemeteries. In fact, it's rather like a miniature town, with its grid-like layout, cast-iron signposts and neat cobbled lanes – a veritable "city of the dead". Size aside, it's also one of the most atmospheric cemeteries that you're ever likely to visit – an eerily beautiful haven, with terraced slopes and some 6000 magnificent old trees that spread their branches over the moss-grown tombs as though shading them from the outside world.

Finding individual graves can be a tricky business. The map overleaf and the free plans given out at the entrance will point you in the right direction, but it's worth buying a slightly more detailed map as it's easy to get lost; the best one is published by Editions Métropolitain Paris (around €2) and should be available in the newsagents and florists near the main entrance on boulevard de Ménilmontant.

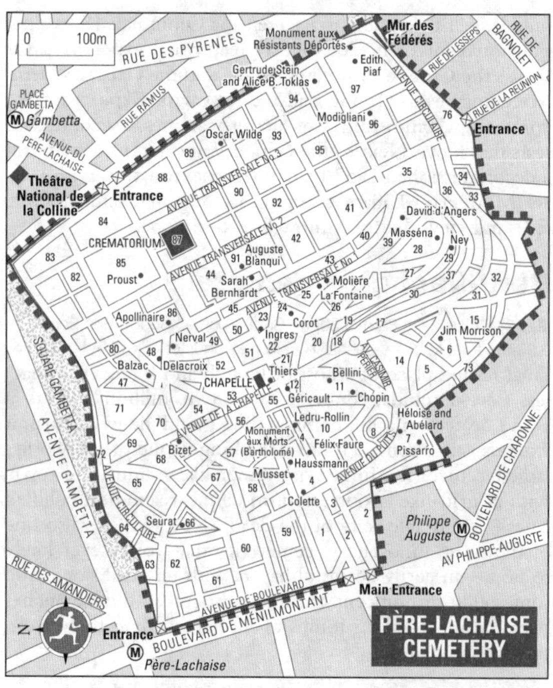

The cemetery was opened in 1804 in response to an urgent stop being put on further burials in the overflowing city cemeteries and churchyards; to be interred in Père-Lachaise quickly became the ultimate symbol of riches and success. Among the most visited graves is that of **Chopin** (Division 11), which has a willowy muse mourning his loss and is often attended by groups of Poles laying wreaths and flowers in the red and white colours of the Polish flag. Swarms also flock to the grave of **Jim Morrison** (Division 6); the ex-Doors lead singer died in Paris in 1971 at the age of 28. Once graffiti-covered and wreathed in marijuana fumes, his grave has been cleaned up and is watched over by a security guard to ensure it stays that way. Another tomb that's not short of visitors is **Oscar Wilde**'s (Division 89), the base of which is covered in lipstick kisses left by devoted fans. It's topped with a sculpture by Jacob Epstein of a mysterious Pharaonic winged messenger (sadly vandalized of its once prominent member, which was last seen being used as a paper weight by the director of the cemetery). The inscription behind is a grim verse from *The Ballad of Reading Gaol*.

Most of the celebrated dead have unremarkable tombs. Femme fatale Colette's tomb, close to the main entrance in Division 4, for example, is very plain, though always covered in flowers. The same is true of Sarah Bernhardt's (division 44) and the great chanteuse Edith Piaf's (division 97). Marcel Proust lies in his family's conventional tomb (division 85). Just across the way is the rather incongruous-looking **Crematorium** (Division 87), crudely modelled on the Aghia Sophia in Istanbul, with domes and minarets. Here among others of equal or lesser renown lie the ashes of Max Ernst, Georges Pérec, Stéphane Grapelli and American dancer Isadora Duncan, who was strangled when her scarf got tangled in the rear axle of her open-top car.

Among illustrious representatives of the arts, Corot (Division 24) and Balzac (Division 48) both have fine busts. Delacroix lies in a sombre sarcophagus in Division 49, while Jacques-Louis David's heart rests in Division 56 (the rest of him is buried in Belgium, where he died). His pupil Ingres reposes in Division 23. In Division 96 is the grave of Modigliani and his lover Jeanne Herbuterne, who killed herself in crazed grief a few days after he died in agony from meningitis.

It is the monuments to the collective, violent deaths, however, that have the power to change a sunny outing to Père-Lachaise into a much more sombre experience. In

Division 97 are the memorials to the victims of the Nazi concentration camps, to executed Resistance fighters and to those who were never accounted for in the genocide of World War II. The sculptures are relentless in their images of inhumanity, of people forced to collaborate in their own degradation and death.

Marking one of the bloodiest episodes in French history, the Mur des Fédérés (Division 76) is the wall where the last troops of the revolutionary Paris Commune were lined up and shot in the final days of the battle in 1871. A total of 147 were rounded up and killed, after a frenetic chase through the tombstones, and the remains of around a thousand other Communards were brought here and thrown into a grave-pit. The wall soon became a place of pilgrimage for the Left, and remains so today. The man who ordered the execution, Adolphe Thiers, lies in the centre of the cemetery in Division 55.

Belleville

Map 4, G3-G4.

Strung out along the western slopes of a ridge that rises from the Seine, the district of **Belleville** is not exactly "belle", but you do glimpse something of the old Paris here. In among the nondescript apartment blocks some characterful streets survive, little changed since the 1930s, especially the little cul-de-sacs of terraced houses and gardens **east of rue des Pyrénées**. The colourful, if somewhat run-down, main street, **rue de Belleville**, abounds with Vietnamese, Chinese and Turkish shops and restaurants, which spill south along boulevard de Belleville and rue du Faubourg-du-Temple. African and oriental fruits, spices, music and fabrics attract shoppers to the **boulevard de Belleville market** on Tuesday and Friday mornings. A visit to either the **Parc de Belleville** or **Parc des Buttes-Chaumont** is well worth it for the views over the city. The best place to watch the sun set over Paris is from the heights of the Parc de Belleville (Map 4, I4; M° Couronnes/Pyrénées).

Parc des Buttes-Chaumont

Map 4, H1. Daily: May & mid-Aug to end Sept 7am–9pm; June to mid-Aug 7am–10pm; Oct–April 7am–8pm; M° Buttes-Chaumont/ Botzaris.

A short walk from La Villette is the **parc des Buttes-Chaumont**, constructed by Haussmann in the 1860s to camouflage what until then had been a desolate warren of disused quarries and miserable shacks. Out of this rather unlikely setting, a romantic, fairy-tale-like fantasy was created – there's a grotto with a cascade and artificial stalactities, and a picturesque lake from which a huge rock rises up, topped with a delicate Corinthian temple. From the temple you get fine views of the Sacré-Cœur and beyond.

Ménilmontant

Map 4, H1-H6.

Like Belleville, much of **Ménilmontant**, to the south, aligns itself along one straight, steep, long street, the **rue de Ménilmontant** and its lower extension rue Oberkampf. Although seedy and dilapidated in parts, its popularity with students and artists has brought a cutting-edge vitality to the area. Alternative shops and trendy bars and restaurants have sprung up among the grocers and cheap hardware stores, especially along **rue Oberkampf**, which now hosts a thriving bar scene (see p.235): some of the most popular hang-outs are *Café Charbon*, a renovated dance hall, the nearby *Cithéa* club and *Le Mécano*. **Boulevard Ménilmontant**, west of Père-Lachaise, is also prime bar-crawling territory, with places like *La Mère Lachaise* and *Les Lucioles* drawing a young *bobo* (bourgeois-bohemian) crowd. The upper reaches of rue de Ménilmontant, above rue Sorbier, are quieter and, looking back, you find yourself dead in line with the roof top of the Pompidou Centre, a measure of how high you are above the rest of the city.

For bar listings in Ménilmontant see p.235.

Musée Edith Piaf

Map 4, H6. 5 rue Crespin-du-Gast. Mon–Thurs 1–6pm; closed Sept; admission by appointment only on ⓣ01.43.55.52.72; donation; M° Ménilmontant/St-Maur.

Edith Piaf, so the story goes, was abandoned as a baby on the steps of 72 rue de Belleville, and there's a small museum dedicated to her nearby in rue Crespin-du-Gast. Piaf was not an acquisitive person: the few clothes (yes, a little black dress), letters, toys, paintings and photographs that she left are almost all here, along with every one of her recordings. The venue is a small flat lived in by her devoted friend Bernard Marchois, and the "Amis d'Edith Piaf" will show you around and tell you stories about her life.

14

Western Paris

Paris's well-manicured **western** arrondissements, the 16e (seizième) and 17e (dix-septième), commonly referred to as the Beaux Quartiers, are mainly residential with few specific sights, the chief exception being the **Musée Marmottan**, with its excellent collection of late Monets. The best area for strolling is around the old villages of **Auteuil** and **Passy**; they exude an almost provincial air, with their tight knot of streets and charming *villas* – leafy lanes of attractive old houses, fronted with English-style gardens full of roses, ivy and wisteria. Auteuil and Passy were only incorporated into the city in 1860, and soon became the capital's most desirable districts. Well-to-do Parisians commissioned new houses here and, as a result, the area is rich in fine examples of **early-twentieth-century architecture**: Hector Guimard, designer of the swirly green Art Nouveau métro stations, worked here, and there are some rare Parisian instances of work by interwar architects Le Corbusier and Mallet-Stevens, who created the first "Cubist" buildings. Running all the way down the west side of the 16e is the extensive **Bois de Boulogne**, former playground of the wealthy, while further west, modern architecture comes bang up to date with the gleaming, purpose-built business district of **La Défense**, dominated by the enormous **Grande Arche**.

Auteuil

Map 1, B5. M° Église d'Auteuil.

The Auteuil district is now an integral part of the city, but there's still a village-like feel about its streets, and it has some attractive little *villas*, not to mention some notable early-twentieth-century architecture. The ideal place to start an exploration of the area is the **Église d'Auteuil** métro station. Nearby are several of Hector Guimard's **Art Nouveau** buildings: at 8 avenue de la Villa-de-la-Réunion; 41 rue Chardon-Lagache; 142 avenue de Versailles; 39 boulevard Exelmans; and 34 rue Boileau. This last was one of Guimard's first commissions, in 1891. A high fence and wisteria obscure much of the view, but you can see some of the decorative tile-work under the eaves and around the doors and windows. At the end of rue Boileau, beyond boulevard Exelmans, you'll find a series of pretty *villas* backing onto the Auteuil cemetery.

For more Guimard buildings, follow the old village high street, **rue d'Auteuil**, west from the métro exit to **place Lorrain** and turn right onto rue de la Fontaine where you'll find examples at nos. 14, 17, 19, 21 and 60. Of these, no. 14, the "Castel Béranger" (1898), is the most famous, with exuberant Art Nouveau decoration in the bay windows, roof line and chimney. If you start to tire of the bulgy curves of Art Nouveau, you could head up rue du Dr-Blanche for the cool, rectilinear lines of Cubist architects Le Corbusier and Mallet-Stevens.

Auteuil bus routes

Handy **bus routes** for exploring Auteuil are the #52 and the #72. The #52 runs between M° Opéra in the centre and M° Boulogne-Pont-de-St-Cloud near the Parc de Princes, stopping at rue Poisson en route, while the #72's route extends between métro Hôtel de Ville in the Marais and M° Boulogne-Pont-de-St-Cloud, stopping en route by the Exelmans crossroads near some of Guimard's buildings on avenue de Versailles.

Villa La Roche and around

Mon 1.30–6pm, Tues–Thurs 10am–12.30pm & 1.30–6pm, Fri 1.30–5pm, Sat 10am–5pm; closed Aug; €2.40; M° Jasmin.

In a cul-de-sac off rue du Dr-Blanche stand the first private houses built by **Le Corbusier** (1923). One of them, the **Villa La Roche**, is in the care of the Fondation Le Corbusier and is open to the public. It's built in strictly Cubist style, very plain, with windows in bands, the only extravagances the raising of one wing on piers and a curved frontage. They look commonplace enough now from the outside, but were a radical departure from anything that had gone before, and once you're inside, the spatial play still seems ground-breaking. The interior, appropriately enough, is decorated with Cubist paintings.

Further north along rue du Dr-Blanche and off to the right, the tiny **rue Mallet-Stevens** was built entirely by the architect of the same name, also in Cubist style. No. 12, where Robert Mallet-Stevens had his offices, has been altered, along with other houses in the street, but you can still see the architectural intention of sculpting the entire street space as a cohesive unit.

Musée Marmottan

Daily except Mon 10am–6pm; €7; ⓦwww.marmottan.com; M° Muette.

The collection of the **Musée Marmottan** consists largely of works by **Monet**. These were bequeathed, along with the family's former residence – a nineteenth-century *hôtel particulier* – to the Académie des Beaux-Arts by the wealthy industrialist Jules Marmottan and his son, art historian and collector, Paul Marmottan. Among the paintings is Monet's *Impression, Soleil Levant* ("Impression, Sunrise"; 1872), a rendering of a misty sunrise over Le Havre, whose title was borrowed by critics to give the Impressionist movement its name. The painting was stolen from the gallery in October 1985, along with eight other paintings. After a police operation lasting five years, they were discovered in a villa in southern Corsica, and were put back on show with greatly increased security. There's a dazzling selection of works from Monet's last years at Giverny, including several *Nymphéas* (Waterlilies), *Le Pont Japonais*, *L'Allée des Rosiers* and *La Saule Pleureur*, where rich colours are laid on in thick, excited whorls and lines. These are virtually abstractions, much more advanced than, say, the work of Renoir, Monet's exact contemporary, some of whose paintings are also on display. Two rooms are devoted to another Impressionist, **Berthe Morisot**, whose work is characterized by vigorous, almost aggressive, brushwork, seen to best effect in paintings such as *Branches d'oranger* (1889) and *Le Jardin à Bougival* (1884).

Passy

Map 1, C4 & map 7 A6–9. M° La Muette/Passy.

The heart of the Passy quartier, northeast of Auteuil, is pleasant little **place de Passy**, with its crowded but leisurely *Le Paris Passy* café. Leading off from here is the old high street, rue de Passy, with its eye-catching parade of boutiques, and the cobbled, pedestrianized **rue de l'Annonciation**, an agreeable blend of genteel affluence and the down-to-earth. At the end of the street you'll find the house that Balzac once lived in, now a museum.

Trocadéro (see p.108), with its stunning view of the Eiffel Tower, is a leisurely walk from place de Passy.

The Maison de Balzac

Map 7, A9. 47 rue Raynouard. Tues–Sun 10am–5.40pm; free; M° Passy/Av-du-Prés-Kennedy–Maison-de-Radio-France.

Tucked away down some steps among a tree-filled garden is the **Maison de Balzac**, a delightful, summery little house with pale-green shutters and a decorative iron entrance porch. Balzac moved to this secluded spot in 1840 in the hope of evading his creditors. He lived under a pseudonym, and visitors had to give a special password before being admitted. Should any unwelcome callers manage to get past the door, Balzac would escape via a back door and down to the river via a network of underground cellars. It was here that he wrote some of his best-known works, including *La Cousine Bette* and *Le Cousin Pons*. The museum preserves his study, simple writing desk and monogrammed cafetière – frequent doses of caffeine kept him going during his long writing stints, which could extend for up to eighteen hours a day for weeks on end. Other exhibits include letters to Mme Hanska, whom he eventually married after an eighteen-year courtship, and a highly complex family tree of around a thousand of the four thousand-plus characters that feature in his *Comédie Humaine*.

Bois de Boulogne

Map 1, A3–B4. M° Porte-Maillot/Porte-Dauphine.

The **Bois de Boulogne** was designed by Baron Haussmann and supposedly modelled on London's Hyde Park – though it's a very French interpretation. The "bois" of the name is somewhat deceptive, though the extensive parklands (just under 900 hectares) do contain some remnants of the once-great Forêt de Rouvray. As its location would suggest, the Bois was once the playground of the wealthy, although it also established a reputation as the site of the sex trade and its associated crime. The same is true today and it's best avoided at night.

By day, however, the park is an extremely pleasant spot, with trees, lakes, cycling trails and the beautiful floral displays of the **Parc de Bagatelle**. The best, and wildest, part for walking is towards the southwest corner. Bikes are available for rent (bring your passport) at the entrance to the **Jardin d'Acclimatation** adventure park and you can go boating on the Lac Inférieur.

More information about the Jardin d'Acclimatation and activities for children in the Bois de Boulogne is given on p.289.

Parc de Bagatelle

Daily 9am–7pm; €1.50; M° Port-de-Neuilly, then bus #43 or M° Porte-Maillot, then bus #244.

Comprising a range of garden styles from French and English to Japanese, the Parc de Bagatelle is renowned for its stunning **rose garden** featuring some 1200 varieties in all, at their best in June. In other parts of the garden there are beautiful displays of tulips, hyacinths and daffodils in early April, irises in May, and waterlilies in early August. The park's attractive orangerie is the setting for candlelight recitals of Chopin's music during the Festival Chopin in late June (see p.279).

La Défense

Map 1, A2. M°/RER Grande-Arche-de-la-Défense.

A futuristic complex of gleaming skyscrapers occupied by Elf, IBM, banks and other big businesses, **La Défense** is Paris's prestige business district and an extraordinary monument to late-twentieth-century capitalism. Its most popular attraction is the huge **Grande Arche**, built in 1989 for the bicentenary of the Revolution. It's a beautiful and astounding 112-metre-high arch, clad in white marble. Standing 6km out and at a slight angle from the Arc de Triomphe, the Grande Arche completes the western axis of a monumental east–west vista. Suspended within the arch's hollow, large enough to enclose Notre-Dame with ease, is a "cloud" canopy, which looks like the top half of a circus tent. Transparent lifts (daily 10am–8pm; close an hour earlier in winter; €7.50) make for a thrilling ride to the roof top, though the views are no more impressive than from the series of steps that lead up to the base of the arch – from here you can see as far as the Louvre on a clear day.

Between the Grande Arche and the river, skyscrapers and state-of-the-art apartment blocks compete to dazzle and dizzy you. The dominant features of concrete and glass are relieved by avant-garde sculptures by artists such as Joan Miró and Torricini, dotted around the place de la Défense and the Esplanade du Géneral de Gaulle.

It's best to get off a stop early, at M° Esplanade-de-la-Défense, for the most dramatic approach to the Grande Arche and to see the sculptures.

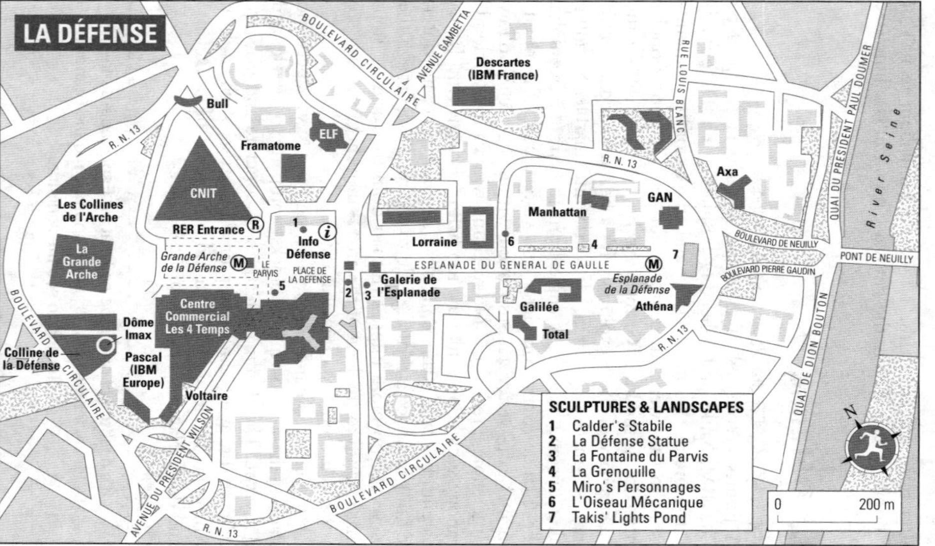
LA DÉFENSE
SCULPTURES & LANDSCAPES
1 Calder's Stabile
2 La Défense Statue
3 La Fontaine du Parvis
4 La Grenouille
5 Miro's Personnages
6 L'Oiseau Mécanique
7 Takis' Lights Pond
Bull
Framatome
ELF
Descartes (IBM France)
CNIT
RER Entrance
Grande Arche de la Défense
LE PARVIS
PLACE DE LA DEFENSE
Info Défense
Les Collines de l'Arche
La Grande Arche
Centre Commercial Les 4 Temps
Dôme Imax
Colline de la Défense
Pascal (IBM Europe)
Voltaire
Galerie de l'Esplanade
Lorraine
Manhattan
GAN
Axa
Galilée
Total
Athéna
Esplanade de la Défense
ESPLANADE DU GENERAL DE GAULLE
BOULEVARD CIRCULAIRE
AVENUE GAMBETTA
RUE LOUIS BLANC
R. N. 13
QUAI DU PRESIDENT PAUL DOUMER
River Seine
PONT DE NEUILLY
BOULEVARD DE NEUILLY
BOULEVARD PIERRE GAUDIN
QUAI DE DION BOUTON
AVENUE DU PRESIDENT WILSON
N
0
200 m

15

St-Ouen and St-Denis

Few visitors head beyond the official city limits – aside from those on day-trips – thanks in part to the *périphérique* ring-road, which quarantines the centre from its less salubrious suburbs. Just north of Montmartre, however, are two sights that should tempt you that little bit further along the métro lines. The sprawling **St-Ouen market** is a veritable kingdom of antiques and curio shops, while the **basilique St-Denis** is an island beacon of stony history, set amid a gritty, post-industrial sea.

St-Ouen market

Sat–Mon 9am–6:30pm, varies depending on weather and many stalls closed Mon; M° Porte-de-Clignancourt.

The **St-Ouen market**, sometimes called the **Clignancourt** market, is located just outside the northern edge of the 18^{e} arrondissement, in the suburb of St-Ouen. Its popular name of **les puces de St-Ouen**, or the St-Ouen flea market, dates from the days when secondhand mattresses, clothes and other infested junk was sold here in a free-for-all zone

outside the city walls. Nowadays, however, it's predominantly a proper – and very expensive – **antiques** market, selling mainly furniture, but also old *zinc* café counters, telephones, traffic lights, posters, jukeboxes and so on.

From the métro it's a five-minute walk up the busy avenue de la Porte-de-Clignancourt. You have to pass through the market's genuinely flea-bitten fringe before you get to the real thing; shaded by the flyover, **rue Jean-Henri-Fabre** is the heart of this light-fingered area, lined with stalls flogging cheap jeans and leather jackets, pirated DVDs and African souvenirs. Watch your wallet, and don't fall for the gangs pulling the three-card monte scams.

The official market complex lies just beyond rue Jean-Henri-Fabre, with over a dozen separate markets covering some two thousand shops. Most have their entrances on **rue des Rosiers**, the main thoroughfare, but a few lie on **rue Jules-Vallès**. For the chance to buy something you could feasibly carry home by yourself, restrict yourself to one of three markets: Vernaison, Jules-Vallès and Malik. Marché **Vernaison**, the oldest in the complex, is the closest thing to a real flea market. Its mazey, creeper-covered alleys are great fun to wander along, threading your way between stalls selling all kinds of bric-a-brac. Marché **Jules-Vallès** is smaller but similar, stuffed with books and records, vintage clothing, colonial knick-knacks and other curiosities. While you won't find any breathtaking bargains, there's plenty to titillate the eye at both. Marché **Malik** stocks mostly discount and vintage clothes and bags, as well as some high-class couturier stuff. The other markets mostly contain expensive antiques and curios.

There are plenty of **cafés** on rue Paul Bert and rue des Rosiers, or you could brave the rather touristy *buvette* buried at the end of Marché Vernaison's Allée 10, *Chez Louisette*.

St-Denis

M° St-Denis-Basilique.

For most of the twentieth century, **St-Denis**, 10km north of the centre of Paris and accessible by métro, was one of the most heavily industrialized communities in France and a bastion of the Communist party. Since those days, however, factories have closed, unemployment has run rife and immigration has radically altered the ethnic mix. The area immediately abutting the historic eponymous **basilica** has been transformed into an extraordinary fortress-like housing and shopping complex, where local youths hang out on mopeds, women shop for African groceries and men, fresh from the latest conflict zone, beg for a few cents. The centre is at its liveliest during the thrice-weekly **market**, on the main place Jean-Jaurès (Tues, Fri & Sun mornings).

About ten minutes' walk south of the cathedral, down rue Gabriel-Péri, is the métro stop St-Denis-Porte-de-Paris. Just beyond it, a broad footbridge crosses the motorway and Canal St-Denis to the dramatic **Stade de France**, scene of France's 1998 World Cup victory.

The basilica

April–Sept Mon–Sat 10am–6pm, Sun noon–6pm; Oct–March Mon–Sat 10am–5pm, Sun noon–5pm; closed during weddings and funerals; free. Necropolis €6.10 (closed during services).

Close by the métro station, the **Basilique St-Denis**, generally regarded as the birthplace of the Gothic style in European architecture, was built in the first half of the twelfth century by Abbot Suger. Inside, his novel use of rib vaulting made possible the huge, luminous windows that fill the choir with light. Today, the upper storeys of the choir are still airier than they were in Suger's day, having been rebuilt in the mid-thirteenth century, at the same time as the nave.

A much earlier abbey church was probably named after its mid-third-century founder, a Parisian bishop decapitated for his beliefs at Montmartre – hence the "Mount of the Martyr". Legend has it that **St Denis** picked up his own head and walked all the way to the site of his new church. It's not in fact all that far – just over 5km – though as a friend of the writer Edward Gibbon's once remarked, "the distance is nothing, it's the first step that counts".

The site's **royal history** began with the coronation of Pepin the Short in 754, but it wasn't until the reign of Hugues Capet, in 996, that St-Denis became the customary burial place of the kings of France. Since then, all but three of France's kings have been interred here, and their very fine tombs and effigies are distributed throughout the **necropolis** in the transepts and ambulatory, which is entered separately via the south portal. Note especially the enormous Renaissance memorials to **François I**, next to the entrance, and **Henri II** and **Catherine de Médicis**, and **Louis XII** and **Anne de Bretagne**, both on the far side of the isle. Up the steps on the south side of the ambulatory, a florid Louis XVI and a busty **Marie-Antoinette** – often graced by bouquets of flowers – kneel in prayer.

16

Day-trips

If you're in Paris for any more than a long weekend, taking a day-trip makes sense. Not only are the four sights described here unmissable in themselves, but they also provide a refreshing balance to Paris's sometimes relentless urbanity – and they're all within an hour's easy train ride of the capital. The Classical **château de Versailles** is best known as the apotheosis of French royal self-indulgence; it also has extensive and delightful gardens. The Renaissance **château de Fontainebleau** is equally superb, if much quieter and less overwhelming; you can also take long walks in the ancient forest that surrounds it. **Chartres cathedral** is certainly one of the finest buildings in the world; its twin spires soar over a pretty provincial town, set in the flat countryside of the Beauce region. Lastly, Monet's house at **Giverny** is most loved for its idyllic Japanese-influenced gardens; you can linger by the lily ponds and let your gaze go blurry on the famous green bridge.

Versailles

Tues–Sun: April–Oct 9am–6.30pm; Nov–March 9am–5.30pm; €7.50; Ⓦwww.chateauversailles.fr; RER line C5 to Versailles-Rive Gauche (frequent; 40min); right out of station and then immediately left to approach palace (5min).

Twenty kilometres southwest of Paris, the **château de Versailles** is France's most staggeringly extravagant palace. It was built for the "sun king", Louis XIV, by the élite design team of architect Le Vau, painter Le Brun and gardener Le Nôtre. Construction began in 1664 and lasted virtually until Louis' death in 1715. Thereafter, the château remained a secondary residence of the royal family until the Revolution of 1789, when the furniture was sold and the pictures dispatched to the Louvre. Today, restoration proceeds apace, the château's management scouring the auction houses of the world in search of furnishings from the day of Louis XVI – the last king of the *ancien régime*.

In Louis XIV's heyday, Versailles was the headquarters of every arm of the state, and the entire French court of around 3500 nobles lived in the palace under a rigid code of royal etiquette centred on the king's equally rigid daily schedule. The astonishingly splendid rooms you can visit on the standard ticket (without a guide) are known as the **State Apartments**, as they were used for all the king's official business. Starting at entrance A, in the main courtyard, the route leads past the grand Baroque royal chapel and a procession of gilded drawing and throne rooms to the dazzling **Galerie des Glaces** (Hall of Mirrors), where the Treaty of Versailles was signed after World War I. If you want to see other, often less crowded areas of the palace, make for entrance D, also in the main courtyard, where you can book yourself on one of the excellent English-language **guided tours** (€4–8). Turn up reasonably early in the day to make sure of a place.

The Park

Daily dawn–dusk; free. Grand and Petit Trianons: daily April–Oct noon–6.30pm; Nov–March noon–5.30pm; combined ticket for both €5.

You could spend the whole day just exploring the **park** at Versailles, along with its lesser outcrops of royal mania: the Italianate **Grand Trianon**, designed by Hardouin-Mansart in 1687 as a "country retreat" for Louis XIV; and the more modest **Petit Trianon**, built by Gabriel in the 1760s for Louis XV's mistress, Mme de Pompadour. Just beyond these is the bizarre **Hameau de la Reine**, a play village and thatch-roofed farm built in 1783 for Marie-Antoinette to indulge her fashionable fantasy of returning to the natural life.

The terraces between the château and the park form Le Nôtre's statue-studded **gardens**, for which you have to pay entry between April and October (€3). Distances in the park are considerable. There's a tourist train, and you can rent **bikes** and **boats** at the Grand Canal, next to a pair of **café-restaurants** – picnics are officially forbidden.

The Potager du Roi

April–Oct daily 10am–6pm; Nov–March Mon–Fri 10am–6pm; Mon–Fri €4.50, Sat & Sun €6.50.

The rather snobby town of Versailles offers little to drag you away from the château, unless you're desperate to see the **Potager du Roi**, the king's reconstructed kitchen-garden, which lies five minutes' walk east of the château's main gate, with its entrance on rue Joffre.

Fontainebleau

Daily except Tues: June–Sept 9.30am–6pm; Oct–May 9.30am–5pm; €5.50; Ⓦwww.musee-chateau-fontainebleau.fr; trains from Gare de Lyon to Fontainebleau-Avon (hourly; 50min) then bus #A or #B (15min); combined train/bus/château ticket €20.

The **château of Fontainebleau**, 60km south of Paris, owes its existence to the magnificent forest that still surrounds it. In the days when France had a monarchy, this vast, tree-filled expanse made the castle the perfect base for royal hunting expeditions; it still makes Fontainebleau a refreshingly rural excursion from Paris. A lodge stood here as early as the twelfth century, but its transformation into a luxurious palace only took place in the sixteenth century under François I, who imported a colony of Italian artists to carry out the decoration, notably the Mannerists Rosso Fiorentino, Primaticcio and Niccolò dell'Abate. The palace enjoyed royal favour well into the nineteenth century, and even Napoleon spent huge amounts of money on it, as did Louis-Philippe. As a result, the château has a gloriously chaotic profusion of styles with staircases, wings and towers jostling around hidden courtyards and gardens.

The palace's highlights, however, are the sumptuous **interiors** worked by François I's Italians, chiefly the dazzlingly frescoed **Salle de Bal** and the celebrated **Galerie François I**, which is resplendent in gilt, carved, inlaid and polished wood, and adorned down its entire length by intricate stucco work and painted panels covered in vibrant Mannerist brushwork. Utterly contrasting in style is the sobre but elegant decor of Napoleon's **Petits Appartements** (mornings only: guided tour only; €3), the private rooms of the emperor, his wife, and their intimate entourage.

The **gardens** are equally splendid and in the summer months you can rent boats on the Étang des Carpes. If you want to escape into the relative wilds, head for the **Forest of Fontainebleau**, which is crisscrossed by signposted walking and cycling trails, all marked on Michelin map #196 (*Environs de Paris*).

Chartres

Daily 8.30am–7.30pm; free. North Tower: Mon–Sat 9am–12.30pm & 2–4.30pm, Sun 2–4.30pm; May–Aug open until 5.30pm; €4. Trains from Gare du Montparnasse (hourly; 1hr), 5min walk from station to cathedral.

An excursion to **Chartres**, 80km southwest of Paris, can seem a long way to go just to see one building; but then you'd have to go a very long way indeed to find a building to beat it. The sheer size of the cathedral was originally a necessity. In the twelfth century, tens of thousands of pilgrims would have come here each year to venerate Sancta Camisia, supposed to have been the robe Mary wore when she gave birth to Jesus (it still exists, though now rolled up and in storage). But Chartres is famous not for its scale but for its astounding architectural harmony – a result of its unusually fast construction between 1194 and 1260 and the fact that, uniquely, it has stood almost unaltered since its consecration.

The cathedral's most famous feature, its stunning **stained glass**, is almost entirely original. It's best experienced on a day of mixed sunshine and cloud, when the colours pulse and fade with the sunlight. Even on a cloudy winter's day, however, you can appreciate the amazing artistry of the windows. Particularly superb is the largely twelfth-century "Blue Virgin" window, in the first bay beyond the south transept, which is filled with a primal image of Mary that has been adored by pilgrims for centuries.

The cathedral's stonework is captivating, particularly the **choir screen**, which curves around the ambulatory, and the hosts of sculpted figures that stand like guardians at each entrance portal. On the floor of the nave, the elaborate medieval labyrinth has a diameter exactly the same size as that of the rose window above the main doors. Be sure to climb the **north tower** and take in its bird's-eye view of the sculptures and structure of the cathedral. There are also pleasant **gardens** at the back from where you can contemplate the apse's flying buttresses.

The Town

Museum: April–Oct Mon & Wed–Sat 10am–noon & 2–6pm, Sun 2–6pm; Nov–March closes 5pm; €2.60.

It's worth leaving an hour or two to explore the **town** of Chartres. There's a peaceful **Musée des Beaux Arts**, in the former Episcopal palace just north of the cathedral, but the most tempting activity is to walk alongside the reedy river Eure. Behind the museum, rue Chantault leads past old town houses to the Pont du Massacre, from where you can follow the right bank a short way upstream past ancient wash houses. A right turn at rue du Bourg, by the Porte

Guillaume, will take you straight up into the appealingly ancient town centre, situated around place de la Poissonnerie, where a carved salmon decorates a sixteenth-century house. Nearby, the daily **food market** is located on place Billard and rue des Changes, and there's a **flower market** on place du Cygne (Tues, Thurs & Sat).

Giverny

April–Oct Tues–Sun 9.30am–6pm; house and gardens €5.50; ⓦwww.fondation-monet.com; train from Paris-St-Lazare to Vernon (4–5 daily; 45min); bus from Vernon to gardens (6km); bikes (€12) available at Café du Chemin de Fer, opposite station; walk (1hr): cross river and turn right on D5, take care as you enter Giverny to follow the left fork.

Claude Monet considered his **gardens at Giverny** to be his greatest masterpiece. They're 65km from Paris in the direction of Rouen, but well worth the trip. Monet lived in Giverny from 1883 till his death in 1926, painting and repainting the effects of the changing seasonal light on the gardens he laid out between his house and the river. Every month from spring to autumn has its own appeal, but May and June, when the rhododendrons flower around the lily pond and the wisteria bursts into colour over the famous Japanese bridge, are the prettiest months to visit – though you'll have to contend with crowds photographing the waterlilies. **Monet's house**, an idyllic pastel pink building with green shutters, stands at the top of the gardens. Inside, the painter's original collection of Japanese prints still hangs on the walls.

Just up rue Claude Monet from the gardens, the swish **Musée d'Art Américain** (April–Oct Tues-Sun 10am–6pm; €5.50; ⓦwww.maag.org) shows paintings by John Singer Sargent and James Whistler, as well as a plethora of works by various American Impressionists who lived in the small colony that grew up around Monet.

17

Disneyland Paris

Children will love **Disneyland Paris** – there are no two ways about it. At just 25km east of the capital, it's easy to visit in a day-trip from Paris, and there are some good roller coasters as well as the Disney-themed rides. The complex is divided into four main areas: **Disneyland Park**, the original Magic Kingdom, with most of the big rides; **Walt Disney Studios Park**, a more technology-based attempt to re-create the world of cartoon film making, along with a few rides; **Disney Village** and the hotels, where you can eat and sleep if you're determined to see both of the other attractions; and lastly the giant retail opportunity that is **La Vallée Outlet Shopping Village**.

Practicalities

Opening hours vary depending on the season and whether it's a weekend, but opening times are either 9 or 10am, while the gates close at either 6 or 8pm – or 11pm in midsummer. Check when you buy your ticket. The best **time to go** is on an off-season weekday, when you'll probably get round every ride you want, though queuing for and walking between rides is purgatorial in wet or very cold weather.

Two- or three-day **tickets** can be purchased in advance at Paris tourist offices (see p.22), all Disney shops, at major métro and RER stations and **online** (Ⓦwww.disneylandparis.

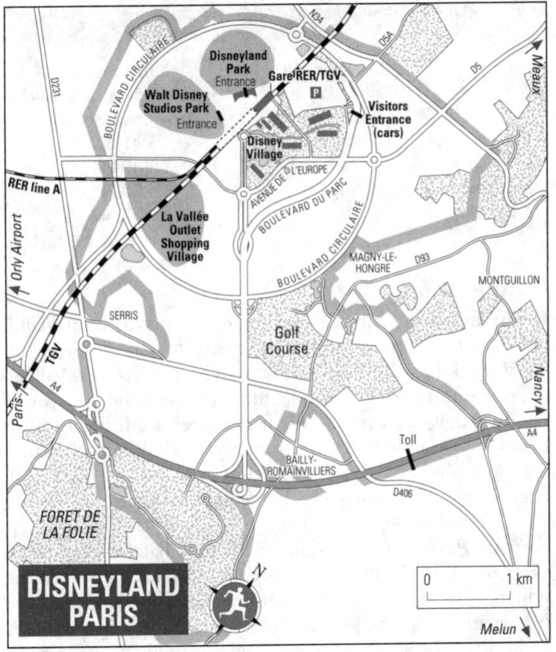

com). The **one-day one-park pass** (only available at the park entrance) allows you to visit either the main Disneyland Park or the Walt Disney Studios Park. You can't move between both areas, but if you choose the Walt Disney Studio, you're entitled to move on to the Disneyland Park section (which stays open later) after the Studios close in the evening. If you buy a **Hopper pass** you can move freely between both park areas. If you buy a two- or three-day Hopper you don't have to use the ticket on consecutive days.

Ticket prices

	Low season (Oct–March excl Christmas hols)	High season (April–Sept & 3rd week Dec–1st week Jan)
1-day 1-park	€40/30	€41/33
1-day Hopper	€49/39	€49/39
2-day Hopper	€89/69	€90/72
3-day Hopper	€108/80	€108/89

Getting there

From London, Eurostar runs trains straight to Disneyland, but it can sometimes be less expensive to change onto the TGV at Lille; all these trains arrive at Marne-la-Vallée/ Chessy station, right outside the main entrance. If you're coming straight **from the airport**, there's a shuttle bus from Charles de Gaulle and Orly (roughly every 30min; 8.30am–7.45pm; for recorded information call ☎01.49.64.47.08). Tickets cost €14 one-way, but children under twelve pay €11.50, and under-3s go free.

From Paris, take RER line A (from Châtelet-Les Halles, Gare-de-Lyon, Nation) to Marne-la-Vallée/Chessy station, which is right next to the train terminal, and opposite the main park gates. The journey takes around forty-five minutes and costs €11.90 round-trip (children under twelve €5.94, under-3s free). A Mobilis travel card (zones 1–5; see p.19) costs €12.10.

Hotels and food

Disney's six themed **hotels** are a mixed bag of hideous eyesores and over-ambitious kitsch that are only worth staying in as part of a multi-day package including park entry, which you can book through Disney or major travel agents. From the UK, for example, you can get a three-day pass, with a return ticket on Eurostar and two nights' accommodation at the *Hotel Santa Fe* (see below) for around £300 per adult and £140 per child. For details look online or call ⓣ0033/1.60.30.60.81 from the US, ⓣ0870/503 0303 in the UK, and ⓣ01.60.30.60.53 in France.

In the two-star *Hotel Santa Fe* you could pay around €150 per adult in low season, while prices rise to over €600 for a peak-season room in the top-flight *Disneyland Hotel*. The budget alternative, as long as you have a car, is the park's *Davey Crockett Ranch*, a fifteen-minute drive away, with self-catering log cabins. Free bright-yellow **shuttle buses** run between the hotels (but not to the ranch) and the single stop for the train station and both park entrances.

Sadly, the **food** in Disneyland Paris is generally overpriced American-style fare. It's safest to avoid the swankier restaurants in Disney Village and go for hamburger-style snacks at the various themed eateries around the park. You're not supposed to bring your own snacks, though whether Donald will turn nasty if he spots you with an apple is anyone's guess.

Disneyland Park

Main Street USA, a mythical vision of a 1900s American town with its own **City Hall**, leads up to **Central Plaza**, the hub of the park. Clockwise from Main Street are the four "lands", connected to each other and Main Street Station by an impressive steam-train **railroad** which runs right round the park. **Luggage** can be left in lockers in "Guest Storage" under Main Street Station (€1.50). While there are a few green patches, there is no lawn to loll on: renting a pushchair (from the building opposite City Hall; €5) for even an older child might be a good idea.

One-hour waits for the popular rides are not uncommon, so bring sunhats or umbrellas, and make sure your kids have all been to the toilet before you begin to queue; keep snacks and drinks handy, too. A number of rides use the **Fastpass** scheme, in which you insert your entry card into a ticket machine by the entrance to the ride; the machine then spews out a time at which you should come back and join the much shorter fastpass queue.

Parades

The main Wonderful World of Disney **Parade** happens every day at 4pm and lasts for half an hour, featuring all the top box-office Disney movie characters, from Snow White to Hercules, with Mickey, Minnie Mouse and Donald Duck making an appearance. Smaller events such as costumed Dixie bands take place throughout the day, while on summer and Halloween-period nights at 7.30pm, the **Fantillusion Parade** follows the main parade route, with a procession of skilfully lit floats adorned by dancing, costumed Disney characters, the whole thing accompanied by zany music. **Firework displays** happen about twice a week during the summer.

The rides

For the youngest kids, **Fantasyland**, home of the distinctive castle, is likely to hold the most thrills. There are no height restrictions here, and rides are mostly gentle. Among the more enjoyable rides are Peter Pan's Flight, a jerky ride over London; Dumbo the Flying Elephant, where you can control the rise and fall of your own pod; and Mad Hatter's Tea Cups, where you slide along a chequered floor. Le Pays des Contes de Fées and It's A Small World are boat rides through fairy-tale scenes, Alice's Curious Labyrinth is a maze with surprises, while Blanche-Neige et les Sept Nains is a kind of ghost train – potentially frightening for younger children. Sadly, Sleeping Beauty's Castle is disappointingly empty inside.

Discoveryland emphasizes technology and the space age, and is centred on its two extreme indoor, space-themed roller coasters: Space Mountain and Space Mountain 2. Star Tours, a simulated ride in a spacecraft through a Star

Wars-style set, goes down well with fans, while Orbitron is a relatively sedate aerial ride and Autopia lets you drive a futuristic car (on rails). Most of the other rides are either high-tech shows presented by actors or walk-through sets, and not especially gripping.

Adventureland has the most outlandish, jungly sets, put to good effect in the cave-playground of Adventure Isle (which for once allows children to run around freely) and The Robinsons' Cabin, complete with a 27-metre mock banyan tree reached by walkways and 170 steps. The two best rides are Indiana Jones and the Temple of Peril: Backwards!, a moderate roller coaster that takes you backwards through a classic Indy landscape; and Pirates of the Caribbean, a satisfyingly long ride that takes you underground, on water and down waterfalls, past scary animated scenes.

The best ride at **Frontierland**, set in the Wild West, is Big Thunder Mountain, a classic (not too excessive) roller coaster mimicking a runaway train round a "mining mountain". In Phantom Manor holographic ghosts appear before cobweb-covered mirrors, but nothing actually jumps out and screams at you, while Thunder Mesa Riverboat Landing takes you on a cruise around the lake on a paddle-boat steamer.

Manchester United Soccer School

Sessions at 9am, 1pm & 4.30pm; children 7-14 only; €25.

The **Manchester United Soccer School** offers three two-and-a-half-hour football training sessions a day during which your budding Beckham will be put through his or her paces along with a group of similar-aged children. The six twenty-minute sessions may not markedly improve their penalty-taking, dribbling, passing or ball-control abilities, but the free-kick wall, passing gates and ball-speed monitoring device are bound to please. To top it off they get a Man Utd "diploma" at the end – though the Disney logo does rather diminish its credibility. You can usually just turn up, but it's

Roller coasters

Each of the park's areas, apart from the tinies-focused Fantasyland, centres on its roller coaster. The runaway train on Frontierland's **Big Thunder Mountain** and the mine-carts of Adventureland's **Indiana Jones and the Temple of Peril: Backwards!** are fast and exciting, but the emphasis is on thrills rather than sheer terror – you can tell that things aren't going to be too bad because you're kept in your seat by a bar, rather than being fully strapped in. **Space Mountain** and its newer sibling **Space Mountain Mission 2**, in Discoveryland, and the **Rock 'n' Roller Coaster Starring Aerosmith**, over in the Walt Disney Studios section, are a different matter altogether. Their upside-down loops, corkscrews and terrifying acceleration require a lock-in padded brace to keep you in place, and you'll need a strong constitution to really enjoy it.

All four rides have different height restrictions, and as you queue for the latter two you'll be bombarded with warnings to discourage pregnant women or people with neck or back problems. You can avoid queues on all of them by using the Fastpass scheme, and arriving early can also be a good strategy. Be warned: the experience can be so intense that the park's gentler rides may seem disappointing. Children, in particular, may want to return again and again.

easy enough to book at the park entrance or with a Disney hotel concierge.

Walt Disney Studios Park

Other than the Rock 'n' Roller Coaster Starring Aerosmith, a terrifyingly fast, corkscrew-looping, Metal-playing white-knuckler, the new **Walt Disney Studios Park** complex lacks the big rides offered by its older, larger neighbour. In some ways it's a more satisfying affair, focusing on what Disney was and is still renowned for – animation. At Art of Disney Animation you watch an actor playing a cartoonist having a conversation with an on-screen animated creation, explaining to the creature how it came to look as it did, after which children are taught to draw identical Mickey Mouse faces. Cinémagique is a screening of a century of movie moments, with actors appearing to jump into and out of the on-screen action, helped by special effects, while Walt Disney Television Studios produces a show with the help of a ready-to-hand live audience.

At the rather impressive Armageddon Special Effects your group of fifty or so is ushered into a circular chamber decked out as a space station; as meteors rush towards the screens on all sides, the whole ship seems about to break up. Studio Tram Tour Featuring Catastrophe Canyon is a sedate circuit of various bits and pieces of film sets, culminating in the halt among the Wild West rocks of Catastrophe Canyon – sit on the left for the scariest ride.

Moteurs ... Action! Stuntshow Spectacular is a full-on show (listen out for announcements of start times) featuring some spectacular stunts: jumping rally cars, sliding motorbikes, leaping jet skis and so on.

La Vallée Outlet

May–Sept Mon–Sat 10am–8pm, Sun 11am–8pm; Oct–April closes 7pm; ⓦwww.lavalleevillage.com; RER Val d'Europe/Serris-Montévrain (line A4) then special shuttle bus.

Just inside the Disney complex's boundaries, **La Vallée Outlet Shopping Village** is an outdoor shopping mall that's designed to look like a village. It's best for discounted labelled clothing, with the previous season's collections sold on at discounts of a third or more. Agnès b, Armani, Burberry, Cacharel, Christian Lacroix, Diesel, Givenchy, Reebok, Tommy Hilfiger and Versace are just a few of the international brands found here, each represented by their own, individual shop. For a full list, see the official website.

Listings

Listings

18

Accommodation

Accommodation in Paris is often booked up well in advance, particularly in the spring and autumn. It's wise to reserve a place as early as you can, especially if you fancy staying in one of the more characterful places. You can simply call – all receptionists speak some English – but it's also worth bearing in mind that more and more hotels offer online booking as well. If you book by phone, many places will ask for a credit card number, others for written or faxed confirmation, while a few inexpensive places may even ask for a deposit to be sent in the post. If you find yourself stuck on arrival the main tourist office at rue des Pyramides and the branches at the Gare de Lyon and Eiffel Tower will find you a room in a hotel or hostel free of charge.

Not surprisingly, hotels in Paris are the most expensive in France, though compared with other European capitals, they are not exorbitant, and there is a wide range of comfort, prices and locations. It's possible to find a decent, centrally located double room for around €40, sometimes even less, though at this level you will probably have to accept a room with just a sink (*lavabo*) and a shared bathroom on the landing – and a few such places still charge for use of the shower. Two of the best central areas for budget-priced hotels are the 10e and the 11e, especially around place de la République. Quieter areas, further out, where you can get some good deals include the 13e and 14e, south of Montparnasse.

Bed and breakfasts, apartment hotels, hostels and campsites are listed separately on pp.186–191.

Hotels

Our **hotel** recommendations are listed by area, following the same chapter divisions used in the guide. Most hotels have a selection of rooms – singles, doubles, twin-bedded and triples – at different prices. In our listings we give prices for doubles and also cite tariffs for single rooms where these are particularly good value. Some hotels lower their prices slightly in slack periods, usually August, November, December (apart from Christmas) and January to March; and even if they don't, it's still sometimes possible, especially in smaller places, to negotiate a reduction of up to ten percent or more on the advertised rate, depending on your length of stay.

The Islands

Henri IV Map 2, F7. 25 place Dauphine, 1er ⓣ01.43.54.44.53. M° Pont-Neuf/Cité. An ancient and well-known cheapie on a beautiful square right in the centre of Paris. It's best to go for one of the renovated rooms with shower, as the rest come with nothing more luxurious than a *cabinet de toilette* and are very run down. Book well in advance and ring to confirm nearer the time. Doubles €32–56.

Hôtel du Jeu de Paume Map 2, I9. 54 rue St-Louis-en-l'Île, Île St-Louis, 4e ⓣ01.43.26.14.18, ⓦwww.jeudepaumehotel.com. M° Pont-Marie. Located on the most desirable island in France, this quiet, charming four-star hotel occupies the site of a tennis court built for Louis XIII in 1634 ("jeu de paume" is "real tennis"). The wood-beam court is now a breakfast room, from which a glass lift whisks you up to the 28 rooms, which are decorated in soothing colours. Doubles from €240.

The Champs-Élysées and around

Hôtel Brighton Map 2, B3. 218 rue de Rivoli, 1er ⓣ01.47.03.61.61, ⓕ01.42.60.41.78, ⓔhotel.brighton@wanadoo.fr. M° Tuileries.

An elegant hotel dating back to the late nineteenth century and affording magnificent views of the Tuileries gardens from the front-facing rooms on the upper floors – if your budget stretches to it, go for one with a balcony right at the top. Around twenty of the 65 rooms have recently been renovated; the standard of the others varies, though many retain period charm and ambience. Doubles €154–233.

Hôtel des Champs-Élysées Map 7, I2. 2 rue d'Artois, 8e ⓣ01.43.59.11.42, ⓕ01.45.61.00.61. M° St-Philippe-du-Roule. The rooms are small but nicely decorated in warm colours and all come with shower or bath, plus satellite TV, minibar, hairdryer and safe. Breakfast is served in a cool, relaxing converted stone cellar. Doubles €98.

Hôtel Lancaster Map 7, G3. 7 rue de Berri, 8e ⓣ01.40.76.40.76, ⓕ01.40.76.40.00, ⓦwww.hotel-lancaster.fr. M° George V. The rooms in this elegantly restored nineteenth-century town house retain original features and are chock full of Louis XVI and rococo antiques, but with a touch of contemporary chic. The hotel was the *pied-à-terre* for the likes of Garbo, Dietrich and Sir Alec Guinness, and is still a favourite among those fleeing the paparazzi. Doubles start at €470.

Hôtel de Lille Map 2, E4. 8 rue du Pélican, 1er ⓣ01.42.33.33.42. M° Palais-Royal-Musée-du-Louvre. This small budget hotel on a quiet street is a bargain for the area, and the rooms, some en suite, are attractively decorated in belle époque style. There's no lift to serve the five floors, and no breakfast. Singles €35; doubles €48–55; triples €60–65.

Hôtel du Lion d'Or Map 2, C3. 5 rue de la Sourdière, 1er ⓣ01.42.60.79.04, ⓕ01.42.60.09.14, ⓦwww.hotelduliondor.com. M° Tuileries. Ideal central location, with twenty en-suite, functional, but clean rooms. Drawbacks include the absence of a lift, and light sleepers might be troubled by traffic noise on the rue de Rivoli, double glazing notwithstanding. Breakfast (€6.80), served in a room that doubles as a cybercafé, is a bit disappointing, with drinks dispensed from a machine. Doubles €85.

L'Hôtel Pergolèse Map 7, B1. 3 rue Pergolèse, 16e ⓣ01.53.64.04.04, ⓦwww.hotelpergolese.com. M° Argentine. A classy four-star boutique hotel in a tall, slender building on a quiet sidestreet near the Arc de Triomphe. The decor is all contemporary – wood floors, cool colours, chic styling – but without chilliness: sofas and friendly service add a cosy touch.

Rooms on six floors (facing the street or the internal courtyard) are comfortable and well-appointed, with great designer bathrooms. Doubles start from €220, but frequent special deals bring prices down well below advertised rates.

Relais St Honoré Map 2, C3. **308 rue St Honoré, 1er ⓣ01.42.96.06.06, ⓕ01.42.96.17.50. M° Tuileries.** A snug little hotel run by friendly and obliging staff, and set in a stylishly renovated seventeenth-century town house. The pretty wood-beamed rooms are done out in warm colours and rich fabrics. Facilities include free broadband Internet access and flat-screen TVs. Doubles from €190.

The Grands Boulevards and around

Hôtel Chopin **Map 3, H8. 46 passage Jouffroy, 9e; entrance on bd Montmartre, near rue du Faubourg-Montmartre ⓣ01.47.70.58.10, ⓕ01.42.47.00.70. M° Grands-Boulevards.** A charming, quiet hotel set in an atmospheric period building hidden away at the end of a picturesque 1850s *passage*. Rooms are pleasantly furnished, though the cheaper ones are on the small side and a little dark. Doubles from €77.

Hôtel Tiquetonne **Map 2, H3. 6 rue Tiquetonne, 2e ⓣ01.42.36.94.58. M° Étienne-Marcel.** Located on a pedestrianized street, the excellent-value, old-fashioned *Tiquetonne* dates back to the 1920s and looks as though it's changed little since. Colour-clash decor notwithstanding, the rooms are nice enough and well maintained, many quite spacious by Parisian standards, though walls are paper-thin. Non-en-suite rooms are equipped with a sink and bidet. Breakfast is served in your room. Singles €30, doubles €40–50.

Hôtel Victoires Opéra **Map 2, G3. 56 rue de Montorgueil, 2e ⓣ01.42.36.41.08, ⓕ01.45.08.08.79, ⓦwww.hotelVictoiresOpera.com. M° Les Halles/Étienne-Marcel.** A stylish boutique hotel on the trendy rue Montorgueil, a pedestrianized market steet. The rooms are warmly decorated in chocolate-brown and coffee tones, and the walls are hung with prints of Modigliani drawings. Doubles €213–274, though occasional special offers (check website) can bring the price down to around €150.

Hôtel Vivienne **Map 3, G8. 40 rue Vivienne, 2e ⓣ01.42.33.13.26, ⓕ01.40.41.98.19, ⓔparis@hotel-vivienne.com. M° Grands-Boulevards/Bourse.** A welcoming place, with good-sized, cheery rooms done up in rather nice woods and prints, several of which have recently seen a full renovation. Doubles with shower and shared WC €69; doubles with full bath €81.

Beaubourg and Les Halles

Agora Map 2, G5. 7 rue de la Cossonnerie, 1er ⓣ01.42.33.46.02, ⓦwww.hotel-paris-agora.com. M° Châtelet-Les-Halles. Located on a pedestrianized street in the heart of Les Halles, this two-star has attractive, individually decorated rooms, some with antique furnishings. Doubles €96–132.

Hôtel Flor Rivoli Map 2, G6. 13 rue des Deux Boules, 1er ⓣ01.42.33.49.60, ⓦwww.hotel-paris-florrivoli.com. M° Châtelet. A good, friendly two-star just off rue de Rivoli. The miniature lift whisks you up to rooms that are nearly as small, but not without charm. Doubles €85.

Relais du Louvre Map 2, E6. 19 rue des Prêtres St-Germain l'Auxerrois, 1er ⓣ01.40.41.96.42, ⓕ01.40.41.96.44, ⓦwww.relaisdulouvre.com. M° Palais-Royal-Musée-du-Louvre. A discreet hotel with eighteen rooms set on a quiet back street opposite the church of St-Germain l'Auxerrois; you can admire the flying buttresses from the front-facing rooms. The decor is traditional but not stuffy, with rich, quality fabrics, old prints, Turkish rugs and solid furniture. The relaxed atmosphere and charming service attract a faithful clientele. Doubles €145–180.

The Marais

Hôtel du Bourg Tibourg Map 4, B10. 19 rue du Bourg-Tibourg, 4e ⓣ01.42.78.47.39, ⓕ01.40.29.07.00, ⓔwww.hotelbourgtibourg.com. M° Hôtel-de-Ville. Oriental meets medieval, with a dash of Second Empire, at this sumptuously designed boutique hotel. Rooms are tiny, but cosseted with rich velvets, silks and drapes. A perfect romantic hideaway. Doubles €200–250.

Hôtel de la Bretonnerie Map 4, A10. 22 rue Ste Croix de la Bretonnerie, 4e ⓣ01.48.87.77.63, ⓕ01.42.77.26.78, ⓦwww.bretonnerie.com. M° Hôtel-de-Ville. A charming place on one of the Marais' liveliest streets; the rooms, all different, are decorated with exquisite care with quality fabrics, oak furniture and, in some cases, four-poster beds. Doubles from €110.

Hôtel du Cantal Map 4, B7. 7 rue des Vertus, 3e ⓣ01.42.77.65.52, ⓕ01.42.77.64.95, ⓔhcantal@wanadoo.fr. M° Arts-et-Métiers. Located on a very quiet back street near the Picasso Museum, this small one-star is very well priced for the area. The nine rooms are simple, but not without character, and the bathrooms are nicely tiled and well maintained. There's also a small family suite (€91) on the top floor. Singles €30–54, doubles with shower €60.

Caron de Beaumarchais Map 4, B11. 12 rue Vieille-du-Temple, 4e ⓣ01.42.72.34.12, ⓕ01.42.72.34.63, ⓦwww.carondebeaumarchais.com. M° Hôtel-de-Ville. Named after the eighteenth-century French playwright Beaumarchais, who would have felt quite at home here: all the furnishings – the original engravings and Louis XVI furniture, not to mention the pianoforte in the foyer – evoke the refined tastes of high-society pre-Revolution Paris. Rooms overlooking the courtyard are petite, while those on the street are a little more spacious. Doubles €122–152.

Hôtel Central Marais Map 4, B10. 33 rue Vieille-du-Temple, 4e; entrance on Rue Sainte-Croix-de-la-Bretonnerie ⓣ01.48.87.56.08, ⓕ01.42.77.06.27, ⓦwww.hotelcentralmarais.com. M° Hôtel-de-Ville. The only self-proclaimed gay hotel in Paris, whose famous and popular gay bar, *Le Central*, is just downstairs. Six small boxy rooms with shared bathrooms, and only one with en-suite bath and WC. Doubles €87.

Grand Hôtel Jeanne d'Arc Map 4, C11. 3 rue de Jarente, 4e ⓣ01.48.87.62.11, ⓕ01.48.87.37.31, ⓦwww.hoteljeannedarc.com. M° St-Paul. An excellent-value hotel in an old Marais town house, just off lovely place du Marché Sainte-Catherine. The rooms are a decent size, with nice individual touches, plus cable TV. It's very popular, so booking well in advance is advised. Doubles €80.

Grand Hôtel du Loiret Map 4, A11. 8 rue des Mauvais-Garçons, 4e ⓣ01.48.87.77.00, ⓕ01.48.04.96.56, ⓔhotelduloiret@hotmail.com. M° Hôtel-de-Ville. A budget hotel, grand in name only, though it has recently renovated its foyer and installed a lift. The rooms are essentially uneventful, but acceptable for the price; cheaper ones have washbasin only, all have TV and telephone. Doubles €45 with shared toilet, €60 with full bath.

Hôtel de Nice Map 4, A11. 42bis rue de Rivoli, 4e ⓣ01.42.78.55.29, ⓕ01.42.78.36.07, ⓦwww.hoteldenice.com. M° Hôtel-de-Ville. A delightful old-world charm pervades this six-storey establishment, its pretty rooms hung with prints and furnished with richly coloured fabrics and Indian-cotton bedspreads. Singles €75, doubles €105.

Hôtel Pavillon de la Reine Map 4, D11. 28 pl des Vosges, 4e ⓣ01.40.29.19.19, ⓕ01.40.29.19.20, ⓦwww.pavillon-de-la-reine.com. M° Bastille. A perfect honeymoon or romantic-weekend hotel in a beautiful ivy-covered mansion secreted away off the Place des Vosges. Rooms are sumptuously decorated with antique furnishings and four-poster beds, and come with all the modern comforts of a four-star hotel. Doubles start at €335.

Hôtel Sévigné Map 4, C11. 2 rue Malher, 4e ⓣ01.42.72.76.17, ⓕ01.42.78.68.26, ⓦwww.le-sevigne.com. M° St-Paul. A comfortable, pleasant hotel, just off rue de Rivoli. The rooms are small but well maintained and double-glazed, and all have either full bath or shower. Doubles €73.

Quartier Latin and the south-east

Hôtel du Commerce Map 2, G10. 14 rue de la Montagne-Ste-Geneviève, 5e ⓣ01.43.54.89.69, ⓦwww.commerce-paris-hotel.com. M° Maubert-Mutualité. Brightly renovated budget hotel aimed at backpackers and families, in the heart of the Quartier Latin. Communal kitchen and dining area. Rooms come at a range of prices, from washbasin-only cheapies (€40) up to en-suite rooms (€60), and there are singles and three- and four-bed rooms.

Hôtel Esmeralda Map 2, G9. 4 rue St-Julien-le-Pauvre, 5e ⓣ01.43.54.19.20, ⓕ01.40.51.00.68. M° St-Michel/Maubert-Mutualité. In an ancient house on square Viviani, this discreet old hotel is run by a friendly elderly Colombian couple and offers small, cosy rooms with an old-fashioned feel – done up head to toe in red velvet – some with superb views of Notre-Dame. A trio of smallish singles come with washbasin only for €35, otherwise en-suite doubles go for €65.

Hôtel des Grandes Écoles Map 2, H12. 75 rue du Cardinal-Lemoine, 5e ⓣ01.43.26.79.23, ⓦwww.hotel-grandes-ecoles.com. M° Cardinal-Lemoine. A cobbled private alleyway leads through to a big surpise: a large and peaceful garden, right in the heart of the Quartier Latin. Rooms (€130) are pretty, with floral wallpaper and old-fashioned furnishings, and the welcome is sincere. Reservations are taken three and a half months in advance.

Hôtel Marignan Map 2, G10. 13 rue du Sommerard, 5e ⓣ01.43.54.63.81, ⓦwww.hotel-marignan.com. M° Maubert-Mutualité. One of the best bargains in town, with breakfast thrown in. Totally sympathetic to the needs of rucksack-toting foreigners, with free laundry and ironing facilities, plus a room to eat your own food in – plates, fridge and microwave provided – and rooms for up to five people. Doubles €60–90, depending on the season and the facilities – the least expensive have shared bathrooms.

Hôtel Port-Royal Map 5, F5. 8 bd Port-Royal, 5e ⓣ01.43.31.70.06, ⓦwww.hotelportroyal.fr. M° Les Gobelins. A one-star hotel at its very best, this friendly address has been in the same family since the 1930s. It's located out at the southern edge of the quarter, at the rue Mouffetard end of the boulevard, but near the métro. Double rooms (€73) are fairly large, immaculately clean and attractive; fifteen rooms are available with shared bathroom facilities (€48, but showers cost €2.50 extra). No credit cards.

Résidence Les Gobelins Map 2, F6. 9 rue des Gobelins, 13e ⓣ01.47.07.26.90, ⓦwww.hotelgobelins.com. M° Les Gobelins. An old-fashioned, quiet establishment within walking distance of the Quartier Latin's rue Mouffetard. With its large, simple but comfortable rooms going for €73, this is a well-known bargain, so book far in advance.

Select Hôtel Map 2, F10. 1 place de la Sorbonne, 5e ⓣ01.46.34.14.80, ⓦwww.selecthotel.fr. M° Cluny-La Sorbonne/RER Luxembourg. A designer-styled hotel right on the *place*. The cool interior here is about stone arches, tidy leather and stylish, recessed wood trim. A large plant-filled atrium adds warmth and the helpful staff are pleasantly un-snooty. Doubles at €140.

Le Vert-Galant Map 5, F7. 41 rue Croulebarbe, 13e ⓣ01.44.08.83.50, ⓕ01.44.08.83.69. M° Les Gobelins. Set on a quiet backwater overlooking the verdant Square René-le-Gall, with a large garden behind, this family-run hotel seems to belong to a provincial French town rather than Paris – they'll even do your laundry and let you park your car on site, and in the evening you can eat downstairs at the *Auberge Etchegorry*. The rooms (€90) are modern but pleasantly airy; those giving onto the garden (€100) come with French windows and kitchenettes.

St-Germain

Hôtel de l'Angleterre Map 2, D7. 44 rue Jacob, 6e ⓣ01.42.60.34.72, ⓦwww.hoteldangleterre.com. M° St-Germain-des-Prés. Classy and extremely elegant hotel in an imposing building that once housed the British Embassy and, later,

Ernest Hemingway, although in those days he only paid three francs a night. The decor throughout mixes classical luxury with stone walls and giant roof-beams. Standard rooms (€140) are good value, while the more expensive rooms (€195–230) are sumptuously huge.

Ferrandi St-Germain Map 2, A11. 92 rue du Cherche-Midi, 6e ⓣ01.42.22.97.40, ⓔhotel.ferrandi@wanadoo.fr. M° Vaneau/St-Placide. Genteel, independent hotel with a timeless feel, hidden away in a residential corner of St-Germain. Rooms are charmingly homely, and cost €130–180, depending on size.

Hôtel du Globe Map 2, E9. 15 rue des Quatre-Vents, 6e ⓣ01.43.26.35.50, ⓦwww.hotel-du-globe.fr. M° Odéon. Extremely welcoming hotel in a tall, narrow, seventeenth-century building decked out in an appealingly eccentric medieval theme: four-posters, stone walls, roof beams and even a suit of armour. Doubles (no twins) cost €105–120, depending on season.

Hôtel de Nesle Map 2, E7. 7 rue de Nesle, 6e ⓣ01.43.54.62.41, ⓦwww.hoteldenesleparis.com. M° St-Michel. Friendly, offbeat hotel with historical- and literary-themed rooms decorated with wacky cartoon murals you'll either love or hate. Doubles are well priced at €75.

Hôtel de l'Odéon Map 2, E9. 13 rue St-Sulpice, 6e ⓣ01.43.25.70.11, ⓦwww.paris-hotel-odeon.com. M° St-Sulpice/Odéon. Old-fashioned luxury: flowers, antique furniture, some four-poster beds, and great service. Doubles €120–160, depending on season.

Hôtel Récamier Map 2, D9. 3bis place St-Sulpice, 6e ⓣ01.43.26.04.89, ⓕ01.46.33.27.73. M° St-Sulpice/St-Germain-des-Prés. Comfortable, old-fashioned hotel, superbly situated on a corner tucked away behind the grand church of St-Sulpice. Rooms are small and quite plain for the price of €110, or €130 with a view onto the square, but if you're willing to use a shared bathroom, you can have the same view for just €90.

Relais Christine Map 2, E8. 3 rue Christine, 6e ⓣ01.40.51.60.80, ⓦwww.relais-christine.com. M° Odéon/St-Michel. Highly elegant and luxurious four-star in a sixteenth-century building set around a deliciously hidden courtyard. At this level, it's well worth paying the small premium for one of the stunning *supérieure* rooms, at €385.

Relais Saint-Sulpice Map 2, D9. 3 rue Garancière, 6e ⓣ01.46.33.99.00, ⓦwww.relais-saint-sulpice.com. M° St-Sulpice/St-

Germain-des-Prés. Set in a beautiful, aristocratic town house on a side street immediately behind St-Sulpice's apse, this is a discreetly classy hotel with well-furnished rooms painted in cheery Provençal colours. All the mod cons, including a sauna off the dining room. Doubles from €170.

The Eiffel Tower quarter

Hôtel du Champs-de-Mars Map 6, B4. 7 rue du Champs-de-Mars, 7e ⓣ01.45.51.52.30, ⓦwww.hotel-du-champ-de-mars.com. M° École-Militaire. Friendly and well-run hotel in a handsome area just off the rue Cler market. The rooms are decidedly cosy, with swathes of colourful fabrics adorning the bedsteads, curtains and chairs. Excellent value at €79 for a double.

Hôtel du Palais Bourbon Map 6, E4. 49 rue de Bourgogne, 7e ⓣ01.44.11.30.70, ⓦwww.hotel-palais-bourbon.com. M° Varenne. This substantial, handsome old building in a sunny street by the Musée Rodin has homely, spacious and prettily furnished double rooms that are a bargain at €120. Family rooms are available, as well as one tiny double and a few miniature singles that are a steal. The immediate area isn't the liveliest, but it's quiet and classy.

Hôtel Saint-Dominique Map 6, C2. 62 rue Saint-Dominique, 7e ⓣ01.47.05.51.44, ⓦwww.hotel-stdominique.com. M° Invalides/La Tour-Maubourg. Welcoming hotel in the heart of this upmarket, village-like neighbourhood, which sits in the shadow of the Eiffel Tower. The smallish but tastefully wallpapered rooms (€119 for a double) are arranged around a bright little courtyard with tables and chairs amid the greenery.

Montparnasse

Hôtel de la Loire Map 6, off F14. 39bis rue du Moulin Vert, 14e ⓣ01.45.40.89.07, ⓔhoteldelaloire@wanadoo.fr. M° Pernety/Alésia. Behind the pretty blue shutters lies a delightful family hotel with a genuinely homely feel. Rooms all have charming personal touches and spotless bathrooms, and are a real bargain at €59, or €52 for the slightly darker rooms in the annex, which runs the length of the garden. (Just off the map: head south down rue Didot and turn left onto rue du Moulin Vert.)

Hôtel Mistral Map 6, G13. 24 rue de Cels, 14e ⓣ01.43.20.25.43, ⓦwww.mistralhotel.multimania.com. M° Pernety/Alésia. Inviting and pleasantly refurbished hotel on a very quiet street, with a little courtyard garden and breakfast room behind. The good-value rooms come with showers and shared WC facilities (€52), or en suite (€68).

Hôtel des Voyageurs Map 6, H14. 22 rue Boulard, 14e ⓣ01.43.21.08.02, ⓔhotel.des.voyageurs2@wanadoo.fr. M° Denfert-Rochereau. A friendly and great-value Montparnasse establishment with an original, warm spirit – there are paintings all over the walls and cultural events in the back garden. All rooms cost €50 and are comfortable and modern, with air conditioning and private, free Internet access.

Montmartre and around

Hôtel Bonséjour Map 3, F2. 11 rue Burq, 18e ⓣ01.42.54.22.53, ⓕ01.42.54.25.92. M° Abbesses. In a marvellous location on a quiet un-touristy street on the slopes of Montmartre, this hotel is run by friendly and conscientious owners. The rooms, which are basic but clean and spacious, are Montmartre's, if not Paris's, best deal – €25 for a simple double room with just a sink, or €42 with a private shower. Ask for the corner rooms 23, 33, 43 or 53, all of which have a balcony.

Hôtel Caulaincourt Map 3, F1. 2 sq Caulaincourt (by 63 rue Caulaincourt), 18e ⓣ01.46.06.46.06, ⓦwww.caulaincourt.com. M° Lamarck-Caulaincourt. One of the nicest and friendliest of Paris's budget hotels. The rooms are well kept, and decent value at €59–69, or €69–79 en suite. From the larger dormitory room of the hostel section (€24 a night), the lucky backpackers get a fine view.

Hôtel du Commerce Map 3, G3. 34 rue des Trois-Frères, 18e ⓣ01.42.64.81.69 ⓦwww.commerce-paris-hotel.com. M° Abbesses/Anvers. Cheerfully basic hotel for the hardened traveller only. Arrive in the morning for a room that night. The cheapest singles go for €29, doubles for €39, though to get an en-suite toilet you'll have to shell out at least €59.

Hôtel Eldorado Map 3, C3. 18 rue des Dames, 17e ⓣ01.45.22.35.21, ⓦwww.eldoradohotel.fr. M° Rome/Place-de-Clichy. Not quite the golden kingdom, but idiosyncratic and enjoyable nonetheless, with its own little wine bar and an attractive annex at the back of the sizeable courtyard garden. Rooms (€60 for a double) are thoughtfully and charmingly decorated, with bright colour schemes and antique furnishings. A few rooms with shared bath are also available.

Ermitage Map 3, H1. 24 rue Lamarck, 18e ⓣ01.42.64.79.22 ⓦwww.ermitagesacrecoeur.fr. M° Lamarck-

Caulaincourt/Château-Rouge. Sitting right on top of the hill of Montmartre, this discreet family-run hotel has rooms caught in time, characterfully decorated with glorious florals in deep colours and antique objets d'art. Only a stone's throw from the Sacré Cœur but it's best to approach via M° Anvers and the *funiculaire* to avoid the steep climb. Doubles cost around €90 – no credit cards.

Hôtel Langlois Map 3, E6. 63 rue St-Lazare, 9e ⓣ01.48.74.78.24, ⓦwww.hotel-langlois.com. M° Trinité. This superbly genteel hotel feels as if it has scarcely changed in the last century, though it has all the facilities you'd expect of a two-star. Every room is different, but they're all large and handsome with high ceilings, antique furnishings, fire-places and other period details. Some have enormous bathrooms. There are only 27 rooms, with prices around €100, so book well in advance.

Hôtel Regyns Montmartre Map 3, F3. 13 place des Abbesses, 18e ⓣ01.42.54.45.21, ⓦwww.paris-hotels-montmartre.com. M° Abbesses. A friendly place with tidy, country-style rooms, a number of which give onto the quiet place Abbesses. If available, get one of the six rooms on the top floors, which have grand views of either the city or Sacré Cœur. Doubles at €84, though you pay a €25 premium for a view.

Perfect Hotel Map 3, H5. 39 Rue Rodier, 9e ⓣ01.42.81.18.86, ⓕ01.42.85.01.38. M° Anvers. This welcoming, well-kept hotel on a lively street lined with restaurants sees many happy return visitors. Rooms are simple and clean, though the walls are notoriously paper-thin. While the hotel doesn't quite live up to its name, for the price it's a great find. Doubles without bath €40, otherwise €52.

Style Hôtel Map 3, C2. 8 rue Ganneron (av Clichy end), 18e ⓣ01.45.22.37.59, ⓕ01.45.22.81.03. M° Place-de-Clichy. Wooden floors, marble fireplaces, a secluded internal courtyard, and friendly service. Simple, but great value, especially in the rooms with shared bathrooms. Doubles at €50, or €35 with shared facilities. No lift.

Timhotel Montmartre Map 3, F2. pl Emile-Goudeau, 11 rue Ravignan, 18e ⓣ01.42.55.74.79, ⓦwww.timhotel.com. M° Abbesses/Blanche. Rooms are modern, comfortable and freshly decorated in a nondescript chain-hotel way. The location, however, is unbeatable – on the beautiful shady square where Picasso had his studio in 1900, with views across the city from the more expensive rooms. Doubles start at €130, running to €160 for the larger rooms with vistas.

The Bastille and around

Nouvel Hôtel Map 1, H6. **24 av du Bel Air, 12e ⓣ01.43.43.01.81, ⓕ01.43.44.64.13, ⓦwww.nouvel-hotel-paris.com. M° Nation.** You'd hardly know you were in the big city at this quiet, family-run hotel, with its provincial, country-cottage air – lent partly by its little garden and patio. The small rooms are immaculate and prettily decorated in pastels and white-painted furniture; no. 9, opening directly onto the garden, is the one to go for. Doubles €72 (shower), €82 (bath).

Hôtel de la Porte Dorée Map 1, H6. **273 av Daumesnil, 12e ⓣ01.43.07.56.97, ⓕ01.49.28.08.18, ⓦwww.hoteldelaportedoree.com. M° Porte-Dorée.** A charming, tastefully decorated two-star. Traditional features such as ceiling mouldings, fireplaces and the elegant main staircase have been retained and many of the furnishings are antique. The Bastille is seven mintues away by métro or a pleasant twenty-minute walk along the Promenade Plantée. Doubles €64.

Eastern Paris

Hôtel Beaumarchais Map 4, E8. **3 rue Oberkampf, 11e ⓣ01.53.36.86.86, ⓕ01.43.38.32.86, ⓦwww.hotelbeaumarchais.com. M° Filles-du-Calvaire/Oberkampf.** Fashionable, funky and gay-friendly hotel with colourful, 1950s-inspired decor; all 31 rooms are en suite with air conditioning, safes and cable TV. There's a little patio for breakfast (€10) on fine days. Singles €75, doubles €110.

Hôtel Gilden-Magenta Map 4, D5. **35 rue Yves Toudic, 10e ⓣ01.42.40.17.72, ⓕ01.42.02.59.66, ⓦwww.multi-micro.com/hotel.gilden.magenta. M° République/Jacques-Bonsergent.** A friendly hotel, with fresh, colourful decor; rooms 61 and 62, up in the attic, are the best and have views of the Canal St Martin. Breakfast is served in a pleasant patio area. Doubles €68–75.

Hôtel Mondia Map 4, E6. **22 rue du Grand Prieuré, 11e, ⓣ01.47.00.93.44, ⓕ01.43.38.66.14, ⓦwww.hotel-mondia.com. M° République/Oberkampf.** A welcoming place on a fairly quiet street. The 23 rooms are modestly furnished in pastel colours and floral prints; those facing the street on the fifth floor have little balconies, and the two attic hideaways (nos. 602 and 603) have a certain charm. For stays of three nights or more in quieter periods you'll get a ten percent reduction on presentation of your Rough Guide. Doubles/twins €58–69; triples €80.

Hôtel de Nevers Map 4, D6. 53 rue de Malte, 11e ⓣ 01.47.00.56.18, ⓕ01.43.57.77.39, ⓦwww.hoteldenevers.com. M° Oberkampf/République. The entrance to this hospitable, good-value one-star is patrolled by three smoky-grey cats. Needless to say, there's no room to swing one, but otherwise these are for the most part decent, if slightly tatty, cheerfully decorated rooms – the best are the en-suite doubles at the front; courtyard-facing rooms are rather dark and poky. Doubles €34–48.

Western Paris

Hameau de Passy Map 1, C5. 48 rue Passy, 16e ⓣ01.42.88.47.55, ⓕ01.42.30.83.72, ⓦwww.hameaudepassy.com. M° Muette/Passy. An utterly peaceful modern hotel with a country sensibility, set back from the main street. Rooms are pleasantly decorated in bright hues of green and orange and look out onto a pretty tree-lined patio. Faultless service is assured by a charming, polyglot staff. Singles €103, doubles €113.

Queen's Hotel Map 1, B5. 4 rue Bastien-Lepage, 16e ⓣ01.42.88.89.85, ⓦwww.queens-hotel.fr. M° Michel-Ange-Auteuil. A three-star hotel run by helpful staff and offering modern comfort on a lovely side street in the centre of old Auteuil. The 22 rooms, individually styled, come with some nice touches such as mahogany mirrors and each is hung with a painting by a contemporary artist. Some rooms have showers (€98), others have baths with Jacuzzi tubs (€118 with baths).

Apartments and bed and breakfast

Rented apartments are attractive alternatives for families with young children or visitors planning an extended visit who want a bit more independence and the option to do their own catering. Staying on a **bed-and-breakfast** basis in a private house is also worth considering if you want to get away from the more impersonal set up of a hotel and is a reasonably priced option.

France Lodge 2 rue Meissonier, 17e ⓣ01.56.33.85.80, ⓕ01.56.33.85.89, ⓦ www.apartments-in-paris.com. M° Le-Peletier. Offers bed-and-breakfast rooms inside and outside Paris. Prices start at €23 single or €40 double, plus a €15 booking fee.

Good Morning Paris 43 rue Lacépède, 5e ⓣ01.47.07.28.29, ⓦwww.goodmorningparis.fr. Bed-and-breakfast accommodation in central Paris, starting at €46 for a single room, €59 for a double. You have to stay at least two nights but there's no reservation fee – payment in full confirms your booking.

Lodgis 47 rue de Paradis, 10e ⓣ01.70.39.11.11, ⓦwww.lodgis.com. A well-run agency with a large number of furnished flats on its books. A studio flat in the 8e starts from around €475 a week.

Paris B and B ⓣ1-800 872 2632, ⓦwww.parisbandb.com. US-based online bed-and-breakfast booking service. The rooms offered are on the luxurious side and start from $90 for a double. Apartments from $120.

Studio-in-paris.com ⓦwww.studio-in-paris.com. Small, friendly Paris-based accommodation service, with nine pleasant flats in the Marais, Palais Royal and Montorgueil areas. Studios from €420 a week.

Hostels, student accommodation and campsites

Hostels are an obvious choice if you're keeping to a tight budget. Most places take **advance bookings**, including all three main hostel groups, FUAJ (part of Hostelling International, or HI), UCRIF and MIJE. Paris has only two central HI hostels, both part of the Fédération Unie des Auberges de Jeunesse (FUAJ; ⓦwww.fuaj.fr), but they can put you in touch with two more HI hostels, Cité des Sciences and Léo Lagrange, both just outside the city limits. You need **membership**, but it's available on the spot. It's advisable to book ahead in summer – this can be done anywhere in the world via their computerized International Booking Network (contact your nearest Hostelling International office before leaving home or look up details on the Internet). In

Paris itself, the central **FUAJ** office is near the Pompidou Centre at 9 rue Brantôme, 3ᵉ (Ⓣ01.48.04.70.40). A second, larger hostel group is run by **UCRIF** (Union des Centres de Rencontres Internationaux de France; Ⓦwww.ucrif.asso.fr), which caters mainly to groups. We've detailed only the most central hostels, but a complete list is available online, and individual hostels should help you find a room elsewhere if they're full. Alternatively, UCRIF's main office at 27 rue de Turbigo, 2ᵉ (Mon–Fri 9am–6pm; Ⓣ01.40.26.57.64; M° Étienne-Marcel) can tell you where there are free places. A third group, **MIJE** (Maison Internationale de la Jeunesse et des Etudiants; Ⓦwww.mije.com), runs three hostels in historic buildings in the Marais district. All are very pleasant places to stay and need to be booked a long time in advance. Independent hostels tend to be noisier, more party-oriented places, often with bars attached and mostly attracting young visitors from Europe and the United States.

Student accommodation is let out during the summer vacation. Rooms are spartan, part of large modern university complexes and often complete with self-service kitchen facilities and shared bathrooms. Space tends to fill up quickly with international students, school groups and young travellers, so it's best to make plans well in advance. Expect to pay €15–30 per night for a room. The organization to contact for information and reservations is **CROUS**, Académie de Paris, 39 avenue Georges-Bernanos, 5ᵉ (Mon–Fri 9am–5pm; Ⓣ01.40.51.55.55, Ⓦwww.crous-paris.fr; M° Port-Royal).

Except where indicated, there is no effective age limit at any of these places.

D'Artagnan Map 4, off I8. 80 rue Vitruve, 20ᵉ Ⓣ01.40.32.34.56, Ⓕ01.40.32.34.55, Ⓦwww.fuaj.fr. M° Porte-de-Bagnolet. A colourful, funky, modern HI hostel, with a fun atmosphere and lots of facilities including a small cinema, restaurant and bar, and a local swimming pool nearby. Located on the eastern edge of the city near Charonne, which has some good bars. Huge, but very popular so try to get here early – you can reserve online, by fax, or by calling the central reservations number on ⓣ01.44.89.87.27. No private rooms, but some dorms have three or four beds. Dorm beds cost €20.60.

BVJ Paris Quartier Latin Map 2, H10. 44 rue des Bernardins, 5e ⓣ01.43.29.34.80, ⓦwww.bvjhotel.com. M° Maubert-Mutualité. Typically institutional UCRIF hostel, but spick and span and in a good location. Dorm beds (€26), plus single or double rooms (€28–35 per person), all with shared toilet.

Le Fauconnier Map 4, B12. 11 rue du Fauconnier, 4e ⓣ01.42.74.23.45, ⓕ01.40.27.81.64. M° St-Paul/Pont-Marie. MIJE hostel in a superbly renovated seventeenth-century building with a courtyard. Dorms (€24–26 per person) sleep three to eight, and there are some single (€30) and double rooms too (€40 with shower). Breakfast included.

Le Fourcy Map 4, B11. 6 rue de Fourcy, 4^{e} ⓣ01.42.74.23.45. M° St-Paul. Another MIJE hostel (same prices as *Le Fauconnier*, above) housed in a beautiful mansion, this one has a small garden and a restaurant with *menus* from €9.50. Dorms and some doubles and triples.

Foyer International d'Accueil de Paris Jean Monnet Map 5, B8. 30 rue Cabanis, 14e ⓣ01.43.13.17.00, ⓦwww.fiap.asso.fr. M° Glacière. A huge, efficiently run UCRIF hostel in a fairly sedate area, with singles (€53), doubles (€34 each) and dorms (€24–30, depending on number of beds). Facilities include a disco; ideal for groups.

Jules Ferry Map 4, E6. 8 bd Jules-Ferry, 11e ⓣ01.43.57.55.60, ⓦwww.fuaj.fr. M° République. Fairly central HI hostel, in a lively area at the foot of the Belleville hill. Very difficult to get a place, but when full they will help you find a bed elsewhere. Only two to four people in each room; beds €19.

Maubuisson Map 4, A11. 12 rue des Barres, 4e ⓣ01.42.74.23.45. M° Pont-Marie/Hôtel-de-Ville. An MIJE hostel in a magnificent medieval building on a quiet street. Shared use of the restaurant at nearby *Le Fourcy* (see above). Dorms only, sleeping four (€25 per person). Breakfast included.

Independent hostels

Auberge Internationale des Jeunes Map 4, G13. 10 rue Trousseau, 11^{e} ⓣ01.47.00.62.00, ⓦwww.aijparis.com. M° Bastille/Ledru-Rollin. Despite the official-sounding name, this is a laid-back (but very noisy) independent hostel in a great location five minutes' walk from the Bastille. Clean and professionally run with 24hr reception, generous breakfast (included) and free luggage storage. Rooms for two, three and four people. €13 Nov–Feb, €14 March–Oct.

Hôtel Caulaincourt Map 3, F1. 2 sq Caulaincourt (by 63 rue Caulaincourt), 18e ⓣ01.46.06.42.99, ⓦwww.caulaincourt.com. M° Lamarck-Caulaincourt. Friendly hotel with a useful dormitory section (€24 a night) from which there's a fine view over Paris; very good value for the location.

Centre International de Paris/Louvre Map 2, E4. 20 rue Jean-Jacques-Rousseau, 1er ⓣ01.53.00.90.90. M° Louvre/Châtelet-Les-Halles. A clean, modern and efficiently run hostel for 18- to 35-year-olds. Bookings can be made up to ten days prior to your stay. Accommodation ranges from single rooms to dorms sleeping eight. From €18.30 per person.

Maison Internationale des Jeunes Map 4, I13. Rue Titon, 11e ⓣ01.43.71.99.21, ⓔmij.cp@wanadoo.fr. M° Faidherbe-Chaligny. A clean, well-run establishment located between Bastille and Nation, geared to 18- to 30-year-olds for stays of between three and five days. Doors are open from 6am till 2am. Rooms range from doubles to dorms sleeping eight. €22.50 per person including shower, breakfast and sheets. Reservations should be made in advance and a fifty percent deposit is required.

Three Ducks Hostel Map 1, C5. 6 place Étienne-Pernet, 15e ⓣ01.48.42.04.05, ⓦwww.3ducks.fr. M° Commerce/Félix-Faure. Private youth hostel very popular with Eurorailing students. Kitchen facilities as well as a bar with very cheap beer. Lockout 11am–4pm, curfew at 2am. Essential to book ahead between May and Oct: send the price of the first night or leave a credit card number online. In high season, beds cost €23 in dorm rooms (sleeping from four to ten people), €26 per person in a double; there are discounts in winter.

Le Village Hostel Map 3, H3. 20 rue d'Orsel, 18e ⓣ01.42.64.22.02, ⓦwww.villagehostel.fr. M° Anvers. Brand-new hostel in an attractively renovated nineteenth-century building, with good facilities such as phones in the rooms. There's a view of the Sacré-Cœur from the terrace. Dorms (€23) or twin rooms (€27 per person); price includes breakfast.

Woodstock Hostel Map 5, H5. 48 rue Rodier, 9e ⓣ01.48.78.87.76, ⓦwww.woodstock.fr. M° Anvers/St-Georges. A reliable hostel in the *Three Ducks* group. Has its own bar, and is set in a great location on a pretty street, not far from Montmartre. Dorms €20/17, depending on season. Twin rooms available (€23/17); price includes breakfast. Book ahead, as a trendy crowd quickly fills all the beds.

Camping

With the exception of the one in the Bois de Boulogne, most of Paris's **campsites** are some way out of town, although the two listed here are linked by public transport. For other possibilities, contact the tourist office or look online at Ⓦwww.camping-fr.com.

Camping du Bois de Boulogne Map 1, A4. Allée du Bord-de-l'Eau, 16e Ⓣ01.45.24.30.00, Ⓦwww.abccamping.com/boulogne.htm. M° Porte-Maillot then bus #244 to Moulins Camping (bus runs 6am–9pm). Extra shuttle bus between campsite and M° Porte-Maillot April–Sept 8.30am–12.30am and 6pm–midnight. By far the most central campsite, with space for 436 tents, next to the River Seine in the Bois de Boulogne, and usually booked out in summer. The ground is pebbly, but the site is well equipped and has a useful information office. Prices start at €11 for a tent with two people; there are also bungalows for four to six people starting at €49 for four per night.

Camping la Colline Map 9, I4. Route de Lagny, Torcy Ⓣ01.60.05.42.32, Ⓦwww.camping-de-la-colline.com. RER line A4 to Torcy, then phone from the station and they will collect you; or take bus #421 to stop Le Clos. Pleasant wooded lakeside site to the east of the city near Disneyland (minibus shuttle to Disneyland costs €12 return), offering rental of anything from luxury tents to bungalows; erecting your own tent costs €15 per night for two people.

19

Cafés and restaurants

The French seldom separate the major pleasures of eating and drinking, and there are thousands of establishments in Paris where you can do both. A restaurant may call itself a *brasserie*, *bistrot*, *café*, or indeed *restaurant*; equally, a *café* can be a place to eat, drink, listen to music or even dance. To simplify matters, we've split our listings for each area into two parts: under **cafés and wine bars**, you'll find venues we recommend primarily for light snacks, and daytime or relaxed evening drinks – though many also serve a *plat du jour* (daily special) or even a full menu; under **restaurants**, you'll find any establishment we recommend specifically for a meal. Alongside cafés, we've listed **wine bars** or *bistrots à vin* which may offer cheeses, cold meats and regional dishes too; also included in this category, you'll find genteel **salons de thé** (tea rooms), which typically serve tea, pastries and light meals. If you're looking for cocktails, pints or full-on **nightlife**, you'll find the best venues listed separately in chapter 20, under "**bars**" (see p.227).

Cafés and restaurants often **close** on Sunday or Monday. It's common for cafés to stay open to 2am, and even extend

Breakfast and snacks

Most cafés are able to make you up a filled baguette or a *tartine* on request. This is generally the best way to eat **breakfast**, and works out cheaper than the rate charged by most hotels (typically around €8–12). In the mornings, you may see a basket of croissants or some hard-boiled eggs on the counter. The drill is to help yourself – the waiter will keep an eye on how many you've eaten and bill you accordingly. Brasseries are also possibilities for cups of coffee, eggs, snacks and other breakfast-type food, while the concept of **le brunch** in a café has taken Paris by storm in recent years, becoming a Sunday institution in areas like the Marais.

For **snacks**, stand-up sandwich bars are found in all but the poshest areas of Paris, while most boulangeries sell savoury quiches, tarts and sometimes sandwiches. For picnic treats, head for a charcuterie or the delicatessen counter in a good supermarket; some of the city's most specialized or luxurious food shops are listed on pp.259–262 of the "Shopping" chapter. For hot take-away food, *crêperies* sell *galettes* (wholewheat pancakes) as well as sweet and savoury *crêpes* (flat pancakes). More common are Turkish or North African kebab-and-fries shops, the latter also serving couscous plates with *merguez* (spicy sausage), chicken or lamb, and a spicy, tomato-rich vegetable soup.

hours on a Friday and Saturday night, closing earlier on Sunday. Restaurants won't usually serve after 10pm, though some **brasseries** serve meals till the early hours. Many restaurants and shops take a **holiday** between the middle of July and the end of August. For the more upmarket or trendy places, and at weekends, it's wise to make **reservations** – usually easily done on the same day, except for the most fashionable or gastronomically renowned places, for which you may need to book weeks in advance. At the élite, Michelin-starred end of the market, you'd be advised to **dress up**, too.

At restaurants, there is often a choice between one or more fixed-price **menus** (or sometimes a budget two-course

Paris for vegetarians

Paris's gastronomic reputation is largely lost on **vegetarians**. In most restaurants, aside from the usual salads and cheeses, there is precious little choice for those who don't eat meat, as almost every dish, if not made almost entirely of beef, chicken, or fish, is invariably garnished with *lardons* (bacon), *anchois* (anchovies), or *jambon* (ham). That said, some of the newer, more innovative places will often have one or two vegetarian dishes on offer, and ethnic restaurants are a good bet. *Salons de thé*, too, offer lighter fare such as soups and quiches (*tartes*), which tend to be vegetarian. It's also possible to put together a meal at even the most meat-oriented brasserie by choosing dishes from among the starters (*crudités*, for example, are nearly always available) and soups, or by asking for an omelette. Useful French phrases to help you along are *Je suis végétarien(ne)* ("I'm a vegetarian") and *Il y a quelques plats sans viande*? (Are there any non-meat dishes?).

The few purely vegetarian restaurants that do exist tend to be based on a healthy diet principle rather than haute cuisine, but at least you get a choice.

Aquarius 40 rue de Gergovie, 14e; p.217.
Au Grain de Folie 24 rue de La Vieuville, 18e; p.220.
La Petite Légume 36 rue Boulangers, 5e; p.209.
Piccolo Teatro 6 rue des Ecouffes, 4e; p.205.
Le Potager du Marais 22 rue Rambuteau, 4e; p.205.
Les 5 Saveurs d'Anada 72 rue du Cardinal-Lemoine, 5e; p.207.
La Victoire Suprême du Cœur 41 rue des Bourdonnais, 1er; p.202.

formule), often particularly good value at lunch time. Eating *à la carte*, by contrast, gives you access to everything on offer, though you'll pay a fair bit more. **Service** is legally included in your bill at all restaurants, bars and cafés, but you may want to leave a one- or two-euro coin as a **tip**. **Waiters** answer to *monsieur* or *madame* or *excusez-moi* – never *garçon*; to ask for the bill, the phrase is *l'addition, s'il vous plaît*.

The Islands

Cafés and wine bars

Berthillon Map 2, I9. 31 rue St-Louis-en-l'Île, 4e. M° Pont-Marie. Wed–Sun 10am–8pm. As the long queues outside attest, *Berthillon* serves the best ice cream and sorbets (€4 a triple) in Paris. They come in all sorts of unusual flavours, such as rhubarb and

Gourmet restaurants

Paris is the perfect place to blow out on the meal of a lifetime. Top rated is *Alain Ducasse* at the *Plaza Athénée* hotel (see p.198), considered one of the best restaurants in Europe. The first-ever chef to have been awarded six Michelin stars (shared between two restaurants), Alain Ducasse swept like a tidal wave through the world of French cuisine in the early 1990s and hasn't looked back. Other greats include *L'Ambroisie* (see p.204), *Pierre Gagnaire* (see p.197) and *Taillevent* (see p.198). Over on the Left Bank, you'll find three gastronomic restaurants, each unusual in a different way. The *Restaurant Hélène Darroze* (see p.213) is run by a woman, the Ducasse-trained Mme Darroze herself; Alain Reix's *Le Jules Verne* (see p.215) is actually located up on the first floor of the Eiffel Tower: while Alain Passard's *L'Arpège*, 84 rue de Varenne, 7e (ⓣ02.45.51.47.33, ⓦwww.alain-passard.com), eschews all red meat in favour of superb fish and vegetable dishes (and has an unusually steep €300 price-tag on its *menu dégustation*).

Prices at most of these restaurants are often cheaper if you go at midday during the week, and some offer a set lunch *menu* for around €70. In the evening, prices average at about €150, and there's no limit on the amount you can pay for top wines. Recently, some of the star chefs have made their fine cuisine more accessible to a wider range of customers by opening up less expensive, more casual, but still high-quality establishments. In addition to presiding over the *Plaza Athénée*, for example, Alain Ducasse has taken over *Aux Lyonnais* bistro (see p.200), while Hélène Darroze has her tapas-style *Salon d'Hélène* (see p.213) underneath the main restaurant.

glazed chestnut, and are also available at other island sites listed on the door.

Taverne Henri IV Map 2, F7. 13 place du Pont-Neuf, 1er. Mº Pont-Neuf. Mon–Fri 11.30am–9.30pm, Sat noon–5pm; closed Aug. An old-style wine bar that's probably changed little since Yves Montand used to come here with Simone Signoret. It's best to drop in at lunch time when it's at its buzziest, usually full of lawyers from the nearby Palais de Justice. Wine by the glass starts at €3; *tartines*, with a choice of cheeses, hams, pâté and *saucisson*, are €5.

Restaurants

Brasserie de l'Île St-Louis Map 2, I7. 55 quai de Bourbon, Île St-Louis, 4e ☎01.43.54.02.59. M° Pont-Marie. Thurs–Tues noon–midnight. A friendly brasserie with a rustic, dark-wood interior and a sunny terrace, serving moderately priced Alsatian cuisine, such as sauerkraut with ham and sausage.

Le Relais de l'Île Map 2, I9. 37 rue St-Louis-en-l'Île, Île St-Louis, 4e ☎01.46.34.72.34. M° Pont-Marie. Mon & Wed–Fri 7–11pm, Sat & Sun noon–2.30pm. A cosy, candlelit jazz-restaurant, serving good, if not exceptional, French cuisine; you'll pay around €35 for three courses, with mains like rabbit in prune sauce or lemon chicken with honey. But it's the ambience that makes this place special: the convivial atmosphere, friendly service and the pianist tinkling away.

Champs-Élysées and around

Cafés and wine bars

Angélina Map 2, B3. 226 rue de Rivoli, 1er. Mº Tuileries. Mon–Fri 9.15am–7pm, Sat & Sun 9.15am–7.30pm; closed Tues in July & Aug. This elegant old *salon de thé*, with its murals, gilded stucco work and comfy leather armchairs, does the best hot chocolate in town – a generous jugful with whipped cream on the side costs around €6. The other house speciality is the Mont Blanc, a chestnut cream, meringue and whipped cream dessert.

Le Fouquet's Map 7, F3. 99 av des Champs-Élysées, 8e ☎01.47.23.70.60. M° George-V. Daily 8am–1.30am. Dating from 1899, *Le Fouquet's* is the favourite venue for celebrations after the annual César film awards. You can just enjoy a drink on the terrace, a prime spot for people-watching on the Champs, or eat in the comfortable restaurant (last orders 11.30pm) amid red velvet drapes and chandeliers; meals aren't cheap (count on around €60), but the food is good.

Musée Jacquemart-André Map 7, J1. 158 bd Haussmann, 8e. M° St-Philippe-du-Roule/Miromesnil. Daily 11.30am–5.30pm. Part of the Musée Jacquemart-André, but with independent access, this is the most sumptuously appointed *salon de thé* in the city. Admire the ceiling frescoes by Tiepolo while savouring the fine pastries or salads (around €10).

Café Véry (also known as Dame Tartine) Map 7, L3. Jardin des Tuileries, 1er. M° Concorde. Daily noon–11pm. The best of a number of café-restaurants in the gardens, with tables outside under shady horse chestnuts, frequented by Louvre curators and other aesthetes. Snacks and more substantial meals available (€5–8).

Restaurants

Le Chiberta Map 7, F2. 3 rue Arsène Houssaye, 8e ⓣ01.53.53.42.00. M° Charles-de-Gaulle-Etoile. Mon–Fri noon–2.30pm & 7.30–11pm, Sat 7.30–11pm. Visually striking minimalist design is the setting for a delicious menu of nouvelle French cuisine under the aegis of wunderchef Guy Savoy. Lemon-grass ginger prawns with herbs make a nice starter (€25), and the rib of beef with béarnaise sauce and mushrooms is actually a great deal at €70 for two. Otherwise there are *menus* at €60 and €100. The wine cellar has some absurdly rare vintages, and service is impeccable.

Lasserre Map 7, I5. 17 av Franklin D. Roosevelt, 8e ⓣ01.43.59.53.43. M° Franklin-D.-Roosevelt. Mon–Sat 7.30–10pm, plus Thurs & Fri noon–2pm; closed Aug. A classic haute-cuisine restaurant with a beautiful belle époque dining room, decorated with flower-draped balustrades and fine ceiling frescoes. Highlights on the menu are lemon-crust seabass and sublime duck à l'orange, though you can't go wrong whatever you choose. *Á la carte* you'll pay upwards of €130, not including wine, though you can eat more cheaply if you come at lunch time and opt for the €75 *menu*.

Pierre Gagnaire Map 7, G1. Hôtel Balzac, 6 rue Balzac, 8e ⓣ01.58.36.12.50, ⓦwww.pierre-gagnaire.com. M° George-V. Mon–Fri noon–1.30pm & 7.30–9.30pm, Sun 7.30–9.30pm. Judged sixth-best restaurant in the world by *Restaurant* magazine in 2005, *Pierre Gagnaire* is a gastronomic adventure. The tasting menu (€225) has nine courses, featuring such treats as black rice, Mallemort asparagus, chicken crest and veal dumpling (and that's just one course). *Á la carte* around €125, lunch *menu* for €90.

Plaza-Athénée Map 7, H5. Hôtel Plaza-Athénée, 25 av Montaigne, 8e ☎01.53.67.65.00. M° Alma-Marceau. Mon–Wed 7–9pm, Thurs & Fri noon–2pm & 7–9pm; closed mid-July to mid-Aug. One of Paris's top haute cuisine temples, run by Alain Ducasse, whose sublime and inventive offerings are likely to revive even the most jaded palate. The menu might include Bresse chicken with truffle sauce or prawns with Iranian caviar. The decor is Louis XV with a modern gloss and the service is exceptional. From about €200 per head.

Le Relais de l'Entrecôte Map 7, G4. 15 rue Marbeuf, 8e ☎01.49.52.07.17. M° Franklin-D.-Roosevelt. Daily noon–2.30pm & 7–11.30pm. There's no main-course menu here, the only dish being steak and *frites*. This is no ordinary steak though – it's served with a delicious sauce, the ingredients of which are a closely kept secret. You'll pay €20.80 a head, including a salad first course; the desserts are well worth investigating too. Second branch at 20bis rue St-Benoit, 6e (M° St-Germain-des-Prés).

Rue Balzac Map 7, G1. 3 rue Balzac, 8e ☎01.53.89.90.91. M° George-V. Mon–Fri noon–2pm & 7.30–11pm, Sat & Sun 7.30–11pm. The low lighting and subdued reds and yellows of the decor of this super-stylish, buzzing restaurant provide an atmospheric back-drop to classy cuisine, available in small or large servings (*petit modèle* and *grand modèle*); most people find the former filling enough. Three courses with wine comes to around €70.

Taillevent Map 7, G2. 15 rue Lamennais, 8e ☎01.44.95.15.01, ⓦwww.taillevent.com. M° George-V. Mon–Fri noon–2.30pm & 7.30–11pm; closed Aug. One of Paris's finest gourmet restaurants, sporting three Michelin stars. The Provencal-influenced cuisine is outstanding and the wine list out of this world. Elegant dining room and clientele to match. Reckon on €150 a head.

Yvan Map 7, J3. 1bis rue J-Mermoz, 8e ☎01.43.59.18.40. M° Franklin-D-Roosevelt. Mon–Fri noon–2.30pm & 8pm–midnight, Sat 8pm–midnight. An elegant restaurant with a deep-red, plush interior, *Yvan* is frequented by a cool crowd and run by staff with similar attitude. The excellent *nouveau* menu includes interesting dishes such as caramelized cod and polenta pigeon. Three courses cost around €60 with wine and it's best to book.

The Grands Boulevards and around

Cafés and wine bars

L'Arbre à Cannelle Map 3, H8. 57 passage des Panoramas, 2e. M° Grands-Boulevards. Mon–Sat 11.30am–6pm. Tucked away in an attractive *passage*, this early twentieth-century *salon de thé* with its exquisite wood panelling, frescoes and painted ceilings makes an excellent spot to treat yourself to salads (from €10) and tarts both savoury and sweet (€4.55).

Aux Bons Crus Map 2, E3. 7 rue des Petits-Champs, 1er. M° Palais Royal-Musée du Louvre. Mon 9am–3pm, Tues–Sat 7.30am–11pm. A relaxed, workaday place that has been serving good wines and cheese, sausage and ham for more than eighty years. A carafe from €6; plate of cold meats from €13.

Le Dénicheur Map 2, H3. 4 rue Tiquetonne, 2e ☎01.42.21.31.03. M° Étienne-Marcel. Tues–Sat 12.30–3.30pm & 7pm–midnight, Sun 12.30–3.30pm. A chic, gay-friendly café-restaurant. The place is a hodgepodge of wacky decor: bright-blue globes above, Snow White and the Seven Dwarves at the door and bin-shaped lampshades all about. Salads are the main event here, though you can find lasagne and *tartines* too, all at reasonable prices. Big, popular weekend brunches for €13.

Juvéniles Map 2, D3. 47 rue de Richelieu, 1er. M° Palais Royal-Musée du Louvre. Tues–Sat 11am–11pm, Sun noon–2pm, Mon 7.30–11pm. Very popular tiny wine *bistrot* run by a Scot. Wine costs from €13 a bottle and there are usually around ten varieties available by the glass (from €3); *plats du jour* cost €11, cheese plates and other light dishes €7.

Ladurée Map 7, M4. 16 rue Royal, 8e. M° Madeleine. Mon–Sat 8.30am–7pm. Lavishly decorated with gilt-edged mirrors and ceiling frescoes, this classy tearoom, with a high Hermès-scarf count, is renowned for its melt-in-your-mouth macaroons.

Verlet Map 2, D4. 256 rue St-Honoré, 1er. M° Palais Royal-Musée du Louvre. Mon–Sat 9am–7pm. A heady aroma of coffee greets you as you enter this old-world coffee merchant's-cum-café, with its wood furnishings, green-leather benches and caddies lining one wall. The menu features 25 varieties of coffee and there's a good selection of teas and light snacks, too.

The World Bar Map 3, C7. Floor 5, Printemps de l'Homme, 64 bd Haussmann, 9e. M° Havre-Caumartin. Mon–Sat 10am–7pm. British designer Paul Smith created the quirky decor of this bar on the fifth floor of Printemps' men's department. Newspapers from round the world plaster the walls and ceiling, while exposed concrete beams and metal workshop chairs lend an air of industrial-chic. A long zinc bar rounds off the masculine look. *Plat du jour* €13.

Restaurants

Chartier Map 3, H8. 7 rue du Faubourg-Montmartre, 9e ☎01.47.70.86.29. M° Grands-Boulevards. Daily 11.30am–3pm & 6–10pm. Brown linoleum floor, dark-stained woodwork, brass hat racks, waiters in long aprons – the original decor of an early twentieth-century soup kitchen. Worth seeing and, though crowded and rushed, the food is not bad at all. Three courses for €16, and a bottle of wine from €5.80.

Dilan Map 2, G3. 13 rue Mandar, 2e ☎01.40.26.81.04. M° Les Halles/Sentier. Mon–Sat noon–3pm & 7.30–11.30pm. An excellent-value Kurdish restaurant, with cosy, kilim-strewn interior. You could do worse than start with the delicious *babaqunuc* (stuffed aubergines), followed by *beyti* (spiced minced beef wrapped in pastry, with yoghurt, tomato sauce and bulgar wheat). Around €18 for two courses; €9 for half a litre of Kurdish wine.

Gallopin Map 2, F2. 40 rue Notre-Dame-des-Victoires, 2e ☎01.42.36.45.38. M° Bourse. Daily noon–midnight. An utterly endearing old brasserie, with all its original brass and mahogany fittings and a beautiful painted glass roof in the back room. The place heaves at lunch time with journalists, business people and glamorous Parisiennes. The classic French dishes, especially the *foie gras maison*, are well above par; *menus* range from €23 to €33.50.

Higuma Map 2, D3. 32bis rue Ste Anne, 1er ☎01.47.03.38.59. M° Pyramides. Daily 11.30am–10pm. Authentic Japanese canteen with cheap, filling ramen dishes and a variety of set menus starting at €10.

Aux Lyonnais Map 2, F1. 32 rue St Marc, 2e ☎01.42.96.65.04. M° Bourse/Richelieu-Drouot. Tues–Fri noon–2pm & 7.30–11pm, Sat 7.30–11pm. This old *bistrot*, with its belle époque tiles and mirrored walls, has been taken over by star chefs Alain Ducasse and Thierry de la Brosse. They've preserved the old-fashioned ambience and done wonders with the cuisine, serving up delicious Lyonnais fare – try the *quenelles* (light and delicate fish dumplings) followed by the heavenly Cointreau soufflé for dessert. Service is friendly and there's a buzzy atmosphere. Three-course set menu €28.

Le Vaudeville Map 3, G9. 29 rue Vivienne, 2e ⓣ01.40.20.04.62. M° Bourse. Daily noon–3pm & 7pm–1am. There's often a queue to get a table at this lively, late-night brasserie, attractively decorated with marble and mosaics. Dishes include grilled cod with truffle sauce and *belle tête de veau*. À la carte from €30; lunch-time *formule* €23.50.

Beaubourg and Les Halles

Cafés and wine bars

Café Beaubourg Map 2, H5. 43 rue St-Merri, 4e. M° Rambuteau/Hôtel-de-Ville. Mon–Thurs & Sun 8am–1am, Sat 8am–2am. A seat under the expansive, not to say expensive, awnings of this stylish café, bearing the trademark sweeping lines of designer Christian de Portzamparc, is one of the best places for people-watching on the Pompidou Centre's piazza.

A la Cloche des Halles Map 2, F4. 28 rue Coquillière, 1er. M° Châtelet-Les Halles/Louvre. Mon–Fri noon–10pm, Sat noon–4pm. The bell hanging over this little wine bar is the one that used to mark the end of trading in the market halls, and the great ambience is owed to the local vendors who spend their off-hours here. You are assured of some very fine wines, best sided with the *jambon d'Auvergne* or one of their delectable cheeses, all very reasonably priced.

Le Petit Marcel Map 4, A9. 63 rue Rambuteau, 4e. M° Rambuteau. Daily 10am–1am. This bar boasts speckled table tops, mirrors and painted tiles, a cracked and faded ceiling and about eight square metres of drinking space as well as friendly bar staff and local atmosphere. There's a dining area, too, where you can get cheap and filling dishes such as omelette and *frites* (€9).

Restaurants

Georges Map 2, H5. Centre Georges Pompidou, 4e ⓣ01.44.78.47.99. M° Rambuteau/Hôtel-de-Ville. Wed–Mon 11am–2am. On the top floor of the Pompidou Centre, this trendy, ultra-minimalist restaurant commands stunning views over the roof tops of Paris and makes a stylish place for lunch or dinner. The French-Asian fusion cuisine is somewhat overpriced (main courses €18–32), but then that's not the main reason you come. Reservations are a must for dinner.

Lô Sushi Map 2, F6. 1 rue du Pont-Neuf, 8e ☎01.42.33.09.09. M° Pont-Neuf. Daily noon–midnight. Bubble-shaped sushi bar with a conveyer belt. The sushi itself (€2–7) is nothing to write home about; the real draw is the computer screens at each place setting, allowing you to email your friends over lunch, or even chat online with fellow diners.

La Robe et le Palais Map 2, G6. 13 rue des Lavandières Ste-Opportune, 1er ☎01.45.08.07.41. M° Châtelet. Mon–Sat noon–2.30pm & 7.30–11pm. Small, busy *restaurant à vin* serving traditional cuisine and a *tête*-boggling selection of 250 wines *au compteur* (priced according to how much you consume). Although the food here can be rough on your cholesterol level, it is excellently prepared. The two-course lunch *menu* is decent value at €18, and large meat or cheese platters for €10 are also available.

La Tour de Montlhéry (Chez Denise) Map 2, F5. 5 rue des Prouvaires, 1er ☎01.42.36.21.82. M° Louvre-Rivoli/Châtelet. Mon–Fri 24hr; closed mid-July to mid-Aug. An old-style, unpretentious Les Halles *bistrot* serving substantial portions of meaty French staples, accompanied by excellent French fries. It's always crowded and smoky. Carte from €38.

La Victoire Suprême du Cœur Map 2, G5. 41 rue des Bourdonnais, 1er ☎01.40.41.93.95. M° Louvre-Rivoli/Châtelet. Mon–Fri 11.45am–2.30pm & 6.45–10pm, Sat noon–3pm & 6.45–10pm. While the interior takes some getting used to – photos and drawings of Indian guru Sri Chimnoy plaster the place – this restaurant does some of the best vegetarian food in Paris, including tasty salads, quiches and wholesome *plats du jour*, such as *roti champignons* with blackberry sauce. Lunch *menu* for just over €10.

Au Vieux Molière Map 2, H4. Passage Molière, 157 rue Saint-Martin, 3e ☎01.42.78.37.87. M° Étienne-Marcel/Rambuteau/RER Châtelet. Mon–Fri noon–2pm & 7.30–10.30pm, Sat & Sun 7.30–10.30pm. French *chansons* playing softly in the background add to the mellow atmosphere of this cosy, candlelit restaurant hidden away down a characterful *passage*. The traditional cuisine is well prepared and flavoursome and includes dishes such as garlic-roasted chicken and mullet in saffron sauce. Lunch-time *formule* €15.25, in the evening *à la carte* from €35.

The Marais

Cafés and wine bars

L'Apparemment Café Map 4, C9. 18 rue des Coutures-St-Gervais, 3e. M° St-Sébastien-Froissart. Mon–Fri noon–2am, Sat 4pm–2am, Sun 12.30pm–midnight. Chic, cosy café resembling a series of comfortable sitting rooms, with quiet corners and deep sofas. Recommended are the salads, which you compose yourself by ticking off your chosen ingredients and handing your order to the waiter. The popular Sunday brunch (until 4pm) costs €15.

L'As du Falafel Map 4, C11. 34 rue des Rosiers, 4e. M° St-Paul. Sun–Thurs noon–midnight. The sign above the doorway of this falafel shop in the Jewish quarter reads "Toujours imité, jamais égalé" ("Always copied, but never equalled"), a boast that few would challenge, given the quality of the food and the queues outside. Falafels to take away cost only €3.50, or pay a bit more and sit in the buzzy little dining room.

Le Loir dans la Théière Map 4, C11. 3 rue des Rosiers, 4e. M° St-Paul. Mon–Fri 11am–7pm, Sat & Sun 10am–7pm. Comfy, battered sofas and *Alice in Wonderland* murals create a homely atmosphere at this laid-back *salon de thé*, serving enormous portions of home-made cakes and excellent vegetarian quiches.

Mariage Frères Map 4, B10. 30 rue Bourg-Tibourg, 4e. M° Hôtel de Ville. Tues–Sun 3–7pm. The ultimate tea-room, serving over five hundred varieties of the stuff, and with no shortage of tempting pastries. The decor is elegant and faintly colonial while service is assured by handsome white-suited waiters. Around €15 for tea and pastry.

Café Martini Map 4, D11. 11 rue du Pas-de-la-Mule, 4e. M° St-Paul. Daily 8.30am–2am. Happy hour 7–10pm. Just off place des Vosges, this airy and relaxing little café offers low prices and taped jazz in the background. Hard to squeeze into, but you can always take the sandwiches away and picnic on the grass of the nearby *place*. Panini from €3.80, good cappuccino, and a *demi* is only €2.40.

Le Pain Quotidien Map 4, A10. 18 rue des Archives, 4e. M° Hôtel-de-Ville. Daily 7am–10.30pm. Trendy Belgian café-bakery with an air of a monks' refectory about it: plenty of natural wood, and diners have the option of sitting at a long, communal *table d'hôte*. It specializes in hearty breads, huge salads (around €11) and *tartines* and is especially popular for its delicious weekend brunch.

Le Petit Fer à Cheval Map 4, B10. 30 rue Vieille-du-Temple, 4e. M° St-Paul. Mon–Fri 9am–2am, Sat & Sun 11am–2am; food served noon–midnight. Very attractive small *bistrot*/bar with original fin-de-siècle decor, including a marble-topped bar in the shape of a horseshoe (*fer à cheval*). It's a popular drinking spot, with agreeable wine, and you can snack on sandwiches or *plats* (around €11) in the little back room furnished with old wooden métro seats.

Restaurants

404 Map 4, A7. 69 rue des Gravilliers, 3e ☎01.42.74.57.81. M° Arts-et-Métiers. Daily noon–midnight. Very popular trendy Moroccan restaurant, with a lanterned, dimly-lit interior that screams colonialist romance. The standard North African fare here is good enough, but surely it's the casbah fetish ambience you're paying for. Reckon on €35 exclusive of drinks or go for the bargain €17 lunch *menu*. Their famed weekend Berber Brunch requires reservations (Sat & Sun noon–4pm).

Ambassade d'Auvergne Map 4, A8. 22 rue de Grenier St-Lazare, 3e ☎01.42.72.31.22. M° Rambuteau. Daily noon–2pm & 7.30–11pm; closed last two weeks in Aug. Suited, moustachioed waiters serve scrumptious Auvergnat cuisine that would have made Vercingétorix proud. There's a set menu for €27, but you may well be tempted by some of the house specialities, such as the *blanquette d'Agneau* (white Roquefort lamb stew, €18). Reservations recommended.

L'Ambroisie Map 4, D11. 9 place des Vosges, 4e ☎01.42.78.51.45. M° Chemin-Vert/St-Paul. Tues–Sat noon–10.15pm; closed Aug. Scoring 19 out of 20 in the gourmet's bible *Gault et Millau* and run by celebrity chef Bernard Pacaud, *L'Ambroisie* offers exquisite food in a magnificent pre-1700s dining room hung with tapestries. Reckon on upwards of €200 a head and book well in advance or hope to get a last-minute cancellation.

Auberge de Jarente Map 4, C11. 7 rue Jarente, 4e ☎01.42.77.49.35. M° St-Paul. Tues–Sat noon–2.30pm & 7.30–10.30pm; closed Aug. This hospitable and friendly Basque restaurant serves up first-class food at moderate prices: *cassoulet*, hare stew, *magret de canard*, and *piperade*. Lunch *menu* €13, evening €19.

Au Bourgignon du Marais Map 4, B11. 52 rue François Miron, 4e ☎01.48.87.15.40. M°

St-Paul. Mon–Fri noon–3pm & 8–11pm; closed two weeks in Aug. Friendly and laid-back restaurant and *cave à vins* with tables outside in summer, serving excellent Burgundian cuisine with carefully selected wines to match. Reckon on €30 a head for three courses, excluding wine.

Le Coude Fou Map 4, B10. 12 rue du Bourg-Tibourg, 4e ☎01.42.77.15.16. M° Hôtel-de-Ville. Daily noon–2.45pm & 7.30–midnight. A popular, relaxed wine *bistrot*, with wooden beams and brightly painted murals. The menu offers some unusual wines from all over France to accompany traditional and more adventurous dishes, such as *filet de cannette aux kumcoats* and *entrecôte au bleu d'Auvergne*. Lunch-time *formule* €16.50, including a glass of wine; dinner *menu* for €24 (weekdays only). Booking is advisable on weekends.

L'Enoteca Map 4, C12. 25 rue Charles-V, 4e ☎01.42.78.91.44. M° St-Paul. Daily noon–11.30pm; closed one week in Aug. Situated in an old Marais building, this fashionable Italian *bistrot à vin* boasts an impressive wine list (22 pages). Food doesn't take a back seat either: choose from an array of *antipasti*, fresh pasta (€11) or more substantial dishes like *cochon de lait* (spit-roasted pork, €13). Two-course lunch-time *menu* for €13 including a glass of wine.

Piccolo Teatro Map 4, B11. 6 rue des Ecouffes, 4e ☎01.42.72.17.79. M° St-Paul. Tues–Sun noon–3pm & 7–11pm; closed Aug. Atmospheric low lighting, stone walls and thick-beamed ceilings characterize this fine vegetarian restaurant. The speciality is *gratin*s with poetic-sounding names, such as the *douceur et tendresse* made of spinach, mint, mozzarella and gruyere. The rhubarb crumble (€5.90) comes recommended. Midday *menu* at €8.90, evening €14.70. It's best to book on weekends.

Pitchi-Poï Map 4, C11. 7 rue Caron, cnr place du Marché-Ste-Catherine, 4e ☎01.42.77.46.15. M° St-Paul. Daily 10am–midnight. A warm and welcoming restaurant with outdoor seating on one of the Marais' most attractive squares. The cuisine revolves around central European/Jewish dishes like *tchoulent* (hearty bean stew) and salmon coulibiac. Don't leave without sampling one of the Polish flavoured vodkas – the honey one goes down a treat. €21.50 lunch and dinner *menu*, childrens' *menu* €11.50.

Le Potager du Marais Map 4, A9. 22 rue Rambuteau, 4e ☎01.42.74.24.66. M° Rambuteau. Mon–Sat noon–10.30pm & Sun 1–10.30pm. Come early or book in advance for a place at this tiny vegetarian restaurant, with only 25 covers at a long communal table. The ingredients are all organic and there's plenty for vegans, too. Dishes include goat's cheese with honey, vegetarian shepherd's pie and ravioli with basil. Lunchtime menu for €12, dinner for €15.

Le Rouge Gorge Map 4, C12. 8 rue St-Paul, 4e ☎01.48.04.75.89. M° St-Paul. Mon–Sat noon–3pm & 7–11pm; closed last fortnight in Aug. Small, friendly *restaurant à vin* with bare stone walls and jazz or classical music playing in the background. €10 lunch menu, €28 for dinner. Wine by the glass starts at €2.30; if you're taken by a particular vintage you can buy a bottle to take home.

The Quartier Latin and the southeast

Cafés and wine bars

Café de la Mosquée Map 2, I13. 39 rue Geoffroy-St-Hilaire, 5e. M° Monge. Daily 9am–midnight. Drink mint tea and eat sweet cakes in the courtyard of the Paris mosque – a haven of calm. The indoor salon has a beautiful Arabic interior, where meals are served for around €15 and up. Sheesha pipes can be had for €6, and there's even a hammam-massage-meal option for €58.

Café de la Nouvelle Mairie Map 2, F12. 19 rue des Fossés-St-Jacques, 5e. M° Cluny-La Sorbonne/RER Luxembourg. Mon, Wed & Fri 9am–9pm, Tues & Thurs 9am–midnight. Sleek café-wine bar with a relaxed feel and a university clientele (note it's shut at weekends). Serves good food like lamb curry or linguine, as well as *assiettes* of cheese or charcuterie (all around €10). On warm days there are outside tables on the picturesque square.

L'Ecritoire Map 2, F10. 3 pl de la Sorbonne, 5e. M° Cluny-La Sorbonne/RER Luxembourg. Daily 7am–midnight. This classic university café is right beside the Sorbonne, with outside tables by the fountain and little booths concealed at the back. Don't expect polite, unhurried service; do expect a lot of black polo necks.

La Fourmi Ailée Map 2, G9. 8 rue du Fouarre, 5e. M° Maubert-Mutualité. Daily noon–midnight. Simple, filling fare is served in this former feminist bookshop, now a relaxed *salon de thé*. A high, mural-painted ceiling and background jazz contribute to the atmosphere.

Around €10 for a *plat*.

Les Pipos Map 2, G11. 2 rue de l'École-Polytechnique, 5e. M° Maubert-Mutualité/Cardinal-Lemoine. Mon–Sat 8am–1am; closed two weeks in Aug. This antique bar has a decor that's heavy on old wood, and a local clientele. Serves wines from €3 a glass along with simple plates of Auvergnat charcuterie, cheese and the like (€5–10).

Le Reflet Map 2, F10. 6 rue Champollion, 5e. M° Cluny-La Sorbonne. Daily 10am–2am. This cinema café has a strong flavour of the *nouvelle vague*, with its scruffy black decor and rickety tables packed with artsy film-goers. Perfect for a drink either side of a film at one of the arts cinemas on rue Champollion, perhaps accompanied by a steak or quiche from the blackboard specials.

Le Verre à Pied Map 2, H14. 118bis rue Mouffetard, 5e. M° Monge. Tues-Sat 7am–5pm, Sun 8am–noon. Deeply old-fashioned market bar where traders take their morning *vin rouge*, or sit down to eat a *plat du jour* for €9. Some have been doing it so long they've got little plaques on their table.

Restaurants

Les 5 Saveurs d'Anada Map 2, H12. 72 rue du Cardinal-Lemoine, 5e ☎01.43.29.58.54. M° Cardinal-Lemoine. Tues–Sun noon–2.30pm & 7.30–10.30pm. Airy and informal restaurant serving delicious organic vegetarian food. Salads (€6.50) are good, or you could try one of the creative meat-substitute dishes (around €12), such as tofu soufflé or confit of tempeh with ginger.

L'Avant Goût Map 5, G8. 37 rue Bobillot, 13e ☎01.45.81.14.06. M° Place d'Italie. Tues–Fri noon–2.30pm & 7.30–10.45pm; closed three weeks in Aug. Small neighbourhood restaurant with a big reputation for excitingly good modern French cuisine and wines to match. Cool contemporary decor, bright red leather banquettes. Superb value lunch *menu* at €13.50, and evening *menus* at €28 and €40.

Le Bambou Map 5, just off J9. 70 rue Baudricourt, 13e ☎01.45.70.91.75. M° Tolbiac. Tues–Sun 11.30am–3.30pm & 6.30–10.30pm. Tiny Asian-quarter restaurant crammed with punters, French and Vietnamese alike, tucking into sublime Vietnamese food. Serves giant portions of powerful pho soups, and a full menu of delicious specialities. Last orders at 10.30pm, but you can stay till midnight.

Au Bistrot de la Sorbonne Map 2, F11. 4 rue Toullier, 5e ☎01.43.54.41.49. RER Luxembourg. Daily noon–2.30pm & 7–11pm.

Traditional French and delicious North African food is served at reasonable prices; locals and students crowd the lively, muralled interior. €12 for the lunch *menu*; evening *menus* from €18.

Brasserie Balzar Map 2, F10. 49 rue des Écoles, 5e ☏01.43.54.13.67. M° Maubert-Mutualité. Daily 8am–11.30pm. This classic, high-ceilinged brasserie is something of an institution. The decor isn't jaw-dropping, but it feels almost intimidatingly Parisian – though if you're unlucky, or choose to eat early, the tourist clientele can spoil the Left Bank mood. *À la carte* is around €35.

Le Buisson Ardent Map 2, I11. 25 rue Jussieu, 5e ☏01.43.54.93.02. M° Jussieu. Mon–Fri noon–2pm & 7–11pm, Sat 7–11pm; closed two weeks in Aug. Copious helpings of inventive, first-class cooking is served in a warm-coloured, pleasantly traditional dining room. Lunch *menu* costs €15; evenings €29. Reservations are recommended.

Chez Gladines Map 5, F8. 30 rue des Cinq-Diamants, 13e ☏01.45.80.70.10. M° Corvisart. Mon & Tues noon–3pm & 7pm–midnight; Wed–Sun noon–3pm & 7pm–1am. This tiny, Basque-run corner *bistrot* is always warm, welcoming and packed with young people. Serves excellent wines and hearty Basque and south-west dishes such as magret de canard. Giant salads cost under €10, and you'll pay less than €20 for a (very) full meal.

L'Ecurie Map 2, G11. 58 rue de la Montagne Ste-Geneviève, cnr rue Laplace, 5e ☏01.46.33.68.49. M° Maubert-Mutualité/Cardinal-Lemoine. Mon–Sat noon–3pm & 7pm–midnight, Sun 7pm–midnight. Shoe-horned into a former stables, this family-run restaurant is bustling and very lovable. Outside tables provide a few extra seats, but not many, so book ahead. Expect well-cooked meat dishes served without flourishes – grilled with *frites*, mostly – for less than €15.

Les Fontaines Map 2, F11. 9 rue Soufflot, 5e. RER Luxembourg. Mon–Sat noon–3pm & 7.30–11pm. The dated brasserie-cum-diner decor looks unpromising, but the welcome inside this family-run place is warm and genuine, and the cooking is in the same spirit, with honest French meat and fish dishes, or game in season. Main courses €11–18.

Lao-Thai Map 5, H9. 128 rue de Tolbiac, 13e ☏01.44.24.28.10. M° Tolbiac. Mon, Tues & Thurs–Sun noon–2.30pm & 7.30–11pm. A big, glass-fronted resto situated on a busy interchange and serving fine Thai and Laotian food. They offer a midday *menu* at €7.95, and several large, two-person *menus* for around €25.

Perraudin Map 2, F11. 157 rue St-Jacques, 5e. RER Luxembourg. Mon–Fri noon–2pm & 7.30–10.15pm; closed last two weeks in Aug. One of the classic *bistrots* of the Left Bank, featuring solid, homely cooking. The place is brightly lit, packed in and thick with Parisian chatter. There's a midday *menu* at €18, while in the evening the *menu* costs €18. No reservations, but you can wait at the bar.

La Petite Légume Map 2, H11. 36 rue des Boulangers, 5e ☎01.40.46.06.85. M° Jussieu. Mon–Sat noon–2.30pm & 7.30–10pm. This health-food grocery doubles as a vegetarian restaurant and tearoom, serving homely, organic *plats* for €8–12, along with fresh-tasting organic Loire wines.

Le Pré-Verre Map 2, G10. 8 rue Thénard 5e ☎01.43.54.59.47. M° Maubert-Mutualitié. Tues–Sat noon–2pm & 7.30–10.30pm; closed three weeks in Aug. This sleek and slightly posey *bistrot à vin* has a great wine list, and the food is just as interesting – you might find swordfish on a bed of quinoa grain or wild boar ragout with quince. *Menus* at €25, or just €12 at lunch.

Le Reminet Map 2, H9. 3 rue des Grands Degrés, 5e ☎01.44.07.04.24. M° Maubert-Mutualité. Mon & Thurs–Sun noon–2.30pm & 7.30–11pm; closed two weeks in Aug. This artful little *bistrot*-restaurant shows its class through small touches such as snowy-white tablecloths and fancy chandeliers. Imaginative sauces grace high-quality traditional French ingredients. Gastronomic *menu* at around €50, but you can get away *à la carte* for about half that.

Tashi Delek Map 2, F12. 4 rue des Fossés-St-Jacques, 5e ☎01.43.26.55.55. RER Luxembourg. Mon–Sat noon–2.30pm & 7.30–11pm; closed two weeks in Aug. Elegantly styled Tibetan restaurant serving everything from hearty, warming noodle soups to the addictive, ravioli-like momok and yak butter tea. There's a good evening menu at €19, but you can eat well for much less.

Le Temps des Cerises Map 5, F9. 18–20 rue Butte-aux-Cailles, 13e ☎01.45.89.69.48. M° Place-d'Italie/Corvisart. Mon–Fri noon–2.15pm & 7.30–11.40pm, Sat 7.30pm–midnight. Truly welcoming cooperative restaurant with elbow-to-elbow seating and a daily choice of hearty French dishes. The atmosphere is perfect. Lunch *menu* at €10 and evening *menus* at €13.50 and €22.

Tricotin Map 1, F7. Kiosque de Choisy, 15 av de Choisy, 13e ☏01.45.85.51.52 & 01.45.84.74.44. M° Porte-de-Choisy. Daily 9am–11.30pm. Glazed in like a pair of overgrown fish tanks, *Tricotin* sits right next to a Chinese-signed McDonalds. Restaurant no. 1 (closed Tues) does Thai and grilled dishes alongside the Chinese classics, while no. 2 has more Vietnamese, Cambodian and steamed foods. Expect to spend around €18.

St-Germain

Cafés and wine bars

Bistrot des Augustins Map 2, F8. 39 quai de Grands Augustins, 6e. M° St-Michel. Daily 9am–11pm. Small, traditional wine bar conveniently located on the riverbank between the Pont Neuf and Place St-Michel. Serves good charcuterie, salads and hot *gratins*, all for around €10, and filling *tartines* – perfect with a glass of wine.

Le Bonaparte Map 2, D8. CNR rue Bonaparte and pl St-Germain, 6e. M° St-Germain-des-Prés. Daily 7.30am–2am. Less touristy than the nearby *Deux Magots* or *Flore*, and situated at the quieter, sunnier end of the square. Hot and cold snacks served at reasonable prices.

Chez Georges Map 2, D9. 11 rue des Canettes, 6e. M° Mabillon. Tues–Sat noon–2am; closed Aug. This thoroughly old-fashioned and atmospherically delapidated old wine bar has its old shop front still in place, though sadly Georges himself is not.

Á la Cour de Rohan Map 2, E9. Cour du Commerce, off rues St-André-des-Arts and Ancienne-Comédie, 6e. M° Odéon. Daily noon–7.30pm; closed mid-July to mid-Aug. This genteel, chintzy drawing-room *salon de thé* is tucked down a picturesque eighteenth-century alleyway just off the Odéon. Cakes, tartes, poached eggs, and the like as well as *plats du jour* from around €10. No smoking.

Les Deux Magots Map 2, D8. 170 bd St-Germain, 6e. M° St-Germain-des-Prés. Daily 7.30am–1am; closed one week in Jan. This famous café on the corner of place St-Germain-des-Prés is the victim of its own reputation as the historic hang out of Left Bank intellectuals, but it's still great for people-watching. A coffee costs €4.50.

Le Flore Map 2, D8. 172 bd St-Germain, 6e. M° St-Germain-des-Prés. Daily 7am–1.30am. The great rival of *Les Deux Magots* has a unique hierarchy: tourists on the *terrasse*, beautiful people inside, intellectuals upstairs. Sartre, De Beauvoir, Camus and Marcel Carné used to hang out here. Especially enjoyable for the hot chocolate.

Bar du Marché Map 2, E8. 75 rue de Seine, 6e. M° Mabillon. Daily 7am–2am. A thrumming café where the *serveurs* are cutely kitted out in flat caps and aprons. It's a fashionable place for a *kir* or a Sauternes but, admittedly, you pay a little extra for the colours of the rue de Buci market on the doorstep.

Café de la Mairie Map 2, D9. 8 pl St-Sulpice, 6e. M° St-Sulpice. Daily 7.30am–1am. A peaceful, pleasant café on the sunny north side of the square, opposite the church of St-Sulpice. Reputedly an old haunt of Henry Miller, now a fashionable place to bask with a coffee or an apéritif.

Café du Musée d'Orsay Map 2, B5. 1 rue Bellechasse, 7e. RER Musée-d'Orsay/M° Solférino. Tues–Sun 11am–5pm. The Musée d'Orsay's roof-top café offers one of the city's quirkier views – over the Seine and towards Montmartre – seen through the giant clock face dominating the room. Serves snacks and drinks, with a wonderful outdoor terrace for sunny days.

M's Coffee Room Map 2, B10. 71 rue du Cherche-Midi, 6e. M° Vaneau/Rennes. Daily noon–7pm. Ideal for a tea break while shopping, or a light *plat du jour* (around €12). The wonderful decor is inherited from a turn-of-the-century butcher's shop, but the comfy sofas, board games, teas, brownies and apple crumble are distinctly Anglo.

La Palette Map 2, E7. 43 rue de Seine, 6e. M° Odéon. Mon–Sat 9am–2am. This once-famous Beaux-Arts student hang-out is now frequented by art dealers, though it's still very relaxed. The decor is superb, including, of course, a large selection of paint-spattered palettes hanging on the walls. There's a roomy *terrasse* outside, and some good daily specials on the menu.

Au Petit Suisse Map 2, E10. 16 rue de Vaugirard, 6e. RER Luxembourg/M° Cluny-La Sorbonne. Daily 6.30am–midnight. The perfect retreat from the Jardin du Luxembourg, with everything you'd need from a café: an outdoor terrace; an in-house *tabac*; a two-hundred-year history; an Art Deco interior; a menu of sandwiches and *plats du jour*; and a mezzanine level that's made for people-watching.

Veggie Map 2, C7. 38 rue de Verneuil, 7e. M° Solférino. Mon–Fri 10.30am–2.30pm & 4.30–7.30pm. Excellent, wholesome organic takeaway from a health-food shop near the Musée d'Orsay.

Restaurants

Allard Map 2, F8. 41 rue St-André-des-Arts, 6e ☎01.43.26.48.23. M° Odéon. Mon–Sat noon–2.30pm & 7.30–11pm. Expect the menu at this proudly unreconstructed Parisian restaurant to be meaty and rich rather than sophisticated or imaginative and you'll be very satisfied. The atmosphere is unimpeachably antique – apart from the international clientele. From around €30 for dinner.

L'Atlas Map 2, E8. 11 rue de Buci, 6e ☎01.40.51.26.30. M° Mabillon. Daily 6.30am–1am. Despite a few Art Deco details, the decor at *L'Atlas* is functional rather than classic, but that's half the charm of this unpretentious market brasserie. Good seafood, and simple, meaty main dishes at around €17.

Au 35 Map 2, D7. 35 rue Jacob, 6e ☎01.42.60.23.24. M° St-Germain-des-Prés. Mon–Fri noon–2.30pm & 7.30–11pm, Sat 7.30–11pm. This adorably intimate *bistrot* is filled with Art Deco lamps, mirrors and old posters, but the food's the thing. You might have an exotic, rich *pastilla d'agneau* (lamb in pastry with honey and spices), or a perfectly simple duck breast. Count on around €30 without wine.

Les Bouquinistes Map 2, F8. 53 quai des Grands Augustins, 6e ☎01.43.25.45.94. M° Odéon/RER St-Michel-Notre-Dame. Mon–Fri noon–2pm & 7.30–10.30pm, Sat 7.30–10.30pm. The suavely modern interior has a few token books to add a touch of Left Bank sophistication, but the focus is on Guy Savoy's serious, contemporary culinary inventions. You might have a starter of warm oysters on fennel jelly followed by spiced lamb shank with confit garlic. Count on €50 a head, without wine.

Brasserie Lipp Map 2, D8. 151 bd St-Germain, 6e ☎01.45.48.53.91. M° St-Germain-des-Prés. Daily noon–12.45am. One of the most celebrated of all the classic Paris brasseries; the haunt of the very successful and very famous, with a wonderful 1900s wood-and-glass interior. There are decent *plats du jour*, including the famous *choucroute* (sauerkraut), for under €20, but gastro-exploring *à la carte* can get expensive.

Le Petit St-Benoît Map 2, D8. 4 rue St-Benoît, 6e ☎01.42.60.27.92. M° St-Germain-des-Prés. Mon–Sat noon–2.30pm & 7.30–10.30pm; closed Aug. Another of the tobacco-stained St-Germain institutions, all rickety wooden tables and brass coat racks. Serves the sort of homely, meaty, comfort food your *grand-mère* would cook: try the *hachis parmentier* (shepherd's pie) or the *boudin noir* with potatoes. Around €20, including house wine.

Polidor Map 2, E10. 41 rue Monsieur-le-Prince, 6e ⓣ01.43.26.95.34. M° Odéon. Mon–Sat noon–2.30pm & 7pm–12.30am, Sun noon–2.30pm & 7–11pm. Eating at *Polidor* is a classic of Left Bank life. Open since 1845, it's bright and bustling with aproned waitresses and packed with noisy regulars until late in the evening. The food is generally good, solid French classics, with mains like *confit de canard* or guinea fowl with *lardons* for around €12. No bookings; just turn up and wait.

Le Salon d'Hélène Map 2, B10. 4 rue d'Assas, 6e ⓣ01.42.22.00.11. M° St-Sulpice/Sèvres-Babylone. Tues 7.30–10.15pm, Wed–Sat 12.30–2.15pm & 7.30–10.15pm; closed Aug. Underneath celebrity chef Hélène Darroze's gastronomic southwest-French restaurant, *Le Restaurant d'Hélène*, the trendier and more relaxed ground-floor *bistrot*-tapas bar offers some expertly created dishes drawing on Basque cuisine – and even on Spanish and Asian influences too. Beware: even the tapas *menu* is expensive at €79, or €99 with selected wines. Book well in advance.

La Tourelle Map 2, F9. 5 rue Hautefeuille, 6e ⓣ01.46.33.12.47. M° St-Michel. Mon–Fri 12.15–2.15pm & 7–10pm, Sat 7–10pm; closed Aug. This splendidly medieval little bistro is packed into a low, stone-walled, convivial room. The meaty cuisine is fresh, simple and very traditional. Service is particularly considerate and the three-course *menu* good value at €18. No reservations, so turn up and wait.

Vagenende Map 2, E8. 142 bd St-Germain, 6e ⓣ01.43.26.68.18. M° Mabillon. Daily noon–1am. This Art Nouveau marvel is registered as a historic monument, all mirrors, marble pillars, chandeliers and dark wood that has been polished for decades to a lustrous glow. Worthwhile if you go for the ambience rather than the food – stick to the straightforward brasserie dishes (mains at €16-24) or seafood specials.

Ze Kitchen Galerie Map 2, F8. 4 rue des Grands-Augustins, 6e ⓣ01.44.32.00.32. M° St-Michel. Mon–Fri noon–2.30pm & 7.30–10.30pm, Sat 7.30–10.30pm. Hovering halfway between restaurant and trendy art gallery in atmosphere, the food is equally studied, mixing Asian influences with contemporary Mediterranean cuisine – try gnochetti with squid and nori, or calf's sweetbreads with lemongrass jus. Expect to pay €50 for three courses, without wine.

The Eiffel Tower quarter

Cafés and wine bars

Café du Marché Map 6, B4. 38 rue Cler, 7e. M° La Tour-Maubourg. Mon–Sat 7am–midnight. Big, busy café-brasserie serving excellent-value meals, with a *plat du jour* for under €10 that's as fresh-tasting as you'd expect, given the position in the middle of the rue Cler market. There's outdoor seating, or a covered-over *terrasse* in winter.

Le Poch'tron Map 6, G3. 25 rue de Bellechasse, 7e. M° Solférino. Mon–Fri 9am–10.30pm. With a good selection of snacks and wines by the glass, this is a relaxing place to revive yourself after visiting the museums in the arrondissement. Also serves lunch and dinner, with main dishes such as *confit de canard* or pike stew at around €17.

Salon de Porcelain Map 7, D5. Place d'Iéna, 16e ☎01.47.23.58.03. M° Trocadéro. Wed–Mon 10am–5.30pm. The shortage of decent places to eat and drink around Trocadéro make the café-restaurant of the Musée Guimet a good bet, albeit more for its interesting menu of speciality teas and dishes from all over Asia – dim sum, Thai, Japanese – than for its basement ambience. *Menus* between €16 and €20.

Restaurants

L'Arpège Map 6, E4. 84 rue de Varenne, 7e ☎01.45.05.09.06. M° Varenne. Mon–Fri noon–2.30pm & 8–11pm. Exceedingly upscale restaurant just across from the Rodin museum. Celebrity chef Alain Passard has given vegetarian dishes the spotlight, though fish is still served for traditionalists. *Haute cuisine* dishes like grilled turnips with chestnuts or Chausey lobster *aiguillette* are €50 and up, though a six-courser runs at a cool €180. Reserve well in advance.

Au Babylone Map 6, G6. 13 rue de Babylone, 7e ☎01.45.48.72.13. M° Sèvres-Babylone. Mon–Sat noon–2pm; closed Aug. The gingham paper tablecloths, old lamps and pictures, and hanging flower baskets give this little restaurant buckets of old-fashioned charm. The menu – €18.50 for the set three-courser – is similarly unreconstructed, with good meaty classics such as *andouillette* and *blanquette de veau*.

La Cave de l'Os à Moëlle Map 1, C6. 181 rue de Lourmel, 15e ☎01.45.57.28.88/28. Tues–Sat noon–2pm & 7pm–midnight; closed 3 weeks in Aug. This no-frills offshoot of *L'Os à Moëlle* has two communal tables at which you can enjoy a €20 *menu* of the same exciting food you'd see at the main restaurant. The ethos is self-service: you help yourself to a steaming pot of stew and cut your own slice of terrine.

Chez Germaine Map 6, F8. 30 rue Pierre-Leroux, 7e ⓣ01.42.73.28.34. M° Duroc/Vaneau. Mon–Fri noon–2.30pm & 7–10pm; Sat noon–2.30pm; closed Aug. Madame hardly has room to squeeze between the tables, the hat stand and the tiny shelf of wines along the back wall at this charming little family restaurant. On the three-course *menu* (€13.50) or two-course lunch time *formule* (€11) you might have anchovy fillets, followed by a meaty pikeperch steak or *tripes à la mode de Caen*.

La Fontaine de Mars Map 6, A3. 129 rue St-Dominique, 7e ⓣ01.47.05.46.44. M° La Tour-Maubourg. Daily noon–3pm & 7.30–11pm. This well-mannered local restaurant is decked out in genteel pinks – tablecloths, napkins and gingham café curtains. Service is attentive, and the blackboard specials might run from a perfect tartare (€17) to a zingy filet de St-Pierre with basil (€20). The summer terrasse, set under a stone arcade, is perfect for lunch (€15 *menu*).

Jules Verne Map 7, D8. South Pillar of the Eiffel Tower, 7e. ⓣ01.45.55.61.44. M° École Militaire. Daily 12.15–1.45pm & 7.15–9.45pm. Genuinely *haute* cuisine – served on the second floor – of the Eiffel Tower. The dining room is a 1980s retro affair of chrome, leather and low spot lighting, but if your eyes aren't locked with your beloved's, there's always the view. Chef Alain Reix's food is top-flight. Book months in advance and dress smart. Lunch *menu* at €49 (weekdays only), evening *menu* at €114.

Aux Marchés du Palais Map 7, E6. 5 rue de la Manutention, 16e ⓣ01.47.23.52.80. M° Iéna. Mon–Fri noon–2pm & 7.30–10.30pm, Sat 7.30–10.30pm. Simple, traditionally styled bistro, with sunny tables on the pavement opposite the side wall of the Palais de Tokyo. There's always a good *entrée* and *plat du jour* – you might find a creamy broccoli *velouté* followed by fillet of perch with lentils and cucumber. Count on around €35 a head with wine.

L'Os à Moëlle Map 1, C6. 3 rue Vasco de Gama, 15e ⓣ01.45.57.27.27. M° Lourmel. Tues–Sat noon–2pm & 7pm–midnight; closed 3 weeks in Aug. The highlight of chef Thierry Faucher's relaxed *bistrot* is the €38 *menu*, which brings you four courses showing off the most rewarding side of traditional French cuisine – from Jerusalem artichoke and black truffle soup, via scallops and giant snails to satisfying steaks. There's an inexpensive lunch menu. Reserve well in advance.

Au Petit Tonneau Map 6, C2. 20 rue Surcouf, 7e ☎01.47.05.09.01. M° Invalides. Daily noon–3pm & 7–11.30pm. Mme Boyer runs this small, friendly, *bistrot*-style restaurant with panache, cooking delicious traditional French cuisine. Wild mushrooms are a speciality, along with a free-range *coq-au-vin*. All prices are *à la carte*: under €10 for starters, around €15–20 for mains.

Au Pied de Fouet Map 6, F6. 45 rue de Babylone, 7e ☎01.47.05.12.27. M° St-François-Xavier/Sèvres-Babylone. Mon–Fri noon–2.30pm & 7–9pm, Sat noon–2.30pm; closed Aug. An atmospheric little place – just four tables and no reservations – where the specials are written up on the mirror. Think home-made *confit* duck, basil ravioli, or haddock fillet with slivers of cabbage. Under €15 for a full meal.

Le P'tit Troquet Map 6, B3. 28 rue de l'Exposition, 7e ☎01.47.05.80.39. M° École Militaire. Mon 7.30–10pm, Tues–Sat noon–2.30pm & 7.30–10pm. This tiny family restaurant has a discreetly nostalgic feel, with its ornate *zinc* bar along the back wall topped by an old brass coffee pot. Serves well-judged, traditional, seasonal cuisine to the diplomats of the *quartier*, with *menus* at around €30.

Thoumieux Map 6, C2. 79 rue St-Dominique, 7e ☎01.47.05.49.75. M° La Tour-Maubourg. Daily noon–3pm & 6.30–11pm. A cavernous, traditional brasserie replete with mirrors, carved wood, hat stands and bustling, black-and-white-clad waiters. Popular with a smart local clientele for carefully prepared classics, many with a southwestern emphasis. Basic *menus* at €20 and €23, or around €40 *à la carte*.

La Varangue Map 6, A4. 27 rue Augereau, 7e ☎01.47.05.51.22. M° École-Militaire. Mon–Fri noon–2.30pm & 5.30–9pm, Sat & Sun 5.30–9pm. Also known as Philippe's restaurant, after the proprietor, who presides over the tiny, homely dining room from his minuscule open kitchen. The food ranges from good salads and vegetarian choices – popular with the loyal American clientele – to more traditional mains (around €12) such as *coq-au-vin*.

Montparnasse

Cafés and wine bars

L'Entrepôt Map 6, E14. 7–9 rue Francis-de-Pressensé, 14e. M° Pernety. Mon–Sat noon–2am. Arty cinema with a spacious, relaxed café and outside seating in the courtyard. Serves a great Sunday brunch, *plats du jour* cost around €10–16, and it holds frequent concerts in the evening.

Le Select Map 6, H10. 99 bd du Montparnasse, 6e. M° Vavin. Daily 7am–2am, Fri & Sat till 4am. If you want to visit one of the great Montparnasse cafés, as frequented by Picasso, Matisse, Henry Miller and F. Scott Fitzgerald, make it this one. It's the most traditional of them all and the prices aren't over-inflated. Only the brasserie-style food is disappointing.

Restaurants

Aquarius Map 6, E14. 40 rue de Gergovie, 14e ☎01.45.41.36.88. M° Pernety/Plaisance. Mon–Sat noon–2.30pm & 7.30–10.30pm; closed three weeks in Aug. This vegetarian restaurant is a homely place serving wholesome if not spectacular main courses such as nut roast, Mexican chilli and lasagne for around €12. There's a *menu* at €15 (€11 at lunch).

La Coupole Map 6, H10. 102 bd du Montparnasse, 14e ☎01.43.20.14.20. M° Vavin. Daily 8am–1am. The largest and most enduring arty-chic Parisian brasserie, *La Coupole* remains a genuine institution, buzzing with conversation and clatter from the diners packed in tightly under the high, chandeliered roof. The menu runs from oysters to Welsh rarebit, with plenty of fishy and meaty classics in between. Evening *menu* at €33.50, but you can have two courses for €23.50 before 6pm and after 10pm.

La Régalade Map 1, D7. 49 av Jean-Moulin, 14e ☎01.45.45.68.58. M° Alésia. Mon 7.30–11.30pm, Tues–Fri noon–2.30pm & 7.30–11.30pm; closed Aug. Star-chef Yves Camdeborde has moved from this famous *bistrot*, but new man Bruno Doucet is keeping up the high standards. Dishes sound deceptively simple – beautifully sauced meats with imaginatively prepared vegetables, for the most part – but the standard €30 *prix fixe* delivers a memorable meal.

La Rotonde Map 6, H10. 105 bd du Montparnasse, 6e ☎01.43.26.68.84. M° Vavin. Daily 7.15am–2am. One of the grand old Montparnasse establishments, frequented in its time by the full roll call of pre-WWI artists and writers. Since those days it has moved upmarket, gaining a plush decor of red velvet and brass, and is now best visited for a reliable meal, served at almost any time of day or night. Mains cost around €20.

Au Vin des Rues Map 6, H14. 21 rue Boulard, 14e. ☎01.43.22.19.78. Mon–Sat noon–3pm & 7.30–11pm, Sun 7.30–11pm. This charmingly old-fashioned restaurant and wine bar has rickety wooden chairs and a menu of solid French classics – *andouillette*, *pavé* of salmon, *foie de veau* and so on. The wines are excellent, and the atmosphere convivial, especially on the rowdy accordion and pot-au-feu evenings (Thurs). Around €30 a head.

Montmartre and around

Cafés and wine bars

Café des Deux Moulins Map 3, E3. 15 rue Lepic, 18e ☎01.42.54.90.50. M° Blanche. Daily 7am–2am. Having seen its early-2000s heyday of fans on the trawl of *Amélie* lore (she waited tables here in the film), this diner-style café is back to what it always was: a down-to-earth neighborhood hang-out, preserved in a bright, charming 1950s interior. Sunday brunch is popular.

L'Été en Pente Douce Map 3, I2. 23 rue Muller, 18e (cnr rue Paul-Albert) ☎01.42.64.02.67. M° Château-Rouge. Daily noon–midnight. An ideal Montmartre lunch or coffee spot, with chairs and tables set out on a terrace alongside the steps leading up to Sacré-Cœur. The food is very good, especially the giant goat's cheese and fig salad; traditional French *plats* cost around €13, but the main reason for coming, summer or winter, is to soak up the pure Montmartre atmosphere.

La Fourmi Café Map 3, G4. 74 rue des Martyrs, 18e. M° Pigalle/Abbesses. Mon–Thurs 8am–2am, Fri & Sat 8am–4am, Sun 10am–2am. A trendy, high-ceilinged café-bar full of conscientiously beautiful young Parisians drinking coffee by day and cocktails at night.

Le Progrès Map 3, H3. 1 rue Yvonne Le Tac, 18e. M° Abbesses/Anvers. Daily 9am–2am. Generous glazed windows overlook this crossroads at the heart of Abbesses, making this café something of a lighthouse for the young *bobos* (bohemian-bourgeoises) of Montmartre. By day a simple, relaxed café serving reasonably priced meals and salads (€12–15), at night it turns into a pub-like venue.

Le Sancerre Map 3, F3. 35 rue des Abbesses, 18e. M° Abbesses. Daily 7am–2am. A fashionable hang-out for the young and trendy of all nationalities under the southern slope of Montmartre, with a row of outside tables perfect for watching the world go by. The food can be disappointing though.

Restaurants

Casa Olympe Map 3, F6. 48 rue St-Georges, 9e ☎01.42.85.26.01. M° St-Georges. Mon–Fri noon–2pm & 8–11pm. As a female chef running her own bistro, Dominique Versini, aka "Olympe", is somewhat unusual in Paris. But then so is her cooking – and at under €40, the set menu is a bargain. Some bold meats are featured, from veal foot to pig's head, while the ambience is classy but not stuffy, with leather banquettes down one wall.

Chez Casimir Map 3, K5. 6 rue de Belzunce, 10e ☎01.48.78.28.80. M° Gare du Nord. Mon 7.30–10.30pm, Tues–Fri noon–2pm & 7.30–10.30pm. In basic, unrenovated *bistrot* surroundings you can enjoy inexpensive but well-sourced and well-cooked dishes. You might be brought an entire *terrine de porc*, from which to help yourself, then enjoy succulent wild-boar steaks – all for €20.

Chez les Fondus Map 3, G3. 17 rue des Trois Frères, 18e ☎01.42.55.22.65. M° Abbesses. Daily 5pm–2am. The €15 *menu* here gets you a hearty fondue – Bourguignonne (meat) or Savoyarde (cheese) – and your personal *biberon*, or baby bottle, full of wine. This idea is unflaggingly popular with a raucous young Parisian crowd, who squeeze onto the banquette tables between the zanily graffitied walls.

Chez Michel Map 3, K5. 10 rue de Belzunce, 10e ☎01.44.53.06.20. M° Gare du Nord. Mon 7.30–10.30pm, Tues–Fri noon–2pm & 7.30–10.30pm. At the more upscale sister restaurant to *Chez Casimir* (see above), you'll pay €30 for a cosier decor and a more adventurous, occasionally Breton-flavoured menu.

La Famille Map 3, G3. 41 rue des Trois-Frères, 18e ☎01.42.52.11.12. M° Abbesses. Tues–Sat 9pm–2am, meals till 11.15pm; closed three weeks in Aug. *La Famille* gets its name from the big table which you share with the other customers – local, designer-clad and thirty-something for the most part. The adventurous menu is characterized by zingy, constrasting flavours: you might have a ceviche with nuts to start (€10) followed by seared tuna with dried fruits and polenta (€18). *Menus* at €27 (two courses) and €33 (three).

Flo Map 3, K8. 7 cour des Petites-Écuries, 10e ⓣ01.47.70.13.59. M° Château-d'Eau. Daily noon–1.30am. Hidden away down what was once Louis XIV's stable yard, this dark, romantic and extremely handsome old-time Alsatian brasserie is a classic. You eat elbow to elbow at long tables, served by old-fashioned waiters in ankle-length aprons. Good-value, traditional *menu*, with lots of fish and seafood options, at €30.50, including wine, or €21.50 on weekday lunch times.

Au Grain de Folie Map 3, G3. 24 rue La Vieuville, 18e ⓣ01.42.58.15.57. M° Abbesses. Mon–Sat 12.30–2.30pm & 7–10.30pm, Sun 12.30–10.30pm. A tiny, simple and colourfully dilapidated vegetarian place where all the food is inexpensive and organic and there's always a vegan option.

L'Homme Tranquille Map 3, G3. 81 rue des Martyrs, 18e ⓣ01.42.54.56.28. M° Abbesses. Mon–Sat 7.30–11.30pm; closed Aug. This genuine, old-fashioned *bistrot* has been in the same family for three generations. It feels like it, too, with its old posters and atmospherically nicotine-coloured paint. The €23 *menu* includes delicious, imaginative French dishes such as chicken in honey, coriander and lemon.

Julien Map 3, K9. 16 rue du Faubourg-St-Denis, 10e ⓣ01.47.70.12.06. M° Strasbourg-St-Denis. Daily noon–1am. Part of the same enterprise as *Flo* (see above), with an even more splendid decor – all globe lamps, hat stands, white linen, brass and polished wood, with frescoes of flowery Art Deco maidens surveying the scene. The cuisine and prices are similar to those at *Flo*, minus the seafood, and with a few specialties unique to Julien.

Le Mono Map 3, F3. 40 rue Véron, 18e ⓣ01.46.06.99.20. M° Abbesses. Thurs-Tues noon–2.30pm & 7.30–11pm. Welcoming, family-run Togolese restaurant. Mains (around €10) are mostly grilled fish or meat served with sour, hot sauces, with rice or cassava meal on the side. Enjoyable but uninsistent Afro atmosphere, with Afro-print tablecloths, soukous on the stereo and Togolese carvings on the walls.

Á la Pomponnette Map 3, F2. 42 rue Lepic, 18e ⓣ01.46.06.08.36. M° Blanche/Abbesses. Tues–Thurs noon–2.30pm & 7–11pm, Fri & Sat noon–2.30pm & 7pm–midnight. A genuine old Montmartre *bistrot*, with posters, drawings and a zinc-top bar. The traditional French food is excellent, with a *menu* at €28.50; otherwise it will cost you €35–50 *à la carte*.

Le Relais Gascon Map 3, G3. 6 rue des Abbesses, 18e ☎01.42.58.58.22. M° Abbesses. Daily 10am–2am. Serving hearty, filling meals all day, this two-storey restaurant provides a welcome blast of straightforward Gascon heartiness in this alternately trendy, run-down and touristy part of town. The enormous warm salads cost €9.50, and there are equally tasty *plats* for around €12, plus a good-value lunch *menu* at €12.50.

Le Restaurant Map 3, F3. 32 rue Véron, 18e ☎01.42.23.06.22. M° Abbesses.Mon–Fri 12.30–2.30pm & 7.30pm–midnight, Sat 7.30–11.30pm. Welcoming, reliable corner restaurant whose decor and clientele seem to follow the same fashion for distressed, arty chic. Most of the food is surprisingly homely, and comes in good-sized portions. The two-course *menu* costs just under €20.

Velly Map 3, G6. 52 rue Lamartine, 9e ☎01.48.78.60.05. M° Notre-Dame-de-Lorette. Mon–Fri noon–2.30pm & 7.30–10.45pm, Sat 7.30–11pm; closed three weeks in Aug. Excellent modern French cooking in an intimate *bistrot* setting with little pretension. You can choose from any of the dishes on the blackboard, which change daily. The sole *menu* costs €21 at lunch time and €28 in the evening, and there are good wines for less than €20.

Au Virage Lepic Map 3, E2. 61 rue Lepic, 18e ☎01.42.52.46.79. M° Blanche/Abbesses. Wed–Mon 7pm–2am. The pink gingham napkins draped over the lamps, and the camp 1970s soundtrack are clues that this isn't an entirely traditional bistro. The warm welcome is old-fashioned, however, as is the cosy atmosphere (tables are very close together) and satisfyingly good *cuisine bourgeoise*, with a two-course *menu* at €16.

The Bastille and around

Cafés and wine bars

Le Baron Rouge Map 4, G14. 1 rue Théophile-Roussel, cnr place d'Aligre market, 12e. M° Ledru-Rollin. Tues–Fri 10am–2pm & 5–10pm, Sat 10am–10pm, Sun 10.30am–3.30pm. This popular *bar à vin* is as close as you'll find to the spit-on-the-floor, saloon stereotype of the old movies. If it's crowded inside you can join the locals on the pavement and stand around the wine barrels lunching on *saucisson*, mussels or Cap Ferret oysters washed down with a glass of Muscadet; *verres* start at €1.30.

Café des Anges Map 4, F11. 66 rue de la Roquette, 11e. M° Bastille. Mon–Sat 8am–2am. A friendly, scruffy corner café hung with retro photos, great for cheap and filling dishes of chips and burgers, salads and quiches and a popular place for evening drinks.

Café de l'Industrie Map 4, F11. 16 rue St-Sabin, 11e. M° Bastille. Daily 10am–2am. One of the best Bastille cafés, packed out at lunch and every evening. There are rugs on the floor around solid old wooden tables, mounted rhinoceros heads, old black-and-white photos on the walls and a young, unpretentious crowd enjoying the comfortable absence of minimalism. *Plats du jour* cost around €12.

Pause Café Map 4, G12. 41 rue de Charonne, cnr rue Keller, 11e. M° Ledru-Rollin. Mon–Sat 8am–2am, Sun 8.45am–8pm. Or maybe "Pose Café" – given its popularity with the *quartier*'s young and fashionable who pack the pavement tables at lunch and aperitif time. *Plats du jour* for about €10.

Restaurants

Le Bistrot du Peintre Map 4, G13. 116 av Ledru-Rollin, 11e ☎01.47.00.34.39. M° Ledru-Rollin. Mon–Sat 7am–2am, Sun 10am–8pm. A charming, traditional *bistrot*, where small tables are jammed together beneath faded Art Nouveau frescoes and wood panelling. The emphasis is on hearty Auvergne cuisine, with *plats* for around €12.

Bofinger Map 4, E12. 7 rue de la Bastille, 4e ☎01.42.72.87.82. M° Bastille. Mon–Fri noon–3pm & 6.30pm–1am, Sat & Sun noon–11pm. This popular fin-de-siècle brasserie, with its splendid, perfectly preserved, original decor, is frequented by Bastille Opera-goers and tourists. Specialities are sauerkraut and seafood. Three courses plus wine around €45, though you can get a *menu* for €33.

Chardenoux Map 4, I12. 1 rue Jules-Vallès, 11e ☎01.43.71.49.52. M° Faidherbe-Chaligny. Daily noon–2.30pm & 7–10.30pm. An authentic oldie, with engraved mirrors dating to 1900 and a great summer terrace. Not a huge wine selection, but they still serve dishes like succulent calf's head tartare or more solid meaty fare like calves' kidneys grilled in mustard. Upwards of €30 *à la carte*.

L'Ebauchoir Map 4, H14. 43–45 rue de Cîteaux, 12e ☎01.43.42.49.31. M° Faidherbe-Chaligny. Tues–Sat noon–2.15pm & 8–11pm. Good *bistrot* fare in a relaxed and convivial atmosphere with soothing sponge-brushed golden walls; midday *menu* for €13; *carte* €30 upwards. It's advisable to book for the evening.

Le Petit Bofinger Map 4, E12. 6 rue de la Bastille, 4e ☎01.42.72.05.23. M° Bastille. Daily noon–3pm & 7pm–midnight. Under the same management as parent-restaurant *Bofinger*, this offshoot serves lighter dishes, with *menus* from €18.50.

Le Petit Keller Map 4, G12. 13 rue Keller, 11e ☎01.47.00.12.97. M° Ledru-Rollin. Mon–Fri 8am–2.30pm & 7.30–11pm, Sat 7.30–11pm. A colourful restaurant, with decorative tiled floor and art exhibitions on the walls, serving very affordable food. The decor may be modern but the cuisine is traditional home cooking – main dishes like rabbit with prunes, and *terrine de campagne* for starters. *Menu* €12.

Le Square Trousseau Map 4, G14. 1 rue Antoine Vollon, 12e ☎01.43.43.06.00. M° Ledru-Rollin. Mon–Sat noon–3pm & 8–11.30pm; closed Aug. A handsome belle époque brasserie with a regularly changing menu featuring excellent New French cuisine and a couple of old stand-bys like *pot-au-feu* and *steak au poivre*. Lunch *menu* for €20, evening is *à la carte* – around €35 excluding wine. Booking is recommended.

Le Train Bleu Map 5, M2. Gare de Lyon, 12e ☎01.43.43.09.06. M° Gare de Lyon. Daily 11.30am–3pm & 7–11pm. The *Train Bleu*'s decor is straight out of a bygone golden era – everything drips with gilt, and chandeliers hang from frescoed ceilings. The traditional French cuisine has a hard time living up to all this, but is more than acceptable, if a tad overpriced. The set *menu* is €43, including half a bottle of wine; for *à la carte* reckon on €70.

Waly Fay Map 4, H12. 6 rue Godefroy-Cavaignac, 11e ☎01.40.24.17.79. M° Charonne/ Faidherbe-Chaligny. Mon–Sat noon–2pm & 7.30–11pm; closed last two weeks of Aug. A West African restaurant with a cosy, stylish atmosphere. Smart, young black and white Parisians come here to dine on perfumed, richly spiced stews and other West African delicacies at a moderate price (mains €12.50).

Eastern Paris

Cafés and wine bars

Chez Prune Map 4, D4. 36 rue Beaurepaire, 10e ☎01.42.41.30.47. M° Jacques-Bonsergent. Mon–Sat 8am–2am, Sun 10am–2am. Patronized by a media and artsy crowd, this is a very friendly and laid-back café with smiley waiting staff and pleasant outdoor seating facing the canal. Lunch-time dishes cost around €12; evening snacks like platters of cheese or *charcuterie* are around €8; cocktails €7.

Le Clown Bar Map 4, D7. 114 rue Amelot, 11e ☎01.43.55.87.35. M° Filles-du-Calvaire. Mon–Sat noon–3pm & 7pm–1am, Sun 7pm–1am. An attractive and popular wine *bistrot* near the Cirque d'Hiver with a circus clientele come the colder months. *Plats du jour*, such as *sauté de boeuf minute au paprika*, for around €10. No credit cards.

La Mère Lachaise Map 1, H4. 78 bd Ménilmontant, 20e ☎01.47.97.61.60. M° Père-Lachaise. Mon–Sat 8am–2am, Sun 9am–1am. The sunny terrace of this bar-restaurant, popular with students and a young, trendy crowd, makes a good place for a drink after a visit to Père-Lachaise, or check out its cosy interior bar, with retro-chic decor of painted wood and wrought-iron lamps.

Restaurants

Les Allobroges Map 1, H4. 71 rue des Grands-Champs, 20e ☎01.43.73.40.00. M° Maraîchers. Tues–Fri noon–2pm & 8–10pm. A charming neighbourhood restaurant, serving traditional French cuisine to consistently high standards. The *menu* at €15 is excellent value, though the wines are a bit pricey. Booking essential.

Astier Map 4, F6. 44 rue Jean-Pierre-Timbaud, 11e ☎01.43.57.16.35. M° Parmentier. Mon–Fri noon–2pm & 8–11pm; closed Aug, Easter & Christmas. This popular restaurant has simple decor, an unstuffy atmosphere, and food renowned for its freshness and refinement, not to mention an outstanding selection of perfectly ripe cheeses. While it's essential to book, lunch is often less crowded (€21 *menu*) and just as enjoyable. Evening *menu* at €26.

Le Bistrot du Parisien Map 4, H6. 25 rue Moret, 11e ☎01.43.38.72.38. M° Couronnes/Ménilmontant. Mon–Fri noon–2.30pm & 7–10.30pm, Sat 7–10.30pm; closed Aug. You almost expect Edith Piaf to walk into this old-fashioned *bistrot* with its retro decor and *chansons* playing in the background. The cosy ambience is matched by reassuringly solid French cuisine, such as *magret de canard* and *tarte tatin*, done to perfection. Around €30 for three courses.

L'Auberge Pyrénées Cévennes Map 4, E6. 106 rue de la Folie Méricourt, 11e ☎01.43.57.33.78. M° République. Mon–Fri noon–2pm & 7–11pm, Sat 7–11pm. Make sure you come hungry to this homely little place serving hearty portions of country cuisine. Highly recommended are the garlicky *moules marinières* for starters and the superb *cassoulet*, served in its own copper pot. Around €30 a head *à la carte*.

Chez Imogène Map 4, E7. Cnr rue Jean-Pierre-Timbaud and rue du Grand-Prieuré, 11e ☎01.48.07.14.59. M° Oberkampf. Mon noon–2.30pm, Tues–Sat noon–2.30pm & 7–11pm. An excellent and friendly little crêperie with a €9 midday *menu* including drink. The good-value three-course €15 dinner *menu* includes a *kir breton* (cassis with cider instead of white wine or champagne). It's best to book for the evening.

L'Homme Bleu Map 4, F6. 57 rue Jean-Pierre-Timbaud, 11e ☎01.48.07.05.63. M° Parmentier. Mon–Sat 7pm–12.45am. A very affordable and pleasant Berber restaurant that's popular with students. Offers a wide range of couscous dishes and a very good meatball *merguez*. *Tagines* are €16.

Lao Siam Map 4, G3. 49 rue de Belleville, 19e ☎01.40.40.09.68. M° Belleville. Mon–Fri noon–3pm & 6–11.30pm, Sat & Sun noon–12.30am. The surroundings are nothing special, but the excellent Thai and Lao food, popular with locals, makes up for it. Dishes start at €7.

Le Verre Volé Map 4, C4. 67 rue de Lancry, 10e ☎01.48.03.17.34. M° Jacques Bonsergent. Tues–Sat 10.30am–11pm, Sun 11am–8pm. This casual *bistrot* is very popular with local young Bohemians, who linger for hours after eating, as the wine is good and cheap. The menu changes often, but if they're available try either the scrumptious *saucisse au couteau* (mushroom-stuffed sausage) or the braised duck, served with beans and salad. Another branch at 38 rue Oberkampf.

Le Villaret Map 4, F7. 19 rue Ternaux, 11e ☎01.43.57.89.76. M° Parmentier. Mon–Fri noon–2pm & 7.30pm–midnight, Sat 7.30pm–midnight. This unassuming-looking place does some of the best creative *bistrot* cuisine in the capital. Typical dishes are roasted country chicken in Arbois wine sauce and there's an exceptional wine list, with bottles from €14. Lunch-time *formules* at €20 and €23, or go all out for the €50 five-course *menu dégustation* in the evening; *à la carte* costs €30–50. Booking is essential.

Le Zéphyr Map 1, H3. 1 rue Jourdain, 20e ⓣ01.46.36.65.81. M° Jourdain. Daily noon–3pm & 7–11pm. Trendy but relaxed 1930s Art Deco-style *bistrot*, with mirrors, frescoes and dark-red leather benches at closely packed tables. You'll pay around €13 for lunch, double that in the evenings, for fine traditional cooking. Service is friendly and boisterous, if sometimes uneven.

Western Paris

Restaurants

Byblos Café Map 1, B4. 6 rue Guichard, 16e ⓣ01.42.30.99.99. M° Muette. Daily 11am–3pm & 5–10.30pm. An excellent Lebanese family restaurant, serving traditional mezes, moussaka and the like in relaxed and convivial surroundings. Prices are very reasonable for the area – for around €7 you get mezes, falafel and Lebanese sausages.

La Gare Map 1, B4. 19 Chaussée de la Muette, 16e ⓣ01.42.15.15.31. M° Muette. Daily noon–3pm & 7pm–midnight. Bar noon–2am. This renovated train station is now an elegant restaurant-bar serving, among other things, two very popular €15 and €17 lunch *menus*. You can sit out on the attractive terrace on sunny days.

20

Bars, clubs and live music

Paris's fame as the quintessential home of decadent, hedonistic **nightlife** has endured for centuries. As the first decade of the new millennium wears on, that reputation seems only to grow stronger, fuelled by a vibrant **bar and club scene** and a world-leading **live music** programme, from rock and world music to jazz and electro-lounge.

To find out **what's on** you need to get hold of one of the city's **listings magazines** – *Pariscope* and *Zurban* are the best bets, and are available from all newsstands. The easiest places to get **tickets** for concerts, whether rock, jazz, Parisian chanson or classical, are at one of Paris's many FNAC stores – the main branch is in the Forum des Halles, 1–5 rue Pierre-Lescot, 1er (Mon–Sat 10am–7.30pm; ⓣ01.40.41.40.00, ⓦwww.fnac.fr; M° Châtelet-Les Halles).

Bars

If you're looking for the city's liveliest venues for **night-time drinking**, from late-opening **cafés** to **beer cellars**, Irish

pubs and **cocktail bars**, we've collected them all here, under "**bars**". You'll find more relaxed, daytime-oriented cafés listed in the "Cafés and restaurants" chapter (see pp.192–226), while full-on nightclubs, with entry fees and proper sound systems, are reviewed separately under "**clubs**" (see p.236).

The Champs-Élysées and around

Buddha Bar Map 7, M4. 8 rue Boissy d'Anglas, 8e. M° Concorde. Bar daily 4pm–2am; restaurant 7pm–12.30am. This is where the *Buddha Bar* phenomenon all began, and while this particular locale no longer profits from the "it" status the place once enjoyed, it's still well worth a stop, either for well-priced cocktails at the beautifully designed bar or a meal in the pan-Asian restaurant, presided over by a giant Buddha.

Costes Map 2, B2. Hôtel Costes, 239 rue St-Honoré, 1er. M° Concorde/Tuileries. Daily 7pm–2am. A favourite haunt of fashionistas and film and media stars, this is a fabulously romantic place for an aperitif or late-night drinks amid decadent nineteenth-century decor of red velvet, swags and columns, set around an Italianate courtyard draped in ivy. Don't expect too much deference from the ridiculously good-looking staff, though. Cocktails around €15.

Impala Lounge Map 7, G3. 2 rue de Berri, 8e. M° George-V. Daily 9.30am–2am. A trendy, *Out of Africa*-themed bar, with great atmosphere and music – mostly remixed reggae, funk and afro-jazz beats. In the evenings a youngish, intellectual crowd settles in to talk shop.

Nirvana Map 7, J3. 3 av Matignon, 8e ☎01.53.89.18.91. M° Champs-Élysées/Clemenceau. Daily 10am–5am. If Bauhaus had furnished a Kalighat temple in the 1970s, it might have looked like this. A hip restaurant-club just off the Champs where you can eat well, sip drinks (cocktails €13) next to tired models flanked by their Hermès bags, and dance in the club downstairs till dawn. The Indian cooking here is some of the best in the city, and you shouldn't pay more than €30 per person.

Grands Boulevards and passages

Bar Hemingway Map 2, C2. Ritz Hôtel, 15 place Vendôme, 1er. M° Tuileries/Opéra. Tues–Sat 6.30pm–2am. Hemingway first came here with F. Scott Fitzgerald in the 1920s at a time when he was too poor to buy his own drinks.

Once he'd made his money, he returned here frequently to spend it; with a classic, authentic decor of warm wood panelling, stately leather chairs and deferential, suited barmen, it's easy to see why. Sip the famed dry martinis or choose from a large selection of malt whiskies, all around €18.

Le Café Map 2, G3. 62 rue Tiquetonne, 2e. M° Étienne-Marcel. Daily noon–2am. A hip, buzzing café-bar with a popular terrace and cosy interior, full of old travel posters, yellowing maps and African sculptures. Drinks are reasonably priced (beer €3, spirits €5.50), and the food is pretty good, too. As it gets quite busy on the weekends, service can lag, but no one seems to mind. *Plats du jour* are €8.

De La Ville Café Map 3, J8. 34 bd de la Bonne Nouvelle, 10e. M° Bonne-Nouvelle. Fri & Sat 11am–4am, Sun–Thurs 11am–2am. This ex-bordello, with grand staircase, gilded mosaics and marble columns, draws in crowds of hip pre-clubbers, who sling back a mojito or two before moving on to one of the area's clubs. On weekends, well-known DJs spin the disks till the early hours. Mojitos cost €8, a demi €3.50.

Le Tambour Map 2, F3. 41 rue Montmartre, 2e. M° Sentier. Daily 24hr. A colourful local habitués' bar, eccentrically furnished with recycled street signs, old paving stones and the like. A demi costs €2.60; hearty salads and snacks available.

Villa Keops Map 2, H4. 56 bd Sebastopol, 3e. M° Étienne-Marcel. Fri & Sat noon–5am, Sun–Thurs noon–2am. Spacious, gay-friendly, modern bar with scruffy, unfinished wood floor and welcoming staff. Burgers, tagines and pasta dishes for around €12. DJs play a varied mix. Happy hour 7–9pm.

Beaubourg and Les Halles

Le Cochon à l'Oreille Map 2, G4. 15 rue Montmartre, 1er. M° Châtelet-Les Halles/Étienne-Marcel. Mon–Sat 6pm–2am. This classic little wooden café-bar, with raffia chairs outside and scenes of fruit and veg stalls on ceramic tiles inside, dates from Les Halles' days as a market. The intellectual conversation is accompanied by Coltrane and other bebopping jazz greats.

Le Comptoir Map 2, G5. 37 rue Berger, 1er ⓣ01.40.26.26.66. M° Châtelet-Les-Halles. Fri & Sat noon–3am, Sun–Thurs noon–2am. Jet-set North African bar/restaurant with plush velvet interior and subdued lighting. A young crowd lounges in comfy sofas sipping sweet mint tea and knock-out cocktails (around €10).

Le Fumoir Map 2, E5. 6 rue de l'Amiral-Coligny, 1er. M°

Louvre-Rivoli. Daily 11am–2am. Animated chatter rises above a mellow jazz soundtrack and the sound of cocktail shakers in this coolly designed bar, popular with a fashionable, thirtysomething crowd. You can browse the international press and there's also a restaurant at the back, walled with books. Cocktails €8.

Kong Map 2, F6. 1 rue du Pont Neuf, 5th floor, 1er ☎01.40.39.09.00. M° Pont-Neuf. Bar daily 12.30pm–2am; restaurant 10.30am–2am. Nights at this über-cool, Philippe Starck-fashioned bar/restaurant atop the flagship Kenzo building are oh-so-swank, and while the gorgeous *demoiselles* meeting the lift will let you in, you might get ignored by the bartenders – and everyone else – if you can't claim the right pedigree. The decor is new Japan meets old, so think geisha girls and manga cartoons. Happy hour daily from 6–8pm. Cocktails €11.

Le Sous-Bock Map 2, F5. 49 rue St-Honoré, 1er. M° Châtelet-Les Halles. Mon–Sat 11am–5am, Sun 3pm–5am. Hundreds of beers – bottled and on tap (from €3.50) – and whiskies to sample, plus simple, inexpensive food. Mussels are a speciality (from €9.50). This place is frequented by *couche-tards* (night owls), as it's one of the few late-night places in the area.

Au Trappiste Map 2, G6. 4 rue St-Denis, 1er. M° Châtelet. Mon–Thurs noon–2.30am, Fri–Sun noon–4.30am. Over 140 draught beers include Jenlain, France's best-known *bière de garde*, Belgian Blanche Riva and Kriek from the Mort Subite (Sudden Death) brewery – plus very good *moules frites* for €12 and various *tartines*. Or, if you've already come on a full stomach, go all out for the €40 giraffe, a table cask bong filled to the brim with three litres of beer.

The Marais

Andy Wahloo Map 4, A7. 69 rue des Gravilliers, 3e. M° Arts-et-Métiers. Mon–Sat 11am–2am. This very popular bar, decked out in original Pop Art-inspired Arabic decor, gets packed to the gills at weekends. Delicious mezze appetizers are served until midnight (the €17 *guassâa* is a good large assortment) and the bar boasts a few original cocktails, including the Wahloo Special (rum, lime, ginger, banana and cinnamon; €9). DJs play a wide range of dance music.

The Lizard Lounge Map 4, B10. 18 rue du Bourg-Tibourg, 4e. M° Hôtel-de-Ville/St-Paul. Daily noon–2am. American-run and popular with young expats, this is a loud and lively, attractive, stone-walled bar on three levels. Choose from around fifty cocktails (€6.50). They also do a popular Sunday brunch (noon–4pm; around €15), with €5 Bloody Marys.

Quiet Man Map 4, B8. 5 rue des Haudriettes, 4e ⓣ01.48.04.02.77. M° Rambuteau. Daily 5pm–2am. Live traditional Celtic music is played by troubadours nightly downstairs at this tiny Irish pub. Lots of locals, but does pull in its share of the tourist crowd as well. Happy hour 5–8pm, music begins shortly thereafter.

Stolly's Map 4, B11. 16 rue Cloche-Perce, 4e. M° St-Paul. Daily 4.30pm–2am. Almost exclusively Anglo bar with very friendly atmosphere and broadcasts of all major sporting events, washed down by €6 pints of Guinness and Kilkenny and a wide selection of spirits and cocktails.

Quartier Latin

Le Bateau Ivre Map 2, H12. 40 rue Descartes, 5e. M° Cardinal-Lemoine. Daily 6pm–2am. Small, dark and ancient, this studenty bar is just clear of the Mouffetard tourist hotspot, though it attracts a fair number of Anglos in the evenings, especially after about 10pm. If it's packed out, the *Pub River* next door is less appealing but more spacious.

Le Piano Vache Map 2, G11. 8 rue Laplace, 5e. M° Cardinal-Lemoine. Mon–Fri noon–2am, Sat & Sun 9pm–2am. Venerable bar crammed with students drinking at little tables. Cool music and a laid-back, grungy atmosphere. A *pression* costs just over €3.

Le Violon Dingue Map 2, G11. 46 rue de la Montagne-Ste-Geneviève, 5e. M° Maubert-Mutualité. Daily 6pm–2.30am. Long, dark student pub that's also popular with young travellers. Noisy and friendly, with English-speaking bar staff and cheap drinks. The cellar bar stays open until 4.30am on busy nights; happy hour 8–10pm.

St-Germain

Le 10 Map 2, E9. 10 rue de l'Odéon, 6e. M° Odéon. Daily 6pm–2am. Classic Art Deco-era posters line the walls of this small, dark bar, and the theme is continued in the atmospherically vaulted cellar bar, where there's a lot of chatting-up among the studenty clientele.

Bar du Marché Map 2, E8. 75 rue de Seine, 6e. M° Mabillon. Daily 7am–2am. This former market café is just as satisfying and just as busy at night as by day. Expect animated conversation rather than banging techno.

Chez Georges Map 2, D9. 11 rue des Canettes, 6e. M° Mabillon. Tues–Sat noon–2am; closed Aug. This thoroughly tobacco-stained wine bar attracts a young, studenty crowd and stays lively well into the small hours.

Les Etages St-Germain Map 2, E8. 5 rue de Buci, 6e. M° Mabillon. Daily 11am–2am. Fashionably distressed café-bar, with a downstairs level open to the street. Upstairs, you can lounge around on dog-eared armchairs, chilling out with a reasonably priced cocktail.

Fubar Map 2, E9. 5 rue St-Sulpice, 6e. M° Odéon. Daily 5pm–2am. Good for a late drink on Tuesdays (student night) or Thursday to Saturday, when there's anything from R&B to French rock playing, and a young, international crowd drinking well past the last métro. The upstairs room is very cosy, with comfy chairs and deep red walls.

La Mezzanine de l'Alcazar Map 2, E8. 62 rue Mazarine, 6e. M° Odéon. Daily 7pm–2am. Both decor and clientele are *très design* at this über-cool cocktail bar, set on a mezzanine level overlooking Conran's Alcazar restaurant. Expensive (€10 for a drink) but exquisite – again, much like the clientele. Most nights start off relaxed and finish with feverish dancing, the harder core moving on to *Le WAGG* club, below. DJs Wed–Sat.

Montparnasse and southern Paris

La Folie en Tête Map 5, E9. 33 rue Butte-aux-Cailles, 13e. M° Place-d'Italie/Corvisart. Mon–Sat 5pm–2am. At night, this friendly, lefty café-bar turns into a vibrant and youthful venue. Regularly hosts great music events, especially on Saturday nights, attracting live world-music acts and experimental DJs.

Le Merle Moqueur Map 5, F9. 11 rue Butte-aux-Cailles, 13e. M° Place-d'Italie/Corvisart. Daily 5pm–2am. Classic narrow, shop-front-style Butte-aux-Cailles bar, which once saw the Paris debut of Mano Negra and Manu Chao. It maintains an alternative edge, though most days serves up 1980s French rock CDs and home-made flavoured rums to young Parisians. If you don't fancy the playlist when you arrive, you can always try the very similar *Le Diapason*, two doors along.

Montmartre and northern Paris

L'Atmosphère Map 5, N7. 49 rue Lucien-Sampaix, 10e. M° Gare-de-l'Est. Tues–Fri 11am–2am, Sat 5.30pm–2am. Lively café-bar by the canal St-Martin, with an alternative flavour and occasional live music on Sundays.

Le Bar du Relais Map 5, G2. 12 rue Ravignan, 18e. M° Abbesses. Mon–Thurs 3pm–2am, Fri–Sun noon–2am. This ancient, ramshackle building has a perfectly picturesque spot on a quiet square on the slopes of the Butte. Cool, youthful and Bohemian-tinged venue, with an *electronique* playlist.

Chez Camille Map 5, F3. 8 rue Ravignan, 18e. M° Abbesses. Tues–Sat 9am–2am, Sun 9am–8pm. *Très chouette* (very cool) is how locals have been describing this little bar for years. In a great spot on the slopes of the Butte, the clientele is typical of Montmartre – think bespectacled, turtlenecked photographers with their beautiful girlfriends.

La Fourmi Café Map 3, G4. 74 rue des Martyrs, 18e. M° Pigalle/ Abbesses. Mon–Thurs 8am–2am, Fri & Sat 8am–4am, Sun 10am–2am. The glamorous decor, long bar and high-ceilinged spaciousness draw the discerning *bobos* of Abbesses and the 10e for cocktails, wine and chatter, to the tune of retro-industrial lounge music.

Le Progrès Map 3, H3. 1 rue Yvonne Le Tac, 18e. M° Abbesses. Daily 9am–2am. Popular, buzzy café–bar on a lively corner of the Abbesses quartier. See p.218.

Au Rendez-Vous des Amis Map 3, G2. 23 rue Gabrielle, 18e. M° Abbesses. Daily 8.30am–2am. Halfway up the Butte, this small, ramshackle, smoky and community-spirited hang-out is a magnet for Montmartre locals, especially the young, artsy and alternative-leaning.

The Bastille and around

Bar des Ferrailleurs Map 4, F12. 18 rue de Lappe, 11e. M° Bastille. Mon–Fri 5pm–2am, Sat & Sun 3pm–2am. Dark and stylishly sinister, with rusting metal decor, an eccentric owner, fun wig-wearing bar staff and a relaxed and friendly crowd.

Café de l'Industrie Map 4, F11. 16 rue St-Sabin, 11e. M° Bastille. Daily 10am–2am. An enduringly popular café, packed out every evening. See p.222.

Iguana Map 4, E12. 15 rue de la Roquette, cnr rue Daval, 11e. M° Bastille. Daily 10am–2am. A place to be seen in. Decor of trellisses, colonial fans and a brushed bronze bar. By day, the clientele studies *recherché* art reviews over excellent coffee, while things hot up at night with a youngish, high-spirited crowd. DJ on Thurs. Cocktails around €9.

SanZSanS Map 4, F13. 49 rue du Faubourg-St-Antoine, 11e. M° Bastille. Mon 9am–2am, Tues–Sat

9am–5am, Sun 6pm–midnight. This gothic get-up of red velvet, oil paintings and chandeliers is popular with a young crowd, especially on Friday and Saturday evenings, when DJs play rare grooves and funky/Brazilian house. Drinks are around €7 and there's a set menu for €23.

Le Wax Map 4, E12. 15 rue Daval, 11e. M° Bastille. Fri & Sat till 5am, Tues–Thurs till 2am. Lose yourself in the huge pod chairs at this popular bar with great early-1970s interior. Full of happy locals and foreigners dancing to the soul, house and electronica DJs.

Eastern Paris

Canal St-Martin

Les Fontaines Map 4, E2. 33 rue Juliette Dodu, 10e ☎01.42.45.36.27. M° Colonel-Fabien. Mon–Sat 7.30am–2am. Excellent bar and café with *soirées* of foot-stomping jazz every evening around 10pm and a great mix of local students and bespectacled music snobs. Gets packed even on week nights, so arrive early if you want a seat.

Favela Chic Map 4, D5. 16 rue du Faubourg-du-Temple, 11e ☎01.40.03.02.66. M° République. Tues–Fri 7.30pm–2am, Sat 7.30pm–4am. Touted eclectic music nights and kitsch furnishings bring twentysomethings of all creeds and persuasions to this Brazilian bar known for its ribald DJ evenings. Table-dancing and dirty hip-grinding are de rigeur.

Le Jemmapes Map 4, D3. 82 quai de Jemmapes, 10e ☎01.40.40.02.35. M° Jacques Bonsergent. Daily 11am–2am. In the summer this neighbourhood resto-bar and boho hang-out is well known for letting its patrons cross the road to nip at their drinks along the banks of the canal. The standard French cuisine is good, but the lure here is the hipster atmosphere.

L'Opus Map 4, D1. 167 quai de Valmy, 10e ☎01.40.34.70.00. M° Louis-Blanc. Mon–Fri 8pm–2am, Sat & Sun 8pm–5am. A stylish modern-chintzy place in a barn-like space used as a British officers' mess during World War I. There's live music every evening: chansons, gospel, soul, funk, African. Drinks cost €9–12 on average, plus there's a €10 entry for the music. There's also a dining area on the mezzanine floor overlooking the action where you can get a three-course *menu* with aperitif for €40.

Point Ephémère Map 4, D1. 200 quai de Valmy, 10e ☎01.40.34.02.48. M° Jaurès/Louis-Blanc. Daily 1pm–2am or later if there's live music. A great energetic atmosphere pervades this creative space for music, dance and visual arts. Set in a dilapidated canal boathouse, the rotating art exhibitions range from the quotidian to the abstract, while the frequent concerts feature cutting-edge rock and electronica bands. The bar serves beer and finger food, and you can even get a decent order of *steak-frites* in the ad hoc restaurant looking out onto the canal.

Ménilmontant and Oberkampf

Café Charbon Map 4, G7. 109 rue Oberkampf, 11e. M° St-Maur/Parmentier. Daily 9am–2am. This very successful and attractive resuscitation of an early-twentieth-century café is particularly popular with the younger, fashionable crowd who are moving into these old working-class districts. *Menu* for €18; snacks around €5; beer is €2.50. There's also a happy hour daily from 5 to 7pm and a DJ Thursday, Friday & Saturday evenings from 10pm to 2am.

Chez Justine Map 4, G7. 96 rue Oberkampf, 11e ☎01.43.57.44.03. M° St-Maur/Parmentier. Mon–Sat 8am–2am, Sun 10am–2am. During the day, a chill candlelit bar-restaurant; after 10pm, things hot up with a DJ and the place gets packed out with a young, hip crowd. Draught beer is €3 and *plats* are €18.

Cithéa Map 4, G7. 112 rue Oberkampf, 11e ☎01.40.21.70.95, ⓦwww.cithea.com. M° St-Maur/Parmentier. Tues–Thurs 10pm–5.30am, Fri & Sat 10pm–6.30am. Popular bar and music venue for Afro funk, funk reggae, world beat, jazz fusion, etc. Cocktails €9. No admission charge for the music.

Le Gast Map 4, H6. 5 rue Crespin-du-Gast, 11e. M° Ménilmontant. Mon–Sat 5pm–2am. Almost exclusively Parisian hipsters nod their heads to goateed drum-and-bass DJs at this small bar, just off the main Oberkampf drag. A demi costs €2.

Lou Pascalou Map 4, I6. 14 rue des Panoyaux, 20e. M° Ménilmontant. Daily 9am–2am. Trendy but friendly place with a zinc bar, this local bobo hangout is a great weekend find for the area, especially if you're interested in leaving with your eardrums intact. Be sure to try some of their delicious mint tea – over a ponderous game of chess if you fancy it. Wide range of beers bottled and on tap from €2, cocktails from €5.

Les Lucioles Map 4, I7. 102 bd Ménilmontant, 20e. M° Père-Lachaise. Daily 9am–2am. This relaxed and friendly neighbourhood bar/restaurant, with an inviting outside terrace in warmer weather, is popular with a youngish crowd. They hold poetry readings on Tuesdays and have live music on weekends creating a party atmosphere. *Demis* for €2.80.

Le Mécano Bar Map 4, G7. 99 rue Oberkampf, 11e. M° Parmentier. Daily 9am–2am. A converted tool shop, with the odd implement left in situ, this cool, atmospheric bar with its stone floor, long wooden bar and comfy seating is a popular fixture on the Oberkampf nightlife scene. Cocktails around €6.

Clubs

20

Paris's **club** scene is moving ever further away from monster-clubs, and where deep house and techno once ruled, you can now find hip-hop, R&B, electro-lounge, tech-funk and more leftfield house. The clubs listed here run good programmes and attract interesting crowds, but the general vibe really depends on who's running the individual *soirée*, and some places also showcase occasional live acts. It's also worth checking the listings for **live music** venues (see p.238), which often hold DJ-led sessions after hours, as well as the **gay and lesbian** club listings (see pp.297–300). Note too that lots of **bars** (see pp.227–236) bring in DJs for weekend nights.

Most clubs **open** between 11pm and midnight, but venues rarely warm up before 1am or 2am. It's worth dressing up, especially for trendier venues. Most **entry prices** include one free drink (*consommation*), and may vary from night to night. Given the difficulty of finding a **taxi after hours** (see p.21), many Parisian clubbers aim to keep going until the métro starts up at around 5.30am, or even later, moving on to one of the city's famous *after* events.

Nightclubs

Batofar Map 5, N6. Opposite 11 quai François Mauriac, 13e ⓣ01.56.29.10.33, ⓦwww.batofar.org. M° Quai de la Gare. Tues–Thurs 8pm–2am, Fri 11pm–dawn, Sat 11pm–noon. This old lighthouse boat moored at the foot of the Bibliothèque Nationale is a small but classic address. Relaunched under new management in 2004, the programme is mostly electro-pop, electroclash, techno, whatever – with the odd experimental funk night or the like thrown in to mix it up a bit. Entry €10–12.

Le Cab Map 2, E4. 2 place du Palais-Royal, 1er ⓣ01.58.62.56.25. M° Palais-Royal. Mon–Sat 11.30pm–5am. Currently one of the most fashionable venues in Paris, somehow dragging the beautiful and designer-clad away from the Champs-Élysées – on weekend nights you'll need to look good to get in. Designer retro-meets-futuristic lounge decor, with a similar music policy. Entry €20.

Le Gibus Map 4, D5. 18 rue Faubourg-du-Temple, 11e ⓣ01.47.00.78.88. M° République. Daily midnight–6am. This basement club has an unappealing low ceiling, but it's an exciting and popular venue, with hardcore and trance on Tuesday and Thursday, R&B on Wednesday, and a famous trance-only night on Friday. Saturday is more mainstream house and attracts a significant gay following. Entry €10–20.

La Loco Map 3, E3. 90 bd de Clichy, 18e ⓣ08.36.69.69.28, ⓦwww.laloco.com. M° Blanche. Tues–Sun 11pm–7am. High-tech monster club with three dance floors, playing mostly house and techno, though you can find all kinds of musical styles on weekday nights and on the two smaller pistes. Not particularly cool, but almost always busy. Entry €12–20.

Le Nouveau Casino Map 4, G6. 109 rue Oberkampf, 11e ⓣ01.43.57.57.40, ⓦwww.nouveaucasino.net. M° Parmentier. Tues & Wed 9pm–2am, Thurs–Sat midnight–5am. Right behind *Café Charbon* (see p.235) lies this excellent venue. An interesting, experimental line-up of live gigs makes way to a relaxed, dancey crowd later on, with music ranging from electro-pop or house to rock. There's a good sound system and ventilation, but the sci-fi decor is a bit off-putting. Entry around €10–15.

Rex Club Map 3, I8. 5 bd Poissonnière, 2e ⓣ01.42.36.28.83. M° Bonne-Nouvelle. Wed–Sat 11.30pm–5am. The clubbers' club: spacious and serious about its music, which is strictly electronic, notably techno. Attracts big-name DJs. Entry €10–13.

La Scène Bastille Map 4, G12. 2bis rue des Taillandiers, 11e ⓣ01.48.06.50.70, restaurant reservations ⓣ01.48.06.12.13, ⓦwww.la-scene.com. M° Bastille. Concerts Mon–Sat 7.30–10.45pm; club Thurs–Sat midnight–6am. A club, concert venue and restaurant all rolled into one, in a converted warehouse, snazzily refurbished in cosy colours. The eclectic music policy embraces rock, afro-beat, funk and reggae, although the emphasis at weekends is on electro, techno and house, with gay-friendly nights most Saturdays. Entry around €12–15.

Le Triptyque Map 2, F2. 142 rue Montmartre, 2e ⓣ01.40.28.05.55, ⓦwww.letriptyque.com. M° Bourse. Daily midnight–6am. *Les physios* (the bouncers) will never turn you away at this unpretentious, grunge-cool club, packed with anyone from local students to lounge lizards. For once, it's all about the music. Concerts earlier on, then themed DJ *soirées* which change nightly – everything from electro to jazz to hip-hop to ska. Entry costs vary; it's sometimes free, it's sometimes up to €15.

Le Twin's Map 3, G8. 44 rue Vivienne, 2e ⓣ01.40.41.05.55. M° Grands-Boulevards. Wed–Sat midnight–6am. This new, pocket venue may be small, but its ideas and status are big. Has an eclectic, exciting music policy, varying from night to night between electro, house, R&B and so on. Entry €8.

Rock and world music

Most of the **venues** listed here are primarily concert venues, though some double up as clubs on certain nights, or after hours. A few of them will have live music all week, but the majority host bands on just a couple of nights. Admission **prices** vary depending on who's playing. Note that the most interesting clubs tend to host gigs earlier on in the evening; jazz venues, too (see p.240) often branch into other genres such as world music and folk.

Rock and world music venues

Le Bataclan Map 4, E7. 50 bd Voltaire, 11e ⓣ01.43.13.35.35, ⓦwww.bataclan.fr. M° Oberkampf. Classic pagoda-styled, ex-theatre venue (seats 1200) with one of the best and most eclectic line-ups covering anything from international and local dance and rock musicians – Francis Cabrel, Chemical Brothers, Khaled, Stereophonics – to opera, comedy and techno nights.

Café de la Danse Map 4, F12. 5 passage Louis-Philippe, 11e ⓣ01.47.00.57.59, ⓦwww.chez.com/cafedeladanse. M° Bastille. Rock, pop, world, folk and jazz music played in an intimate and attractive space. Open nights of concerts only.

La Cigale Map 3, G4. 120 bd de Rochechouart, 18e

Ⓣ01.49.25.89.99, Ⓦwww.lacigale.fr. M° Pigalle. Formerly playing host to the likes of Mistinguett and Maurice Chevalier, since 1987 and a Philippe Starck renovation this historic, 1400-seat Pigalle theatre has become a leading venue for cutting-edge rock and indie acts, especially French and other continental European bands.

Le Divan du Monde Map 3, G4. 75 rue des Martyrs, 18e Ⓣ01.40.05.06.99, Ⓦwww.divandumonde.com. M° Anvers. A youthful venue in a café whose regulars once included Toulouse-Lautrec. One of the city's most diverse and exciting programmes, ranging from techno to Congolese rumba, with dancing till dawn on weekend nights.

Élysée Montmartre Map 3, G4. 72 bd de Rochechouart, 18e Ⓣ01.55.07.06.00, Ⓦwww.elysee-montmartre.com. M° Anvers. A historic Montmartre nightspot that pulls in a young, excitable crowd with its rock and dance acts – Redman, the Pharcyde, Angra, the Hives. Also hosts up-tempo Latin and club nights.

La Guinguette Pirate Map 5, N6. Quai François Mauriac, 13e Ⓣ01.52.61.08.49. M° Quai-de-la-Gare. Beautiful Chinese barge, moored alongside the quay in front of the Bibliothèque Nationale, hosting relaxed but upbeat world music and folk-rock nights from Tuesday to Sunday. A sound bet for an inexpensive (€5–10), perhaps taste-expanding night out.

Maroquinerie Map 1, H3. 23 rue Boyer, 20e Ⓣ01.40.33.30.60, Ⓦwww.lamaroquinerie.fr. M° Gambetta. The smallish concert venue is the downstairs part of a trendy arts centre. The line-up is rock, folk and jazz, with a particularly good selection of French musicians.

Jazz, blues and chansons

Jazz has long enjoyed an appreciative audience in France, especially since the end of World War II, when the intellectual rigour and agonized musings of bebop struck an immediate chord of sympathy in the existentialist hearts of the *après-guerre*.

Gypsy guitarist Django Reinhardt and his partner, violinist Stéphane Grappelli, whose work represents the distinctive

Jazz club prices

For many of the jazz clubs listed, **expense** is a drawback to enjoyment – *Utopia* and *Le Caveau de la Huchette* are among the cheaper venues. Admission charges are generally high, and, when they're not levied, there's usually a whacking charge for your first drink. Subsequent drinks, too, can be absurdly priced – about twice what you'd pay in a similar club in London, and more than double what you'd pay in New York.

and undisputed French contribution to the jazz canon, had much to do with the music's popularity. But it was also greatly enhanced by the presence of many front-rank black American musicians, such as soprano sax player Sidney Bechet, for whom Paris was a haven of freedom and culture after the racial prejudice and philistinism of the States.

Jazz is still alive and well in the city, with a good selection of clubs playing all styles from New Orleans to current experimental. Frequent festivals are also a good source of concerts, particularly in the summer (see "Festivals", p.274). *Bistrots* and bars are a good place to catch musicians carrying on the tradition of Django Reinhardt – Romane and the Ferré brothers are just some of musicians doing the rounds – as well as French traditional chansons. Gigs aren't usually advertised in the press, but you'll see handmade posters in the *bistrots* themselves, or you could check out the site ⓦwww.zingueurs.com.

Mainly jazz

Les 7 Lézards Map 4, B10. 10 rue des Rosiers, 4e ⓣ01.48.87.08.97, ⓦwww.7lezards.com. M° St-Paul. Daily 6pm–2am; concerts at 7pm & 10am. A cosy and intimate jazz club, which encourages young, upcoming musicians and attracts more established names, too. Also hosts the odd world-music gig, and there's a decent, affordable restaurant (noon–midnight) upstairs. Admission €8–15.

Le Baiser Salé Map 2, H6. 58 rue des Lombards, 1er ⓣ01.42.33.37.71. M° Châtelet. Daily 5pm–6am. A small, crowded upstairs room with live music every night from 10pm – usually jazz, rhythm and blues, fusion, reggae or Brazilian. This is one of the less expensive jazz clubs, with free jam sessions, even, on Mondays. The downstairs bar is great for just chilling out. Admission €5–16.

Caveau de la Huchette Map 2, G8. 5 rue de la Huchette, 5e ⓣ01.43.26.65.05, ⓦwww.caveaudelahuchette.fr. M° St-Michel. Daily 9.30pm–2am or later. A wonderful slice of old Parisian life in an otherwise touristy area. Both Sidney Bechet and Lionel Hampton played here. There's live jazz, usually trad and big band, to dance to on a floor surrounded by tiers of benches, and a bar decorated with caricatures of the barman drawn on any material to hand. Admission Friday and Saturday is €13, Sunday to Thursday €10.50; drinks start at €4.50.

Au Duc des Lombards Map 2, H6. 42 rue des Lombards, 1er ⓣ01.42.33.22.88, ⓦwww.ducdeslombards.com. M° Châtelet/Les-Halles. Daily until 3am. Admission €23; drinks from €4.50. Small, unpretentious bar with performances every night from 9pm. This is the place to hear gypsy jazz, as well as jazz piano, blues, ballads and fusion. Sometimes big names.

Lionel Hampton Bar Map1, C2. Hôtel Méridien, 81 bd Gouvion-St-Cyr, 17e ⓣ01.40.68.30.42, ⓦwww.jazzclub-paris.com. M° Porte-Maillot. Daily 10pm–2am. First-rate jazz venue, with big-name musicians. Inaugurated by Himself, but otherwise the great man is only an irregular visitor. There's no entry fee but your first drink will cost at least €25 (refills €11).

New Morning Map 3, K7. 7–9 rue des Petites-Ecuries, 10e ⓣ01.45.23.51.41, ⓦwww.newmorning.com. M° Château-d'Eau. Usually Mon–Sat 8pm–1.30am, concerts 9pm. The decor's somewhat spartan, a bit like an underground garage, but this is the place where the big international names in jazz come to play and it attracts true aficionados. It's often standing room only unless you get here early. Blues and Latin, too. Admission is around €20.

Le Petit Journal Map 2, E11. 71 bd St-Michel, 5e ⓣ01.43.26.28.59. RER Luxembourg. Mon–Sat 9pm–2am; closed Aug. Small, smoky bar, with good, mainly French, traditional and mainstream sounds. These days rather middle-aged and tourist-prone. Admission and first drink costs €16, while subsequent drinks are €6; it's €43-48 if you include a meal.

Le Petit Journal Montparnasse Map 6, F12. 13 rue du Commandant-Mouchotte, 14e ⓣ01.43.21.56.70,

Ⓦ www.petitjournal-montparnasse.com. **M° Montparnasse-Bienvenüe. Mon–Sat 8.30pm–2am, concerts 10pm.** Under the *Hôtel Montparnasse*, and sister establishment to the above, with bigger visiting names, both French and international. Admission free, but first drink around €18. There's also the option of dining (three courses and wine, with no extra charge for music €50–80).

Le Petit Opportun Map 2, G6. 15 rue des Lavandières-Ste-Opportune, 1er Ⓣ 01.42.36.01.36. M° Châtelet-Les Halles. Tues–Sat 9pm–dawn, music from 10.30pm; closed Aug. It's worth arriving early to get a seat for the live music in the dungeon-like cellar, where the acoustics play strange tricks and you can't always see the musicians. Fairly eclectic policy and a crowd of genuine connoisseurs. Admission with first drink starts at €10.

Le Sunset/Le Sunside Map 2, H6. 60 rue des Lombards, 1er Ⓣ 01.40.26.46.20, Ⓦ www.sunset-sunside.com. M° Châtelet/Les-Halles. Daily 9pm–2.30am. Two clubs in one: *Le Sunside* on the ground floor features mostly traditional jazz, whereas the downstairs *Sunset* is a venue for electric and fusion jazz. The *Sunside* concert usually starts at 9pm and the *Sunset* at 10pm, so you can sample a bit of both. Attracts some of the best musicians – the likes of pianist Alain Jean Marie and Turk Mauro. Admission is €18–25.

Utopia Map 6, E14. 1 rue de l'Ouest, 14^{e} Ⓣ 01.43.22.79.66. M° Pernety. Mon–Sat 9.30pm–6am; closed Aug. No genius here, but good French blues singers interspersed with jazz and blues tapes, and a mostly young and studentish crowd. Generally very pleasant atmosphere. Admission is free; drinks start at €8.

Mainly chansons

Casino de Paris Map 3, D6. 16 rue de Clichy, 9e Ⓣ 01.49.95.99.99, Ⓦ www.casinodeparis.fr. M° Trinité. Most performances 8.30pm. Tickets from €23. This decaying, once-plush casino in one of the seediest streets in Paris is a venue for all sorts of performances – chansons, poetry combined with flamenco guitar, cabaret. Check the listings magazines under "Variétés" and "Chansons".

Au Limonaire Map 3, I8. 18 Cité Bergère, 9e Ⓣ 01.45.23.33.33. M° Grands Boulevards. Tiny back-street venue, perfect for Parisian chanson nights showcasing young singers and zany music/poetry/performance acts. Dinner beforehand – traditional, inexpensive, and fairly good – guarantees a seat for the show at 10pm – otherwise you'll be crammed up against the bar, if you can get in at all.

Le Magique Map 6, E14. 42 rue de Gergovie, 14e ☎01.45.42.26.10. M° Pernety. Wed–Sat 10pm–2am. A bar and "chanson cellar", with traditional French chansons performances by lesser-known stars during the week. At weekends the owner takes to the piano. Admission is free, payment for the show is at your own discretion, and drinks are very reasonably priced.

21

Shops and markets

When it comes to **shopping**, Paris is an epicurean wonderland. Despite pressures to concentrate consumption, Parisians, for the most part, remain fiercely loyal to their small local traders. Some of the most entertaining and memorable experiences of a trip to Paris are to be had just browsing in small shops.

The most distinctive and unusual shopping possibilities are in the nineteenth-century arcades, or *passages,* in the **2e and 9e arrondissements**, almost all now smartly renovated. On the streets proper, the square kilometre around **place St-Germain-des-Prés** is hard to beat: to the north of the square lie rows of antique shops and arts and interior design boutiques, while to the south you'll find every designer clothing brand you can think of.

The **Les Halles** and **Sentier** districts are also well-shopped, good for everything from records through to designer clothes. The aristocratic **Marais**, the hip quartier of the **Bastille** and northeastern Paris (**Oberkampf** and the **Canal St-Martin**) have filled up with dinky little boutiques, interior design, arty and specialist shops and galleries. For Parisian **haute couture**

– Hermès and the like – the traditional bastions are avenue Montaigne, rue François 1er and the upper end of **rue du Faubourg-St-Honoré** in the 8e.

Markets, too, are a grand spectacle. Though food is perhaps the best offering of the Paris markets, there are also street markets dedicated to secondhand goods (the *marchés aux puces*), clothes and textiles, flowers, birds, books and stamps.

Clothes

As long as there's a strong euro, visitors from outside the eurozone will find shopping relatively expensive. That said, you can snap up some excellent bargains if you're able to time your visit to coincide with the **sales**, officially held twice a year, beginning in mid-January and mid-July and lasting a month.

Department stores and hypermarkets

Le Bon Marché Map 6, G6. 38 rue de Sèvres, 7e. M° Sèvres-Babylone. Mon–Wed & Fri 9.30am–7pm, Thurs 10am–9pm, Sat 9.30am–8pm. Paris's oldest department store, founded in 1852. The range of moderately priced labels is better than at the more chic Galeries Lafayette and Printemps, but there's still plenty of high-end Paris fashion. Excellent kids' department and a legendary food hall (see p.259).

Galeries Lafayette Map 3, E7. 40 bd Haussmann, 9e ⓦwww.galerieslafayette.com. M° Havre-Caumartin. Mon–Sat 9.30am–7.30pm, Thurs till 9pm. The store's forte is high fashion, with two floors given over to the latest creations by leading designers; the third floor is dedicated almost entirely to lingerie, plus there's a large section devoted to clothes for children on the fourth floor. Then there's a host of big names in men's and women's accessories and a huge parfumerie – all under a striking 1900 dome. Just down the road at no. 35 is a new addition to the emporium, Lafayette Maison, five floors of quality kitchenware, linen and furniture.

Printemps Map 3, C7. 64 bd Haussmann, 9e ⓦwww.printemps.com. M° Havre-Caumartin. Mon–Sat 9.35am–7pm, Thurs till 10pm. The main store has an excellent

Where to shop for clothes in Paris

If you're looking for a one-stop hit of Paris fashion, the department stores **Galeries Lafayette** and **Printemps**, just behind the Opéra on boulevard Haussmann, have unrivalled selections. Alternatively, the streets around M° St-Sulpice, on the Left Bank, make up one of the most appealing of Paris's clothes shopping quarters. You'll find rich pickings along rues du Vieux Colombier, de Rennes, Madame, de Grenelle and du Cherche-Midi, as well as the excellent Bon Marché department store, on rue de Sèvres. Rues du Cherche-Midi and de Grenelle are particularly good for shoes.

For **couture** and seriously expensive **designer wear**, make for the wealthy, manicured streets around the Champs-Élysées, especially avenue François 1er, avenue Montaigne and rue du Faubourg-St-Honoré. In recent years, younger designers have begun colonizing the lower reaches of rue du Faubourg-St-Honoré, between rue Cambon and rue des Pyramides. In the heart of this area, luxurious place Vendôme is the place to come for **serious jewellery**.

On the eastern side of the city, around the Marais and Bastille, the clothes, like the residents, are younger, cooler and more relaxed. **Chic boutiques** line the Marais' main shopping street, rue des Francs-Bourgeois, and young, trendy designers and hippie outfits congregate on Bastille streets rue de Charonne and rue Keller. At the more alternative and avant-garde end of the spectrum, there's a good concentration of **one-off designer boutiques** around M° Abbesses, at the foot of Montmartre – try rues des Martyrs, des Trois Frères, de la Vieuville, Houdon and Durantin. For more **streetwise clothing**, rue Étienne-Marcel and pedestrianized rue Tiquetonne, near the Forum des Halles, are good for young, **trendy fashion** boutiques.

fashion department for women, plus a parfumerie even bigger than rival Galeries Lafayette's. The sixth-floor restaurant is right underneath the beautiful Art Nouveau glass dome. Next door is a huge men's store, stocking a wide range of labels.

La Samaritaine Map 2, F6. 75 rue de Rivoli, 1er, ⓦ www.lasamaritaine.fr.

M° Pont-Neuf. Deemed unsafe by Paris city council, this venerable old belle époque department store closed in 2005 for a major refit and will be closed for at least five years.

Tati Map 3, J3. 4 bd de Rochechouart, 18e ⓦwww.tati.fr. M° Barbès. Mon–Fri 10am–7pm, Sat 9.15–7pm. Map 6, G12. Galerie Gaîté Montparnasse, 68 av du Maine, 14e. M° Gaîté. Budget department store chain with a distinctive pink gingham logo that sells reliable and utterly cheap clothing, among a host of other items.

Classic style

APC Map 2, C11. 3 & 4 rue de Fleurus, 6e. M° St-Placide. Mon, Fri & Sat 11am–7pm, Tues–Thurs 9am–7.30pm. The clothes here are young and urban, but still effortlessly classic in that Parisian way. The men's and women's shops face each other across the road. The same gear, but discounted over-stock fare, can be found at Surplus APC, 45 rue Madame, 6e.

Comptoir des Cotonniers Map 2, D8. 30 rue de Buci & 58 rue Bonaparte, 6e. M° Mabillon/St-Germain-des-Prés. Map 2, F4. 29 rue du Jour, 1er. M° Les Halles. Map 4, B10. 33 rue des Francs Bourgeois 4e. M° St-Paul. Mon 11am–7pm, Tues–Sat 10am–7.30pm. Utterly reliable little chain stocking comfortable, well-cut women's basics that nod to contemporary fashions without being modish. Trousers, shirts and dresses for around €100.

Isabel Marant Map 4, F13. 16 rue de Charonne, 11e. M° Bastille. Mon–Sat 10.30am–7.30pm. Marant excels in feminine and flattering clothes in quality fabrics such as silk and cashmere. Prices are €90 upwards for skirts, around €250 for coats.

Kabuki Map 2, G3. 25 rue Étienne-Marcel, 1er. M° Etienne-Marcel. Mon–Sat 10.30am–7.30pm. A one-stop store for all your Prada, Issey Miyake and Calvin Klein needs.

Loulou de la Falaise Map 6, F2. 7 rue de Bourgogne, 7e. M° Varenne. Mon–Sat 11am–7pm. This is the first store for Loulou, the former head of accessories at Yves Saint Laurent, and it's fashioned in the same international-chic look that has made her clothing line so popular. The derivative style is very multicultural, and there's everything from bangles to tartan kilts to mandarin-collared bodices.

Patricia Louisor Map 3, G3. 16 rue Houdon, 18e. M° Abbesses. Daily noon–8pm. Vibrant and sassy designs that spring from a solid base of classic Parisian style. Trousers, skirts and pullovers all come in at around €70–120.

Sabbia Rosa Map 2, C8. 71–73 rue des Saints-Pères, 6e. M° St-Germain-des-Prés. Mon–Sat 10am–7pm. Supermodels' knickers – literally, they all shop here – at supermodel prices. Beautiful lingerie creations in silk, fine cotton and Calais lace. An ensemble will cost around €150, and you could pay three times that.

Spree Map 3, G3. 16 rue de la Vieuville, 18e. M° Abbesses. Mon 2–7pm, Tues–Sat 11am–7.30pm. So fashionable it actually looks like an art gallery. The hip, feminine clothing collection is led by individual designers such as Vanessa Bruno, Isabel Marant and Christian Wijnants, and there are often a few vintage pieces too, as well as accessories. Clothing mostly falls in the €100-250 range.

Vanessa Bruno Map 2, D9. 25 rue St-Sulpice, 6e. M° Odéon. Mon–Sat 10.30am–9.30pm. Bright, breezy and effortlessly beautiful women's fashions – trainers/sneakers, dresses and bags – with a hint of updated hippy chic.

Zadig & Voltaire Map 2, C9. 1 & 3 rue du Vieux Colombier, 6e. M° St-Sulpice. Map 2, F4. 15 rue du Jour, 1er. M° Les Halles. Map 2, C3. 9 rue du 29 Juillet, 1er. M° Tuileries. Map 2, G4. 11 rue Montmartre, 1er. M° Les Halles. Map 4, C11. 36 rue de Sévigné, 4e. M° St-Paul. Mon–Sat 10am–7pm. The women's clothes at this small, moderately expensive Parisian chain are pretty and feminine. In style it's not a million miles from agnès b. (see p.249) – and her shop's just opposite too – only with a more wayward flair.

Trendy and avant-garde

Anne Willi Map 4, G12. 13 rue Keller, 11e. M° Ledru-Rollin/Voltaire. Mon 2–8pm, Tues–Sat 11.30am–8pm. Completely original pieces of clothing that respect classic French sartorial design. The works are done in gorgeous, luxurious fabrics and run the gamut from layered casual-chic sets to one-piece geometric studies of the body. Prices from €60.

Art Brutal Map 4, B11. 4 rue Ferdinand Duval, 4e. M° St-Paul. Daily 11am–9pm. Unique clothing designed in-house by Spanish conceptual artist Miguel Amate and his daughter. The artsy jackets and shirts are splotched, cut, stretched, patched and otherwise wrangled beyond recognition, but still wearable and very cool. €80–260.

D2G Map 2, C3. 249 rue St-Honoré, 1er. M° Tuileries/Pyramides. Mon–Sat 10am–7pm. With exclusive but affordable brands like Garella, Batiste and Nathalie Garçon, this new boutique has perfected the posh-meets-ethnic aesthetic.

Many of the funky vests, jackets and shirts are striped, quilted and accented with embroidery and gorgeous chicken-stitching.

FuturWare Lab Map 3, G3. 23 rue Houdon, 18e. M° Abbesses. Map 4, C9. 64 rue Vieille du Temple, 3e. M° Hôtel-de-Ville. Tues–Sat 11am–2pm & 2.30–7pm. Tatiana Lebedev's one-woman boutique has found a secure perch on the trendy designer scene with her innovative use of contemporary fabrics. It's not all high tech, however, and graceful touches soften the look.

Heaven Map 3, G3. 83 rue des Martyrs, 18e. M° Abbesses. Tues–Sat 11am–7.30pm, Sun 2–7.30pm. English-bred Lea-Anne Wallis has a wild streak, designing luxurious, sometimes brash, sometimes classically elegant clothing for men and women. Her husband, Jean-Christophe Peyrieux, handles the adjacent lighting department.

Le Shop Map 2, F3. 3 rue d'Argout, 2e. M° Étienne Marcel. Mon 2–8pm, Tues–Sun 11.30am–8pm. Excellent place to stock up on all your urban gear, or get that perfect gift for your favourite baggy-jeaned skater-boy. Men's and women's brands like Carhartt and Chipie, Stussy and Sessun are sold in a funky setting with DJs spinning round the clock. Tattooing and piercing on the ground floor.

S2A Map 2, F6. 46 rue de l'Arbre Sec, 1er. M° Pont Neuf. Mon–Sat 12.30–7.30pm. Fronting as an art-collective and studio space, this trendy clothing boutique generally sells to the popular nouveau skater look, but has a number of very interesting one-of-a-kind, artsy garments. Also sells books, magazines and the latest can't-do-without accessories, and hosts occasional openings and parties.

The big designer names

Below is a selection of the main or most conveniently located outlets of Paris's **top designers**. For a more complete list, including branch boutiques and websites, get online at Ⓦ www.modemonline.com or Ⓦ www.stargonaut.com/fashion.htm. Nearly all the shops below operate normal French boutique **opening hours** of Mon–Sat 10am–7pm.

agnès b. Map 2, F4. 6 rue du Jour, 1er. M° Châtelet-Les Halles. Map 2, C9. 6 & 10 rue du Vieux Colombier, 6e. M° St-Sulpice. Born in Versailles, this queen of understatement rebels against heavily styled and elaborate garments, favouring anti-elitist staples for women of all persuasions. While the line has expanded into watches, sunglasses and cosmetics, her clothing remains chic, timeless and, best of all, relatively affordable.

Chanel Map 7, I4. 42 av Montaigne, 8e. M° Franklin-D.-Roosevelt. Born in 1883, Gabrielle "Coco" Chanel engendered a way of life that epitomized elegance, class and refined taste. Her most famous signatures are the legendary No. 5 perfume, the black evening dress and the once-omnipresent tweed suit.

Chloé Map 7, N4. 54 rue du Faubourg-St-Honoré, 8e. M° Madeleine. Dark, tweed wool pants, light knit tops and lovely semi-formal prêt-à-porter dresses.

Christian Lacroix Map 7, M4. 73 rue du Faubourg-St-Honoré, 8e. M° Concorde. Map 2, B2. 366 rue St-Honoré, 1er. M° Madeleine. Best known for his flamboyant, Zorro-inspired vests and cloaks, this baroque, theatrical designer now does everything from just-woke-up rumpled trousers to sequined and laméd miniskirts. His couture jeans are a steal at €175.

Comme des Garçons Map 7, M4. 54 rue du Faubourg-St-Honoré, 8e. M° Concorde. Led by Tokyo-born Rei Kawakubo, this very popular label favours novel tints and youthful, asymmetric cuts that defamiliarize the body. Exceptional lace sweaters.

Jean-Paul Gaultier Map 7, F3. 44 av George V, 8e. M° George V. Map 2, E2. 6 rue Vivienne, 2e. M° Bourse. The primordial young turk of Paris fashion, his current sets are very industrial-meets-Second Empire. Colouring is quite eclectic, with lots of greys and blacks and the odd chartreuse or fuchsia thrown in to throw you off. The denim collection at the stores is well within reach of those not being chased by paparazzi.

Lagerfeld Gallery Map 2, D7. 40 rue de Seine, 6e. M° Mabillon. Though he still designs for Chanel and Fendi, Karl Lagerfeld's life as an intellectual and auteur clearly shows in his own ready-to-wear line, typified by stalwart tailoring, bold colours and comfy-fitting tops and jackets that make a lasting first impression.

Pierre Cardin Map 7, K4. 27 av Marigny, 8e. M° Place-Clemenceau. Famous early on for his futuristic body suits, Cardin's current label uses irregular cuts in outspoken, brash prints and fabrics.

Sonia Rykiel Map 2, C8. Women 175 bd St-Germain, 6e; Men 194 bd St-Germain, 7e. both M° St-Germain-des-Prés. Map 7, M4. Women 70 rue du Faubourg-St-Honoré, 8e. M° Concorde. Unmistakably Parisian designer who threw out her first line when the *soixante-huitards* threw Europe into social revolution. Her multi-coloured designs – especially sweaters – are all the rage, as is Rykiel Woman, her sister shop for women's erotic toys (4 rue de Grenelle, 6e M° St-Sulpice), and Sonia, her daugher Nathalie's younger, funkier clothing offshoot (61 rue des Saints-Pères, 6e, M° Sèvres-Babylone).

YSL Rive Gauche Map 2, D9. Men 6 place St-Sulpice, 6e. M° St-Sulpice/ Mabillon. Map 7, M4. Women 32–38 rue du Faubourg-St-Honoré, 8e. M° Concorde. When Yves Saint Laurent retired in 2002, he closed shop on his revered couture line and passed the baton over to Tom Ford, who initially designed this prêt-à-porter spin-off. Now run by ex-Prada man Stefano Pilati, the line has been modernized once again, with beige tulip skirts and colourful polka-dot jackets for women. Classic monochrome chic remains the staple for men.

Discount clothing

A number of dedicated "stock" shops (short for *déstockage*) sell end-of-line and last year's models at thirty- to fifty-percent **reductions**. Before you get too excited, however, remember that thirty percent off €750 still leaves a hefty bill – not that all items are this expensive. The best times of year to join the scrums are after the new collections have come out in January and October.

Cacharel Stock Map 1, D6. 114 rue d'Alésia, 14e. M° Alésia. Mon–Sat 10am–7pm. One of a cluster of factory and budget clothes shops on this stretch of rue d'Alésia, with a small but decent range of Cacharel clothes from last season at 40–50 percent discounts. Lots of suits for men and women.

La Clef des Marques Map 6, H10. 124 bd Raspail, 7e. M° Vavin. Mon 2.30–7pm, Tues–Sat 10.30am–7pm. Huge store with a wide choice of inexpensive brand-name clothes for men and women – also lots of lingerie and children's clothes.

Défilé de Marques Map 6, B3. 171 rue de Grenelle, 7e. M° La Tour-Maubourg. Tues–Sat 10am–2pm & 3–7.30pm. *Dépôt-vente* shop selling a wide choice of designer clothes for women – as returned unsold from the big-name boutiques. Labels from Prada to Paco Rabanne discounted to around €200–300.

Kookai Stock Map 2, H2. 82 rue Réamur, 2e. M° Réamur-Sebastopol/Trocadéro. Off Map 7, A5. 2 rue Gustave Courbet, 16e. M° Victor Hugo Tues–Sat 10am–7pm. Trendy young women's clothes; up to seventy percent off end-of-line and old stock.

Le Mouton à Cinq Pattes Map 2, E9. 138 bd St-Germain, 6e. M° Odéon/Mabillon. Mon-Fri 10.30am–7.30pm, Sat 10.30am–8pm. Map 2, B10. 18 rue St-Placide. Women only 8 rue St-Placide, 6e. Both M° Sèvres-Babylone. Mon–Sat 10am–7pm. Names such as Helmut Lang and Gaultier can be found among the racks of smart, discounted end-of-line and last-season's clothes for men and women, though often enough the labels are cut out so you'll have to trust your judgement.

Passé Devant Map 3, G3. 62 rue d'Orsel, 18e. M° Abbesses. Tues–Sat 10.30am–1pm & 2–7pm, Sun 2–7pm. Big-name labels such as Yamamoto, Donna Karan, Miu Miu and D&G hang alongside smaller designers' work, most of it ex-sale or return stock at heavily discounted prices. The €75 Diesel jeans here are a steal.

Secondhand and rétro clothes

Alternatives Map 4, B11. 18 rue du Roi-de-Sicile, 4e. M° St-Paul. Tues–Sat 11am–1pm & 2.30–7pm. Vintage meets designer at this fantastic stop where you can perfect *le look parisien* both with fashionable marks and lesser-known brands. The clothes here are often straight off the bodies of runway models.

Guerrisol Map 3, C3. 29–31 av de Clichy, 17e. M° Clichy. Mon–Sat 10am–7pm. Enormous in size, unbeatable in selection, frequently called the temple of *fripe* (secondhand clothes). Not really Parisian chic, as much of the used clothing here comes from all over the place, but if you have time to sift through the bins, you'll walk off with some great deals such as Levi's 501s for €5.

Kiliwatch Map 2, G3. 64 rue Tiquetonne, 2e. M° Étienne-Marcel. Mon 2–7pm, Tues–Sun 10am–7pm. A clubbers' mecca, where rails of new cheap 'n' chic youth streetwear and a slew of trainers/sneakers meet the best range of unusual secondhand clothes and accessories in Paris. This is the place in Paris to buy jeans for men, with no fewer than fifteen brands stocked and well displayed.

Moda di Andréa Map 3, E6. 79 rue de la Victoire, 9e. M° Trinité/Chaussée d'Antin. Mon–Sat 10.30am–7.30pm. Sounds too good to be true, but this diamond in the rough sells all the big names in footwear – Prada, Miu Miu, Jil Sander and YSL – for up to half what you'll pay in most other shops.

L'Occaserie Map 1, B4. 30 rue de la Pompe, 16e. M° Muette/Passy. Mon–

Sat 11am–7pm. All branches Map 1, B4.16 & 21 rue de l'Annonciation; 14 rue Jean Bologne; 19 rue de la Pompe, all 16e. M° Muette/Passy. Specialists in secondhand haute couture – Dior, Prada, Cartier and the like. "Secondhand" doesn't mean cheap though: Chanel suits are around €720 and Louis Vuitton handbags €300.

Réciproque Map 1, B4. 89, 92, 93–97, 101 & 123 rue de la Pompe, 16e. M° Pompe. Tues–Sat 11am–7pm. A similar series of shops to L'Occaserie's, this one is slightly more chichi and better for couture labels, with expensive finds like Christian Lacroix, Moschino and Manolo Blahnik. Women's design at no. 93–95; accessories and coats for men at no. 101; more accessories and coats for women at no. 123.

Shoes and accessories

Two of the best streets for shoe shopping are rue de Grenelle and rue du Cherche-Midi.

Biberon & Fils Map 2, D4. 334 rue St-Honoré, 1er. M° Pyramides/ Tuileries. Mon–Sat 10.30am–6.30pm. An unexpected find on one of the city's most exclusive shopping streets, this bargain shop sells very stylish French-made leather handbags in citrus colours as well as classic shades (€60–80).

Cécile et Jeanne Map 4, F14. 49 av Daumesnil, 12e. M° Gare-de-Lyon. Mon–Fri 10am–7pm, Sat & Sun 2–7pm. Innovative jewellery design from local artisans in one of the Viaduc des Arts showrooms. Many pieces under €100.

Décalage Map 4, C10. 33 rue des Francs-Bourgeois, 4e. M° St-Paul. Tues–Sat 11am–7pm, Sun & Mon 2–7pm. Beautiful handcrafted jewellery – in classic and contemporary designs. Prices are reasonable: earrings, for example, start at €50.

Editions de Parfums Frédéric Malle Map 2, B8. 37 rue de Grenelle, 7e. M° Rue-du-Bac. Mon–Sat 11am–7pm; closed two weeks in Aug. All the perfumes at this deliciously serious boutique have been created by "authors", which means professional parfumeurs working under their own name through this "publishing house". A 50ml bottle costs upwards of €50, or you could spend a fortune having a perfume individually designed for you.

Eighty Four Map 7, I2. 84 rue St-Honoré, 8e. M° St Philippe du Roule. Mon–Sat 10am–7pm. All of your favourite footers including Zanotti, Michael Kors, and Pedro Garcia, any of whose creations you can try on upstairs in opulent red velvet under a decadent crystal chandelier. An impressive 150 styles of shoes and boots in all, from €300 to €800.

Hermès Map 2, C3. 24 rue du Faubourg-St-Honoré, 8e. M° Concorde. Mon–Sat 10am–6.30pm. Luxury clothing and accessory store; come here for the ultimate silk scarf – at a price.

Jamin-Puech Map 3, K6. 61 rue d'Hauteville, 10e. M° Poissonière. Tues–Sat 10.30am–7pm. Map 4, B10. 68 rue Vieille du Temple, 4e. M° Hôtel de Ville. Tues noon–7pm, Wed–Sat 11am–7pm. An exquisite range of beautifully crafted bags (around €200) in brightly coloured leather, crepe silk and other luxury fabrics.

Jet One Map 2, G4. 21 rue Turbigo, 2e. M° Étienne-Marcel. Tues–Sat 10.30am–7pm. There are some great finds among the Nike, Adidas, Puma and Converse overstocks, many of which are quite stylish, some costing as little as €35.

Patrick Cox Map 2, G3. 62 rue Tiquetonne, 2e. M° Étienne-Marcel. Mon–Sat 10.30am–7.30pm. The chic and friendly Paris outlet of the London-based shoe designer. Clothes to match.

Séphora Map 7, H3. 70 av des Champs-Élysées, 8e. M° Franklin-D-Roosevelt. Mon–Sat 10am–midnight, Sun 11am–midnight. A huge perfume and cosmetics emporium, stocking every conceivable brand.

Virginie Monroe Map 4, G12. 30 rue de Charonne, 11e. M° Ledru-Rollin. Mon–Sat 11.30am–8pm. Delicate and unusual jewellery made from stones, glass, feathers and other non-precious materials. Earrings from €60, rings €50.

Art

The commercial **art galleries** are concentrated in the 8e, especially in and around avenue Matignon; in the Marais; on rue Quincampoix, near the Pompidou Centre; around the Bastille; and in St-Germain. There are literally hundreds of galleries and, for an idea of who is being exhibited where, look up details in *Pariscope* under "Expositions". Entry to commercial galleries is free to all.

Comptoir des Ecritures Map 2, H5. 35 rue Quincampoix, 4e. M° Rambuteau. Tues–Sat 11am–7pm. A delightful shop entirely devoted to the art of calligraphy, with an extensive collection of paper, pens, brushes and inks.

Dubois Map 2, F11. 20 rue Soufflot, 5e. RER Luxembourg. Tues–Sat 9am–7pm. In the same great apothecary-style building since the mid-1800s, the Dubois family still offers an excellent selection of art supplies and paints alongside very knowledgeable service.

Papier Plus Map 4, A11. 9 rue du Pont-Louis-Philippe, 4e. M° St-Paul. Mon–Sat noon–7pm. Fine-quality, colourful stationery, including notebooks, travel journals, photo albums and artists' portfolios.

Design

A small selection of places where contemporary and the best of twentieth-century **design** can be seen is listed below. Also worth checking out are the shops of the art and design museums, and the streets around the Bastille, with a high concentration of shops specializing in particular periods.

Colette Map 2, C3. 213 rue St-Honoré, 1er. M° Tuileries. Mon–Sat 10.30am–7.30pm. This cutting-edge concept store, combining high fashion and design, complete with photo gallery and exhibition space, has become something of a tourist attraction. When you've finished sizing up the Pucci underwear, Stella McCartney womenswear and Sonia Rykiel handbags, you could head for the cool *Water Bar*, with its 80 different kinds of H^2O.

Eugénie Seigneur Map 4, D7. 16 rue Charlot, 3e. M° République. Mon–Fri 10am–7pm, Sat 10am–1pm & 3–7pm. The place to take your print or original for a highly unique frame. Also sells one-off beautiful old floral tiles, mirrors and interesting brooches; prices begin at €40.

Fiesta Galerie Map 4, B10. 45 rue Vieille-du-Temple, 4e. M° Hôtel-de-Ville. Tues–Sat noon–7pm, Sun & Mon 2–7pm. A big selection of twentieth-century kitsch and retro objects.

Galerie Patrick Séguin Map 4, G12. 34 rue de Charonne, 11e. M° Bastille. Tues–Sat noon–7pm. A fine collection of furniture and objects from the 1950s, including pieces by Le Corbusier and Jean Prouvé, though not everything is for sale. There's another showroom nearby in rue des Taillandiers.

Louvre des Antiquaires Map 2, D4. 2 place du Palais-Royal, 1er. M°

Palais-Royal/Musée-du-Louvre. Tues–Sun 11am–7pm; closed Sun in July & Aug. An enormous antiques and furniture hypermarket where you can pick up anything from a Mycenaean seal ring to an Art Nouveau vase – for a price.

Lulu Berlu Map 4, E7. 27 rue Oberkampf, 11e. M° Oberkampf. Mon–Sat 11.30–7.30pm. This shop is crammed with twentieth-century toys and curios, most with their original packaging.

Résonances Map 7, M3. 3–5 bd Malesherbes, 8e. M° Madeleine. Mon–Sat 10am–8pm. Stylish kitchen and bathroom accessories, with an emphasis on French design. Covetable items include elegant wine decanters and a white porcelain hot-chocolate maker.

Le Viaduc des Arts Map 4, F14. 9–129 av Daumesnil, 12^{e}. M° Bastille/Gare de Lyon. Most shops Mon–Sat 10.30am–7.30pm. Practically the entire north side of the street is dedicated to an extremely high standard of skilled workmanship and craft. Each arch of this old railway viaduct houses a shop front and workspace for the artists within, who produce contemporary metalwork, ceramics, tapestry, sculpture and much more.

Books

The most atmospheric areas for **book** shopping are the Seine quais, with their rows of new and secondhand bookstalls perched against the river parapet, and the narrow streets of the Quartier Latin. **English-language bookshops** function as home-away-from-home for expats, often with readings from visiting writers, and sometimes handy noticeboards for flat-shares, language lessons and work.

For a general French-language bookshop, the classic is **Gibert Jeune**, with various branches around place St-Michel, in the Quartier Latin.

English-language books

Galignani Map 2, C3. 224 rue de Rivoli, 1er. M° Concorde. Mon–Sat 10am–7pm. Claims to be the first English bookshop established on the Continent way back in 1802. Stocks a good range, including fine art and children's books.

Shakespeare & Co **Map 2, G9. 37 rue de la Bûcherie, 5e ⓦwww.shakespeareco.org. M° Maubert-Mutualité. Daily noon–midnight.** A cosy and very famous literary haunt (see p.84). Has the biggest selection of secondhand English books in town and every Monday at 8pm there are readings in the library upstairs (where you can sit and read for as long as you like at other times).

Tea and Tattered Pages **Map 6, F9. 24 rue Mayet, 6e. M° Duroc. Mon–Sat 11am–7pm, Sun noon–6pm.** A secondhand bookshop with more than 15,000 titles in English, mostly tatty fiction. You can munch on cheesecake, bagels and the like in the small, attached *salon de thé*.

Village Voice **Map 2, D9. 6 rue Princesse, 6e ⓦwww.villagevoicebookshop.com. M° Mabillon. Mon 2–8pm, Tues–Sat 10am–8pm.** A welcoming recreation of a neighbourhood bookstore, with a good, two-floor selection of contemporary fiction and non-fiction, and a decent list of British and American poetry and classics. Also runs frequent readings and author signings.

W. H. Smith **Map 2, B3. 248 rue de Rivoli, 1er. M° Concorde. Daily 9.30am–7pm.** A Parisian outlet of the British chain with a wide range of new books, newspapers and magazines.

Art, architecture and cookery

Artcurial **Map 7, I4. 7 Rond-Point des Champs Elysées, 8e ⓦwww.artcurial.com. M° Franklin-D-Roosevelt. Mon–Fri 10.30am–7pm; closed two weeks in Aug.** *The* art bookshop in Paris, set in an elegant town house. Sells French and foreign editions, and there's also a gallery, which puts on interesting exhibitions.

FNAC **Map 2, F5. Forum des Halles, niveau 2, Porte Pierre-Lescot, 1er. M°/RER Châtelet-Les Halles. Map 2, B11. 136 rue de Rennes, 6e. M° St-Placide. Map 1, C3. 26 av des Ternes, 17e. M° Ternes. Map 1, A2. CNIT, 2 place de la Défense. M° La Défense. ⓦwww.fnac.com. Mon–Sat 10am–7.30pm.** Lots of *bandes dessinées*, guidebooks and maps, among everything else.

La Hune **Map 2, C8. 170 bd St-Germain, 6e. M° St-Germain-des-Prés. Mon–Sat 10am–11.45pm, Sun 11am–7.45pm.** A good general French range, but the main selling point – apart from its fifty-year history as a Left Bank arts institution – is the art, design, fashion and photography "image" collection on the first floor.

Lardanchet **Map 7, K3. 100 rue du Faubourg-St-Honoré, 8e ⓣ01.42.66.68.32. M° St-Philippe du Roule/Champs-Elysées. Mon–Sat 10am–7pm.** Specializes in Beaux-Arts and out-of-print art books.

A very discerning clientele means this is not where you come to browse your favourite coffee-table books – most of the books are sealed anyway.

Librairie des Archives Map 4, A9. 83 rue du Temple, 3e ⓦwww.librairiedesarchives.com. M° Rambuteau/Hôtel de Ville. Tues–Sat noon–7pm. An extensive selection of fine and decorative arts and fashion, plus a large number of out-of-print books.

Librairie Gourmande Map 2, G9. 4 rue Dante, 5e ⓦwww.librairie-gourmande.fr. M° Maubert-Mutualité. Mon–Sat 10am–7pm. The very last word in books about cooking.

Librairie le Moniteur Map 2, E10. 7 place de l'Odéon, 6e. M° Odéon. Mon–Sat 10am–7pm. Entirely dedicated to architecture, contemporary and historical, with books in English as well as French. There's even an in-house magazine devoted to public building projects.

Librairie du Musée d'Art Moderne de la Ville de Paris Map 7, E6. Palais de Tokyo, 11 av du Président-Wilson, 16e. M° Iéna. Tues–Fri 10am–5.30pm, Sat & Sun 10am–6.30pm. Specialist publications on modern art, including foreign works.

Librairie du Musée des Arts Décoratifs Map 2, D4. 107 rue de Rivoli, 1er. M° Palais-Royal. Daily 10am–7pm. Design, posters, architecture, graphics, and the like.

Comics (Bandes Dessinées)

Album Map 2, G9. 6–8 rue Dante, 5e. M° Maubert-Mutualité. Map 2, E10. 60 rue Monsieur-le-Prince, 6e. M° Odéon. ⓦwww.album.fr. Tues–Sat 10am–8pm. Serious collection of French BDs, some of them rare editions with original artwork. This block of rue Dante houses no fewer than five separate comic book shops.

Editions Déesse Map 2, H10. 8 rue Cochin, 5e. M° Maubert-Mutualité. Mon 4.30–7pm, Tues–Fri 11am–1pm & 2.30–7pm, Sun 11am–7pm. Specializes in older, rarer comics. The well-informed owner speaks excellent English and should be able to help you locate whatever you need.

Thé-Troc Map 4, F6. 52 rue Jean-Pierre-Timbaud, 11e. M° Parmentier. Mon–Fri 9.30am–8pm, Sat 11am–8pm. The friendly owner publishes *The Fabulous Furry Freak Brothers* in French and English (he is a friend of the author of the famous 1970s comics, who lives nearby). There are other comic books and memorabilia on sale, too, as well as a wide selection of teas and teapots, secondhand records, jewellery and assorted junk. The attached *salon de thé* (until 7pm) is comfy, colourful and restful, with board-games.

Food and drink

Paris has resisted the march of mega-stores with admirable resilience. Almost every quartier still has its *charcuterie*, *boulangerie* and **weekly market**, while some streets, such as rue Cler, in the 7e and rue des Martyrs, in the 9e, are literally lined with groceries, butchers' shops, delicatessens, pâtisseries, cheese shops, and wine merchants. Shopping at these places is an aesthetic experience.

As for buying food with a view to economic eating, you will be best off shopping at the street markets or supermarkets – though save your bread-buying at least for the local boulangerie. Useful **supermarkets** with branches throughout Paris are Félix Potin, Prisunic and Monoprix. The cheapest supermarket chain is Ed l'Epicier.

Gourmet food shops

Any list of food shops in Paris has to have at its head three palaces:

Fauchon Map 7, N3. 24–30 place de la Madeleine, 8e. M° Madeleine. Mon–Sat 9am–8pm. An amazing range of extravagantly beautiful groceries, exotic fruit and vegetables, charcuterie, wines both French and foreign – almost anything you can think of, all at exorbitant prices. The quality is assured by blind testing, which all suppliers have to submit to.

La Grande Epicerie Map 2, A10. 38 rue de Sèvres, 7e. M° Sèvres-Babylone. Mon–Sat 8.30am–9pm. This edible offshoot of the famous Bon Marché department store may not be quite as nakedly epicurean as Fauchon and Hédiard, but it's a fabulous emporium of fresh and packed foods. Popular among choosy Parisians, mon-eyed expats (for its country-specific favourites) and gastro-tourists alike.

Hédiard Map 7, N3. 21 place de la Madeleine, 8e. M° Madeleine. Mon–Sat 8am–10pm. The aristocrat's grocer since the 1850s. Superlative-quality coffees, spices and confitures. You can also eat at the restaurant upstairs.

Bread, cheese and charcuterie

Barthélémy Map 2, B8. 51 rue de Grenelle, 7e. M° Bac. Tues–Sat 8.30am–1pm & 4–7.15pm; closed Aug. Purveyors of carefully ripened and meticulously stored seasonal cheeses to the rich and powerful.

Aux Ducs de Gascogne Map 4, C11. 111 rue St-Antoine, 4e. M° St-Paul. Mon–Sat 10am–8pm. Excellent range of high-quality charcuterie, as well as enticing – and expensive – deli goods ranging from little salads to caviar. Sevice is ever so friendly.

Flo Prestige Map 2, C3. 42 place du Marché-St-Honoré, 1er. M° Pyramides. Daily 8am–11pm. Stocks all sorts of super delicacies, plus wines, champagne and exquisite ready-made dishes.

Labeyrie Map 2, G4. 6 rue Montmartre, 1er. M° Châtelet-Les Halles. Tues–Fri 11am–2pm & 3–7pm. Specialist in products from the Landes region, pâtés in particular: Bayonne hams, goose and duck pâtés, conserves, etc.

La Maison du Fromage Map 2, H14. 118 rue Mouffetard, 5e. M° Censier-Daubenton. Map 6, F8. 62 rue de Sèvres, 6e. M° Duroc. Tues–Sat 9am–1pm & 4–7.30pm, Sun 9am–1pm. Offers a wonderful selection, beautifully displayed. Specializes in goat's, sheep's and mountain cheeses.

Petrossian Map 6, C2. 18 bd de Latour-Maubourg, 7e. M° Latour-Maubourg. Mon–Sat 10am–7pm. Not just gilt-edged fish eggs, but other Russian and French delicacies too. You can try delights such as smoked salmon sorbet at the restaurant next door.

Poilâne Map 2, C9. 8 rue du Cherche-Midi, 6e. M° Sèvres-Babylone. Mon–Sat 6.15am–8.15pm. The source of the famous Pain Poilâne – a type of bread baked using traditional methods (albeit ramped up on an industrial scale) as conceived by the late, legendary Monsieur Poilâne himself.

Poujauran Map 6, C3. 20 rue Jean-Nicot, 7e. M° Latour-Maubourg. Tues–Sat 8am–8.30pm. Poujauran was a pioneer in the revival of traditional breads; he recently sold this shop, but the quality of the baguettes is still good, the pâtisseries wonderful, and the decor exquisite, with its original belle époque painted glass panels and tiles.

Chocolates and pâtisseries

Cacao et Chocolat Map 2, E8. 29 rue de Buci, 6e. M° Mabillon. Map 2, I9. 63 rue St-Louis-en-l'Île, 4e. M° Pont-Marie. Mon–Sat 10.30am–7.30pm, Sun 11am–7pm. The aroma alone makes it worth stopping in at this chocolate shop, which crafts confections of cacao from around the world and offers its own version of liquid chocolate in the small salon area.

Debauve and Gallais Map 2, D7. 30 rue des Saints-Pères, 7e. M° St-Germain-des-Prés/Sèvres-Babylone. Mon–Sat 9am–7pm. A beautiful shop specializing in chocolate and elaborate sweets that's been around since chocolate was taken as a medicine – and an aphrodisiac.

Pâtisserie Stohrer Map 2, G3. 51 rue Montorgueil, 2e. M° Sentier. Daily 7.30am–8pm; closed first two weeks Aug. Bread, pâtisseries, chocolate and charcuterie have been baked here since 1730. Discover what *pain aux raisins* should really taste like.

Tea and coffee

Mariage Frères Map 4, B10. 30 rue du Bourg-Tibourg, 4e. M° Hôtel-de-Ville. Daily 10.30am–7.30pm. Hundreds of teas, neatly packed in tins, line the floor-to-ceiling shelves of this 100-year-old tea emporium. There's also a classy *salon de thé* (see p.203) on the ground floor.

Verlet Map 2, D4. 256 rue St-Honoré, 1er. M° Palais Royal-Musée du Louvre. Mon–Sat 9am–7pm. An old-fashioned *torréfacteur* (coffee merchant), one of the best known in Paris, selling both familiar and less common varieties of coffee and tea from around the world. There's also a tearoom, perfect for a pick-me-up espresso.

Wine

Les Caves Augé Map 7, L2. 116 bd Haussmann, 8e. M° St-Augustin. Mon 1–7.30pm, Tues–Sat 9am–7.30pm. This old-fashioned, wood-panelled shop is the oldest *cave* in Paris and not only sells fine wines, but also a wide selection of port, armagnac, cognac and champagne.

La Crèmerie Map 2, E9. 9 rue des Quatre-Vents, 6e. Tues–Sat 10am–10pm; closed Aug. M° Odéon. Excellent wine shop set behind an attractive old dairy shop front. The Miard family, who run it, can recommend some fine lesser-known wines, especially from the Loire and Burgundy. Like an Italian *enoteca*, they offer wines by the glass, with plates of hams and cheeses (€6-11) to aid tasting.

Lavinia Map 2, B1. 3–5 bd de la Madeleine, 8e. M° Madeleine. Mon–Fri 10am–8pm, Sat 9am–8pm. The largest wine and spirits store in Europe. The gorgeous, modern interior displays thousands of bottles of wines from over 43 countries, and the wine cellar holds some of the rarest bottles in the world. Attached wine library and bar allow you to read up, then drink up. Prices range €3–36,000.

De Vinis Illustribus Map 2, G11. 48 rue de la Montagne-Ste-Geneviève, 5e. M° Maubert-Mutualité. Tues–Sat 11–8pm. International wine dealer and connoisseur extrarordinaire Lionel Michelin set up shop ten years ago in this ancient cellar where Hemingway used to buy his wine. He still specializes in very old and very rare vintages (the 1969 Romanee Conti at €4900 is one of his finest), but is just as happy selling you an €8 bottle of 2002 Coteaux du Languedoc and orating eloquently on its tannins.

A miscellany

Abdon Map 4, E11. 6 bd Beaumarchais, 11e. M° Chemin-Vert. Tues–Sat 9.30am–12.30pm & 1.30–6.30pm. New and secondhand photographic equipment. If they don't have what you're looking for, try the half-dozen other camera shops on the same street.

Archives de la Presse Map 4, B9. 51 rue des Archives, 3e. M° Rambuteau. Mon–Sat 10.30am–7pm. A fascinating shop for a browse, trading in old French newspapers and magazines, with vintage Vogues giving a good insight into the changing fashion scene.

Boîte à Musique Anna Joliet Map 2, E3. Jardin du Palais Royal, 9 rue de Beaujolais, 1er. M° Palais Royal-Musée du Louvre. Mon–Sat 10am–7pm. A delightful, minuscule boutique selling every style of music box, from inexpensive self-winding toy models to grand cabinets costing thousands of euros. Prices begin at €8.50 and quickly go up from there.

Ciné-Images Map 6, E6. 68 rue de Babylone, 7e. M° Sèvres-Babylone. Tues–Fri 10am–1pm & 2–7pm, Sat 2–7pm. Suitably located right opposite the famous Pagode cinema, this classy shop sells original and mainly French film posters. Prices range from €30 for something small and recent to €15,000 for the historic advert for the Lumière brothers' *L'Arroseur Arrosé*.

Le Pot à Tabac Map 7, M1. 28 rue de la Pépinière, 8e. M° St-Augustin. Daily 7.30am–7.30pm. Classy selection of pipes, cigars, tobacco and thermidors, plus an enormous choice of international cigarettes.

Pylones Map 4, B13. 57 rue St-Louis-en-l'île, 4e. M° Sully-Morland. Daily 11am–7.30pm. Playful and silly things, including inflatable fruit bowls, grasshopper can crushers, hand-puppet face-washers and sparkly resin jewellery.

Trousselier Map 7, M2. 73 bd Haussmann, 8e. M° St-Augustin. Mon–Sat 10am–7pm. Described in French Vogue as *the* artificial flower shop. Every conceivable species of flora fashioned from man-made fibre. Decadent and pricey, but fun.

Music

La Chaumière Map 2, E10. 5 rue de Vaugirard, 6e. M° Odéon/RER Luxembourg. Mon–Fri 11am–8pm, Sat 10am–8pm, Sun 2–8pm. The friendly staff here can advise on a wide selection of classical music and some jazz, with more than 15,000 CD recordings to choose from, many discounted.

Crocodisc Map 2, G10. 40–42 rue des Écoles, 5e. M° Maubert-Mutualité. Tues–Sat 11am–7pm. Folk, Oriental, Afro-Antillais, raï, funk, reggae, salsa, hip-hop, soul, country. New and secondhand, at some of the best prices in town.

Crocojazz Map 2, G11. 64 rue de la Montagne-Ste-Geneviève, 5e. M° Maubert-Mutualité. Tues–Sat 11am–7pm. Sells mainly new imports of jazz and blues, but a big grab-bag of inexpensive used titles for around €7.

FNAC Musique Map 4, E12. 4 place de la Bastille, 12e, next to the opera house. M° Bastille. Mon–Sat 10am–8pm, Wed & Fri till 10pm. Extremely stylish shop in black, grey and chrome with computerized catalogues, every variety of music, books, and a concert booking agency. The other FNAC shops (see under "Bookshops") also sell music and hi-fi.

Jussieu Music Map 2, I12. 16-19 rue Linné, 5e. M° Jussieu. Mon–Sat 11am–7.30pm. A hundred thousand or so new and used CDs and DVDs ranging from rock and hip-hop to jazz, classical and world.

Maison Sauviat Map 3, J3. 124 bd de la Chapelle, 18e. M° Barbès-Rochechouart. Mon–Sat 9am–7.30pm. Wonderful shop that's been going strong since the 1920s. Now specializing in North and West African and Middle Eastern music.

Paul Beuscher Map 4, E11. 15–27 bd Beaumarchais, 4e. M° Bastille. Mon 2–7pm, Tues–Sat 10.15am–7pm. A music department store that's been going strong for more than a hundred years. Instruments, scores, books, recording equipment, etc.

Virgin Megastore Map 7, H3. 52 av des Champs-Elysées, 8e. M° Franklin-D-Roosevelt. Map 2, D5. Carrousel du Louvre, under the Louvre, 1er. M° Palais-Royal-Musée-du-Louvre. Map 3, H8. 5 bd Montmartre, 2e. M° Rue Montmartre. Mon 10am–9pm, Tues 10am–8pm, Wed–Sun 10am–10pm. This is one of the biggest music stores in the country, and is a great place to get acquainted with French music, as you can listen to much of the music through digital listening-posts. Also houses a concert-booking agency.

Markets

Many of Paris's biggest and most historic markets, such as those on rue Mouffetard (5^{e}) and rue des Martyrs (9^{e}) have become proper streets lined with food shops, but it's still remarkably easy to find fresh fruit, vegetables and even meat, fish and cheese on the city's streets. There are also a number of specialist markets, from those selling books and art to the famous "flea markets" – which nowadays are really giant antiques emporia.

Books, stamps and art

For books and old posters, don't forget the **bouquinistes**, who hook their green, padlocked boxes onto the riverside quais of the Left Bank.

Marché du Livre Ancien et d'Occasion Map 1, D6. Pavillon Baltard, Parc Georges-Brassens, rue Brancion, 15e. M° Porte-de-Vanves. Sat & Sun 8am–1pm. Secondhand and antiquarian books.

Marché aux Timbres Map 7, K4. junction of avs Marigny & Gabriel, on the north side of place Clemenceau in the 8e. M° Champs-Elysées–Clemenceau. Thurs, Sat, Sun & hols 10am–7pm. *The* stamp market in Paris.

Clothes and flea markets

Paris has three main **flea markets** (*marchés aux puces*) of ancient descent gathered about the old gates of the city. No longer the haunts of the flamboyant gypsies and petty crooks of literary tradition, they are nonetheless good entertainment.

Porte de Montreuil Map 1, H5. Av de Porte de Montreuil, 20e. M° Porte-de-Montreuil. Sat, Sun & Mon 7.30am–5pm. Cheap new clothes have begun to dominate what was the best of Paris's flea markets for secondhand clothes – still cheapest on Monday when leftovers from the weekend are sold off. Also old furniture, household goods and assorted junk.

Porte de Vanves Map 1, D7. Av Georges-Lafenestre/av Marc-Sangnier, 14^{e}. M° Porte-de-Vanves. Sat & Sun 7am–1.30pm. The best choice for bric-a-brac and little Parisian knick-knacks. Professionals deal alongside weekend amateurs.

St-Ouen/Porte de Clignancourt Map 1, E1. 18^{e}. M° Porte-de-Clignan-

court. Mon, Sat & Sun 7.30am–7pm. The biggest and most touristy flea market, with nearly a thousand stalls selling new and secondhand clothes, shoes, records, books and junk of all sorts. The majority of the covered market, however, is now given over to expensive antiques. For a full description, see pp.151–153.

Food markets

For a full list of all Paris's many street food markets, see online at Ⓦwww.paris.fr/fr/marches/. The most historic markets – the rue Mouffetard (5e), rue Cler (7e), rue des Martyrs (9e) and rue de Lévis (17e) – are now more market street than street market, with their stalls mostly metamorphosed into permanent, often fairly luxurious shops. For real **street markets** the Left Bank offers a tempting scattering in the 5e – notably on place Maubert and place Monge – and larger markets at Montparnasse, in boulevard Edgar-Quinet; opposite Val-de-Grâce in boulevard Port-Royal; and on rue de la Convention, in the 15e. On the Right Bank, the rue Lepic market (Tues–Sun), in Montmartre is satisfyingly authentic. On Sunday mornings a very fancy organic market takes over boulevard Raspail, 7e, in the vicinity of rue du Cherche-Midi. For a different feel and more exotic **foreign produce**, take a look at the Mediterranean/Oriental displays in boulevard de Belleville, 20e, rue d'Aligre, 12e and rue Dejean, 18e.

Food markets are traditionally **morning** affairs, usually starting between 7 and 8am and tailing off sometime between 1 and 2.30pm. However, in a break with Parisian tradition a few afternoon-only markets have recently opened, and so far they have been very well received by those who prefer to sleep in, among others.

Film, theatre and dance

Movie-goers have a choice of around three hundred **films** showing in Paris in any one week, covering every country and era. The city also has a vibrant **theatre** scene and several superstar directors are based here, including Peter Brook and Ariane Mnouchkine, known for their highly innovative, cutting-edge productions. Dance enjoys a high profile, enhanced by the recent opening of the Centre National de la Danse, Europe's largest dance academy.

Listings for all films and stage productions are detailed in *Pariscope* and other weekly listing magazines (see p.22).

Film

Despite the success of the multiscreen cinema chains, Paris's smaller and more historic cinemas continue to screen splendidly varied programmes of art-house and international cinema. Aside from new and recent film releases, the repertoires of outstanding directors from the world over are regularly shown as part of retrospective seasons. These will be listed along with other cinema-clubs and museum screenings under "Séances exceptionnelles" or "Ciné-clubs", and are usually cheaper than ordinary cinemas.

To watch foreign films in the original language (with subtitles in French) look for version originale or "v.o." in the listings, and avoid version française or "v.f.", which means it's dubbed into French – usually badly.

For the seriously committed film freak, the best movie venue in Paris is the **Cinémathèque Française**, 51 rue de Bercy, 12e (Ⓣ01.71.19.33.33, Ⓦwww.cinemathequefrancaise.com), with its museum of cinema and wonky Frank Gehry architecture. It gives a choice of around two dozen different films a week, many of which would never be shown commercially, and tickets are only €5. Alternatively, the **Forum des Images** (Tues–Sun 1–9pm, Thurs till 10pm; Ⓣ01.44.76.62.00, Ⓦwww.forumdesimages.net), in the Porte St-Eustache side of the Forum des Halles (see p.70), is another great venue for the bizarre or obscure. The €5.50 entrance fee allows you access all day to as many screenings as you can stomach, as well as private video viewings in the archive, or *vidéothèque*. Cultural institutions also have their own cinémathèques, notably the **Pompidou Centre**, place Georges-Pompidou, 4e (M° Rambuteau; Ⓣ01.44.78.12.33) and the **Institut du Monde Arabe**, 23 quai des Fossés St-Bernard, 5e (M° Jussieu; Ⓣ01.40.51.34.77).

Cinemas

L'Arlequin Map 2, C10. 76 rue de Rennes, 6e. M° St-Sulpice.

Owned by Jacques Tati in the 1950s, L'Arlequin has now been renovated and is once again *the* cinephile's palace in the

Latin Quarter. There are special screenings of classics every Sunday at 11am, followed by debates in the café opposite.

L'Entrepôt Map 6, E14. 7–9 rue Francis-de-Pressensé, 14e ⓦwww.lentrepot.fr. M° Pernety. One of the best alternative Paris cinemas, with a great bookshop and bar/restaurant.

L'Escurial Map 5, F5. 11 bd de Port-Royal, 13e. M° Gobelins. Combines plush seats, a big screen, and more art than commerce in its programming policy – and no dubbing.

Grand Action and Action Écoles Map 2, F10. 5 & 23 rue des Écoles, 5e, M° Cardinal-Lemoine/Maubert-Mutualité); Action Christine Odéon, 4 rue Christine, 6e, M° Odéon/St-Michel (Map 2, E8). The Action chain specializes in new prints of old classics and screens contemporary films from around the world.

Le Grand Rex Map 3, I8. 1 bd Poissonnière, 2e. M° Bonne-Nouvelle. This outrageously huge 1930s ciné-palace, has a *Metropolis*-style tower blazing its neon name, 2750 seats and a ceiling of stars and a Moorish city skyline on the wall. Sadly, it shows mostly dubbed blockblusters.

MK2 Bibliothèque Map 5, N7. 128–162 av de France, 13e. M° Bibliothèque/Quai de la Gare. Architecturally cutting-edge cinema with a very cool café and fourteen screens showing a varied range of French films – mostly new, some classic – and *v.o.* foreign movies.

La Pagode Map 6, E6. 57bis rue de Babylone, 7e. M° François-Xavier. The most beautiful of the city's cinemas, transplanted from Japan at the end of the nineteenth century. Walls are silk-embroidered, while golden dragons and elephants hold up the candelabra. Shows a mix of arts films and documentaries, and commercial movies in *v.o.*

Reflet Medicis Le Quartier Latin Map 2, F10. 3, 5, 7 & 9 rue Champollion, 5e. M° Cluny-La-Sorbonne/Odéon. A cluster of inventive little cinemas, tirelessly offering up rare screenings and classics, including frequent retrospective cycles covering great directors (always in *v.o*). The small cinema café *Le Reflet*, on the other side of the street, is a little-known cult classic in itself.

Le Studio 28 Map 3, F2. 10 rue de Tholozé, 18e. M° Blanche/Abbesses. This historic art-house cinema still hosts avant-garde premières as well as regular festivals.

Le Studio des Ursulines Map 2, F13. 10 rue des Ursulines, 5e. RER Luxembourg. Screens and sometimes premières avant-garde movies, arts films and documentaries, often followed by in-house debates with the directors and actors.

Cinema tickets rarely need to be purchased in advance, and they're cheap by European standards. The average price is €7–10; and some cinemas have lower rates on Monday or Wednesday, as well as reductions for students from Monday to Thursday. Some matinée séances also have discounts.

Theatre

Certain directors in France do extraordinary things with the medium of **theatre**; classic texts are shuffled into theatrical moments, where spectacular and dazzling sensation takes precedence over speech. Their shows can be overwhelming: huge casts, vast sets, exotic lighting effects, original music scores. It adds up to a unique experience, even if you haven't understood a word.

Ariane Mnouchkine, whose **Théâtre du Soleil** is based at the Cartoucherie in Vincennes, is the director par excellence of this form. **Peter Brook**, the English director based at the Bouffes du Nord theatre, is another great magician of the all-embracing show. Any production by these two should not be missed, and there are often other weird and wonderful productions by younger directors, such as **Jérôme Savary**, who is artistic director at the Opéra Comique.

At the same time, bourgeois farces, postwar classics, Shakespeare, Racine and the like are staged with the same range of talent, or lack of it that you'd find in London or New York. The great generation of French or Francophone dramatists, which included Anouilh, Genet, Camus, Sartre, Adamov, Ionesco and Cocteau, came to an end with the death of **Samuel Beckett** in 1989 and **Ionesco** in 1994. Their plays, however, are still frequently performed and can now be included alongside Corneille and Shakespeare in the programme of the **Comédie Française**, the national theatre for the classics.

Parisian suburbs are a great source of excellent theatre productions, thanks to the ubiquitous **Maisons de Culture**. Ironically, however, although they were designed to bring culture to the masses, their productions are often among the most "difficult" and intellectually inaccessible.

Another plus is the Parisian theatre's openness to **foreign influence** and foreign work. The troupe at the Théâtre du Soleil is made up of around twenty different nationalities, and foreign artists and directors are frequent visitors. In any month there might be an Italian, Mexican, German or Brazilian production playing in the original language.

Buying theatre tickets

The easiest places to get **tickets** to see a stage performance in Paris are from the FNAC shops or Virgin Megastores (see pp.257 and 263). You can also buy tickets through their websites ⓦwww.fnac.com and ⓦwww.virginmega.fr, and then pick them up in one of their stores; alternatively Virgin will send them to your home address for a fee of €10 if you book more than seven days in advance. Another booking service is offered by ⓦwww.theatreonline.com; you pay for your tickets online and then you're given a reference number that you present to the box office half an hour before the performance to claim your tickets.

Same-day tickets with a fifty-percent discount and a small commission are available from the **half-price ticket kiosks** on place de la Madeleine, 8e, opposite no. 15, and on the Esplanade de la Gare du Montparnasse, 14e (Tues–Sat 12.30–8pm, Sun 12.30–4pm), but queues can be very long and the tickets are likely to be for the more commercial plays. Booking well in advance is essential for new productions and all shows by the superstar directors.

Prices vary between around €10 and €35. Previews at half price are advertised in Pariscope, etc, and there are weekday discounts at some places for students. Most theatres are closed on Sunday and Monday, and during August.

The best time of all for theatre lovers to come to Paris is for the **Festival d'Automne**, from the end of September to December (see p.277), an international celebration of all the performing arts, which attracts stage directors of high calibre.

Theatres

Bouffes du Nord Map 3, M3. 37bis bd de la Chapelle, 10e. ☎01.46.07.34.50. Mº La Chapelle. Peter Brook resurrected the derelict Bouffes du Nord in 1974 and has been based there ever since, mounting innovative, unconventional and controversial works. The theatre also invites renowned international directors and hosts top-notch chamber music recitals.

Cartoucherie Map 1, I6. Rte du Champ-de-Manoeuvre, 12e. Mº Château-de-Vincennes. Notable as home to the Théâtre du Soleil (☎01.43.74.24.08), the Cartoucherie is also the base for other good theatre companies.

Comédie Française Map 2, D4. 2 rue de Richelieu, 1er ☎01.44.58.15.15. Mº Palais-Royal. This venerable national theatre is a longstanding venue for the classics – Molière, Racine, Corneille – as well as twentieth-century greats, such as Anouilh and Genet.

Odéon Théâtre de l'Europe Map 2, E10. 1 place Paul-Claudel, off place de l'Odéon, 6e ☎01.44.41.36.36. Mº Odéon. Contemporary plays, as well as *version originale* productions by well-known foreign companies. During May 1968, the Odéon was occupied by students and became an open parliament with the backing of its directors, Jean-Louis Barrault (of Baptiste fame in *Les Enfants du Paradis* and who died in 1994) and Madeleine Renaud, one of the great French stage actresses.

Opéra Comique Map 3, G8. Rue Favart, 2e ☎01.42.44.45.46. Mº Richelieu-Drouot. Artistic director Jérôme Savary blends all forms of stage arts: modern and classical opera, musicals, comedy, dance and pop music, creating a bold and exciting programme.

Théâtre de la Huchette Map 2, G8. 23 rue de la Huchette, 5e ☎01.43.26.38.99. Mº St-Michel. Fifty years on, this small theatre is still showing Ionesco's *Cantatrice Chauve* (*The Bald Prima Donna*; 7pm) and *La Leçon* (8pm), two classics of the Theatre of the Absurd. Reserve by phone or at the door from 5pm; tickets €18 for one play or €28 for two.

Théâtre national de Chaillot Map 7, B7. Palais de Chaillot, place du

Trocadéro, 16e ⓣ01.53.65.30.00, ⓦwww.theatre-chaillot.fr. Mº Trocadéro. Puts on an exciting programme and regularly hosts foreign productions; Deborah Warner and Robert Lepage are regular visitors.

Théâtre national de la Colline Map 1, H4. 15 rue Malte-Brun, 20e. ⓣ01.44.62.52.52, ⓦwww.colline.fr. Mº Gambetta. Known for its modern and cutting-edge productions under director Alain Françon.

Dance

The status of dance in the capital received a major boost with the inauguration in 2004 of the Centre National de la Danse, a long overdue recognition of the importance of dance in a nation that boasts six hundred dance companies. A huge complex on the scale of the Pompidou, the CND is committed to promoting every possible dance form from classical to contemporary, and including ethnic traditions. Its creation also reflects an increased interest in the capital in dance, especially in contemporary dance, and while Paris itself has few homegrown companies (government subsidies go to regional companies expressly to decentralize the arts) it makes up for this by regularly hosting all the best contemporary practitioners. Names to look out for are **Régine Chopinot**'s troupe from La Rochelle, **Maguy Marin**'s from Rilleux-le-Pape and **Angelin Preljocaj**'s from Aix-en-Provence. Creative choreographers based in or around Paris include José Montalvo, Karine Saporta and the Californian Carolyn Carlson.

Many of the **theatres** listed above include dance in their programmes. Plenty of space and critical attention are also given to **tango**, **folk** and to visiting **traditional dance** troupes from all over the world. As for **ballet**, the principal stage is at the Palais Garnier, home to the Ballet de l'Opéra National de Paris, directed by Brigitte Lefèvre. It still bears the influence of Rudolf Nureyev, its charismatic, if controversial, director from 1983 to 1989, and frequently revives his productions, such as *Swan Lake* and *La Bayadère*.

Festivals combining theatre, dance and classical music include the Festival Exit in Créteil, the Paris Quartier d'Été from mid-July to mid-August and the Festival d'Automne from mid-September to mid-December (see "Festivals", overleaf).

Dance venues

Centre Mandapa Map 5, D9. 6 rue Wurtz, 13e ☎01.45.89.01.60. M° Glacière. Hosts mainly classical Indian dance.

Centre National de la Danse 1 rue Victor Hugo, Pantin ☎01.41.83.27.27, Ⓦwww.cnd.fr. M° Hoche/RER Pantin. The capital's major new dance centre occupies an impressively large building, ingeniously converted from a disused 1970s monolith into an airy and light high-tech space. Though several of its eleven studios are used for performances, the main emphasis of the centre is to promote dance through training, workshops and exhibitions.

Opéra de Bastille Map 4, E13. Place de la Bastille, 12e ☎08.36.69.78.68, Ⓦwww.opera-de-paris.fr. M° Bastille. Stages some productions by the Ballet de l'Opéra National de Paris, usually large-scale or contemporary works.

Palais Garnier Map 3, E8. Place de l'Opéra, 9e ☎08.36.69.78.68, Ⓦwww.opera-de-paris.fr. M° Opéra. Main home of the Ballet de l'Opéra National de Paris and the place to see ballet classics.

Théâtre des Abbesses Map 3, F3. 31 rue des Abbesses, 18e. M° Abbesses. The Théâtre de la Ville's sister company where you'll find slightly more off-beat performances by the likes of controversial choreographers Robyn Orlin and Jan Fabre.

Théâtre des Champs-Élysées Map 7, G5. 15 av Montaigne, 8e ☎01.49.52.50.50. M° Alma-Marceau. This prestigious venue occasionally hosts foreign troupes, eg the Tokyo Ballet, and stars, such as Sylvie Guillem.

Théâtre de la Ville Map 2, G6. 2 place du Châtelet, 4e ☎01.42.74.22.77, Ⓦwww.theatredelaville-paris.com. M° Châtelet. Specializes in avant-garde dance by top European choreographers, such as Anne Teresa de Keersmaeker and Pina Bausch.

23

Festivals

Paris hosts an impressive roster of **festivals** and **events**. Arguably the city's biggest jamboree is Bastille Day on July 14 but throughout the year there's invariably something on to add extra colour to your stay. The tourist office produces a biannual "Saisons de Paris – Calendrier des Manifestations", which gives details of all the mainstream events; otherwise, check the **listings** and other Paris magazines (see p.22) like *Pariscope* or look up "What's on" on the tourist board's website Ⓦwww.parisinfo.com. Many Parisian quartiers like Belleville and Montmartre have *portes ouvertes* (open doors) weeks, when artists' studios are open to the public and some festivities are laid on, generally in May and June – keep an eye open for posters and flyers.

The following listings give a selection of the most important or entertaining festivals and events in the Paris calendar.

January

La Grande Parade Jan 1. New Year's Day parade from Porte St-Martin to Madeleine Ⓦwww.parisparade.com.

February

Chinese New Year Paris's Chinese community brings in the New Year in the 13e around Avenue d'Ivry.

March

Banlieues Bleus Mid-March to mid-April. International jazz festival in the towns of Seine-St-Denis – Blanc-Mesnil, Drancy, Aubervilliers, Pantin, St-Ouen, Bobigny Ⓦwww.banlieuesbleues.org.
Festival Exit Usually last week of March. International festival of contemporary dance, performance and theatre at Créteil Ⓦwww.maccreteil.com.
Festival de Films des Femmes Second week of March. Major women's film festival at Créteil Ⓦwww.filmsdefemmes.com.
Festival du Film de Paris End of March to beginning of April. Mostly mainstream films on preview at the Cinéma Gaumont Marignan, 27–33 avenue des Champs-Élysées, 8e Ⓦwww.festivaldeparisidf.com.
Paris Fashion Week First week of March (and also first week of October). Next to Milan, the fashion event of the year. Technically for fashion professionals only, but surely there's a door left ajar somewhere Ⓦwww.modeaparis.com.

April

Poisson d'Avril April 1. April Fools' Day, with spoofs in the media and people sticking paper fishes on the backs of the unsuspecting.
Foire de Paris End of April to beginning of May. Food, wine, house and home fair at the Parc des Expositions, Porte de Versailles Ⓦwww.foiredeparis.fr.
Foire du Trône April to May. Centuries-old funfair with an actual freak show located in the Pelouse de Reuilly, Bois de Vincennes, 12e Ⓦwww.foiredutrone.com.

May

Fête du Travail May Day (May 1). Everything closes and there are marches and festivities in eastern Paris and around place de la Bastille.
Printemps des Rues End of May. Free street performances in the areas of La Villette, Gambetta, Nation and République Ⓦwww.leprintempsdesrues.com.
Jazz in the Parc Floral May to July. Big jazz names give free concerts in the Parc Floral at the Bois de Vincennes Ⓦwww.parcfloraldeparis.com.

June

Festival Agora First week of June. Contemporary theatre/dance/music festival organized by IRCAM and the Pompidou Centre Ⓦwww.ircam.fr.
Festival de St-Denis All June. Classical and world-music festival

with opportunities to hear music in the Gothic St-Denis basilica Ⓦwww.festival-saint-denis.fr.

Fête de la Musique June 21. Live bands and free concerts throughout the city Ⓦwww.fetedelamusique.culture.fr.

Feux de la Saint-Jean Around June 24. Fireworks for St-Jean's Day at the Parc de la Villette and quai St-Bernard.

Gay Pride End of June. Gay and Lesbian Pride march Ⓦmarche.inter-lgbt.org.

Foire St-Germain June to July. Concerts, antique fairs, poetry and exhibitions in the 6e Ⓦwww.foiresaintgermain.org.

Festival de Chopin Mid-June to mid-July. Chopin recitals by candlelight, held in the Orangerie de Bagatelle, in the Bois de Boulogne Ⓦwww.frederic-chopin.com.

July

Arrivée du Tour de France Cycliste Third or fourth Sun of July. The Tour de France cyclists cross the finishing line in the avenue des Champs-Élysées.

Bastille Day July 14 and the evening before. The 1789 surrender of the Bastille is celebrated with official pomp: tanks parade down the Champs-Élysées, firework displays and concerts are put on. At night there is dancing in the streets around place de la Bastille to good French bands.

La Goutte d'Or en Fête First week of July. A music festival of rap, reggae and raï with local and international performers Ⓦwww.gouttedorenfete.org.

Paris Quartier d'Été Mid-July to mid-Aug. Music, cinema, dance and theatre events around the city Ⓦwww.quartierdete.com.

Paris Plage Mid-July to mid-Aug. A popular initiative launched by the mayor, Bertrand Delanoë, in which 3km of the Seine quais are closed to traffic and transformed into mini-beaches, complete with imported sand and palm trees.

Festival de Cinéma en Plein Air End of July to end of Aug. Free open-air cinema at Parc de la Villette Ⓦwww.cinema.arbo.com.

August

Cinéma au Clair de Lune. First three weeks of Aug. Open-air screenings of films shot in Paris and shown near the location where they were filmed.

Fête de l'Assomption Aug 15. A procession from Notre-Dame around the Île de la Cité to celebrate the Assumption of the Virgin Mary.

September

Fête de l'Humanité Second weekend of Sept. Sponsored by the French Communist Party and *L'Humanité* newspaper, this annual three-day event just north of Paris at La Courneuve (M° La Courneuve, then bus #177 or special shuttle from RER) attracts people in their tens of thousands and of every political persuasion. Food and drink (all very cheap), and music and crafts from every corner of the globe, are the predominant features, rather than political platforms.

Villette Jazz Festival Early Sept. One of the city's best jazz festivals, with music played by legendary greats and local conservatory students, held in the park and Grande Halle at la Villette Ⓦwww.villette.com.

Journées du Patrimoine One weekend in mid-Sept. A nationwide event where normally off-limits buildings – like the Palais de l'Élysée – are opened to a curious public. Details in local press and on Ⓦwww.jp.culture.fr.

Techno Parade Mid-Sept. Floats and sound systems parade from Place de la République to Pelouse de Reuilly and celebrations culminate in a big party Ⓦwww.technopol.net.

Festival d'Automne Mid-Sept to mid-Dec. Theatre and music festival including companies from Eastern Europe, America and Japan; multilingual productions; lots of avant-garde and multimedia stuff, most of it very exciting Ⓦwww.festival-automne.com.

October

Fête des Vendanges First or second weekend in Oct. The grape harvest festival takes place in the Montmartre vineyard, at the corner of rue des Saules and rue St-Vincent Ⓦwww.fetedesvendangesdemontmartre.com.

Foire Internationale d'Art Contemporain (FIAC) End Oct. International contemporary art fair held at Paris Expo, Porte de Versailles Ⓦwww.fiaconline.com.

Nuit Blanche Early Oct. All-night cultural events at unusual venues Ⓦwww.paris.fr.

November

Festival FNAC-Inrockuptibles Early Nov. Dubbed *Les Inrocks*, rock festival featuring lots of new names at various venues around town is put on by the book and record chain-store FNAC. Ⓦwww.lesinrocks.com.

Paris Photo Mid–Nov. From early works to modern masterpieces, this is actually one of the best events anywhere for seeing some of the world's greatest photography. This month also sees photographic exhibitions held in museums, galleries and cultural centres throughout the city Ⓦwww.parisphoto.fr.

Lancement des Illuminations des Champs-Élysées End of Nov. Jazz bands, the Republican Guard and an international star turning on the Christmas lights on the Champs-Élysées.

Festival d'Art Sacré de la Ville de Paris End of Nov to mid–Dec. Concerts and recitals of church music in Paris's churches and concert halls Ⓦwww.festivaldart-sacre.new.fr.

December

Noël Dec 24–25. Christmas eve is a huge affair all across France, and of much more importance than the following day. Both Notre-Dame and Église de la Madeleine hold lovely midnight mass services, though you'll want to arrive early to avoid standing. The doors open at 10pm and the ceremony begins at 10.30pm.

Le Nouvel An December 31. New Year's Eve means fireworks, drinking and kissing, notably on the Champs-Élysées.

Patinoire de l'Hôtel de Ville Mid–Dec to end of Feb. Ice-skating rink erected in front of the town hall. Free entry but you pay €5 for rental of ice skates Ⓦwww.paris.fr.

24

Activities

If you've had enough of following crowds through museums, shopping or just wandering through the city, then there are saunas to soak in, ice-skating rinks to fall on, and swimming pools to dive into. You can also rent a bike, go on a boat trip or view the city from a helicopter.

Pariscope has useful listings of **sports** facilities, pools, *hammams* and so on (under "Sport et bien-être"). **Information** on municipal facilities is available from the town hall, the Mairie de Paris; check the comprehensive website Ⓦwww.paris.fr.

Boat trips

On a **Bateau-Mouche** you may not be able to escape the running commentary, but the rides certainly give a close-up view of the classic, glamorous buildings along the Seine. Trips start from the Embarcadère du Pont de l'Alma, on the Right Bank in the 8e (information Ⓣ01.40.76.99.99, Ⓦwww.bateaux-mouches.fr; reservations Ⓣ01.42.25.96.10; M° Alma-Marceau). The rides, which usually last an hour, run roughly hourly to every half hour, depending on the season. Summer departures are 10am–10.30pm, winter 11am–9.30pm. Tickets cost €7.

The main **competitors** to the Bateaux-Mouches can all be found detailed in *Pariscope* under "Croisières" in the "Visites-Promenades" section. An alternative way of riding on the Seine – one in which you are mercifully spared the commentary – is the **Batobus** (ⓣ01.44.11.33.99), a river transport system operating from May to September. See "City transport" (p.21) for more details.

Great views of the city

Few cities present such a uniform skyscape as Paris. Looking down on the ranks of seven-storey apartment buildings from above, it's easy to imagine the city as a lead-roofed plateau split by the leafy canyons of the boulevards and avenues. Spires, towers, and parks – not to mention multicoloured art museums and glass pyramids – stand out all the more against the solemn grey backdrop. Here are some of the best vistas in town:

Arc de Triomphe (see p.49): look out on an ocean of traffic and enjoy impressive vistas of the Voie Triomphale.

Pompidou Centre (see p.66): a stunning backdrop to modern art.

Grande Arche de la Défense (see p.149): take the long view.

Eiffel Tower (see p.103): the classic, best at night.

Institut du Monde Arabe (see p.90): sip mint tea on the rooftop overlooking the Seine.

Musée d'Orsay (see p.99): peer through the old station clock towards Montmartre.

Notre-Dame (see p.31): perch among the gargoyles.

Parc André-Citroën (see p.104): a tethered balloon rises 150m above this quirky park.

Parc de Belleville (see p.140): watch the sunset over the city.

Sacré-Cœur (see p.118): this puffball dome soars over Montmartre.

Tour Montparnasse (see p.111): stand eye to eye with the Eiffel Tower.

Canal trips

Less overtly touristy than the Bateaux-Mouches and their clones are the **canal-boat trips**. Canauxrama (reservations ⓣ01.42.39.15.00, ⓦwww.canauxrama.com) chugs up and down between the Port de l'Arsenal (opposite 50 bd de la Bastille, 12e; M° Bastille) and the Bassin de la Villette (13 quai de la Loire, 19e; M° Jaurès) on the Canal St-Martin (see p.132).

A more stylish vessel for exploring the canal is the **catamaran** of Paris-Canal, with trips between the Musée d'Orsay (quai Anatole-France by the Pont Solférino, 7e; M° Solférino) and the Parc de la Villette (La Folie des Visites Guidées, on the canal by the bridge between the Grande Salle and the Cité des Sciences, 19e; M° Porte-de-Pantin), which also last three hours. The catamaran departs from the Musée d'Orsay at 9.30am; daily mid-March to mid-November, Sunday only other months. Parc de la Villette departures are at 2.30pm. Trips cost €16, 12–25s and over-60s €12 (except Sun and holiday afternoons), 4–11s €9; reservations ⓣ01.42.40.96.97.

Guinguettes

For the ultimate Parisian retro experience, head for a traditional riverbank **guinguette** or open-air dance hall. You can usually eat good, homely French food, but the real draw is the orchestra. Families, older couples and trendy young things from the city sway with varying degrees of skill to foxtrots, tangos and lots of well-loved accordion numbers – especially good for a Sunday afternoon.

Chez Gégène 162bis quai de Polangis, Joinville-le-Pont ⓣ01.48.83.29.43. Open April–Oct. RER Joinville-le-Pont. Just the other side of the Bois de Vincennes, this original *guinguette* was established in the 1900s, though the band now mixes in pop anthems with the accordion classics. There's a decent restaurant, but the time to come is on Saturday nights (9pm–2am) and Sunday afternoons (3–7pm), when a live band plays ballroom classics and traditional French numbers. Admission €16 for non-diners.

Guinguette de l'Île du Martin-Pêcheur 41 quai Victor-Hugo, Champigny-sur-Marne ⓣ01.49.83.03.02, ⓦwww.guinguette.fr. Dancing mid-March to Dec Thurs–Sat 9.30pm–2am, Sun 2–6pm. RER A2 to Champigny-sur-Marne. Traditional and charming *guinguette* situated on an island in the River Marne. You don't have to dine – or pay – to dance.

Le Petit Robinson 164 quai de Polangis, Joinville-le-Pont ⓣ01.48.89.04.39, ⓦwww.le-petit-robinson.com. Dancing Fri–Sat 9.30pm–2am, Sun 3–7pm. RER Joinville-le-Pont. Fifty metres along from *Chez Gégène* and a bit more upmarket, this is the place where serious dancers go to show off their immaculate waltzes, foxtrots and tangos. Like its neighbour, it has a huge dance floor, but it also boasts a live orchestra and is open year-round. Admission and drink €14–16.

Swimming pools and gyms

For €2.60, you can go swimming in most of Paris's **municipal pools.** If you plan to go swimming a lot, the carnet of ten tickets (each good for one entrance) is good value. **Privately run pools**, whether owned by the city or not, are usually much more expensive.

As for **gyms**, you'll find any number of aerobics classes, dance workouts and anti-stress fitness programmes offered, along with yoga, t'ai chi and martial arts.

Gyms and fitness

Aquaboulevard Map 1, C6. 4 rue Louis-Armand, 15e ⓣ01.40.60.10.00, ⓦwww.aquaboulevard.com. M° Balard/Porte de Versailles/RER Bd-Victor. The biggest in town, with a state-of-the-art fitness centre, squash and tennis courts, a climbing wall, golf tees, aquatic diversions, *hammams*, dance floors, shops and restaurants. To gain access to the full range of facilities, most importantly the gym, you're supposed to be accompanied by a member, but exceptions are sometimes made. €20 for a day pass.

Club Quartier Latin Map 2, H10. 19 rue de Pontoise, 5e ⓣ01.55.42.77.88, ⓦwww.clubquartierlatin.com. Mon–Fri 7am–11.45pm, Sat 10am–6.45pm, Sun 8am–6.45pm. M° Maubert-Mutualité. Dance, gym, swimming and squash; €16 day pass for the pool and gym.

Espace Vit'Halles Map 2, H5. Place Beaubourg, 48 rue Rambuteau, 3e ⓣ01.42.77.21.71, ⓦwww.vithalles.fr. Mon–Fri 8am–10.30pm, Sat 10am–7pm, Sun 10am–6pm. M° Rambuteau. One of the flashiest fitness clubs in the city, with endless classes of every kind, weight rooms, various gyms, a sauna and *hammam*, and everything else you'd expect. Quite popular among Americans. For €20, the day pass gives access to all of the above.

Swimming pools

At weekends, all the municipal pools listed below, except the Butte-aux-Cailles pool, are open Saturday 7am–5.30pm, Sunday 8am–5.30pm; on weekdays, they typically open for an hour in the early morning and at lunch, then close for the morning and afternoon school sessions and re-open in the early evening until about 6–8pm. It's best to ring in advance, check the Mairie's website (ⓦwww.paris.fr) or choose a pool nearby and consult their timetable. Many municipal pools are also closed on Monday in school terms.

Aquaboulevard Map 1, C6. 4 rue Louis-Armand, 15e ⓣ01.40.60.10.00, ⓦwww.aquaboulevard.com. M° Balard/Porte de Versailles/RER Bd-Victor. The private pool has wave machines and some incredible water slides, and there are jacuzzis and a grassy outdoor sunning area. €20 (€10 for children aged 3–11).

Les Amiraux Map 1, F1. 6 rue Hermann-Lachapelle, 18e ⓣ01.42.52.34.20. M° Simplon. Municipal pool where Juliette Binoche memorably swam in the Kieslowski film *Three Colours Blue*.

Butte aux Cailles Map 5, G9. 5 place Paul-Verlaine, 13e ⓣ01.45.89.60.05. Sat 7–8am & 10am–6pm, Sun 8am–5.30pm. M° Place-d'Italie. Housed in a spruced-up 1920s brick building with an Art Deco ceiling, this is one of the most pleasant municipal pools in the city. There's a children's pool inside, and a 25-metre outside pool.

Les Halles Suzanne Berlioux Map 2, G5. 10 place de la Rotonde, niveau 3, Porte du Jour, Forum des Halles, 1er ⓣ01.42.36.98.44. RER Châtelet-Les Halles/M° Châtelet. Very centrally located, this private, 50-metre pool with vaulted concrete ceiling sports a glass wall looking through to a tropical garden. €3.80.

Henry-de-Montherlant Map 1, B3. 32 bd Lannes, 16e ⓣ01.40.72.28.30. M° Porte-Dauphine. This municipal facility has two pools, one 25-metre and one 15-metre, plus a terrace for sunbathing, a solarium – and the Bois de Boulogne close by.

Jean Taris Map 2, G12. 16 rue Thouin, 5e ⓣ01.55.42.81.90. M° Cardinal-Lemoine. A 25-metre unchlorinated municipal pool in the centre of the Latin Quarter. A student favourite, with a small pool for children.

Pontoise-Quartier Latin Map 2, H10. 19 rue de Pontoise, 5e ⓣ01.55.42.77.88. M° Maubert-Mutualité. This private pool offers Art Deco architecture, beautiful blue mosaic interior and a 33-metre pool. On weekdays outside school terms, features night sessions until 11.45pm. Pool €3.80.

Hammams

Hammams, or Turkish baths, are one of the unexpected delights of Paris. Much more luxurious than the standard Swedish sauna, these are places to linger and chat, and you can usually pay extra for a massage and a *gommage* – a rub down with a rubber glove – followed by mint tea to recover. Don't let modesty get the better of you; all are quite restrained in terms of nudity and the staff are consummate professionals. You're provided with a strip of linen, but swimsuits are almost always required for mixed men-and-women sessions.

Les Bains du Marais Map 4, B10. 31–33 rue des Blancs-Manteaux, 4e ⓣ01.44.61.02.02, ⓦwww.lesbainsdumarais.com. M° Rambuteau/St-Paul. As much a posh health club as a *hammam*, with a rather chichi clientele and glorious interior. Offers facials, massage and haircuts, and you can lounge about in a robe with mint tea and a newspaper. Sauna and steam room entry costs €30, massage/*gommage* is €30 extra; there are mixed sessions on Wednesday evenings (7–11pm), Saturdays (10am–8pm) and Sundays (11am–11pm) for which you have to bring a swimsuit.

Hammams des Grands Boulevards Map 3, J8. 28 bd Bonne-Nouvelle, 10^{e} ⓣ01.48.24.33.65, ⓦwww.hammam-paris.com. M° Bonne Nouvelle. Fashionable new *hammam* with a good central location and a range of massage styles on offer, as well as a number of mixed sessions that are ideal for couples. Women: Saturday 1–5pm; mixed (swimsuit obligatory): Monday 2–10pm, Wednesday 1–5pm, Saturday 5–9pm, Sunday 1–9pm; Men: Tuesday 1–10pm & Friday 1–8pm; nude sessions: Wednesday 5–10pm (mixed; female partner obligatory for men), Thursday 1–10pm (mixed). Monday–Wednesday & Friday €21, Thursday, Saturday & Sunday €26; massage, *gommage* and towels €55.

Hammam de la Mosquée Map 2, I13. 39 rue Geoffroy-St-Hilaire, 5e ⓣ01.43.31.38.20. M° Censier-Daubenton. One of the most atmospheric baths in the city, with its vaulted cooling-off room and marble-lined steam chamber, and it's not intimidating if you've never taken a public bath before. It's very good value for €15, though towels are extra, and you can also have a reasonably priced massage and *gommage*. After your bath you can order mint tea and honey cakes around a fountain in the little courtyard café. Times may change, so check first, but generally women: Monday, Wednesday, Thursday & Saturday 10am–9pm, Friday 2–9pm; men: Tuesday 2–9pm, Sunday 10am–9pm.

Blading and skateboarding

Rollerblading has become so popular in Paris that it takes over the streets most Friday nights from 9.45pm, when expert skaters – up to 25,000 on fine evenings – meet on the esplanade of the Gare Montparnasse in the 14^{e} (M° Montparnasse) for a demanding three-hour circuit of the city; check out ⓦwww.pari-roller.com for details. A more sedate outing – and a better choice for families – takes place on Sundays, departing at 2.30pm from the Place de la Bastille and returning at 5.30pm (ⓦwww.rollers-coquillages.org).

The best places to find more information and hire blades (around €10 for a half day) are: Vertical Line, 4 rue de la Bastille, 4e (Ⓣ01.42.74.70.00, Ⓦwww.vertical-line.com; M° Bastille); and Nomades, 37 bd Bourdon, 4e (Ⓣ01.44.54.07.44, Ⓦwww.nomadeshop.com; M° Bastille); both hold their own roller events.

Ice skating

One of Paris's most touted winter attractions is the 200-square-metre **ice-skating rink** suspended between two legs of the **Eiffel Tower**. It can only hold eighty skaters at a time, but at nearly 60m above ground, the rink offers unsurpassed views of the city (Dec to mid-Jan; free admission and skate rental with entrance fee to the tower). Back on the ground, a big **outdoor rink** is set up on place de l'Hôtel de Ville, 3e (Dec to mid-March Mon–Thurs noon–10pm, Fri noon–midnight, Sat 9am–midnight, Sun 9am–10pm; M° Hôtel de Ville); you can hire skates (*patins*) for around €5 (bring your passport) and there's a small section cordoned off for children under 6. You can get on the ice year-round at the **Patinoire de Bercy**, at the Palais Omnisports, 8 bd de Bercy, 12e Ⓣ01.40.02.60.60 (Fri 9.30pm–12.30am, Sat 3–6pm & 9.30pm–12.30am, Wed & Sun 3–6pm; M° Bercy).

Cycling

The Mairie de Paris has made great efforts to introduce dedicated **cycle lanes** in the city, which now add up to some 250km. If you prefer cycling in a more natural environment, the Bois de Boulogne and the Bois de Vincennes have extensive bike tracks. "Paris Breathes," a town hall-sponsored scheme, closes off the following roads on Sundays and public holidays year-round, making them popular places for cyclists and rollerbladers to meet up: the right bank of the Seine in the 8e and 12e arrondissements, along voie Georges Pompidou (9am–7pm); the left bank from quai Anatole-France to quai Branly, in the 7e (9am–7pm); around rue Mouffetard, rue Descartes and rue de l'École Polytechnique in the 5e (10am–6pm); on quai de Valmy and quai de Jemmapes, in the 10e (2–6pm; 2–8pm in summer).

Several outlets detailed below **rent bikes**. Prices average about €15–20 a day. If you want a bike for Sunday, when all of Paris takes to the quais, you'll need to book in advance. Some companies also offer **bike tours**.

Bike 'n' Roller Map 6, D3. 38 rue Fabert, 7e ⓣ01.45.50.38.27, ⓦwww.bikenroller.fr. Daily 10am–7pm. M° Invalides. Also rents out rollerblades.

Bois de Boulogne See p.147. At the roundabout near the Jardin d'Acclimatation. M° Les Sablons. For rides through the wood. €5 for a three-hour rental; bring your passport.

Bois de Vincennes See p.129. M° Porte Dorée. Bikes for the several trails here can be rented from Paris Cycles just at the western entrance to the park at Porte Dorée. €5 for a three-hour rental.

Paris a Vélo C'est Sympa/Vélo Bastille Map 4, D13. 37 bd Bourdon, 4e ⓣ01.48.87.60.01, ⓦwww.parisvelosympa.com. Daily 9am–7pm, closed weekdays 1–2pm. M° Bastille. One of the least expensive (from €24 for the weekend) and most helpful for bike rental. Their excellent three-hour tours of Paris – including one at night and another at dawn – all cost €32.50.

Paris-Vélo Map 2, I14. 2 rue du Fer-à-Moulin, 5e ⓣ01.43.37.59.22. Mon–Sat 10am–12.30pm & 2–7pm. M° Censier-Daubenton. Offers 21-speed and mountain bikes. €14 per day, €64 per week.

25

Kids' Paris

The French are extremely welcoming to **children** on the whole and Paris's vibrant atmosphere, with its street performers and musicians, lively pavement cafés and brightly lit carousels is certainly family friendly. The obvious pull of Disneyland aside (covered in Chapter 00), there are plenty of other attractions and activities to keep kids happy, from circuses to rollerblading. As you'd expect, museum-hopping with youngsters in Paris can be as tedious as in any other big city, but remember that while the Louvre and Musée d'Orsay cater to more acquired tastes, the Musée des Arts et Métiers, the Pompidou Centre, Parc de la Villette and some of the other attractions listed below will interest children and adults alike. Travelling with a child also provides the perfect excuse to enjoy some of the simpler pleasures of city life – the playgrounds, ice-cream cones, toy shops and pastries that Paris seems to offer in endless abundance.

In terms of **practicalities**, many cafés, bars or restaurants offer *menus enfants* (special children's set menus) or are often willing to cook simpler food on request, and hotels tack only a small supplement for an additional bed or cot on to the regular room rate. You should have no difficulty finding disposable nappies/diapers, baby foods and milk powders for infants. Throughout the city the RATP (Paris Transport) charges half-fares for 4- to 10-year-olds; under-4 travel free. It's worth remembering that **Wednesday afternoons**, when primary school children have free time, and **Saturdays** are the peak times for children's activities and entertainment; Wednesdays continue to be child-centred even during the school holidays.

Parks and gardens

Children are well catered to by the **parks and gardens** within the city. There's even a park designed especially for kids, the **Jardin d'Acclimatation**, in the Bois de Boulogne, with an impressive array of activities and attractions. On the other side of the city in the Bois de Vincennes, the **Parc Floral** also offers a host of treats, and the high-tech **Parc de la Villette** (described on pp.133–137), in the northeast, will keep children entertained for hours. Most of the city's other parks have some activities for children, usually an enclosed playground with swings, climbing frames and often a sandpit. Many also have **guignol** (puppet) shows, the French equivalent of Punch and Judy.

The Jardin d'Acclimatation Map 1, B3–4. Bois de Boulogne. €2.70, under-3s free; rides €2.50, or buy a carnet of 15 tickets for €30; ⓦwww.jardindacclimatation.fr. M° Les Sablons & M° Porte-Maillot. A little train takes you there from M° Porte-Maillot (behind L'Orée du Bois restaurant) 11am–6pm (every 15min); €5.20 return, includes admission. Daily: June–Sept 10am–7pm, Oct–May 10am–6pm; special attractions Wed, Sat, Sun & all week during school hols. The Jardin d'Acclimatation is a cross between a funfair, zoo and amusement park, with temptations ranging from bumper cars, go-karts, pony and camel rides, sea lions, birds, bears and monkeys, to a magical mini-canal ride ("la rivière enchantée"), distorting mirrors, a huge trampoline, scaled-down farm buildings and a puppet theatre. There are also two museums: the high-tech Exploradôme (daily 10am–6pm; e5, free for under-4s) is designed to help children discover science, the five human senses and art, through interactive computer-based exhibits and the usual array of hands-on activities. The Musée en Herbe (Mon–Fri & Sun 10am–6pm, Sat 2–6pm) aims to bring art history alive through workshops and games. The park also has its own theatre, the Théâtre du Jardin, which puts on musicals, ballets and poetry readings. Outside the *jardin*, in the Bois de Boulogne (see p.147), older children can amuse themselves with mini-golf and bowling, boating on the Lac Inférieur or roaming the wood's 14km of cycle trails (rentals near the entrance to the *jardin*; bring your passport).

Free guignol puppet shows in the Jardin d'Acclimatation take place at 3pm and 4pm daily during the school holidays and on Wednesday and weekend afternoons year round; see the "Enfants" section of Pariscope for more details.

Parc Floral Map 1, H–I6. Bois de Vincennes, on rte de la Pyramide (Mº Château-de-Vincennes, then bus #112 or a 10min walk past the Château Vincennes). Daily: March–Sept 9.30am–7pm; Oct–Feb 9.30am–5pm. €1, 7- to 26-year-olds €0.50 plus supplements for some activities, under-7s free. Ⓦwww.parcfloraldeparis.com. To the delight of kids, the Parc Floral has much more than just flowers. It's known for its excellent playground, with slides, swings, ping-pong (racket and ball €6) and pedal carts (from 2pm; €7–10 per 30min), mini-golf (from 2pm; €5, children under 12 €3), an electric car circuit, and a little train touring all the gardens (April–Oct daily 1–5pm; €1). Tickets for the paying activities are sold at the playground between 2 and 5.30pm weekdays and until 7pm on weekends; activities stop fifteen minutes afterwards. Note that many of these activities are available from March/April to August only and on Wednesdays and weekends only in September and October. On Wednesdays at 2.30pm (May–Sept) there are free performances by clowns, puppets and magicians. A further programme of mime and other shows is put on at the Théâtre Astral (Wed & Sun 3pm, school hols Mon–Fri & Sun 3pm; €6; Ⓣ01.43.71.31.10). Another hit with kids is the wonderful *butterfly garden* (mid-May to mid-Oct Mon–Fri 1.30–5.15pm, Sat & Sun 1.30–6pm).

Jardin des Enfants aux Halles Map 2, F–G4. 105 rue Rambuteau, 1er Ⓣ01.45.08.07.18. Mº/RER Châtelet-Les Halles. April–Oct Tues, Thurs & Fri 9am–noon & 2–6pm, Sat & Wed 10am–6pm, Sun & hols 1–6pm; Nov–March till 4pm; closed Mon & during bad weather; €0.50 for a 1hr slot; 7- to 15-year-olds only except Sat am. Right in the centre of town, just west of the Forum des Halles, the Jardin des Enfants aux Halles is a series of cleverly designed fantasy landscapes supervised by professional child-carers. In order to drop off your child, you have to reserve a place an hour or so in advance. Under-7s are allowed in on Saturday mornings (10am–2pm) only, provided they are accompanied by an adult. Several languages are spoken, including English. Opening times vary a little in the middle of the day, so it might be best to phone ahead, but in any case you'll want to arrive early as only sixty kids are allowed in per hour and it's quite popular.

Funfairs

Three big **funfairs** (*fête foraines*) take place in Paris each year. The season kicks off in late March with the Fête du Trône in the Bois de Vincennes (running until late May), followed by the funfair in the Tuileries gardens in mid-June to late August, with more than forty rides including a giant ferris wheel, and ending up with the Fête à Neu Neu, held near the Bois de Boulogne from early September to the beginning of October. Look up "Fêtes Populaires" under "Agendas" in *Pariscope* for details if you're in town at these times.

Out of season, rue de Rivoli around M° St-Paul occasionally hosts a mini-fairground, and there's usually a merry-go-round at the Forum des Halles and beneath Tour St-Jacques at Châtelet. Merry-go-rounds for smaller children are to be found on place de la République, at the Rond-Point des Champs-Élysées by avenue Matignon, at place de la Nation, and at the base of the Montmartre funicular in place St-Pierre.

Circuses

Circuses (*cirques*) are taken seriously in France and come under the heading of culture as performance art (and there are no qualms about performing animals). As circuses tend to travel, you'll find details of the seasonal ones under "Cirques" in the "Jeunes" section of *L'Officiel des Spectacles* and under the same heading in the "Enfants" section of *Pariscope*. The Cirque Diana Moreno Bormann, Grands Sablons, at the Jardin d'Acclimatation, 16e (Ⓦwww.cirque-diana-moreno.com; M° Sablons) is a perennial favorite; admission prices start at €10.

Museums

One of the city's best treats for children of every age from 3 upwards is the **Cité des Sciences** (described on pp.133–136) in the Parc de la Villette. Most children will also enjoy the **Grande Galerie de l'Evolution** (see p.90), which has a children's discovery room on the first floor with child-level microscopes, glass cases with live caterpillars and moths and a burrow of Mongolian rodents. The **Pompidou Centre** (see p.66) has a children's *espace*, consisting of a room filled with hands-on exhibits. Paris has two excellent **planetariums**, in the Palais de la Découverte (see p.49) and the Cité des Sciences (p.135). Two fun ways for children to find out about Paris itself and its history are the **Paris-Story** (see p.58), an enjoyable, if highly romanticized, 45-minute, wide-screen film on the history of Paris; and the Musée Grévin (see p.57), with its mock-ups of key events in French history, especially the more grisly ones.

For a more earthy experience, you could visit **les égouts** – the sewers – at place de la Résistance, in the 7e. Dank, damp, dripping, claustrophobic and filled with echoes, this is just the sort of place pre-teens love; for further details, see p.105. Another underground experience popular with youngsters is the **catacombs** at 1 place Denfert-Rochereau, 14e, described on p.115.

Shops

The fact that Paris is filled with beautiful, enticing, delicious and expensive things all artfully displayed is not lost on most modern youngsters. Below is a small selection of shops to seek out, be dragged into or to avoid at all costs.

Books

The following stock a good selection of English books.

Brentano's Map 3, E9. 37 av de l'Opéra, 2e ⓦwww.brentanos.fr. M° Opéra. Mon–Sat 10am–7.30pm. Story-telling sessions, singing and crafts on Wednesday afternoons and Saturday mornings. Check on the website for details.

Chantelivre Map 2, B9.13 rue de Sèvres, 6e. M° Sèvres-Babylone. Mon 1–6.50pm, Tues–Sat 10am–6.50pm; closed mid-Aug. A huge selection of everything to do with and for children, including good picture books for the younger ones, an English section, and a play area.

Toys and games

In addition to the shops below, be sure to check out the superb selection of toys at the department stores Le Bon Marché and Samaritaine, the latter of which even has an entertainment section to keep your kids occupied while you try out some retail therapy.

Le Ciel Est à Tout le Monde Map 2, F12. 10 rue Gay-Lussac, 5e ⓦwww.lecielestatoutlemonde.com (RER Luxembourg); 7 av Trudaine, 9e ⓣ01.48.78.93.40 (M° Anvers). Mon–Sat 10am–7pm. The best kite shop in Europe also sells frisbees, boomerangs, etc, and, next door, books, slippers, mobiles and traditional wooden toys.

JouéClub Map 3, G8. Passage des Princes, 2e. M° Richelieu-Drouot. Mon–Sat 10am–8pm. This toy emporium is the largest in Paris and takes up the whole of the renovated passage des Princes. This is the place to buy French Trivial Pursuit or two-thousand-piece jigsaws of French paintings such as Renoir's *Moulin de la Galette* (€19).

Au Nain Bleu Map 7, N4. 406–410 rue St-Honoré, 8e ⓦwww.au-nain-bleu.com. M° Madeleine. Mon–Sat 10am–6.30pm; closed Mon in Aug. Since opening in the 1830s, Au

Nain Bleu has become expert at delighting children with wooden toys, dolls and faux-china tea-sets galore.

Pains d'Epices Map 3, H8. 29 passage Jouffroy, 9e. M° Grands-Boulevards. Mon 12.30–7pm, Tues–Sat 10am–7pm, Thurs 10am–9pm. Fabulous dolls' house necessities from furniture to wine glasses, and puppets.

Puzzles Michèle Wilson Map 6, F14.116 rue du Château, 14e ⓦwww.pmw.fr. M° Pernety. Mon & Wed–Sat 9am–7pm, Tues 10am–7pm. Puzzles galore and a workshop on the premises.

Si Tu Veux Map 2, 1E. 68 galerie Vivienne, 2e ⓣ01.42.60.59.97. M° Bourse. Mon–Sat 10.30am–7pm. Well-made traditional toys, plus do-it-yourself and ready-made costumes.

Clothes

Besides the specialist shops listed here, most of the big department stores and the discount shops have children's sections.

agnès b. Map 2, F4. 2 rue du Jour, 1er. M°/RER Châtelet-Les Halles. Mon–Sat 10am–7pm. Very fashionable and desirable clothes as you'd expect from this chic Parisian designer. Just opposite is Le Petit B for babies, selling lots of very French-looking outfits in navy-blue and white.

Bain – Plus Enfants Map B10. 23 rue des Blancs Manteaux, 4e. M° Hôtel de Ville. Tues–Sat 11am–7.30pm. Aimed at infants to 12 year-olds, this stylish shop has an irresistible range of bed and bath items: chic pyjamas, hooded robes, fluffy towels and cuddly bears.

Du Pareil au Même Map 4, G13. 122 rue du Faubourg-St-Antoine, 12e ⓦwww.dpam.fr. M° Ledru-Rollin. Mon–Sat 10am–7pm. Beautiful kids' clothing at very good prices. Gorgeous inexpensive floral dresses, cute jogging suits, and bright-coloured basics. Branches all over Paris.

Pom d'Api Map 2, F4. 13 rue du Jour, 1er. M°/RER Châtelet-Les Halles. Mon–Sat 10.30am–7pm. The most colourful, imaginative and well-made shoes for kids in Paris, up to size 40/UK7, and from €40.

See Chapter 21 for listings of department stores and other clothes shops.

26

Gay and lesbian Paris

Paris is one of the world's best cities in which to be **gay**, with numerous bars, clubs, restaurants, saunas and shops catering to a gay clientele. The focal point of the gay scene is the **Marais**, whose central street, rue Ste-Croix-de-la-Bretonnerie, has visibly gay-oriented businesses at almost every other address. **Lesbians** are less well served commercially.

In general, the French consider sexuality to be a private matter, and most Parisians are remarkably tolerant. **Legally**, homosexuality was decriminalized over twenty years ago, and the age of consent is now fixed at 16.

The high points on the calendar are the huge annual **Marche des Fiertés LGBT**, or gay pride march, which normally takes place on the last Saturday in June, and the **Bastille Day Ball** (July 13, 10pm–dawn), a wild open-air dance on the quai de la Tournelle, 5ᵉ (M° Pont-Marie), which is free for all to join in.

Information and contacts

The gay and lesbian community is well catered for by the **media**, most prominently by *Têtu*, France's main gay monthly, and *Lesbia*, both available from most newsagents. Listed below are a handful of the most useful contacts.

Useful contacts and organizations

Association des Médecins Gais (AMG) 48 rue Damrémont, 11e ⓣ01.48.05.81.71. ⓦwww.medecins-gays.org. M° Lamarck-Caulaincourt. Telephone lines Wed 6–8pm, Sat 2–4pm. Gay doctors' association, offering help with all health concerns relative to the gay community.

Centre Gai et Lesbien de Paris 3 rue Keller, 11e ⓣ01.43.57.21.47, ⓦwww.cglparis.org. M° Bastille/Ledru-Rollin/Voltaire. Open Mon–Sat 4–8pm. Fights for political rights and acts as a first port-of-call for information and advice – legal, social, psychological and medical. Also has a good library and puts on small exhibitions.

Inter-LGBT 127 rue Amelot, 11e ⓣ01.53.01.47.01, ⓦwww.inter-lgbt.org. M° St-Sébastien-Froissart. Fights for gay rights and organizes the annual pride march.

Maison des Femmes 163 rue de Charenton, 12e ⓣ01.43.43.41.13, ⓦhttp://maisondesfemmes.free.fr. M° Reuilly-Diderot. Mon–Wed 9am–7pm, Thurs & Fri 9am–5pm. The main women's centre in Paris and home to a number of lesbian groups, who organize workshops and meetings. Frequent gay/straight lunches and parties, too.

Les Mots à la Bouche 6 rue Ste-Croix-de-la-Bretonnerie, 4e ⓣ01.42.78.88.30, ⓦwww.motsbouche.com. M° Hôtel-de-Ville. Mon–Sat 11am–11pm, Sun 2–8pm. The main gay and lesbian bookshop, with exhibition space and meeting rooms; a selection of literature in English, too. Lots of free listings maps and club flyers to pick up, and one of the helpful assistants usually speaks English.

Pharmacie du Village 26 rue du Temple, 4e ⓣ01.42.72.60.71. M° Hôtel-de-Ville. Mon–Sat 8.30am–9.30pm, Sun 9am–8pm. Gay-run pharmacy.

SOS Homophobie ⓣ0810.108.135,ⓦwww.france.qrd.org/assocs/sos/. From mobiles call ⓣ01.48.06.42.41. Mon–Fri & Sun 8–10pm, Sat 2–4pm. First-stop helpline for victims of homophobia, with a local-rate call number.

The media and websites

Citegay Ⓦ **http://citegay.fr** One of the best websites, with lots of links, features and contacts.
e.m@le Free gay and lesbian paper with cultural and nightlife listings, small ads, lonely hearts, services, etc. Comes out every Thursday.
Lesbia Ⓦ **www.lesbiamag.com.** France's leading lesbian monthly. **MAG 106 rue de Montreuil, 11e** Ⓣ **01.43.73.31.63,** Ⓦ **www.mag-paris.org.** Useful online magazine from the Mouvement d'Affirmation des Jeunes Gais et Lesbiennes, a group aimed at young people that organizes occasional tea dances, picnics, and cinema and theatre nights.
Paris Gay Ⓦ **www.paris-gay.com.** Major portal for gay tourists visiting Paris. The online *Guide Gay* has lots of reviews of bars, restaurants, clubs, saunas, etc, though the English translations tend to be rather brief.
Têtu Ⓦ **www.tetu.com.** The glossiest and most readable of France's gay monthlies – the name means "headstrong". The pull-out section, "Agenda", is full of contact details, addresses and reviews, though it's not restricted to Paris.

Nightlife

Parisians like to complain about the bar scene in Paris relative to rival cities like London or New York, but in truth there's a good range of gay bars, especially in the "pink triangle" of the Marais. The reputation of wild hedonism in gay **clubs** has spread beyond the gay community and attracted heterosexuals in search of a good time. Consequently, straights are welcome in some gay establishments – in fact, some clubs have all but abandoned a gay-only policy – the legendary *Le Queen*, for instance, is gay-only just on weekends and Wednesdays now. Check the main club listings on pp.236–238, and keep an eye out for events at *Le Cab*, *Le Twin's* and *La Scène Bastille* in particular.

Mainly women – bars

3W-Kafé Map 4, B11. 8 rue des Ecouffes, 4e ☎01.48.87.39.26. M° Hôtel-de-Ville. Daily 5.30pm–2am. The ex-*Scandaleuses* has had a designer makeover, turning itself into a swish lipstick-lesbian lounge-café. Sophisticated professionals earlier on, but it warms up considerably at weekends, when the cellar bar gets moving.

Bliss Kfé Map 4, B11. 30 rue du Roi de Sicile, 3e ☎01.42.78.49.36. M° St-Paul. Daily 5pm–2am. Small, laid-back bar with a good programme of DJ *soirées*, massage sessions and so on. Draws a friendly, fairly cool crowd of lesbians, straights and gay guys. At weekends, a surprisingly large number of people squeeze in, spilling down the stairs into the cellar bar later on.

Boobsbourg Map 4, A8. 26 rue de Montmorency, 3e ☎01.42.74.04.82. M° Rambuteau. Tues–Sat 5pm–2am. Fashionable mainly lesbian bar, with good food, classy decor and a chic young clientele. Comfy sofas on the first-floor level.

Mainly men – bars

Amnesia Café Map 4, B10. 42 rue Vieille-du-Temple, 4e ☎01.42.72.16.94. M° St-Paul. Daily 11am–2am. Pleasantly trashy gay bar with a relaxed, largely Parisian clientele lounging around on sofas. Later on, the tiny dancefloor in the basement pulls in happy good-timers with a noisy, camp playlist.

Café Cox Map 4, A10. 15 rue des Archives, 3e ☎01.42.72.08.00. M° Hôtel-de-Ville. Daily noon–2am. Muscular, shaved-head body-beautiful clientele up for a seriously good time. Friendly – if your face fits – and has DJs on weekend nights.

Le Carré Map 4, A10. 18 rue du Temple, 4e ☎01.44.59.38.57. M° Hôtel-de-Ville. Daily 10am–4am. Stylish, designer café with good food, comfortable chairs, cool lighting, an excellent *terrasse* on the street, and occasional video projects or fashion shows on the side. Mostly full of sophisticated, good-looking Parisians, but the occasional clued-up tourist finds their way here too.

Le Central Map 4, B10. 33 rue Vieille-du-Temple, 4e ☎01.48.87.99.33. M° Hôtel-de-Ville. Fri–Sun 2pm–2am, Mon–Thurs 4pm–2am. The oldest gay local in the Marais. Small, relatively quiet, friendly and always crowded with tourists and Parisians.

Le Duplex Map 4, A8. 25 rue Michel-le-Comte, 3e ☎01.42.72.80.86. M° Rambuteau. Fri & Sat 8pm–4am, Sun–Thurs 8pm–2am. Popular with intellectual or media types for its relatively relaxed and chatty atmosphere. Friendly rather than cruisy – the barmen know all the regulars by name.

Le Mixer Map 4, A10. 23 rue Ste-Croix-de-la-Bretonnerie, 4e ☎01.42.78.26.20. M° Hôtel-de-Ville. Daily 5pm–2am. Popular and crowded Marais bar with a high-tech decor and a mezzanine level looking down on the bar area. Some say the name comes from the DJ on his podium, raising the pulse of the crowd with a techno and house soundtrack, others from the clientele, which is – unusually for Paris – a genuine mix of gay, straight, black, white, whatever.

L'Open Café Map 4, B8. 17 rue des Archives, 3e ☎01.48.87.80.25. M° Arts-et-Métiers. Tues–Sun 5pm–2am. The first gay café-bar to have tables out on the pavement, and they're still there, with overhead heaters in winter. *L'Open* is *the* most famous gay bar in Paris and, as such, it's expensive and quite touristy, but still fairly cool.

Le Raidd Map 4, A10. 23 rue du Temple, 4e. M° Hôtel-de-Ville. Daily 5pm–2am. All new, and instantly one of the city's premier gay bars, famous for its beautiful staff, topless waiters and go-go boys' shower shows.

Clubs

Amnésia Map 6, G10. 24 rue de l'Arrivée, 15e ☎01.56.80.37.37. M° Montparnasse-Bienvenüe. Tues–Sat 11.30am–6am, Sun 7pm–2am; €20. It was somehow inevitable that Spray, the Sunday "tea dance" (7pm–2am) at Johnny Hallyday's South Beach-themed nightclub, would become one of the hottest events on Paris's gay scene – though be warned that things change fast. Druggy and dance-oriented.

Le Folie's Pigalle Map 3, F4. 11 place Pigalle, 9e ☎01.48.78.25.26. M° Pigalle. Fri & Sat midnight–noon, Sun 6pm–6am, Mon–Thurs midnight–6am; €20. You really have to find out what's on when to get the best out of this former cabaret turned nightclub. There are frequent, early-morning *after* events, which can be superbly trashy, and big, if occasional, themed gay events.

L'Insolite Map 2, D2. 33 rue des Petits-Champs, 1er ☎01.40.20.98.59. M° Pyramides. Daily 11pm–5am; €15–20. Dinky little basement club pulling in a chatty, international mixed crowd, from beautifully dressed PR execs to guys in vests. A classic venue with a lively dance floor. Busy right through the week.

Le Pulp Map 3, I8. 25 bd Poissonnière, 2e ☎01.40.26.01.93. M° Bonne Nouv-

elle. **Wed–Sat midnight–6am; Fri & Sat €9.** Paris's lesbian club par excellence, playing music from techno to Madonna. So cool that it pulls in a huge straight crowd on the free Wednesday (rock) and Thursday (electro) nights.

Le Queen Map 7, G3. 102 av Champs-Elysées, 8e ⓣ01.53.89.08.89, ⓦwww.queen.fr. M° George-V. Daily midnight–6am; €10–20. Le Queen has been far too successful to resist going mainstream, and the decor hasn't really changed since its early 1990s heyday, but it still runs gay R&B nights on Wednesday, and massive, loved-up and very gay house events on Saturday and Sunday.

Le Redlight Map 6, G10. 34 rue du Départ, 14e ⓣ01.42.79.94.53. M° Montparnasse-Bienvenüe. Fri & Sat midnight–noon, Thurs & Sun midnight–6am; €20. Huge club with a serious sound system and two dance floors. The industrial decor fits the largely deep house music policy, though Fridays are more mixed, both in terms of music policy (garage, R&B) and sexual orientation (straights from the suburbs too).

Le Tango Map 4, B7. 13 rue au-Maire, 3e ⓣ01.42.72.17.78. M° Arts-et-Métiers. Fri & Sat 10.30pm–dawn, Sun 5pm–5am; €6.50. Gay and lesbian club with a traditional Sunday afternoon *bal* from 5pm, featuring proper slow dances as well as tangos and camp 1970s and 1980s disco classics. Turns into a full-on club later on, and on Friday and Saturday nights.

Hotels and restaurants

Although gays and lesbians aren't likely to come across any anti-social behaviour in **hotels** and **restaurants**, there is a choice of gay-oriented places to stay and eat in should you wish. You don't need to look any further than the Marais.

Hotels

Hôtel Beaumarchais Map 4, E8. 3 rue Oberkampf, 11e ⓣ01.53.36.86.86, ⓦwww.hotelbeaumarchais.com. M° Filles-du-Calvaire/Oberkampf. **See p.185.**

Hôtel Central Marais Map 4, B10. 33 rue Vieille-du-Temple, 4e ⓣ01.48.87.56.08, ⓦwww.hotelcentralmarais.com. M° Hôtel-de-Ville. **See p.178.**

Restaurants

B4 Le Resto Map 4, A10. 6–8 rue Ste-Croix-de-la-Bretonnerie, 4e ⓣ01.42.72.16.19. M° Hôtel-de-Ville. Daily noon–2.30pm & 7.30–11.30pm. Stylish, up-front café-restaurant with a chic modern decor and a stylish up-front clientele. At lunch and dinner there's delicious modern Mediterranean cuisine. Count on around €30–40 à la carte.

La Coupe Gorge Map 2, H6. Rue de la Coutellerie, 4e ⓣ01.48.04.79.24. M° Hôtel-de-Ville. Mon–Fri noon–2.30pm & 7.30pm–midnight, Sat & Sun 7.30pm–midnight; closed Aug. Traditional in cuisine and decor, with its old-style *zinc* bar counter, rustic upstairs room and great dishes such as *magret de canard*. Set menu at €16.

Le Loup Blanc Map 2, G3. 42 rue Tiquetonne, 2e ⓣ01.40.13.08.35. M° Étienne Marcel. Daily 7.30pm–midnight, Sun brunch 11am–4.30pm. Bustling, trendy restaurant with changing artwork on the walls. Attracts a fun, camp crowd, and serves great *assiettes* of grilled and marinated meats and fish (€10–15), with a selection of delicious sauces on the side.

La Maison Rouge Map 4, A10. 13 rue des Archives, 4e ⓣ01.42.71.69.69. M° Hôtel-de-Ville. Daily noon–midnight. New and trendy restaurant full of the beautiful and well dressed. The food's good too, largely fresh, light and Mediterranean. You'll spend €20–40 for a meal.

Gyms, saunas and sex clubs

Paris's proud history as the erotic capital of Europe is reflected in the modern-day plethora of gay **saunas**, **gyms** and straight-ahead **sex clubs**. A handful of stand-out venues are listed.

Venues

Le Depôt Map 2, H4. 10 rue aux Ours, 3e ⓦwww.ledepot.com. M° Étienne-Marcel/Rambuteau. Daily 2pm–8am. A Parisian institution, this is allegedly "Europe's biggest backroom", spread over a maze of different rooms and levels, with a pumping dance floor. It's usually packed – you'll have to queue for a cubicle, though it's not obligatory. €6–10.

IDM Map 3, H8. 4 rue du Fau-

bourg-Montmartre, 9^{e}. M° Grands Boulevards. Daily noon–1am, Sun 6am–2am. This gay gym and sauna has been well established for some thirty years, and it's still going strong with its beautiful, posey clientele, restaurant, basement backroom, "toy" rooms and, lest it be forgotten, its well-equipped gym. €10–18.

Le Next Map 2, F5. 87 rue St-Honoré, 1er. M° Louvre-Rivoli. Mon–Fri & Sun noon–5am, Sat noon–7am. Brand-new and hence well-equipped sex club with a funky red-and-black decor, dance floor, private cabins and video backroom. €4.50.

Sun City Map 2, H4. 62 bd de Sébastopol, 3e. M° Étienne-Marcel. Daily noon-2am. This huge, Indian-themed sauna on three levels was opened in 2005 by Le Depôt, to lots of media fanfare. With a swimming pool, cinema, jacuzzi and three-room *hammam*, it's likely to become the place to be. €9-15.

Univers Gym Map 2, E4. 20–22 rue des Bons-Enfants, 1er ⓦwww.univers.net. M° Palais-Royal/Les Halles. Mon–Sat noon–2am, Sun 6am–2am. Much more than just a gym, this is a sauna, café and tanning centre, with personal trainers and hairdressers on hand – and a most beautiful clientele. Very flash and very sociable, with frequent party events. €7–17.50.

27

Classical music and opera

Classical music, as you might expect in this Neoclassical city, is alive and well and takes up twice as much room as jazz, pop, folk and rock in the listings magazines. The Paris Opéra, with its two homes – the Palais Garnier and Opéra Bastille – puts on a fine selection of **opera and ballet** and is in for an exciting time under its new, adventurous director Gérard Mortier. The choice of concerts is enormous, ranging from free recitals in the city's atmospheric churches to performances by international names and orchestras, staged in prestigious venues such as the Salle Pleyel and Théâtre des Champs-Élysées. Excellent chamber music can be heard in the fine settings of the Musée du Louvre, Musée d'Orsay and a number of other museums. The capital's two main **orchestras** are the Orchestre de Paris, which has built up a formidable reputation under the leadership of Christopher Eschenbach, and the Orchestre National de France, under the baton of Kurt Masur. If you're interested in the **contemporary** scene of systems composition and the like, check out the state-sponsored experiments at IRCAM, and L'Ensemble Intercontemporain at La Villette's Cité de la Musique.

The city hosts a good number of music **festivals**; the major ones are listed on pp.274–278. One of the most popular is the **Fête de la Musique** held on June 21, a day of music-making throughout the capital. For details of this and other festivals pick up the current year's festival schedule from one of the tourist offices or the Hôtel de Ville.

Tickets for classical concerts in the auditoriums and theatres listed below are best bought at the box offices or FNAC (see pp.257 & 263) or Virgin Megastore (see p.263), though for big names you may find overnight queues, and a large number of seats are always booked by subscribers. The price range is very reasonable. There's often no admission fee for recitals in churches and you can sometimes get free tickets for live broadcasts at the Maison de la Radio, 166 av du Président-Kennedy, 16e; ⓣ01.56.40.15.16, ⓦwww.radiofrance.fr (map 1, C5; M° Passy). All you have to do is turn up half an hour in advance at the Salle Olivier Messiaen to secure a yellow *carton d'invitation*. All concerts are detailed in the **listings magazines** (see p.22).

Classical music venues

Cité de la Musique Map 1, H2. 221 av Jean-Jaurès, 19e ⓣ01.44.84.44.84, ⓦwww.cite-musique.fr. M° Porte-de-Pantin. €16–35. The Cité de la Musique's main concert hall, the Salle des Concerts, has seating for up to 1200 listeners depending on the programme, which can cover anything from traditional Korean music to the contemporary sounds of the centre's own *Ensemble Intercontemporain*. Performances also take place in the museum amphitheatre.

Conservatoire National Supérieur de Musique et de Danse de Paris Map 1, G2. 209 av Jean Jaurès, 19e ⓣ01.40.40.46.46, ⓦwww.cite-musique.fr. M° Porte-de-Pantin. Free. Debates, masterclasses and free recitals from the Conservatoire's students.

IRCAM (Institut de Recherche et Coordination Acoustique/Musique) Map 2, H5. 1 place Igor Stravinsky,

4e ⓣ01.44.78.48.16, ⓦwww.ircam.fr. M° Hôtel-de-Ville. From around €12. IRCAM, the experimental music laboratory set up by Pierre Boulez, hosts regular concerts and also performs in the main hall (Grande Salle) of the nearby Pompidou Centre.

Musée Carnavalet Map 4, C10. 23 rue de Sévigné, 3e ⓣ01.48.04.85.94. M° Saint-Paul. €8–13. Mainly chamber music from the Baroque period, held in one of the museum's elegant salons.

Musée du Louvre Map 2, D5. Palais du Louvre, 1er (Pyramid entrance) ⓣ01.40.20.84.00, ⓦwww.louvre.fr. M° Louvre-Rivoli & M° Palais-Royal-Musée-du-Louvre. Around €10. Midday and evening concerts of chamber music in the auditorium.

Musée d'Orsay Map 2, B5. 1 rue de Bellechasse, 7e ⓣ01.40.49.47.17, ⓦwww.musee-orsay.fr. M° Solférino & RER Musée-d'Orsay. €6–25. Varied programme of midday and evening concerts in the auditorium.

St-Julien-le-Pauvre Map 2, G9. 23 quai de Montebello, 5e ⓣ01.42.08.49.00. M° St-Michel. €13–23. Mostly chamber music and choral recitals.

St-Séverin Map 2, G9. 1 rue des Prêtres St-Séverin, 5e ⓣ01.48.24.16.97. M° St-Michel. €15–23. Varied programmes.

Ste-Chapelle Map 2, F7. 4 bd du Palais, 1er ⓣ01.42.77.65.65. M° Cité. €10–25. A fabulous setting for mainly Mozart, Bach and Vivaldi classics.

Salle Gaveau Map 7, J2. 45 rue de la Boétie, 8e ⓣ01.49.53.05.07, ⓦwww.sallegaveau.com. M° Miromesnil. From €15. Recently renovated, this atmospheric and intimate concert hall, built in 1907, is a major venue for piano recitals by world-class players, such as Stephen Kovacevich, as well as chamber music recitals and full-scale orchestral works.

Salle Pleyel Map 7, G1. 252 rue du Faubourg-St-Honoré, 8e ⓣ01.45.61.53.00. M° Ternes. €15–45. Along with visiting international performers, the Orchestre de Paris, the city's top orchestra, performs most frequently at this venerable concert hall, dating back to 1927.

Théâtre des Champs-Élysées Map 7, G5. 15 av Montaigne, 8e ⓣ01.49.52.50.50, ⓦwww.theatrechampselysees.fr. M° Alma-Marceau. €5–150 A two-thousand-seat capacity in this historic theatre built in 1913. Home to the Orchestre National de France and the Orchestre Lamoureux, but also welcomes international superstar conductors, ballet troupes and opera companies. Buying the lowest-priced tickets will mean you won't have a view, but on average you can reckon

on €30 for a decent seat.
Théâtre Musical de Paris Map 2, G6. Théâtre du Châtelet, 1 place du Châtelet, 1er ⓣ01.40.28.28.00, ⓦwww.chatelet-theatre.com M° Châtelet. From €8. A prestigious concert hall with a varied programme of high-profile operas, ballets, concerts and solo recitals.

Opera

The **Opéra National** de Paris has two homes: the original **Palais Garnier**; and the newer **Opéra Bastille**, Mitterrand's most extravagant legacy to the city. In addition to these main venues, operas are regularly hosted by the **Théâtre des Champs Élysées** (see p.305) and the **Théâtre Musical de Paris** (see above). The **Opéra Comique** (see p.271) gives a platform to solo singers and also puts on opéra bouffe and operettas.

Palais Garnier Map 3, E8. Place de l'Opéra, 9e. M° Opéra. With the arrival of the Bastille opera house, the lavishly refurbished old Palais Garnier tends to concentrate on smaller-scale operatic and ballet productions.
Opéra Bastille Map 4, E13–F14. 120 rue de Lyon, 12e. M° Bastille. Despite the inevitable discussion about the acoustics of the new opera house, opened in 1989, the Bastille orchestra is first rate and nearly every performance is a sell-out. The current musical director, the controversial

Tickets for the Opéra National

Tickets (€5–160) for operas at both venues can be booked Monday to Saturday 9am to 7pm on ⓣ08.36.69.78.68 at least four weeks in advance; via the Internet (ⓦwww.operadeparis.fr) from three months to three days in advance; or at the ticket office (Mon–Sat 11am–6.30pm) within two weeks of the performance – the number of tickets available by this stage, however, is limited. Unfilled seats are sold at a discount to students five minutes before the curtain goes up. For programme details, have a look at their website or call the above number.

Belgian, Gérard Mortier, has been pulling audiences in with some daring and unusual offerings. His first season in 2004, for example, included a six-hour *Saint François d'Assise* by Messiaen and a wacky production of Mozart's *Magic Flute* featuring punks skating on stage, breasts beamed onto video screens and swinging acrobats, while 2005 saw a sell-out performance of Wagner's *Tristan and Isolde*, directed by Peter Sellars and designed by the video artist Bill Viola.

Directory

AIDS/HIV see p.311.

Addresses Paris is divided into twenty districts, or arrondissements. The first arrondissement, or 1er, is centred on the Louvre, in the heart of the city. The rest wind outwards in a clockwise direction like a snail's shell: the 2e, 3e and 4e are in the centre; the 5e, 6e and 7e lie on the inner part of the Left (south) Bank; while the 8e–20e make up the outer districts. Parisian addresses always quote the arrondissement, along with the nearest métro station or stations.

Airport information see pp.15–17.

Banks and exchange On the whole, the best exchange rates are offered by banks, though there's always a commission charge on top. Be wary of bureaux de change, which cluster around arrival points and tourist spots, as they can really rip you off. Standard banking hours are Monday to Friday from 9am to 4 or 5pm, though some may close for lunch. A few are open on Saturday from 9am to noon; all are closed on Sunday and bank holidays. Money-exchange bureaux stay open until 6 or 7pm, tend not to close for lunch and may even open on Sundays in the more touristy areas.

Crime Petty theft sometimes occurs on the métro, at train stations, around Les Halles and at tourist hotspots such as the rue de la Huchette in the Quartier Latin. Serious crime against tourists is rare. The Préfecture de Police de Paris, for reporting theft, is at 7 boulevard du Palais (☎01.53.73.53.73).

Disabled travellers Paris has no special reputation for providing facilities or ease of access for disabled travellers, though things are gradually improving. Up-to-date information is best obtained from organizations at home before you leave or from the French tourist board (ⓦwww.franceguide.com). A handy publication is *Access in Paris* by Gordon Couch and Ben Roberts, a guide to accommodation, monuments, museums, restaurants and travel to the city. It was written over ten years ago now, but much of it is still relevant.

Doctors see Emergencies, below.

Electricity 220V out of double, round-pin wall sockets.

Embassies/Consulates Australia: 4 rue Jean-Rey, 15e ⓣ01.40.59.33.00, ⓦwww.austgov.fr (M° Bir-Hakeim); Britain: 35 rue du Faubourg-St-Honoré, 8e ⓣ01.44.51.31.02, ⓦwww.amb-grandebretagne.fr (M° Concorde); Canada: 35 av Montaigne, 8e ⓣ01.44.43.29.00, ⓦwww.amb-canada.fr (M° Franklin-D-Roosevelt); Ireland: 4 rue Rude, 16e ⓣ01.44.17.67.00 (M° Charles-de-Gaulle–Étoile); New Zealand: 7ter rue Léonardo-de-Vinci, 16e ⓣ01.45.00.24.11 (M° Victor-Hugo); USA: rue St-Florentin, 1er ⓣ01.43.12.22.22, ⓦwww.amb-usa.fr (M° Concorde).

Emergencies Fire brigade (Sapeurs-Pompiers) ⓣ18; Ambulance ⓣ15; Doctor call-out (SOS Médecins) ⓣ01.47.07.77.77; Rape crisis (SOS Viol; Mon–Fri 10am–6pm) ⓣ08.00.05.95.95.

Health British citizens with a European Health Insurance Card (from post offices) can take advantage of French health services. Non-EU citizens are strongly advised to take out travel insurance. See also "Pharmacies" below.

Internet Access Internet access is everywhere in Paris. If it's not in your hotel there will likely be a café nearby. Most post offices, too, have a computer geared up for public Internet access.

Left luggage Located at all the main train stations. You cannot leave luggage at the airports.

Lost baggage Airports: Orly ⓣ01.49.75.04.53; Charles de Gaulle ⓣ01.48.62.10.86.

Lost property Bureau des Objets Trouvés, Préfecture de Police, 36 rue des Morillons, 15e; ⓣ01.55.76.20.00 (Mon & Wed 8.30am–5pm, Thurs 8.30am–8pm, Fri 8.30am–5.30pm; M° Convention). For property lost on public transport, phone the RATP on ⓣ01.40.30.52.00. If you lose your passport, report it to a police station and then your embassy. Airports: Orly ⓣ01.49.75.42.34 or ⓣ01.49.75.34.10; Charles de Gaulle ⓣ01.48.62.13.34 or ⓣ01.48.16.63.83.

Pharmacies All pharmacies, signalled by an illuminated green cross, can give good advice on minor complaints, offer appropriate medicines and recommend a doctor. They are also equipped to give first aid on request (for a fee). They keep normal shop hours (roughly 9am–7pm), and some stay open all night: details of the nearest one open are posted in all pharmacies. You can find a good English-speaking chemist at Swann, 6 rue Castiglione, 1er (☎01.42.60.72.96). Pharmacies open at night include Dérhy/Pharmacie des Champs-Élysées, 84 avenue des Champs-Élysées, 8e (☎01.45.62.02.41; 24hr; M° George-V); Pharmacie Européenne, 6 place de Clichy, 9e (☎01.48.74.65.18; 24hr; M° Place-de-Clichy); Pharmacie des Halles, 10 boulevard Sébastopol, 4e (☎01.42.72.03.23; daily 9am–midnight; M° Châtelet); Pharmacie Internationale de Paris, 5 place Pigalle, 9e (☎01.48.78.38.12; Mon–Fri 8.30am–midnight, Sat & Sun 8.30am–1am; M° Pigalle); Grande Pharmacie de la Nation, 13 place de la Nation, 11e (☎01.43.73.24.03; daily 8am–midnight; M° Nation).

Post Office Post offices are located in every neighbourhood – look for the bright-yellow signs and the words "la Poste" or "le PTT" – and are generally open Mon–Fri 8am–7pm & Sat 8am–noon. The main office at 52 rue du Louvre, Paris 75001 (M° Étienne-Marcel) is open daily 24hr for all postal services (except banking). The easiest place to buy ordinary stamps (*timbres*) is at a *tabac* (tobacconist). Postcards (*cartes postales*) and letters (*lettres*) up to 20g cost €0.55 for the UK and the rest of the EU, €0.90 for the US and Australasia. For anything heavier most post offices now have *guichets automatiques* that weigh your letter or package and give you the correct stamps.

Public holidays January 1, New Year's Day; Easter Sunday; Easter Monday; Ascension Day (40 days after Easter); Pentecost or Whitsun (seventh Sunday after Easter, plus the Monday); May 1, May Day/Labour Day; May 8, Victory in Europe Day; July 14, Bastille Day; August 15, Assumption of the Virgin Mary; November 1, All Saints' Day; November 11, Armistice Day; December 25, Christmas Day.

Public Toilets Ask for *les toilettes* or look for signs for the WC (pronounced "vay say"); when reading the details of facilities outside hotels, don't confuse *lavabo*, which means washbasin, with lavatory. French toilets in bars are still often of the hole-in-the-ground squatting variety, and tend to lack toilet paper. Standards of cleanliness aren't always high. Toilets in railway stations and department stores are commonly staffed by attendants who will expect a bit of spare change. Some have coin-operated locks, as do the tardis-like public toilets found on the streets, so you might want to keep some loose change to hand.

Radio The BBC World Service (Ⓦwww.bbc.co.uk/worldservice) can be found on 648kHz or 198kHz long wave from midnight to 5am (and Radio 4 during the day). The Voice of America (Ⓦwww.voa.gov) transmits on 90.5, 98.8 and 102.4FM. You can listen to the news in English on Radio France International (RFI; Ⓦwww.rfi.fr) at 7am, 2.30pm and 4.30pm on 738KHz AM. For radio news in French, there's the state-run France Inter (87.8FM), Europe 1 (104.7FM), or round-the-clock news on France Info (105.5FM).

Safer sex A warning: Paris has the highest incidence of AIDS of any city in Europe; people who are HIV positive are just as likely to be heterosexual as homosexual. Condoms (*préservatifs*) are readily available at supermarkets, clubs, from dispensers on the street – often outside pharmacies – and in the métro. From pharmacies you can also get spermicidal cream and jelly (*dose contraceptive*), suppositories (*ovules, suppositoires*), and (with a prescription) the pill (*la pillule*), a diaphragm or IUD (*le stérilet*). Pregnancy test kits (*tests de grossesse*) are sold at pharmacies; the morning-after pill (*la pilule du lendemain*) is available from pharmacies without prescription.

Sales tax VAT (Value Added Tax) is referred to as TVA in France (*taxe sur la valeur ajoutée*). The standard rate in France is 20.6 percent; it's higher for luxury items and lower for essentials, but there are no exemptions (children's clothes, for example, are more expensive than in the UK). However, non-EU residents who have been in the country for less than six months are entitled to a refund (*détaxe*) of some or all of this amount (but usually around 14 percent) if you spend at least €175 in a single trip to one shop. Not all stores participate in this scheme though, so you'll have to ask. The procedure is rather complicated: present your passport to the shop while paying and ask for the three-paged *bordereau de vente à l'exportation* form. They should help you fill it in and provide you with a self-addressed envelope. When you leave the EU, get customs to stamp the filled-in form; you will then need to send two of the pages back to the shop in the envelope within three months; the shop will then transfer the refund through your credit card or bank. The Centre de Renseignements des Douanes (Ⓣ08.25.30.82.63, Ⓦwww.douane.gouv.fr) can answer any customs-related questions.

Smoking Laws requiring restaurants to have separate smokers' (*fumeurs*) and non-smokers' (*non-fumeurs*) areas are widely ignored. Non-smokers may well find themselves eating elbow-to-elbow alongside smokers, and waiters are not that likely to be sympathetic; even if there are clearly defined non-smoking areas, they tend to be in the least desirable part of the restaurant, tucked away in a back room, for example. Smoking is not allowed on public transport, including surburban trains, or in cinemas. Smoking, however, is still a socially acceptable habit in France, and cigarettes are cheap in comparison with Britain, for example. Note that you can only buy tobacco in *tabacs.*

Student information (CROUS) 39 av Georges-Bernanos, 5e (Ⓣ01.40.51.36.00, Ⓦwww.crous.fr; RER Port-Royal).

Telephones You can make international phone calls from any telephone box (*cabine*) and can receive calls where there's a blue logo of a ringing bell. You'll need to buy a phonecard (télécarte; 50-unit card for €7.50 or 120 units for €15), since coin boxes have been almost phased out. If you're making a lot of calls it's worth buying a card with a PIN (*une carte à code*), which can be used from a public or private telephone; just dial the toll-free number on the card, followed by your PIN (given on the card) and then the number you want to reach. The cheapest one for calling abroad to Europe or the US is the Kosmos France/Monde card, which gives you one thousand minutes of calling time for €15. All phonecards are available from *tabacs* and newsagents. All calls are timed in France and off-peak charges apply on weekdays between 7pm and 8am, and all day Saturday and Sunday. For calls within France – local or long-distance – dial all ten digits of the number. For international calls, calling codes are posted in the telephone box; remember to omit the initial 0 of the local area code from the subscriber's number. If you're bringing your mobile phone and you haven't used it abroad before you'll probably need to contact your provider to get it activated for foreign use. Remember that you'll pay for people to call you while you're abroad. Note that France operates on the European GSM standard, so US cellphones won't work in France unless you've got a tri-band phone.

Television French TV terrestrial channels include three public (France 2, Arte/La Cinquième and France 3) and two commercial channels (TF1 and M6), plus a subscription channel, Canal Plus. In addition, there are the cable networks, which include LCI (French news), CNN, the BBC World Service and BBC Prime (*Eastenders*, etc). The main French news broadcasts are at 8pm on F2 and TF1.

Time France is one hour ahead of Britain (Greenwich Mean Time), six hours ahead of Eastern Standard Time (eg New York), and nine hours ahead of Pacific Standard Time (eg Los Angeles). Australia is eight to ten hours ahead of France, depending on which part of the continent you're in. Remember also that France uses a 24hr clock, with, for example, 2am written as 2h and 2.30pm written as 14h30. The most confusing are noon and midnight – respectively 12h and 00h. Talking clock ⓣ36.99. Alarm ⓣ36.88, or with a digital phone dial *55* then the time in four figures (eg 0715 for 7.15am) then #. To annul, dial #55* then the time, then # (costs around €0.60).

Tours The best walking tours of Paris in English are those offered by Paris Walks (ⓣ01.48.09.21.40, ⓦwww.paris-walks.com; 2hr; €10, children €5), with subjects ranging from "Hemingway's Paris" to "Historic Marais". The Paris transport authority, RATP, also runs numerous excursions, some to quite far-flung places, which are far less expensive than those offered by commercial operators. Details are available from RATP's Bureau de Tourisme, place de la Madeleine, 1e (ⓣ01.40.06.71.45, ⓦwww.ratp.fr; M° Madeleine).

Trafffic & road conditions For Paris's traffic jams listen to 105.1 FM (FIP) on the radio; for the *boulevard périphérique* and main routes in and out of the city, ring ⓣ01.48.99.33.33.

Weather Paris and Île de France ⓣ08.36.68.02.75; rest of France ⓣ01.36.68.01.01. On the Internet at ⓦwww.meteofrance.com and ⓦwww.weather.com.

Contexts

Contexts

A brief history of Paris

Beginnings

When the **Gauls** or **Celts** began to settle in the Paris region, probably in the third century BC, they called their settlement Lutetia or Lucotetia, from a Celtic root word for "marshland". Back then, the Seine was broader, flowing past a miniature archipelago of five islets. The modern name for the city comes from the local Quarisii or **Parisii** tribe, who built an iron-age fort on the largest island, at the eastern end of what is now the Île de la Cité. This fort commanded a perfect site: defensible and astride the most practicable north–south crossing point of an eminently navigable river.

When Julius Caesar's conquering armies arrived in 52 BC, they found a thriving settlement. Romanized Lutetia prospered too, even if the town was fairly insignificant by **Gallo-Roman** standards, with a population of some eight thousand. The Romans established their basilica on the Île de la Cité, but the town lay almost entirely on the Left Bank, on the slopes of the Montagne Ste-Geneviève.

Although Roman rule in Gaul disintegrated under the impact of **Germanic invasions** around 275 AD, Lutetia itself held out for almost two hundred years. The marauding bands of Attila the Hun were repulsed in 451, supposedly thanks to the prayerful intervention of Geneviève, who became the city's patron saint. The city finally fell to **Clovis the Frank** in 486; the first, and by no means the last, time the city would fall to German troops. Clovis's descendants founded the Christianized but endlessly warring **Merovingian** dynasty, whose bodies were buried in the great basilica at St-Denis.

In the early ninth century, the king **Charlemagne** conquered half of Europe and sparked a mini-Renaissance, but Paris's good fortune plummeted after the break-up of his empire as the city was repeatedly sacked and pillaged by the **Vikings** from the mid-840s onwards. Thereafter Paris lay largely in ruins, a provincial backwater without power, influence, or even a significant population.

The medieval heyday

In the eleventh century, the Paris region was ruled by the **Capetian dynasty**, but as the royal family did not deign to base itself in the miserable capital, regrowth was slow. By 1100, the city's population was only around three thousand. One hundred years later, however, Paris had become the largest city in the Christian world (which it would remain until overtaken by London in the eighteenth century), as well as its intellectual and cultural hub. By the **1320s**, the city's population had swollen even further reaching almost a quarter of a million inhabitants. This rapid expansion was owed to Paris's valuable river-borne trade and the associated growth of the **merchant classes**, coupled with thriving **agriculture** in the wider Paris region. The economic boom was matched by the growth of the city's university on the Left Bank – notably the **Sorbonne** college. Meanwhile, the capital was protected by the novelty of a relatively strong – and largely Paris-based – monarchy.

To defend his burgeoning metropolis, **Philippe-Auguste** (1180–1223), built the **Louvre fortress** and a vast **city wall**, which enclosed an area now roughly traced by the inner ring of modern Paris's 1er–6e arrondissements. The administration of the city remained in the hands of the monarchy until 1260, when **Louis IX** (St Louis) ceded a measure of responsibility to the *échevins* or leaders of the Paris watermen's guild, whose power was based on their monopoly control of all river traffic and taxes thereon. The city's government, when it has been allowed one, has been conducted ever since from the place de Grève/place de l'Hôtel-de-Ville.

A city adrift

From the mid-fourteenth to mid-fifteenth centuries Paris shared the same unhappy fate as the rest of France, embroiled in the long and destructive **Hundred Years War**, which pitted the French and English nobility against each other in a power struggle whose results were misery for the French peasant classes, and penury for Paris. A break in the Capetian line led to the accession of Philippe VI, the first of the **Valois dynasty**, but the legitimacy of his claim to the throne was contested by Edward III of England. Harried by war, the Valois monarchs spent much of their troubled reigns outside the capital, whose loyalty was often questionable. Infuriated by the lack of political representation for merchant classes, the city mayor, or Prévôt des Marchands, **Étienne Marcel**, even let the enemy into Paris in 1357.

Charles V, who ruled from 1364, built a new Louvre and a new city wall that increased Paris's area by more than half again (roughly incorporating what are now the modern 9e–11e arrondissements, on the Right Bank), but the population within his walls was plummeting due to disease and a harsh climate in Europe generally, as well as warfare and political instability. The **Black Death**, which arrived in the summer of 1348, killed some eight hundred Parisians a day, and over the next 140 years, one year in four was a plague year. Harvests repeatedly failed – icebergs even floated on the Seine in 1407 – and, politically, things were no better.

In 1422 the Duke of Bedford set up his government of northern France in Paris. **Joan of Arc** made an unsuccessful attempt to drive the English out in 1429, but the following year the English king, Henry VI, had the cheek to have himself crowned king of France in Notre-Dame. Meanwhile, the Valois kings fled the city altogether for a life of pleasure-seeking irrelevance in the gentle Loire Valley.

Renaissance and rebirth

It was only when the English were expelled – from Paris in 1437 and from France in 1453 – that Paris had the chance to recover. When, in 1528, **François I** decided to bring the royal court back to the capital, Paris's fortunes improved further. Work began on reconstructing the Louvre and building the Tuileries palace for Catherine de Médicis and an economic boom brought peasants in from the countryside in droves, enlarging the city's population well past its medieval peak. Although centralized planning coughed into life to cope with the influx, Paris remained, as Henri II put it, a city of "mire, muck and filth".

In the second half of the century, war interrupted early efforts at civic improvement – this time **civil war** between Catholics and Protestants. Paris swung fanatically behind the Catholic cause, leading to the infamous **St Bartholomew's Day massacre**, on August 25, 1572, when some two thousand Protestants were murdered in the streets. After years of outright war, and the death of some forty thousand Parisians from disease or starvation, the Protestant leader Henri of Navarre entered the city as the Catholic king **Henri IV**. "Paris is worth a Mass", he is reputed to have said, to justify renouncing his Protestantism in order to soothe the Catholic sensibilities.

The Paris Henri IV inherited was filthy and overcrowded, and he quickly set out to revive its fortunes. He instituted tight building regulations and created the splendid place des Vosges and place Dauphine, as well as building the **Pont Neuf**, the first of the Paris bridges not to be cluttered with medieval houses. The tradition of grandiose public building was to continue, reaching its apogee in the seventeenth century under **Louis XIV** – even when the entire court moved outside Paris to the vast palace of **Versailles** in 1671. But civic works also continued, as Paris's old fortifications were cleared to make way for the new **boulevards** and **avenues**, notably the Champs-Elysées. The aristocratic *hôtels*, or private mansions, of the **Marais** were largely erected during the seventeenth century, only to be superseded early in the **eighteenth century** by the **Faubourg St-Germain** as the fashionable quarter of the rich and powerful. Towards the end of the century, coffee-houses or "cafés" were opening by the hundreds to serve the needs of the burgeoning **bourgeoisie**. Obscured by all the glitter, however, were the **poor living conditions** of the ordinary citizens – the centre of the city remained a densely packed and unsanitary warren of medieval lanes and tenements.

Revolution and empire

In 1789, Louis XVI summoned a meeting of the "Estates General" – a parliament of representatives of the clergy (the First Estate), the nobility (the Second) and the middle classes (the Third) – to help sort out his disastrous finances. When the Estates duly met, however, the bourgeois representatives of the Third Estate proved troublesome. When Louis posted troops around Versailles and Paris, the city's deputies entered the Hôtel de Ville and declared a municipal government or **Commune**, setting up a militia – the National Guard – and preparing to defend Paris against attack. When a band of ordinary Parisians stormed the **Bastille** prison on July 14 looking for weapons with which to arm themselves, the National Guard joined in. From this moment on, the ordinary people of Paris – known as the **sans-culottes**, or "people without breeches" – became the shock troops of the Revolution.

At this point the king bowed to pressure and legalized a new National Assembly, which in August 1789 passed the **Declaration of the Rights of Man**, sweeping away the feudal privileges of the old order. In 1791 Louis attempted to flee abroad, but was forced to return to Paris; by August 1792, he was a virtual prisoner of the *sans-culottes*. In September, the monarchy was abolished, the Republic declared, and the king put on trial for treason; Louis was convicted and guillotined on place de la Concorde in January 1793.

The Republican Convention, however, was wracked with infighting and the moderate Girondin faction lost out to the radical **Jacobins**. Under the ruthless Maximilien **Robespierre**, the Committee of Public Safety began the extermination of "enemies of the people", a period known as the **Grande Terreur** – among the first casualties was **Marie-Antoinette**.

The revolutionary chaos ended only after Robespierre himself was sent to the Guillotine, in July 1794, and a new leader emerged. **Napoleon Bonaparte** officially overthrew the Directory in a **coup d'état** in November 1799, subsequently appointing himself first consul for life in 1802 and **emperor** in 1804.

Although Napoleon took France into numerous costly and bloody **wars**, his rule brought relative prosperity and stability to Paris, making it the heart of an efficient and highly centralized bureaucracy, and beginning many grandiose building schemes. He lined the Seine with two and a half miles of stone quais, provided Paris with its modern water supply, and built the Arcs de Triomphe and Carrousel as well as a further extension for the Louvre. After the disastrous **invasion of Russia** in 1812, however, Napoleon was forced to abdicate and **Louis XVIII**, brother of the decapitated Louis XVI, was installed as king. In a last desperate attempt to regain power, Napoleon escaped from exile on the Italian island of Elba and reorganized his armies, only to meet final defeat at **Waterloo** on June 18, 1815.

The nineteenth century

France's glorious and powerful rulers, from Philippe-Auguste to Napoleon, may have created Paris's great landmark buildings but Paris's distinctive cityscape only took shape thanks to the bourgeoisie, in the **nineteenth century**. This was the century of the middle classes, punctuated by brief and often bloody revolts led by Paris's poor.

The first rebellion, however, was bourgeois. When King Charles X refused to accept the result of the 1830 National Assembly elections, **Adolphe Thiers** led the opposition in revolt; barricades were erected in Paris and there followed three days of bitter street fighting, known as *les trois glorieuses*. The outcome of this **July Revolution** was the election of **Louis-Philippe** as a constitutional "bourgeois monarch".

For the **poor**, living and working conditions in Paris only deteriorated, with twenty thousand deaths from cholera in Paris in 1832 alone. Smaller expressions of discontent occurred in Paris in 1832 and 1834, but the real eruption came on June 23, 1848, when working-class Paris – Poissonnière, Temple, St-Antoine, the Marais, Quartier Latin, Montmartre – rose, united, in revolt. In this **1848 Revolution**, men, women and children fought fifty thousand troops in three days of fighting. Nine hundred soldiers were killed; no one knows how many of the insurgents died.

In November 1848, the anxious middle classes elected **Louis Napoléon Bonaparte**, nephew of the Emperor Napoleon, as President. Within three years he brought the tottering republic to an end by announcing a coup d'état. Twelve months later, he had himself crowned Emperor Napoléon III. There followed a period of laissez-faire capitalism, which greatly increased the **economic wealth** of France. Napoléon III's great legacy to Paris, however, was the appointment of **Baron Haussmann** as Prefect of the Seine department. He undertook a total **transformation of the city**, driving 135km of broad new streets and boulevards through the cramped quarters of the medieval city. Haussmann's taste also dictated the uniform grey stone facades, mansard roofs and six to seven storeys – some with elegant ironwork balconies – that are still the architectural hallmark of the Paris street today.

The downside of this urban re-design was that some 350,000 poor Parisians were simply displaced, many moving out to the ever-growing **banlieue**, the city beyond the old walls. These suburbs tripled in population between 1860 and the outbreak of World War I, becoming the home of one and a half million almost-Parisians. Inside the city proper, the working classes were coralled into ever-smaller islands of poverty, where sanitation was nonexistent, and cholera and TB rife.

Haussmann's scheme was at least in part designed to keep the workers under control, the broad boulevards facilitating cavalry manoeuvres and artillery fire. The system was soon tested. In September 1870, Napoléon III surrendered to Bismarck at the border town of Sedan, less than two months after France had declared war on the superior forces of the **Prussian** state. The humiliation was enough for a Republican government to be instantly proclaimed in Paris. The Prussians advanced and by September 19 were laying **siege** to the capital. Daring balloonists kept the city in contact with the outside world, but meanwhile, Parisians starved. Finally, a newly elected Assembly surrendered the city to the Prussians and, on March 1, enemy troops marched down the Champs-Élysées.

Less than three weeks later, working-class Paris rose up in revolt, and the **Commune** was proclaimed from the Hôtel de Ville; it lasted all of 72 days – a festival of the oppressed, Lenin called it. Socialist in inspiration, the Commune had no time to implement lasting reforms, succumbing to the army of Adolphe Thiers' conservative government on May 28, 1871, after a week of street-by-street warfare – the so-called *semaine sanglante*, or "Bloody Week" – during which several of the city's landmark buildings were destroyed, including the Tuileries palace and the original Hôtel de Ville.

Paris at play and at war

Within six or seven years of the Commune, few signs of the fighting remained. Visitors remarked admiringly on Paris's teeming streets, the expensive shops and energetic nightlife: this was the start of the capital's decadent heyday. In 1889 the **Eiffel Tower** stole the show at the great Exposition, and for the 1900 repeat, the **métro** was unveiled. Paris now emerged as the supremely inspiring environment for artists and writers – the so-called Bohemians – both French and foreign. **Impressionism**, **Fauvism** and **Cubism** were all born in Paris in this period, while French **poets** like Apollinaire, Laforgue, Max Jacob, Blaise Cendrars and André Breton were preparing the way for Surrealism, concrete poetry and Symbolism. **Cinema**, too, first saw the light in Paris, with the jerky documentaries of the Lumière brothers and George Méliès' fantastical features both appearing in the mid-1890s. It was a constellation of talents such as Western culture has rarely seen.

As a city, Paris escaped **World War I** relatively lightly. The human cost was rather higher: one in ten Parisian conscripts failed to return. But Paris remained the world's art – and party – capital after the war, with an injection of foreign blood and a shift of venue from Montmartre to Montparnasse. Indeed, the **années folles** (or "mad years") of the 1920s were some of Paris's most decadent and scintillating, consolidating a longstanding international reputation for hedonistic, often erotic, abandon that has sustained its tourism industry for the best part of a century.

As **Depression** deepened in the 1930s and Nazi power across the Rhine became more menacing, the mood changed, and attention turned to politics. The Left won the **1936 elections** but the brave new government soon foundered and returned to opposition, where it remained, with the exception of coalition governments, until 1981. After the outbreak of **World War II** and the fall of France, Paris suffered the humiliation of a four-year Nazi **occupation**. Food, fuel for heating and petrol were all short, and many Parisians were forced to make compromises in order to survive. In 1942, Parisian Jews were rounded up – by other Frenchmen – and shipped off to Auschwitz. The **Resistance**, however, was also very active in the city. As Allied forces drew near to Paris in 1944, the FFI (armed Resistance units) called their troops onto the streets – some said, in a leftist attempt to seize political power. On August 23, Hitler famously gave orders that Paris should be physically destroyed, but the city's commander, Von Cholitz, delayed just long enough. **Liberation** arrived on August 25 in the shape of General Leclerc's tanks, motoring up the Champs-Élysées to the roar of a vast crowd.

Postwar Paris: 1945 to 2000

Postwar Paris remained no stranger to political street battles. Violent demonstrations accompanied the Communist withdrawal from the coalition government in 1947; in the Fifties the Left protested against the colonial wars in Indochina and Algeria; and, in 1961, in one of the most shameful episodes in modern French history, some two hundred Algerians were killed by the police during a civil rights demonstration.

In the extraordinary month of **May 1968**, a radical, leftist movement gathered momentum in Paris's universities. Students began by occupying university buildings, and the extreme reaction of the police and government helped the movement to spread until it represented a mass revolt against institutional stagnation that ended with a general strike by nine million workers. The vicious battles between students, workers and police on the streets of Paris shook large sectors of the population – France's silent majority – to the core.

Elections called in June 1968 returned the Right to power, but French institutions and French society had changed – then president Charles de Gaulle didn't survive a referendum in 1969. His successor, **Georges Pompidou**, only survived long enough to begin the construction of the giant Les Halles development, and the expressways along the quais of the Seine.

When **François Mitterrand** became president in 1981, there was a mood of euphoria on the Left. His chief legacy to the city of Paris, however, was not social reform, but the **Grands Projets**, or great architectural projects. Many were extremely controversial. Most shocking of all to conservative Paris was I.M. Pei's **glass pyramid**, erected in the very heart of the historic Louvre palace. It is a testament to a new spirit in the city that most Parisians have now taken this symbol of thrusting modernity to their hearts, along with the **Institut du Monde Arabe** in the Quartier Latin, the **Grande Arche de la Défense** and the **Bibliothèque Nationale**, in the 13e. Only one *grand projet* has proved less successful: the ugly **Opéra Bastille**.

In the summer following the presidential election of 1995, which brought **Jacques Chirac** to power, a series of shocks hit Paris and the new regime. **Bombs** planted by an extremist Algerian Islamic group exploded in the RER stations of St-Michel and Port Royal. By November, public confidence in the government of Prime Minister **Alain Juppé** had collapsed, and over a period of three weeks some five million people took to the streets of Paris in protest against arrogant, elitist politicians and economic austerity measures – problems that would become the key theme of Paris politics in the new millennium.

The government's standing in the popularity stakes tumbled further as it was hit by a succession of **corruption scandals**. Accusations of cover-ups and perversion of the course of justice followed, punctuated by revelations of illegal funding of election campaigns, politicians taking bribes and dirty money changing hands during privatizations.

The home affairs minister, Charles Pasqua, stepped up **anti-immigration measures** which resulted in some 250,000 people living and working in France having their legal status removed. For many blacks or Arabs seeking work, particularly young men, the ring road dividing the city from its suburbs might as well have been a wall of steel. Paris is often caricatured as a rich ghetto, yet the number of SDF – *Sans Domicile Fixe*, or **homeless** – was estimated at as many as fifty thousand.

In a bid to gain influence for his party, Chirac called a snap parliamentary election in May 1997. His gamble failed spectacularly as he was forced into "cohabitation" with triumphant Socialist Prime Minister **Lionel Jospin**, whose government introduced the famous 35-hour working week. It was soon hit by another series of **scandals**, however, as was the Right. In 1998, Jean Tiberi – conservative Paris mayor since Chirac's move to the presidency in 1995 – was implicated in a scandal involving subsidized real-estate and salaries for fake jobs. As if this wasn't bad enough, Chirac himself was also accused of using millions of francs in cash from illegal sources to pay for luxury holidays for himself and his family and friends between 1992 and 1995. When investigating magistrates tried to question him, he claimed presidential immunity, a position upheld by France's highest court, though only as long as he remained in office.

Lightening the national mood, in July 1998, Paris – or at least the Paris suburb of St-Denis – was the scene of France's victory in the football **World Cup** at the new Stade de France. The team was proudly multi-ethnic and, for once, support for *les bleus* overrode all other colour distinctions; that night, the Champs-Élysées became a river of a million cheering fans.

Contemporary Paris

In the first years of the new millennium, two seismic events shook Parisian politics. The first was the election of the quiet, unassuming Socialist candidate, **Bertrand Delanoë**, as Mayor of Paris in March 2001. The fact that this was the first time the Left had won control of the capital since the Paris Commune in 1871 was far more of a shock to most Parisians than the fact that he was openly gay – in Paris, a politician's private life has almost always been seen as exactly that. Delanoë's brief was to end town-hall corruption, tackle crime and traffic congestion and instill new pride and energy into the city.

Shortly after the election, Delanoë attempted to show he meant business as a reformer. During the summer of

2002, when many Parisians turn the city over to tourists, he caused apoplexy among Paris's fiercely independent car users by closing a three-kilometre length of the riverbank roads and turning them into a public beach from mid-July to mid-August. Dubbed **Paris Plage** ("Paris beach"), the scene was complete right down to palm trees, deck chairs and 150 tonnes of sand – the only thing missing was the chance to take a dip in the river. The next landmark event was October's **Nuit Blanche** ("sleepless night"), in which hundreds of galleries, museums, bars, restaurants and public buildings remained open for a city-wide all-night party of poetry readings, live music and performance art. Both are now established events in the city's calendar.

Less glamorous have been improvements in **city transport**: bus and cycle lanes have been installed throughout Paris; a tramway ringing the entire city is currently under construction; new ferries are to provide a seriously expanded river-bus service by 2008; and, outstripping London's lead, there is even a scheme to limit car use, and eventually to ban cars from the historic centre for all except residents.

On the national level, the greatest cataclysm since the new millennium – not counting the **introduction of the euro** on January 1, 2002 – was the presidential election of spring 2002 and the far-Right candidate **Le Pen's shock success** in the first round, beating the Socialist candidate Lionel Jospin into third place. Chirac and Le Pen were now to stand against each other in the final run-off in May. This result acted like a wake-up call to the nation and on May 1, some 800,000 people packed the boulevards of Paris in the biggest **demonstration** the capital had seen since the student protests of 1968. Chirac's victory in the next round was assured, with the Socialists calling on its supporters to vote for Chirac; the incumbent President duly swept the board, winning 82 percent – 90 percent in Paris – of the vote.

Since 2002, Chirac's second presidency has faced a seemingly unending succession of problems, most stemming from high unemployment and a swollen budget deficit. Proposed **reforms** – including relaxations of labour laws and cuts to the generous provision of pensions and free health care – have divided the country and provoked fierce opposition.

In 2003, the political heat was accompanied by soaring Parisian **summer temperatures** which, in the first half of August, regularly topped 40°C (104°F) – more than ten degrees above the average maximum for the time of year. At the same time, there was trouble on the foreign front. Responding to the US's refusal to give weapons inspectors in **Iraq** more time, Chirac vowed in March 2003 to use France's Security Council veto against any second resolution committing the UN to war. Throughout France, Chirac was feted for "standing up to the Americans", but Paris's tourist industry suffered, as for a time many Americans chose to holiday at home – or at least not in France.

Since Iraq, resistance to economic reforms has proved unflagging, with waves of passionate strikers continuing to flood the city streets at regular intervals – there were half a million on the streets in October 2005. Unfortunately for Paris, one wave of strikes and demonstrations coincided with the arrival in 2005 of the International Olympic Committee in Paris to assess the city's ultimately unsuccessful bid for the **2012 Olympic Games**.

The future

The Olympic Committee's close-run "*non*" neatly echoed the result of France's **referendum** on the **EU constitution** the previous month, at which 55 percent of voters refused what they saw as an attempt to impose an "Anglo-Saxon" neo-liberal system on France. Chirac used the referendum debacle to bring in Dominique de Villepin – foreign minister at the time of the Iraq affair – as Prime Minister. Many saw the appointment as an attempt by Chirac to undermine the political standing of his ambitious, right-wing rival, Nicholas Sarkozy, in the run-up to the **2007 presidential elections**. The Socialists, meanwhile, remained in disarray, terminally split on the issue of Europe, and indeed on every other issue.

The **long-term future** for Paris depends not on political manoeuvring, public transport improvements, or Olympic Games, but on larger structural issues. High rents and higher property prices – up 100 percent since 2000 – have provoked a **flight of residents** from Paris "intra-muros" to the suburbs. There are now 2.1 million residents in central Paris, down from 2.8 million in the late 1950s – although a million more "greater Parisians" travel in to work every weekday. In the city proper, a majority of residents live in one-person households, while retirees make up fifteen percent of the population, and less than five percent of residents hold traditionally working-class jobs – half of these are foreigners.

Parisians, long inclined to judge a city's success by its gastronomic activity, are regularly alarmed by the publication of horrifying statistics such as the fact that the city has lost roughly a quarter of its **small food stores** and butcher's shops in the last decade, and that there is scarcely a single bakery in the vicinity of the Champs-Élysées. They may be comforted to learn that a city with "only" 159 cheese shops, and "just" one grocery for every thirty people is not yet facing a crisis.

While Paris remains one of the developed world's most **densely populated** cities – with double the density of Tokyo – the number of people living in the central arrondissements has halved over the course of the twentieth century. The figure has been roughly stable for the last twenty-five years, but the social mix has undoubtedly changed. Some areas have become virtual ghettoes of the rich, while the **banlieue** remains riven with poverty and unemployment. Mayor Delanoë has ordered that each of the central Paris's twenty arrondissements must ensure that twenty percent of the housing stock is reserved for rent-controlled **social housing**. With rich quartiers such as the 7^{e} and 8^{e} currently maintaining controls on less than two percent of their stock, however, the project to stop Paris becoming a dead, rich ghetto has a long way to go.

One sure way of driving out Paris's remaining residents, it seems, would be to enforce a ban on **smoking**. In 2005, a scheme allowing the city's twelve thousand-odd cafés and bistros to volunteer themselves as smoke-free environments ended ignominiously after only three months. Just thirty establishments had applied.

Books

In the selected listing of books below, publishers are detailed in the form of British publisher/American publisher. Where books are published in one country only, UK or US follows the publisher's name. The abbreviation "o/p" means "out of print", while the ★ symbol marks titles that are particularly recommended.

History and politics

Anthony Beevor & Artemis Cooper *Paris After the Liberation: 1944–1949* (Penguin). Gripping account of a crucial era in Parisian history, featuring de Gaulle, the Communists, the St-Germain scene and Dior's New Look.

Robert Cole *A Traveller's History of Paris* (Windrush Press/Interlink). This brief history of the city from the first Celtic settlement to the present day is an ideal starting point for anyone wishing to delve into the historical archives.

Christopher Hibbert *The French Revolution* (Penguin). Good, concise popular history of the period. The description of events is vivid, but it's not so good on the intellectual background and the meaning of the Revolution.

Alistair Horne *The Fall of Paris* (Pan) and *Seven Ages of Paris* (Pan/Vintage). The former is a very readable and humane account of the extraordinary period of the Prussian siege of Paris in 1870 and the ensuing struggles of the Commune, while the latter is a compelling (if rather old-fashionedly fruity) account of significant episodes in the city's history.

★ **Colin Jones** *Paris: Biography of a City* (Allen Lane/Viking). Jones focuses on the actual life and growth of the city, from the Neolithic past to the future. Five hundred pages flow by easily, punctuated by thoughtful but accessible "boxes" on streets, buildings and characters, whose lives were especially bound up with Paris's. The best single book on the city's history.

Philip Mansel *Paris Between Empires* (Orion/Phoenix). Serious but gripping tale of an often-ignored patch of Paris's history: the turbulent years of revolutions and restorations that followed in the wake of Napoleon. Brilliantly conjures up the events of the streets and the salons.

Theodore Zeldin *A History of French Passions, 1848–1945* (OUP). A subtle, humanistic attempt to understand France through its history, culture and people, tackled by themes such as intellect and taste. Big both in size and ambition, but very readable nonetheless.

Culture and society

John Ardagh *France in the New Century: Portrait of a Changing Society* (Penguin). Probably the most useful book if you want to get to grips with French culture, society and recent political history (it was published in 2000). There's material on food, film, education and holidays as well as the drier political-historical stuff, and there's a fair amount on the relationship between Paris, its suburbs and the rest of France.

Marc Augé *In the Metro* (University of Minnesota Press US). A philosophically minded anthropologist descends deep into métro culture and his own memories of life in Paris. A brief, brilliant and utterly Barthian essay.

Roland Barthes *Mythologies* (Vintage). A classic and superb intellectual rhapsody on how the ideas, prejudices and contradictions of French thought and behaviour manifest themselves, in food, wine, the Citroën DS, travel guides and other cultural offerings.

Barthes' piece on the Eiffel Tower doesn't appear, but it's included in the *Selected Writings* (Vintage), published in the US as *A Barthes Reader* (ed Susan Sontag; Hill and Wang).

Walter Benjamin *The Arcades Project* (Belknap Press/Harvard University Press). An all-encompassing portrait of Paris from 1830–70, in which the passages are used as a lens through which to view Parisian society. Never completed, Benjamin's magnum opus is a kaleidoscopic assemblage of essays, notes and quotations, gathered under such headings as "Baudelaire", "Prostitution", "Mirrors" and "Idleness".

James Campbell *Paris Interzone* (Vintage/Secker and Warburg). The feuds, passions and destructive lifestyles of Left Bank writers in 1946–60 are evoked here. The cast includes Richard Wright, James Baldwin, Samuel Beckett, Boris Vian, Alexander Trocchi, Eugène Ionesco, Sartre, de Beauvoir, Nabokov and Allan Ginsberg.

Rupert Christiansen *Paris Babylon: Grandeur, Decadence and Revolution 1869–1875* (Pimlico UK). Written with verve and dash – some of it slap – Christiansen's account of Paris at the time of the Siege and the Commune is exuberant, original and captivating. Worth reading for its evocative and insightfully chosen contemporary quotations alone – it begins with a delightful 1869 guidebook to "Paris Partout!".

Richard Cobb *Paris and Elsewhere* (John Murray/New York Review of Books). Selected writings on postwar Paris by the acclaimed historian of the Revolution, with a personal and meditative tone.

Adam Gopnik *Paris to the Moon* (Vintage/Random House). Intimate and acutely observed essays from the Paris correspondent of the New Yorker on society, politics, family life and shopping. Probably the most thoughtful and enjoyable book by an expat in Paris.

Ian Littlewood *A Literary Companion to Paris* (Penguin/HarperCollins). A thorough account of which literary figures went where, and what they had to say about it.

Edmund White *The Flâneur* (Bloomsbury). An American expat novelist muses over Parisian themes and places as diverse as the Moreau museum, gay cruising and the history of immigration, as well as the art of being a good *flâneur* – a loiterer or stroller.

Theodore Zeldin *The French* (Harvill Press/Kodansha). A wise and original book that attempts to describe a country through the thoughts and feelings of its people. Draws on the author's conversations with a fascinating range of French people, about money, sex, phobias, parents and everything else.

Art, architecture and photography

Brassaï *Le Paris Secret des Années 30* (Gallimard). Extraordinary photos of the capital's nightlife in the 1930s. Henry Miller accompanied Brassaï on many of his nocturnal expeditions, a friendship captured in his book *Henry Miller: the Paris Years*.

Henri Cartier-Bresson *A Propos de Paris* (Bulfinch Press). Some of the greatest photos ever taken: a brilliant blend of the ordinary and the surreal, of photo-journalism and art photography.

André Chastel *French Art* (Flammarion). The great French art historian tries to define what is distinctively French about French art in this insightful and superbly illustrated three-volume work.

Robert Doisneau *Three Seconds of Eternity* (Te Neues). The famous Kiss in front of the Hôtel de Ville takes the front cover, but there's more to Doisneau than this. A collection chosen by the man himself of photographs taken in France, but mainly Paris, in the 1940s and 1950s. Beautifully nostalgic.

Anthony Sutcliffe *Paris – An Architectural History* (Yale UP). Excellent overview of Paris's changing cityscape, as dictated by fashion, social structure and political power.

Fiction and travel writing

In English

Helen Constantine (translator) *Paris Tales* (OUP). Twenty-two (very) short stories and essays, each chosen for their evocation of a particular place in Paris. From Balzac in the Palais Royal to Perec on the Champs-Élysées.

Charles Dickens *A Tale of Two Cities* (Penguin/Vintage). Paris and London during the 1789 Revolution and before. The plot is pure, breathtaking Hollywood, but the streets and the social backdrop are very much for real.

Julien Green *Paris* (Marion Boyars). Born in Paris in 1900, Green became one of the city's defining writers. This bilingual edition presents twenty-odd short, meditative and highly personal essays on different aspects and quartiers of Paris, from Notre-Dame and the 16e to "stairways and steps" and the lost cries of the city's hawkers. Proust meets travel writing.

Ernest Hemingway *A Moveable Feast* (Arrow/Scribner). Hemingway's memoirs of his life as a young man in Paris in the 1920s. Includes fascinating accounts of meetings with literary celebrities Ezra Pound, F. Scott Fitzgerald, Gertrude Stein and others.

J.K. Huysmans *Parisian Sketches* (Dedalus European Classics). Published in 1880, Huysmans' fantastical, intense prose pieces on contemporary

Paris drip with decadence and cruelly acute observation. If Manet was a novelist, he might have produced this.

Henry Miller *Tropic of Cancer (*Flamingo/Grove Press); *Quiet Days in Clichy* (New Eng Lib/Grove Press). Erratic, wild, self-obsessed writing, but with definite flights of genius.

George Orwell *Down and Out in Paris and London* (Penguin/Harvest). Documentary account of breadline living in the 1930s – Orwell at his best.

Jean Rhys *Quartet* (Penguin/Norton). A beautiful and evocative story of a lonely young woman's existence on the fringes of 1920s Montparnasse society.

French (in translation)

Honoré de Balzac *The Père Goriot* (Oxford Paperbacks). Biting exposé of cruelty and selfishness in the contrasting worlds of the fashionable Faubourg St-Germain and a down-at-heel but genteel boarding house in the Quartier Latin. Like Dickens, but with a tougher heart. Balzac's equally brilliant *Wild Ass's Skin* (Penguin) is a strange moralistic tale of an ambitious young man's fall from grace in early-nineteenth-century Paris.

Louis-Ferdinand Céline *Death on Credit* (Calder/Riverrun Press). A disturbing and powerful semi-autobiographical novel, in which Céline recounts the delirium of the world as seen through the eyes of an adolescent in working-class Paris at the beginning of the twentieth century.

Gustave Flaubert *Sentimental Education* (Penguin). A lively, detailed 1869 reconstruction of the life, manners, characters and politics of Parisians in the 1840s, including the 1848 Revolution.

Victor Hugo *Les Misérables* (Penguin). Set among the Parisian poor and low-life in the first half of the nineteenth century, it's probably the greatest treatment of Paris in fiction – unless that title goes to Hugo's haunting (and shorter) *Notre Dame de Paris* (Penguin/Modern Library), a novel better known in English as "The Hunchback of Notre Dame".

Guy de Maupassant *Bel-Ami* (Penguin/Hatier). Maupassant's chef-d'oeuvre is a brilliant and utterly sensual account of corrupt Parisian high society during the belle époque. Traces the progress of the fascinating journalist and seducer, Georges Duroy.

Daniel Pennac *Monsieur Malaussène* (Harvill Press/Kiepenheuer & Witsch). The last in the "Belleville Quintet" of quasi-detective novels set in the working-class east of Paris is possibly the most disturbing, centred on a series of macabre killings. Witty, experimental and chaotic, somewhat in the mode of Thomas Pynchon.

Marcel Proust *Remembrance of Things Past* (Penguin/Modern Library). Proust's 3000-page novel, much of it set in Paris, is one of the twentieth century's greatest works of fiction.

Georges Simenon *Maigret at the Crossroads* (Penguin/New York Review Books), or any other of the Maigret novels. Literary crime thrillers; the Montmartre and seedy criminal locations are unbeatable. If you don't like crime fiction you should go for *The Little Saint*, the story of a little boy growing up in the rue Mouffetard when it was a down-at-heel market street.

Émile Zola *Nana* (Penguin). The rise and fall of a courtesan in the decadent times of the Second Empire. Not bad on sex, but confused on sexual politics. A great story nevertheless, which brings mid-nineteenth-century Paris alive, direct, to present-day senses. Paris is also the setting for Zola's *L'Assommoir*, *The Masterpiece*, *L'Argent*, *Thérèse Raquin* and *The Debacle* (all Penguin).

Language

Language

French

Paris isn't the easiest place to learn French: many Parisians speak a hurried slang and will often reply to your carefully enunciated question in English. Despite this, it's worth making the effort and knowing a few essentials can make all the difference. Even just saying "Bonjour monsieur/madame" and then gesticulating will usually secure you a smile and helpful service.

What follows is a run-down of essential words and phrases. For more detail, get *French: A Rough Guide Dictionary Phrase Book*, which has an extensive vocabulary, a detailed menu reader and useful dialogues.

Pronunciation

Vowels are the hardest sounds to get right. Roughly:

a	as in hat
e	as in get
é	between get and gate
è	between get and gut
eu	like the u in hurt
i	as in machine
o	as in hot
o/au	as in over
ou	as in food
u	as in a pursed-lip, clipped version of toot

More awkward are the combinations in/im, en/em, on/om, un/um at the end of words, or followed by consonants other than n or m. Again, roughly:

in/im	like the "an" in anxious
an/am, en/em	like "on" said with a nasal accent
on/om	like "on" said by someone with a heavy cold
un/um	like the "u" in understand

Consonants are much as in English, except that ch is always sh, h is silent, th is the same as t, ll is like the y in "yes" when preceded by the letter "i", w is v, and r is growled (or rolled).

Words and phrases

Basics

Yes	Oui
No	Non
Please	S'il vous plaît
Thank you	Merci
Excuse me	Pardon/excusez-moi
Sorry	Pardon/Je m'excuse
Hello	Bonjour
Hello (phone)	Allô
Goodbye	Au revoir
Good morning/afternoon	Bonjour
Good evening	Bonsoir
Good night	Bonne nuit
How are you?	Comment allez-vous?/Ça va?
Fine, thanks	Très bien, merci
I don't know	Je ne sais pas
Do you speak English?	Vous parlez anglais?
How do you say...in French?	Comment ça se dit...en français?
What's your name?	Comment vous appelez-vous?

My name is …	Je m'appelle …
I'm English/	Je suis anglais(e)/
Irish/	irlandais(e)/
Scottish/	écossais(e)/
Welsh/	gallois(e)/
American/	américain(e)/
OK/agreed	D'accord
I understand	Je comprends
I don't understand	Je ne comprends pas
Can you speak slower?	S'il vous plaît, parlez moins vite
Today	Aujourd'hui
Yesterday	Hier
Tomorrow	Demain
In the morning	Le matin
In the afternoon	L'après-midi
In the evening	Le soir
Now	Maintenant
Later	Plus tard
Here	Ici
There	Là
This one	Ceci
That one	Cela
Open	Ouvert
Closed	Fermé
Big	Grand
Small	Petit
More	Plus
Less	Moins
A little	Un peu
A lot	Beaucoup
Half	La moitié
Inexpensive	Bon marché/pas cher

Expensive	Cher
Good	Bon
Bad	Mauvais
Hot	Chaud
Cold	Froid
With	Avec
Without	Sans

Questions

Where?	Où?
How?	Comment?
How many	Combien?
How much is it?	C'est combien?
When?	Quand?
Why?	Pourquoi?
At what time?	À quelle heure?
What is/Which is?	Quel est?

Getting around

Which way is it to the Eiffel Tower?	S'il vous plaît, pour aller à la Tour Eiffel?
Where is the nearest metro?	Où est le métro le plus proche?
Bus	Bus
Bus stop	Arrêt
Train	Train
Boat	Bâteau
Plane	Avion
Railway station	Gare
Platform	Quai
What time does it leave?	Il part à quelle heure?
What time does it arrive?	Il arrive à quelle heure?

A ticket to …	Un billet pour …
Single ticket	Aller simple
Return ticket	Aller retour
Where are you going?	Vous allez où?
I'm going to …	Je vais à …
I want to get off at …	Je voudrais descendre à …
Near	Près/pas loin
Far	Loin
Left	À gauche
Right	À droite

Accommodation

A room for one/two people	Une chambre pour une/deux personnes
With a double bed	Avec un grand lit
A room with a shower	Une chambre avec douche
A room with a bath	Une chambre avec salle de bain
For one/two/three nights	Pour une/deux/trois nuit(s)
With a view	Avec vue
Key	Clef
To iron	Repasser
Do laundry	Faire la lessive
Sheets	Draps
Blankets	Couvertures
Quiet	Calme
Noisy	Bruyant
Hot water	Eau chaude
Cold water	Eau froide
Is breakfast included?	Est-ce que le petit déjeuner est compris?
I would like breakfast	Je voudrais prendre le petit déjeuner

I don't want breakfast	Je ne veux pas le petit déjeuner
Youth hostel	Auberge de jeunesse

Eating out

I'd like to reserve a table…	Je voudrais réserver une table …
…for two people, at eight thirty	…pour deux personnes, à vingt heures et demie
I'm having the €15 menu	Je prendrai le menu à quinze euros
Waiter!	Monsieur/madame! (never "garçon")
The bill, please	L'addition, s'il vous plait

Days

Monday	Lundi
Tuesday	Mardi
Wednesday	Mercredi
Thursday	Jeudi
Friday	Vendredi
Saturday	Samedi
Sunday	Dimanche

Numbers

1	un	11	onze
2	deux	12	douze
3	trois	13	treize
4	quatre	14	quatorze
5	cinq	15	quinze
6	six	16	seize
7	sept	17	dix-sept
8	huit	18	dix-huit
9	neuf	19	dix-neuf
10	dix	20	vingt

21	vingt-et-un	90	quatre-vingt-dix
22	vingt-deux	95	quatre-vingt-quinze
30	trente	100	cent
40	quarante	101	cent un
50	cinquante	200	deux cents
60	soixante	1000	mille
70	soixante-dix	2000	deux mille
75	soixante-quinze	1,000,000	un million
80	quatre-vingts		

Menu glossary

Essentials

déjeuner	lunch
dîner	dinner
menu	set menu
à la carte	individually priced dishes
entrées	starters
les plats	main courses
pain	bread
beurre	butter
œufs	eggs
lait	milk
poivre	pepper
sel	salt
sucre	sugar
fourchette	fork
couteau	knife

cuillère	spoon
bio	organic
à la vapeur	steamed
au four	baked
cru	raw
frit	fried
fumé	smoked
grillé	grilled
rôti	roast
salé	salted/savoury
sucré	sweet
à emporter	takeaway

Drinks

eau minérale	mineral water
eau gazeuse	fizzy water
eau plate	still water
carte des vins	wine list
une pression	a glass of beer
un café	coffee (espresso)
un crème	white coffee
bouteille	bottle
verre	glass
un quart/demi de rouge/blanc	a quarter/half-litre of red/white house wine
un (verre de) rouge/blanc	a glass of white/red wine

Snacks

crêpe	pancake (sweet)
un sandwich/une baguette	sandwich
croque-monsieur	grilled cheese & ham sandwich
panini	flat toasted Italian sandwich

omelette	omelette
nature	plain
aux fines herbes	with herbs
au fromage	with cheese
assiette anglaise	plate of cold meats
crudités	raw vegetables with dressings

Fish (poisson) and seafood (fruits de mer)

anchois	anchovies
brème	bream
brochet	pike
cabillaud	cod
carrelet	plaice
colin	hake
coquilles st-jacques	scallops
crabe	crab
crevettes	shrimps/prawns
daurade	sea bream
flétan	halibut
friture	whitebait
hareng	herring
homard	lobster
huîtres	oysters
langoustines	saltwater crayfish (scampi)
limande	lemon sole
lotte de mer	monkfish
loup de mer	sea bass
maquereau	mackerel
merlan	whiting
morue	dried, salted cod

moules (marinière)	mussels (with shallots in white wine sauce)
raie	skate
rouget	red mullet
saumon	salmon
sole	sole
thon	tuna
truite	trout
turbot	turbot

Meat (viande) and poultry (volaille)

agneau	lamb
andouillette	tripe sausage
bavette beef	flank steak
bœuf	beef
bifteck	steak
boudin noir	black pudding
caille	quail
canard	duck
contrefilet	sirloin roast
dinde	turkey
entrecôte	ribsteak
faux filet	sirloin steak
foie	liver
foie gras	fattened (duck/goose) liver
gigot (d'agneau)	leg (of lamb)
grillade	grilled meat
hachis	chopped meat or mince hamburger
jambon	ham
lapin, lapereau	rabbit, young rabbit
lard, lardons	bacon, diced bacon
merguez	spicy, red sausage
oie	goose

onglet	cut of beef
porc	pork
poulet	chicken
poussin	baby chicken
rognons	kidneys
tête de veau	calf's head (in jelly)
tournedos	thick slices of fillet
veau	veal
venaison	venison

Steaks

bleu	almost raw
saignant	rare
a point	medium
bien cuit	well done

Garnishes and sauces

beurre blanc	sauce of white wine & shallots, with butter
chasseur	white wine, mushrooms & shallots
forestière	with bacon & mushroom
fricassée	rich, creamy sauce
mornay	cheese sauce
pays d'auge	cream & cider
piquante	gherkins or capers, vinegar & shallots
provençale	tomatoes, garlic, olive oil & herbs

Vegetables (légumes), herbs (herbes) and spices (épices)

ail	garlic
artichaut	artichoke
asperges	asparagus

avocat	avocado
basilic	basil
betterave	beetroot
carotte	carrot
céleri	celery
champignons	mushrooms
chou (rouge)	(red) cabbage
chou-fleur	cauliflower
ciboulette	chives
concombre	cucumber
cornichon	gherkin
échalotes	shallots
endive	chicory
épinards	spinach
estragon	tarragon
fenouil	fennel
flageolets	white beans
gingembre	ginger
haricots	beans
verts	string (french)
rouges	kidney
beurres	butter
lentilles	lentils
maïs	corn (maize)
moutarde	mustard
oignon	onion
pâtes	pasta
persil	parsley
petits pois	peas
pois chiche	chickpeas
pois mange-tout	snow peas
pignons	pine nuts

poireau	leek
poivron (vert, rouge)	sweet pepper (green, red)
pommes (de terre)	potatoes
primeurs	spring vegetables
radis	radishes
riz	rice
safran	saffron
salade verte	green salad
tomate	tomato
truffes	truffles

Fruits (fruits) and nuts (noix)

abricot	apricot
amandes	almonds
ananas	pineapple
banane	banana
brugnon, nectarine	nectarine
cacahouète	peanut
cassis	blackcurrants
cerises	cherries
citron	lemon
citron vert	lime
figues	figs
fraises	strawberries
framboises	raspberries
groseilles	redcurrants & gooseberries
mangue	mango
marrons	chestnuts
melon	melon
myrtilles	bilberries
noisette	hazelnut

noix	nuts
orange	orange
pamplemousse	grapefruit
pêche	peach
pistache	pistachio
poire	pear
pomme	apple
prune	plum
pruneau	prune
raisins	grapes

Desserts (desserts or entremets) and pastries (pâtisserie)

bavarois	refers to the mould, could be mousse or custard
brioche	sweet, high yeast breakfast roll
coupe	a serving of ice cream
crème chantilly	vanilla-flavoured & sweetened whipped cream
crème fraîche	sour cream
crème pâtissière	thick eggy pastry-filling
fromage blanc	cream cheese
glace	ice cream
parfait	frozen mousse, sometimes ice cream
petits fours	bite-sized cakes/pastries
tarte	tart
yaourt, yogourt	yoghurt

Cheese (fromage)

There are over four hundred types of French cheese, most of them named after their place of origin. *Chèvre* is goat's cheese and *brebis* is cheese made from sheep's milk. *Le plateau de fromages* is the cheeseboard, and bread – but not butter – is served with it.

ROUGH
GUIDES

ROUGH GUIDES

NOTES

NOTES

NOTES

NOTES

ROUGH
GUIDES

Small print & Index

A Rough Guide to Rough Guides

Published in 1982, the first Rough Guide – to Greece – was a student scheme that became a publishing phenomenon. Mark Ellingham, a recent graduate in English from Bristol University, had been travelling in Greece the previous summer and couldn't find the right guidebook. With a small group of friends he wrote his own guide, combining a highly contemporary, journalistic style with a thoroughly practical approach to travellers' needs.

The immediate success of the book spawned a series that rapidly covered dozens of destinations. And, in addition to impecunious backpackers, Rough Guides soon acquired a much broader and older readership that relished the guides' wit and inquisitiveness as much as their enthusiastic, critical approach and value-for-money ethos.

These days, Rough Guides include recommendations from shoestring to luxury and cover more than 200 destinations around the globe, including almost every country in the Americas and Europe, more than half of Africa and most of Asia and Australasia. Our ever-growing team of authors and photographers is spread all over the world, particularly in Europe, the USA and Australia.

In the early 1990s, Rough Guides branched out of travel, with the publication of Rough Guides to World Music, Classical Music and the Internet. All three have become benchmark titles in their fields, spearheading the publication of a wide range of books under the Rough Guide name.

Including the travel series, Rough Guides now number more than 350 titles, covering: phrasebooks, waterproof maps, music guides from Opera to Heavy Metal, reference works as diverse as Conspiracy Theories and Shakespeare, and popular culture books from iPods to Poker. Rough Guides also produce a series of more than 120 World Music CDs in partnership with World Music Network.

Visit www.roughguides.com to see our latest publications.

Rough Guide travel images are available for commercial licensing at www.roughguidespictures.com

Publishing information

This second edition published March 2006 by
Rough Guides Ltd, 80 Strand, London WC2R 0RL.
345 Hudson St, 4th Floor, New York, NY 10014, USA.
Distributed by the Penguin Group
Penguin Books Ltd, 80 Strand, London WC2R 0RL.
Penguin Group (USA), 375 Hudson Street, NY 10014, USA.
14 Local Shopping Centre, Panchsheel Park, New Delhi 110017, India.
Penguin Group (Australia), 250 Camberwell Road, Camberwell, Victoria 3124, Australia.
Penguin Group (Canada), 10 Alcorn Avenue, Toronto, ON M4V 1E4, Canada.
Penguin Group (New Zealand), Cnr Rosedale and Airborne Roads, Albany, Auckland, New Zealand.
Typeset in Bembo and Helvetica to an original design by Henry Iles.
Printed and bound in Italy by LegoPrint S.p.A.

396pp includes index.
A catalogue record for this book is available from the British Library
ISBN 1-84353-593-9
ISBN 13: 9781843535935

3 5 7 9 8 6 4

Help us update

We've gone to a lot of effort to ensure that the second edition of **The Mini Rough Guide to Paris** is accurate and up to date. However, things change – places get "discovered", opening hours are notoriously fickle, restaurants and rooms raise prices or lower standards. If you feel we've got it wrong or left something out, we'd like to know, and if you can remember the address, the price, the time, the phone number, so much the better.

We'll credit all contributions, and send a copy of the next edition (or any other Rough Guide if you prefer) for the best letters. Everyone who writes to us and isn't already a subscriber will receive a copy of our full-colour thrice-yearly newsletter. Please mark letters: **"Mini Rough Guide Paris Update"** and send to: Rough Guides, 80 Strand, London WC2R 0RL, or Rough Guides, 4th Floor, 345 Hudson St, New York, NY 10014. Or send an email to **mail@roughguides.com**

Have your questions answered and tell others about your trip at **www.roughguides.atinfopop.com**

Rough Guides credits

Text editor: Sarah Eno
Layout: Daniel May
Cartography: Ed Wright
Picture editor: Harriet Mills
Production: Katherine Owers
Proofreader: Helen Cartell
Cover design: Chloë Roberts
Photographer: James McConnachie

Acknowledgements

James would like to say a particular thank you to Ginger Benjafield, Sarah Brody, Marco Calzoni, Professor Clive Gamble, Dr Alice Hunt, Sally Jones, Terry Jones, Sacha Kolev, M et Mme Kolev, Eva Loechner, Pierre Loechner, Gwen and Robin McConnachie, John and Barbara McNaught, William McNaught, Dr Stephen Oppenheimer, Edwin Samuel, Dr Richard Scholar, Alison Telfer and, of course, Ruth Blackmore.

Ruth would like to say a special thank you to Dr Phillipa Tawn, Dr Robin Cleveland, Dylan and Imogen Cleveland; James McConnachie for being such an excellent co-author; Véronique Potelet and Agnès Mignot from the Paris tourist board; Christina Greveldinger, Maryse Courberand, Anne Wencélius, Matthew Teller, Dr M. B. Chadwick, Ursula Williams, Polly Thomas and Dylan Reisenberger.

Readers' letters

Thanks to all the readers who have taken the time to write in with comments and suggestions (and apologies if we've inadvertently omitted or misspelt anyone's name):

Paul Adams, Keith Allan, Colin Armstrong, Kate Armstrong, Lance Balcom, Stanley Blenkinsop, Eoin Brown, Eamonn Coughlan, Charlotte Eastwell, John Ennis, Chris Frean, Peter Gerrard, William Goldman, Ruth Harris, Rory Kelleher, Doug Miles, Muriel Mironneau, Chris Nugent, Roger and Yvonne Perkins, Doug Rew, Kate Santon, Sebastian Schroeder, Martin Smit, Jan Smith, Richard Stansfield, Nadine Vitols-Dixon and William Wang.

Photo credits

All photos © Rough Guides except the following:

Cover
Front cover: Clock, Musée D'Orsay © Getty
Back cover: Eiffel Tower and statue © Alamy

Things not to miss
05 Food market, place Jean-Lorrain, 16e © Roz Belgrave/Icen Photos

Index

Map entries are in colour.

F

G

H

I

J

INDEX

INDEX

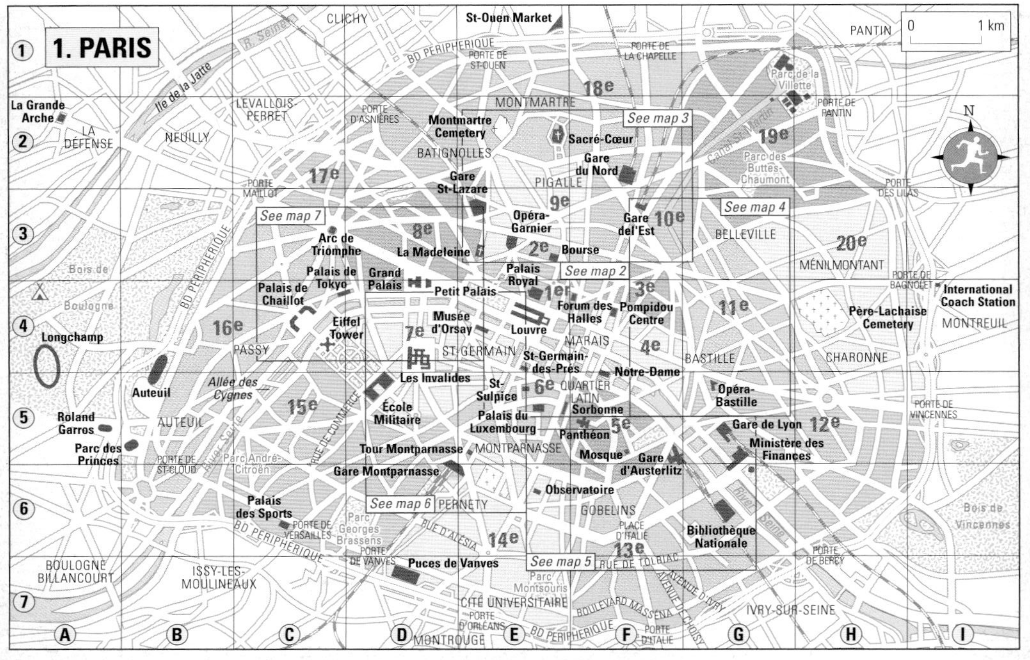
1. PARIS
0
1 km
N
La Grande Arche
LA DÉFENSE
NEUILLY
Ile de la Jatte
R. Seine
LEVALLOIS-PERRET
CLICHY
BD PERIPHERIQUE
PORTE DE ST-OUEN
St-Ouen Market
PORTE DE LA CHAPELLE
PANTIN
Parc de la Villette
PORTE DE PANTIN
18e
MONTMARTRE
PORTE D'ASNIÈRES
Montmartre Cemetery
BATIGNOLLES
See map 3
Sacré-Cœur
Gare du Nord
19e
Canal St-Martin
Parc des Buttes-Chaumont
PORTE MAILLOT
17e
Gare St-Lazare
PIGALLE
9e
PORTE DES LILAS
See map 7
Opéra-Garnier
Gare de l'Est
10e
See map 4
BELLEVILLE
20e
Arc de Triomphe
8e
La Madeleine
2e
Bourse
Bois de Boulogne
Palais de Tokyo
Grand Palais
Palais Royal
See map 2
MÉNILMONTANT
PORTE DE BAGNOLET
International Coach Station
Palais de Chaillot
Petit Palais
1er
3e
Forum des Halles
Pompidou Centre
11e
Père-Lachaise Cemetery
MONTREUIL
16e
Eiffel Tower
Musée d'Orsay
7e
Louvre
MARAIS
4e
Longchamp
PASSY
ST-GERMAIN
St-Germain-des-Prés
BASTILLE
CHARONNE
Les Invalides
Notre-Dame
Allée des Cygnes
Auteuil
St-Sulpice
6e
QUARTIER LATIN
Opéra-Bastille
15e
École Militaire
Sorbonne
Roland Garros
AUTEUIL
RUE DE COMMERCE
Palais du Luxembourg
5e
Gare de Lyon
12e
PORTE DE VINCENNES
Panthéon
Ministère des Finances
Parc des Princes
Tour Montparnasse
MONTPARNASSE
Mosque
PORTE DE ST-CLOUD
River Seine
Parc André-Citroën
Gare d'Austerlitz
Gare Montparnasse
Observatoire
See map 6
PERNETY
GOBELINS
Palais des Sports
River Seine
Bois de Vincennes
PORTE DE VERSAILLES
Parc Georges Brassens
RUE D'ALÉSIA
14e
PLACE D'ITALIE
Bibliothèque Nationale
13e
BD PERIPHERIQUE
PORTE DE VANVES
Puces de Vanves
See map 5
RUE DE TOLBIAC
PORTE DE BERCY
BOULOGNE BILLANCOURT
ISSY-LES-MOULINEAUX
Parc Montsouris
AVENUE D'IVRY
AVENUE DE CHOISY
CITÉ UNIVERSITAIRE
BOULEVARD MASSÉNA
IVRY-SUR-SEINE
PORTE D'ORLÉANS
BD PERIPHERIQUE
PORTE D'ITALIE
MONTROUGE
A
B
C
D
E
F
G
H
I
1
2
3
4
5
6
7

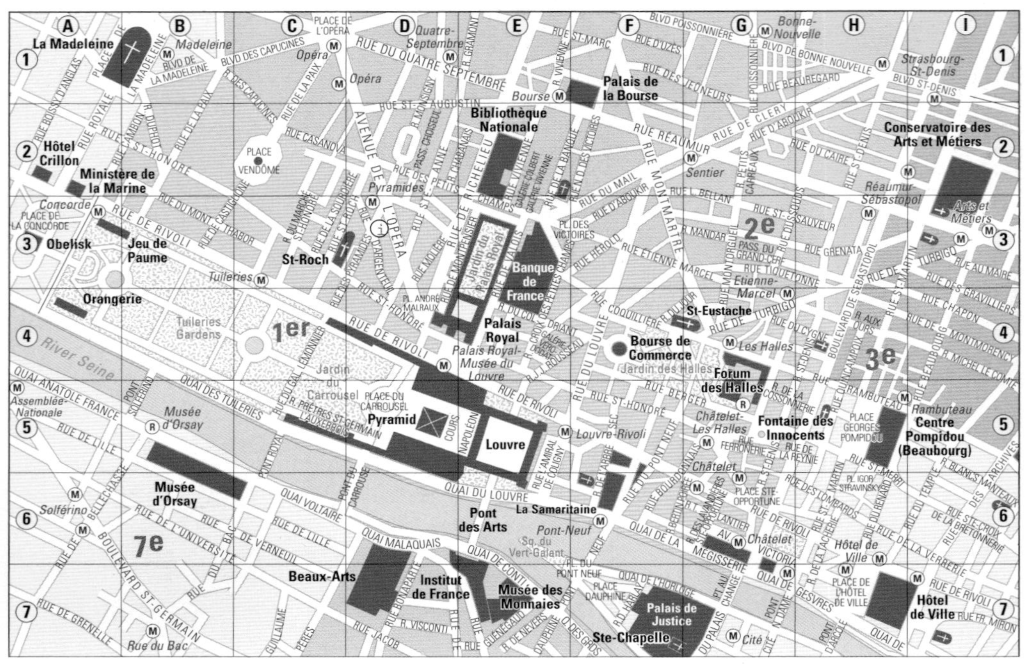

La Madeleine
Hôtel Crillon
Ministère de la Marine
Obelisk
Jeu de Paume
Orangerie
Tuileries Gardens
St-Roch
Place Vendôme
Bibliothèque Nationale
Palais de la Bourse
Banque de France
Palais Royal
Jardin du Palais Royal
Pyramid
Louvre
Musée d'Orsay
Beaux-Arts
Institut de France
Musée des Monnaies
Pont des Arts
La Samaritaine
Palais de Justice
Ste-Chapelle
Bourse de Commerce
St-Eustache
Forum des Halles
Jardin des Halles
Fontaine des Innocents
Centre Pompidou (Beaubourg)
Conservatoire des Arts et Métiers
Hôtel de Ville
River Seine
Jardin du Carrousel
1er
2e
3e
7e

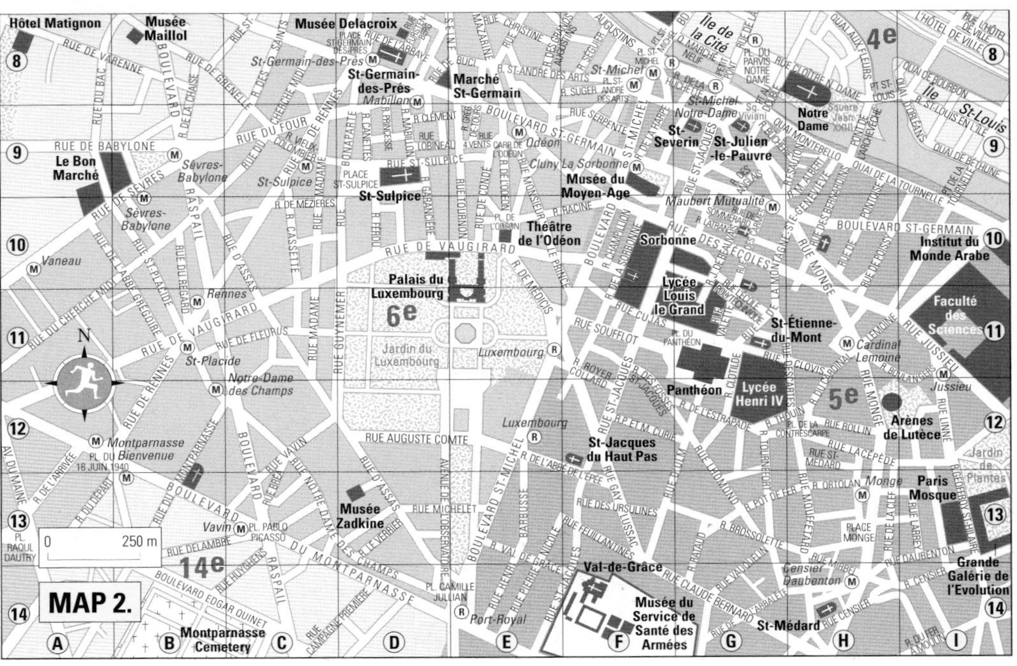
MAP 2.
Hôtel Matignon
Musée Maillol
Musée Delacroix
St-Germain-des-Prés
Marché St-Germain
Île de la Cité
Notre Dame
4e
Île St-Louis
Le Bon Marché
St-Sulpice
St-Severin
St-Julien -le-Pauvre
Musée du Moyen-Age
Théâtre de l'Odéon
Sorbonne
Institut du Monde Arabe
Palais du Luxembourg
6e
Jardin du Luxembourg
Lycée Louis le Grand
Faculté des Sciences
St-Étienne-du-Mont
Panthéon
Lycée Henri IV
5e
Arènes de Lutèce
Jardin de Plantes
St-Jacques du Haut Pas
Paris Mosque
Musée Zadkine
Val-de-Grâce
Musée du Service de Santé des Armées
St-Médard
Grande Galérie de l'Evolution
Montparnasse Cemetery
14e
0 250 m
N
BOULEVARD ST-GERMAIN
RUE DE VAUGIRARD
BOULEVARD ST-MICHEL
BOULEVARD RASPAIL
BOULEVARD DU MONTPARNASSE
RUE DE RENNES
RUE DE SÈVRES
RUE DE BABYLONE
RUE DE VARENNE
RUE MONGE
RUE DES ÉCOLES
RUE SOUFFLOT
RUE MOUFFETARD
RUE CLAUDE BERNARD
RUE AUGUSTE COMTE
AVENUE DE L'OBSERVATOIRE
RUE D'ASSAS
RUE GUYNEMER
RUE MADAME
RUE JUSSIEU
QUAI DE LA TOURNELLE
QUAI DE MONTEBELLO
QUAI DE BÉTHUNE
QUAI D'ORLÉANS
QUAI DE BOURBON
QUAI AUX FLEURS
SEINE
A B C D E F G H I
8 9 10 11 12 13 14

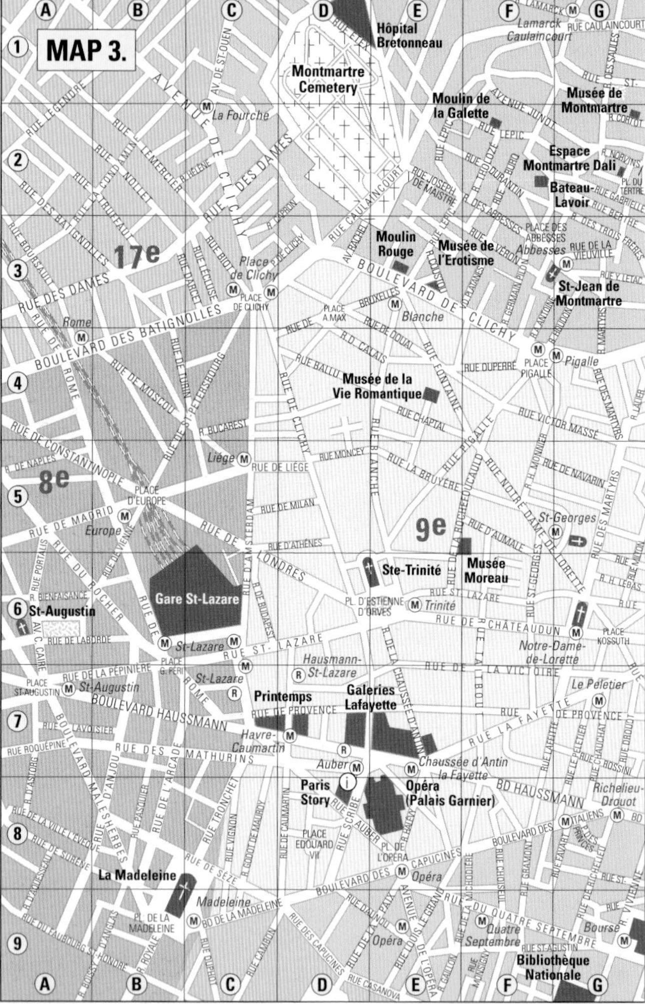
MAP 3.
Hôpital Bretonneau
Montmartre Cemetery
Moulin de la Galette
Musée de Montmartre
Espace Montmartre Dali
Bateau-Lavoir
Moulin Rouge
Musée de l'Erotisme
St-Jean de Montmartre
17e
8e
9e
Musée de la Vie Romantique
Gare St-Lazare
St-Augustin
Ste-Trinité
Musée Moreau
Printemps
Galeries Lafayette
Paris Story
Opéra (Palais Garnier)
La Madeleine
Bibliothèque Nationale
La Fourche
Place de Clichy
Blanche
Pigalle
Abbesses
Lamarck Caulaincourt
Rome
Liège
Europe
St-Lazare
Trinité
St-Georges
Notre-Dame-de-Lorette
Le Peletier
Havre-Caumartin
Auber
Chaussée d'Antin la Fayette
Richelieu-Drouot
Opéra
Madeleine
Quatre Septembre
Bourse
BOULEVARD DE CLICHY
BOULEVARD DES BATIGNOLLES
BOULEVARD HAUSSMANN
AVENUE DE CLICHY
RUE DE ROME
RUE ST-LAZARE
BOULEVARD DES CAPUCINES
BOULEVARD MALESHERBES

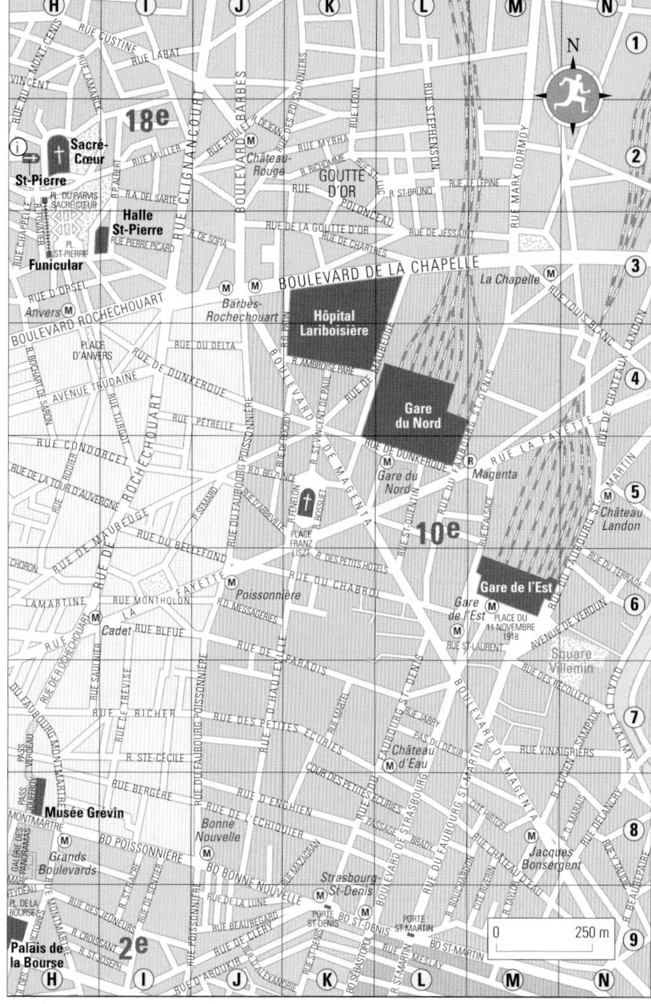

18e
Sacré-Cœur
St-Pierre
Halle St-Pierre
Funicular
Château-Rouge
GOUTTE D'OR
BOULEVARD DE LA CHAPELLE
La Chapelle
Anvers
Barbès-Rochechouart
Hôpital Lariboisière
Gare du Nord
Magenta
10e
Château Landon
Gare de l'Est
Poissonnière
Cadet
Square Villemin
Château d'Eau
Musée Grévin
Grands Boulevards
Bonne Nouvelle
Jacques Bonsergent
Strasbourg-St-Denis
Porte St-Denis
Porte St-Martin
Palais de la Bourse
2e
0 250 m

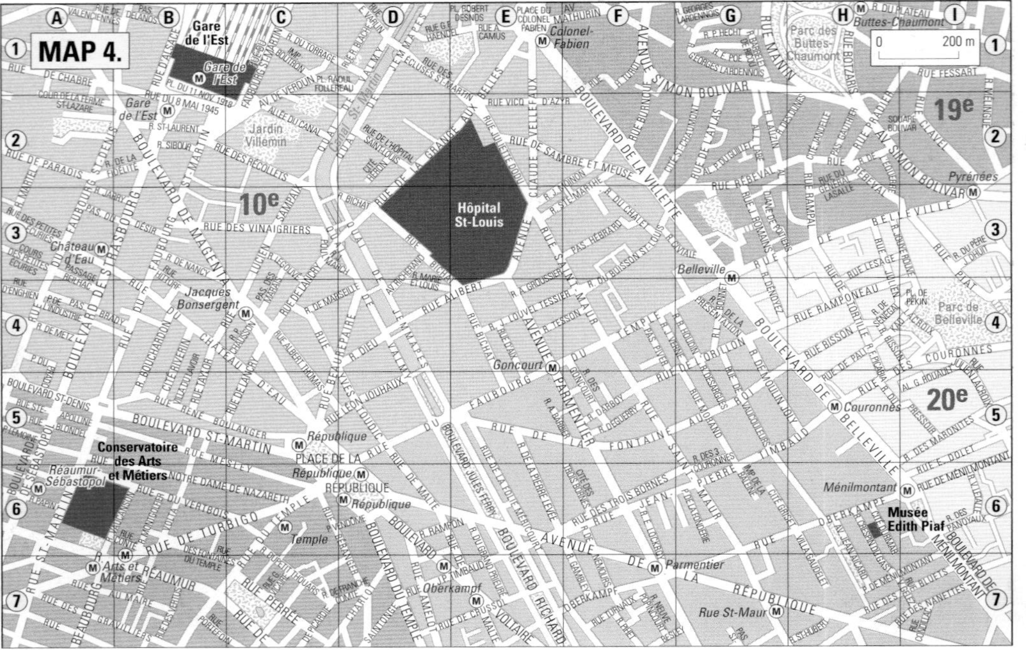
MAP 4.
0
200 m
Gare de l'Est
Jardin Villemin
10e
19e
20e
Hôpital St-Louis
Parc des Buttes-Chaumont
Buttes-Chaumont
Parc de Belleville
Conservatoire des Arts et Métiers
Musée Edith Piaf
Colonel-Fabien
Pyrénées
Belleville
Goncourt
Couronnes
Ménilmontant
Parmentier
Rue St-Maur
Oberkampf
République
Temple
Arts et Métiers
Réaumur-Sébastopol
Château d'Eau
Jacques Bonsergent
PLACE DE LA RÉPUBLIQUE
Canal St-Martin
BOULEVARD DE MAGENTA
BOULEVARD DE STRASBOURG
BOULEVARD ST-MARTIN
BOULEVARD DE LA VILLETTE
BOULEVARD DE BELLEVILLE
BOULEVARD DE MÉNILMONTANT
BOULEVARD DU TEMPLE
BOULEVARD RICHARD
BOULEVARD JULES FERRY
AVENUE SIMON BOLIVAR
AVENUE PARMENTIER
AVENUE DE LA RÉPUBLIQUE
RUE DU FAUBOURG DU TEMPLE
RUE DE TURBIGO
RUE RÉAUMUR
RUE DES VINAIGRIERS
RUE ST-MAUR
RUE MANIN
RUE BOTZARIS

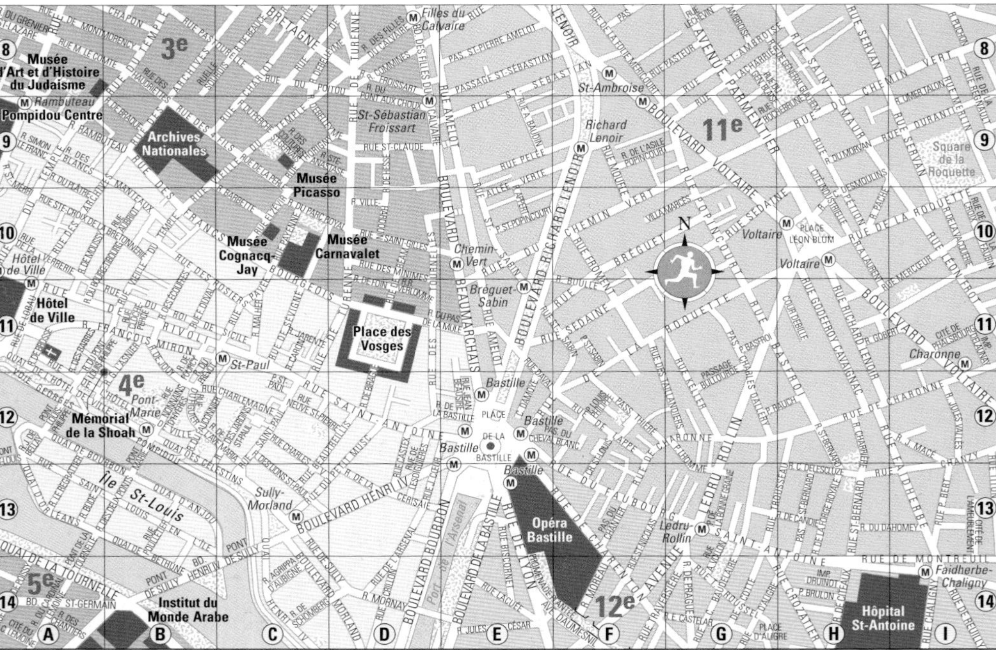

3e
4e
5e
11e
12e
Musée d'Art et d'Histoire du Judaïsme
Rambuteau
Pompidou Centre
Archives Nationales
Musée Picasso
Musée Cognacq-Jay
Musée Carnavalet
Place des Vosges
Hôtel de Ville
St-Paul
Pont-Marie
Mémorial de la Shoah
Île St-Louis
Sully-Morland
Institut du Monde Arabe
Filles du Calvaire
St-Sébastian Froissart
Chemin-Vert
Bréguet-Sabin
Bastille
Place de la Bastille
Opéra Bastille
Ledru-Rollin
Faidherbe-Chaligny
Hôpital St-Antoine
St-Ambroise
Richard Lenoir
Voltaire
Place Léon Blum
Charonne
Square de la Roquette
Port de l'Arsenal
Rue de Rivoli
Rue St-Antoine
Boulevard Beaumarchais
Boulevard Richard Lenoir
Boulevard Voltaire
Avenue Parmentier
Rue de la Roquette
Rue du Faubourg St-Antoine
Avenue Ledru Rollin
Rue de Lyon
Boulevard de la Bastille
Boulevard Bourdon
Boulevard Henri IV
Rue de Turenne
Rue de Bretagne
Rue Oberkampf
Rue de Charonne
Rue Faidherbe
N
A
B
C
D
E
F
G
H
I
8
9
10
11
12
13
14

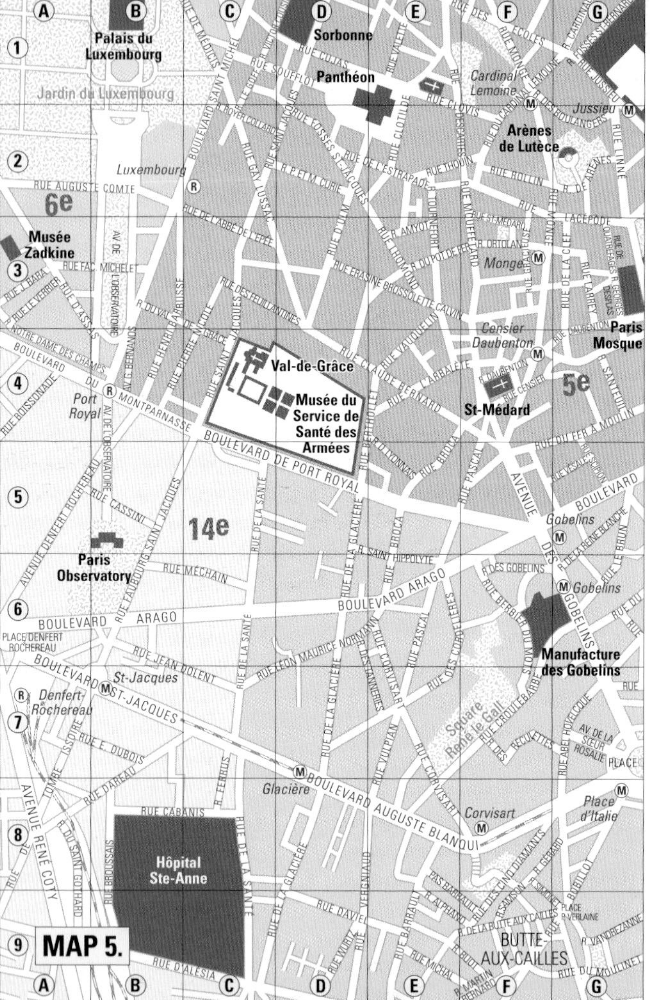

Palais du Luxembourg
Jardin du Luxembourg
Sorbonne
Panthéon
Cardinal Lemoine
Jussieu
Arènes de Lutèce
Luxembourg
6e
Musée Zadkine
Monge
Censier Daubenton
Paris Mosque
Val-de-Grâce
Musée du Service de Santé des Armées
St-Médard
5e
Port Royal
14e
Paris Observatory
Gobelins
Manufacture des Gobelins
Place Denfert Rochereau
St-Jacques
Denfert-Rochereau
Square René le Gall
Glacière
Corvisart
Place d'Italie
Hôpital Ste-Anne
Butte-aux-Cailles
MAP 5.

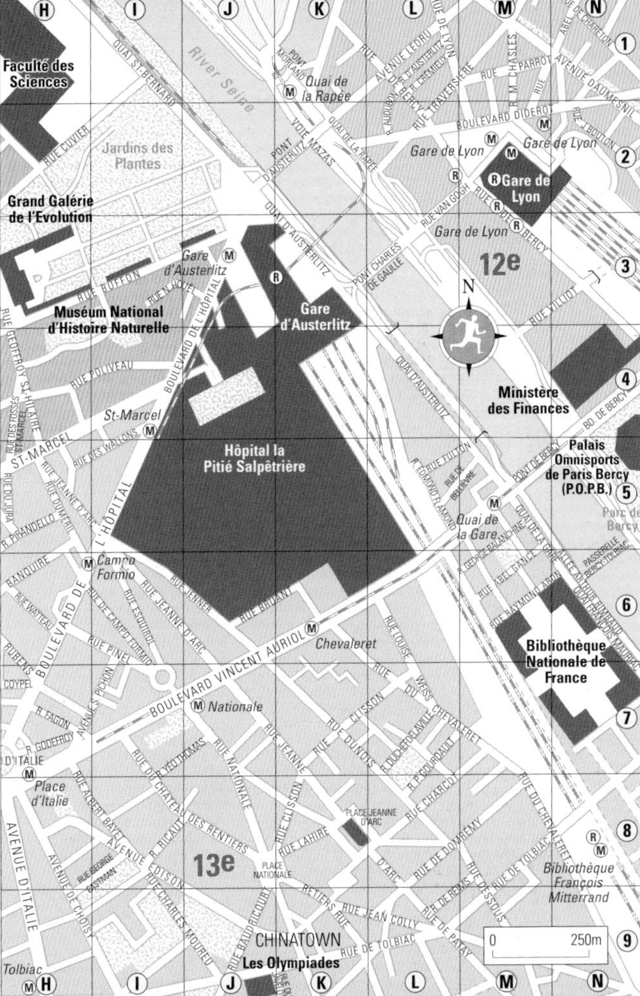
H
I
J
K
L
M
N
1
2
3
4
5
6
7
8
9
Faculté des Sciences
River Seine
Quai de la Rapée
Jardins des Plantes
Grand Galérie de l'Evolution
Gare d'Austerlitz
Gare de Lyon
12e
Muséum National d'Histoire Naturelle
Ministère des Finances
St-Marcel
Hôpital la Pitié Salpêtrière
Palais Omnisports de Paris Bercy (P.O.P.B.)
Parc de Bercy
Quai de la Gare
Campo Formio
Chevaleret
Bibliothèque Nationale de France
Nationale
Place d'Italie
13e
Place Nationale
Place Jeanne d'Arc
Bibliothèque François Mitterrand
CHINATOWN
Les Olympiades
Tolbiac
0
250m
Quai St-Bernard
Rue Cuvier
Rue Buffon
Boulevard de l'Hôpital
Rue Poliveau
St-Marcel
Boulevard Vincent Auriol
Boulevard Diderot
Rue de Bercy
Rue Van Gogh
Quai d'Austerlitz
Pont d'Austerlitz
Pont Charles de Gaulle
Rue de Tolbiac
Rue du Chevaleret
Avenue d'Italie
Avenue de Choisy
Rue Nationale
Rue Jeanne d'Arc
Rue Jean Colly
Avenue Daumesnil
Avenue Ledru
Rue de Lyon
Rue de Charenton

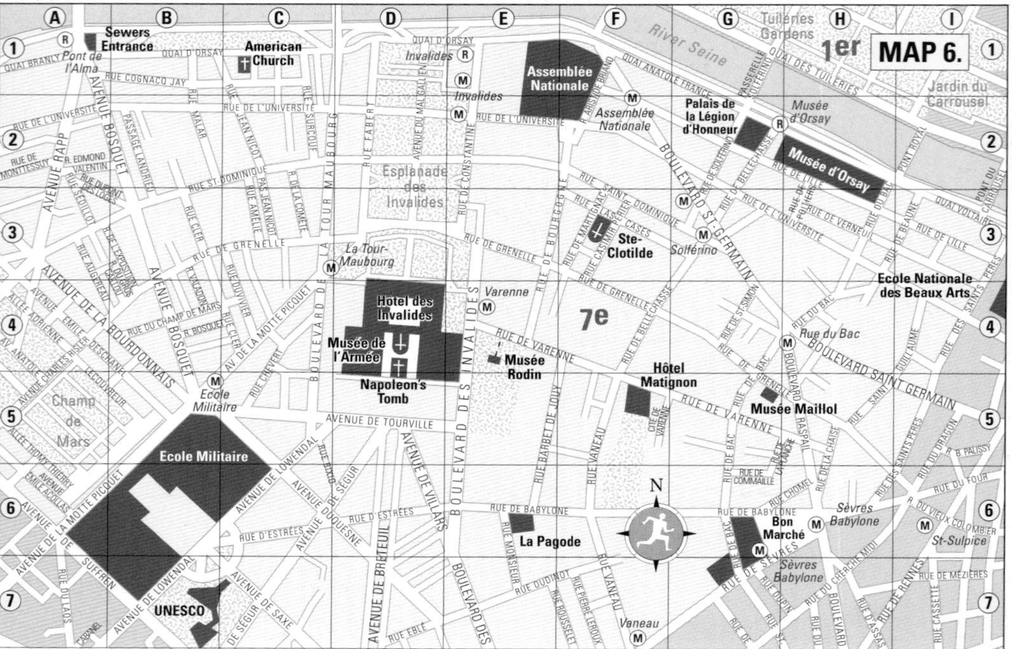

MAP 6.
1er
7e
River Seine
Tuileries Gardens
Jardin du Carrousel
Sewers Entrance
Pont de l'Alma
American Church
Invalides
Assemblée Nationale
Palais de la Légion d'Honneur
Musée d'Orsay
Esplanade des Invalides
La Tour-Maubourg
Ste-Clotilde
Solférino
Ecole Nationale des Beaux Arts
Hotel des Invalides
Musée de l'Armée
Napoleon's Tomb
Varenne
Musée Rodin
Hôtel Matignon
Rue du Bac
Musée Maillol
Ecole Militaire
Champ de Mars
La Pagode
Bon Marché
Sèvres Babylone
St-Sulpice
Vaneau
UNESCO
QUAI BRANLY
QUAI D'ORSAY
QUAI ANATOLE FRANCE
QUAI DES TUILERIES
QUAI VOLTAIRE
AVENUE BOSQUET
AVENUE RAPP
RUE DE L'UNIVERSITÉ
RUE ST-DOMINIQUE
RUE DE GRENELLE
BOULEVARD DE LA TOUR MAUBOURG
BOULEVARD DES INVALIDES
BOULEVARD ST-GERMAIN
BOULEVARD SAINT GERMAIN
BOULEVARD RASPAIL
RUE DE VARENNE
RUE DE BABYLONE
RUE DE SÈVRES
AVENUE DE LA BOURDONNAIS
AVENUE DE LA MOTTE PICQUET
AVENUE DE TOURVILLE
AVENUE DE VILLARS
AVENUE DE BRETEUIL
AVENUE DE SÉGUR
AVENUE DE SUFFREN
AVENUE DE LOWENDAL
AVENUE DUQUESNE
AVENUE DE SAXE
RUE DE RENNES
RUE DU BAC

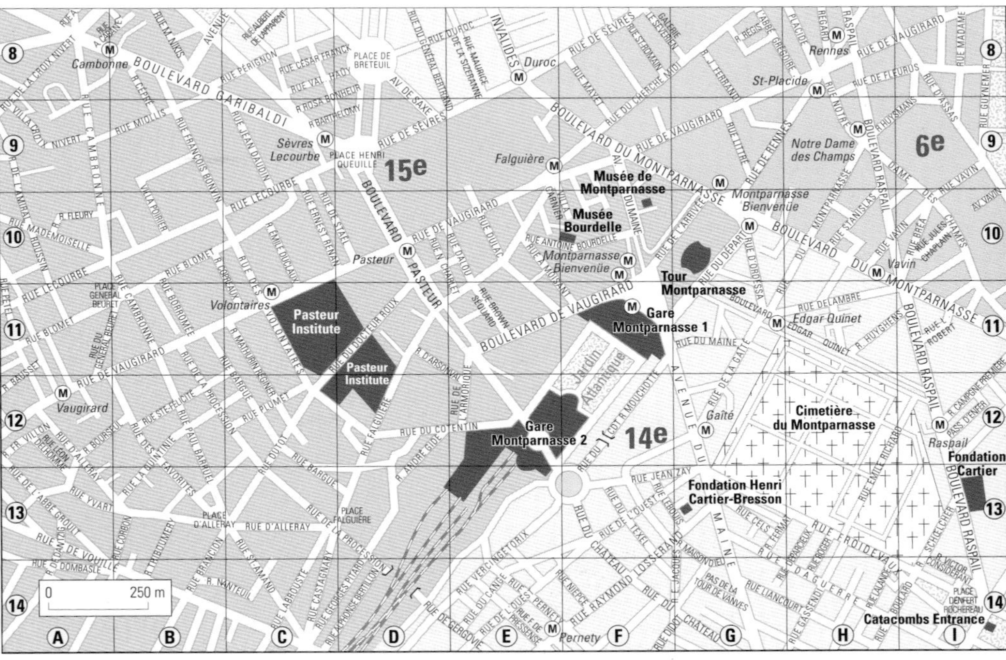

Cambonne
Boulevard Garibaldi
Place de Breteuil
Invalides
Duroc
Rue de Sèvres
Rennes
St-Placide
Rue de Vaugirard
Rue de Fleurus
Rue d'Assas
Rue Madame
Rue Guynemer
6e
Notre Dame des Champs
Boulevard du Montparnasse
Boulevard Raspail
Sèvres Lecourbe
Place Henri Queuille
15e
Falguière
Musée de Montparnasse
Musée Bourdelle
Montparnasse Bienvenüe
Tour Montparnasse
Vavin
Rue Vavin
Rue de Rennes
Rue Lecourbe
Boulevard Pasteur
Pasteur
Volontaires
Pasteur Institute
Rue de Vaugirard
Boulevard de Vaugirard
Gare Montparnasse 1
Edgar Quinet
Rue Delambre
Rue de la Gaîté
Gaîté
Jardin Atlantique
Gare Montparnasse 2
14e
Avenue du Maine
Cimetière du Montparnasse
Raspail
Fondation Cartier
Vaugirard
Rue du Cotentin
Fondation Henri Cartier-Bresson
Rue Froidevaux
Rue Daguerre
Place d'Alleray
Rue d'Alleray
Place Falguière
Rue de la Procession
Rue Raymond Losserand
Rue du Château
Pernety
Rue Vercingétorix
Catacombs Entrance
Place Denfert Rochereau
0 250 m
A B C D E F G H I
8 9 10 11 12 13 14

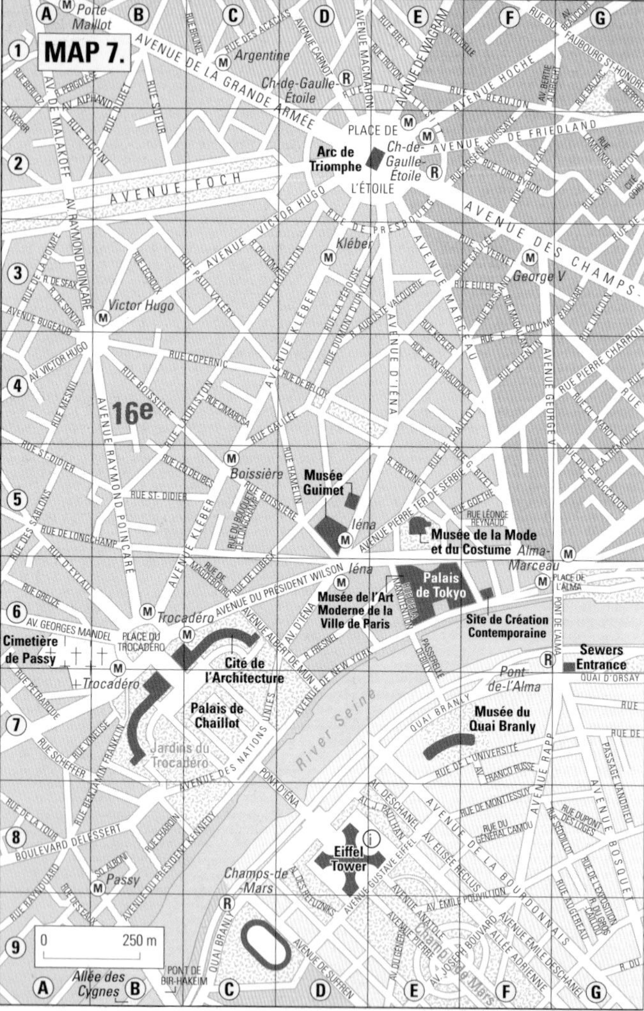

MAP 7.
Arc de Triomphe
Musée Guimet
Musée de la Mode et du Costume
Palais de Tokyo
Musée de l'Art Moderne de la Ville de Paris
Site de Création Contemporaine
Cimetière de Passy
Cité de l'Architecture
Palais de Chaillot
Jardins du Trocadéro
Sewers Entrance
Musée du Quai Branly
Eiffel Tower
River Seine
Champ de Mars
16e
AVENUE DE LA GRANDE ARMÉE
AVENUE FOCH
AVENUE VICTOR HUGO
AVENUE KLÉBER
AVENUE D'IÉNA
AVENUE MARCEAU
AVENUE DES CHAMPS-
AVENUE GEORGE V
AVENUE RAYMOND POINCARÉ
AVENUE DU PRÉSIDENT WILSON
AVENUE DE NEW YORK
AVENUE DE LA BOURDONNAIS
AVENUE BOSQUET
AVENUE RAPP
AVENUE DE FRIEDLAND
AVENUE HOCHE
AVENUE DE WAGRAM
AVENUE MACMAHON
AVENUE DE SUFFREN
QUAI BRANLY
QUAI D'ORSAY
BOULEVARD DELESSERT
AVENUE DU PRÉSIDENT KENNEDY
PLACE DE L'ÉTOILE
PLACE DU TROCADÉRO
PLACE DE L'ALMA
Porte Maillot
Argentine
Ch-de-Gaulle-Étoile
Kléber
George V
Victor Hugo
Boissière
Iéna
Alma-Marceau
Trocadéro
Pont-de-l'Alma
Passy
Champs-de-Mars
Allée des Cygnes
PONT DE BIR-HAKEIM
PONT D'IÉNA
0
250 m

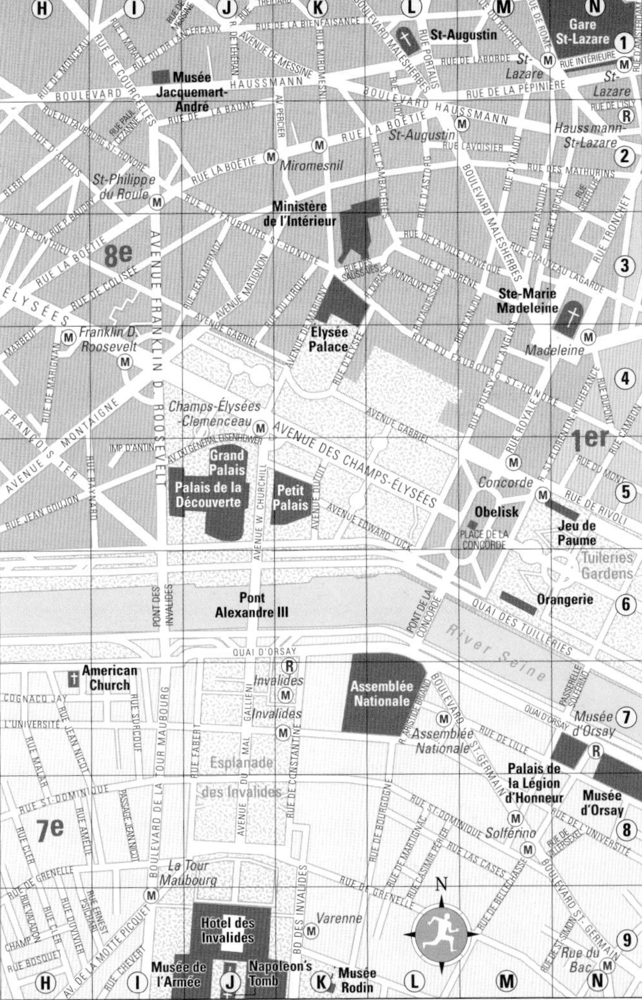

Gare St-Lazare
St-Augustin
Musée Jacquemart-André
St-Philippe du Roule
Miromesnil
Ministère de l'Intérieur
8e
Ste-Marie Madeleine
Madeleine
Élysée Palace
Franklin D. Roosevelt
Champs-Élysées -Clemenceau
Grand Palais
Palais de la Découverte
Petit Palais
Concorde
Obelisk
Jeu de Paume
Tuileries Gardens
Orangerie
1er
Pont Alexandre III
River Seine
American Church
Invalides
Assemblée Nationale
Musée d'Orsay
Esplanade des Invalides
Palais de la Légion d'Honneur
7e
Solférino
La Tour Maubourg
Varenne
Hôtel des Invalides
Musée de l'Armée
Napoleon's Tomb
Musée Rodin
Rue du Bac
AVENUE DES CHAMPS-ÉLYSÉES
AVENUE FRANKLIN D. ROOSEVELT
BOULEVARD HAUSSMANN
BOULEVARD MALESHERBES
RUE DU FAUBOURG ST-HONORÉ
RUE DE RIVOLI
QUAI D'ORSAY
QUAI DES TUILLERIES
BOULEVARD ST-GERMAIN
RUE DE GRENELLE
RUE ST-DOMINIQUE

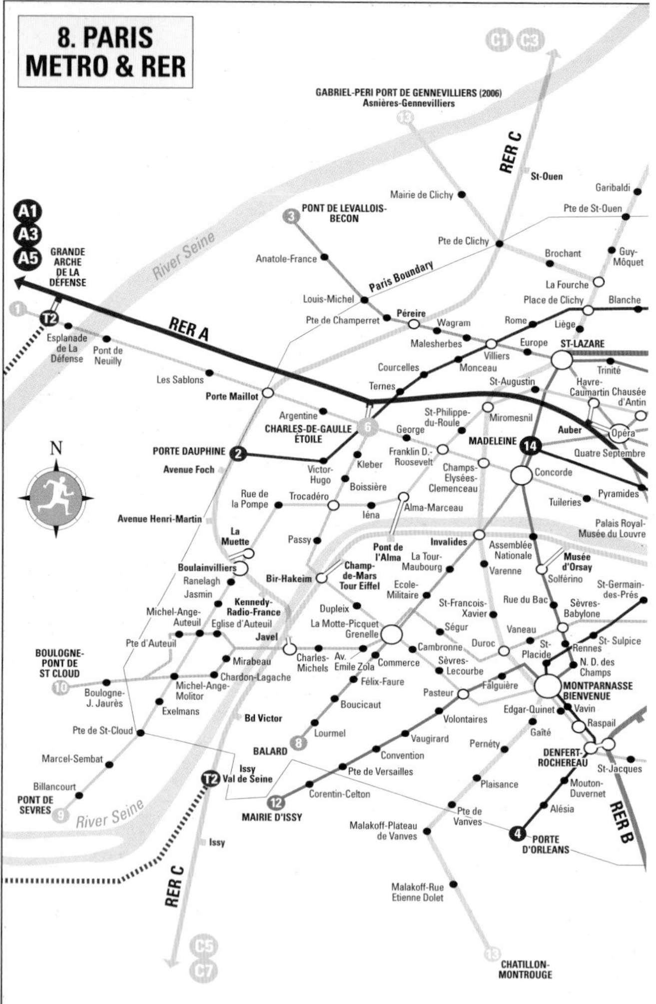

8. PARIS
METRO & RER
C1 C3
GABRIEL-PERI PORT DE GENNEVILLIERS (2006)
Asnières-Gennevilliers
13
RER C
St-Ouen
Garibaldi
Mairie de Clichy
Pte de St-Ouen
PONT DE LEVALLOIS-BECON
3
A1
A3
A5
GRANDE ARCHE DE LA DÉFENSE
River Seine
Anatole-France
Pte de Clichy
Brochant
Guy-Môquet
Paris Boundary
La Fourche
Louis-Michel
Place de Clichy
Blanche
1
T2
Pte de Champerret
Péreire
Wagram
Rome
Liège
RER A
Esplanade de La Défense
Pont de Neuilly
Malesherbes
Villiers
Europe
ST-LAZARE
Courcelles
Monceau
Trinité
Les Sablons
St-Augustin
Havre-Caumartin
Chausée d'Antin
Ternes
Porte Maillot
Argentine
St-Philippe-du-Roule
Miromesnil
CHARLES-DE-GAULLE ÉTOILE
6
George
Auber
Opéra
MADELEINE
14
PORTE DAUPHINE
2
Franklin D.-Roosevelt
Quatre Septembre
N
Avenue Foch
Victor-Hugo
Kleber
Champs-Elysées-Clemenceau
Concorde
Boissière
Rue de la Pompe
Trocadéro
Alma-Marceau
Tuileries
Pyramides
Iéna
Avenue Henri-Martin
Palais Royal-Musée du Louvre
La Muette
Passy
Pont de l'Alma
Invalides
Assemblée Nationale
Musée d'Orsay
La Tour-Maubourg
Boulainvilliers
Champ-de-Mars Tour Eiffel
Varenne
Solférino
Ranelagh
Bir-Hakeim
Ecole-Militaire
St-Germain-des-Prés
Jasmin
Kennedy-Radio-France
Rue du Bac
Sèvres-Babylone
Dupleix
St-Francois-Xavier
Michel-Ange-Auteuil
Eglise d'Auteuil
La Motte-Picquet Grenelle
Ségur
Vaneau
Javel
St- Sulpice
Pte d'Auteuil
Duroc
Cambronne
St-Placide
Rennes
BOULOGNE-PONT DE ST CLOUD
Mirabeau
Charles-Michels
Av. Emile Zola
Commerce
Sèvres-Lecourbe
N. D. des Champs
Chardon-Lagache
10
Michel-Ange-Molitor
Félix-Faure
Falguière
MONTPARNASSE BIENVENUE
Boulogne-J. Jaurès
Pasteur
Exelmans
Boucicaut
Edgar-Quinet
Vavin
Bd Victor
Volontaires
Raspail
Pte de St-Cloud
Lourmel
Vaugirard
Gaîté
8
Pernéty
BALARD
DENFERT-ROCHEREAU
Marcel-Sembat
Convention
St-Jacques
Issy Val de Seine
Pte de Versailles
Billancourt
Mouton-Duvernet
Plaisance
Corentin-Celton
PONT DE SEVRES
9
12
River Seine
MAIRIE D'ISSY
Alésia
Pte de Vanves
RER B
Malakoff-Plateau de Vanves
4
PORTE D'ORLEANS
Issy
RER C
Malakoff-Rue Etienne Dolet
C5
C7
13
CHATILLON-MONTROUGE

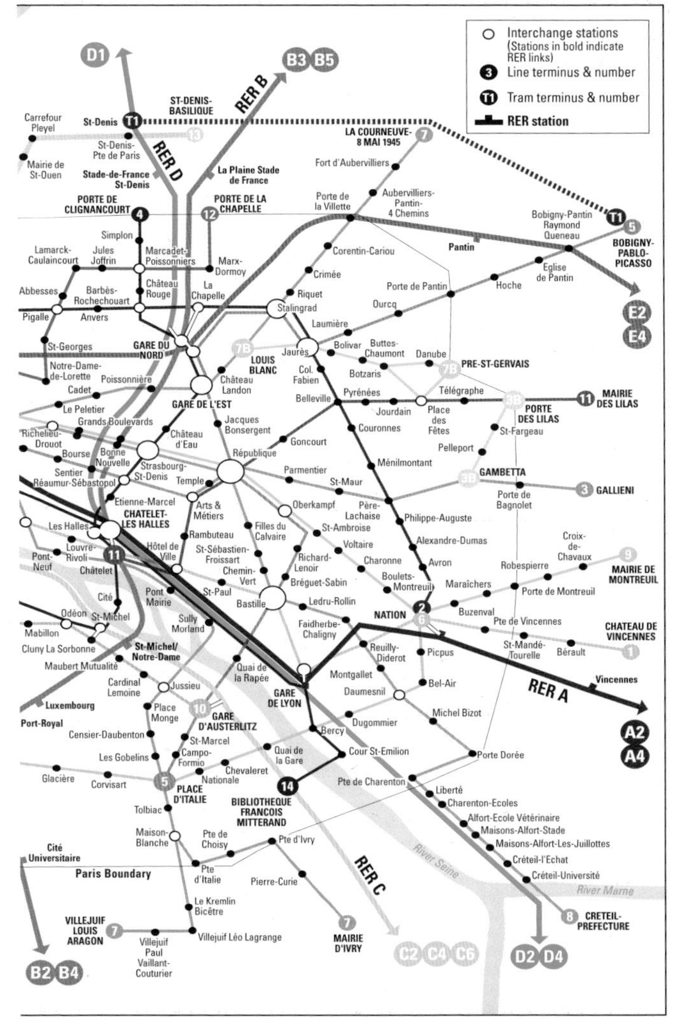

Interchange stations (Stations in bold indicate RER links)
Line terminus & number
Tram terminus & number
RER station
D1
B3 B5
RER B
RER D
ST-DENIS-BASILIQUE
St-Denis
Carrefour Pleyel
Mairie de St-Ouen
St-Denis-Pte de Paris
Stade-de-France St-Denis
La Plaine Stade de France
LA COURNEUVE-8 MAI 1945
Fort d'Aubervilliers
Aubervilliers-Pantin-4 Chemins
Porte de la Villette
PORTE DE CLIGNANCOURT
PORTE DE LA CHAPELLE
Bobigny-Pantin Raymond Queneau
BOBIGNY-PABLO-PICASSO
Pantin
Eglise de Pantin
Hoche
Porte de Pantin
Ourcq
Corentin-Cariou
Crimée
Riquet
Stalingrad
Laumière
Simplon
Lamarck-Caulaincourt
Jules Joffrin
Marcadet-Poissonniers
Marx-Dormoy
Château Rouge
La Chapelle
Abbesses
Barbès-Rochechouart
Pigalle
Anvers
St-Georges
GARE DU NORD
Jaurès
LOUIS BLANC
Bolivar
Buttes-Chaumont
Danube
PRE-ST-GERVAIS
Botzaris
Col. Fabien
E2
E4
Notre-Dame-de-Lorette
Poissonnière
Château Landon
Cadet
GARE DE L'EST
Belleville
Pyrénées
Télégraphe
MAIRIE DES LILAS
Jourdain
Place des Fêtes
PORTE DES LILAS
Le Peletier
Grands Boulevards
Richelieu-Drouot
Château d'Eau
Jacques Bonsergent
Couronnes
St-Fargeau
Goncourt
Pelleport
Bourse
Bonne Nouvelle
République
Ménilmontant
Sentier
Strasbourg-St-Denis
Réaumur-Sébastopol
Temple
Parmentier
GAMBETTA
St-Maur
GALLIENI
Porte de Bagnolet
Etienne-Marcel
CHATELET-LES HALLES
Arts & Métiers
Oberkampf
Père-Lachaise
Philippe-Auguste
Les Halles
Filles du Calvaire
St-Ambroise
Alexandre-Dumas
Rambuteau
Louvre-Rivoli
Hôtel de Ville
Voltaire
Pont-Neuf
Châtelet
St-Sébastien-Froissart
Richard-Lenoir
Charonne
Avron
Croix-de-Chavaux
Robespierre
MAIRIE DE MONTREUIL
Chemin-Vert
Bréguet-Sabin
Boulets-Montreuil
Maraîchers
Porte de Montreuil
Cité
Pont Marie
St-Paul
Bastille
Ledru-Rollin
NATION
Buzenval
Odéon
St-Michel
Sully Morland
Faidherbe-Chaligny
Pte de Vincennes
CHATEAU DE VINCENNES
Mabillon
Cluny La Sorbonne
St-Michel/Notre-Dame
Reuilly-Diderot
Picpus
St-Mandé-Tourelle
Bérault
Maubert Mutualité
Quai de la Rapée
Montgallet
Vincennes
Cardinal Lemoine
Jussieu
GARE DE LYON
Daumesnil
Bel-Air
RER A
Luxembourg
Place Monge
GARE D'AUSTERLITZ
Michel Bizot
Port-Royal
Censier-Daubenton
Dugommier
A2
A4
St-Marcel
Bercy
Les Gobelins
Campo-Formio
Quai de la Gare
Cour St-Emilion
Porte Dorée
Chevaleret
Glacière
Corvisart
Nationale
Pte de Charenton
PLACE D'ITALIE
BIBLIOTHEQUE FRANCOIS MITTERAND
Liberté
Tolbiac
Charenton-Ecoles
Alfort-Ecole Vétérinaire
Maisons-Alfort-Stade
Maison-Blanche
Pte de Choisy
Pte d'Ivry
Maisons-Alfort-Les-Juillottes
Cité Universitaire
RER C
Créteil-l'Echat
Paris Boundary
Pte d'Italie
River Seine
Créteil-Université
Pierre-Curie
River Marne
Le Kremlin Bicêtre
CRETEIL-PREFECTURE
VILLEJUIF LOUIS ARAGON
Villejuif Léo Lagrange
MAIRIE D'IVRY
Villejuif Paul Vaillant-Couturier
C2 C4 C6
D2 D4
B2 B4

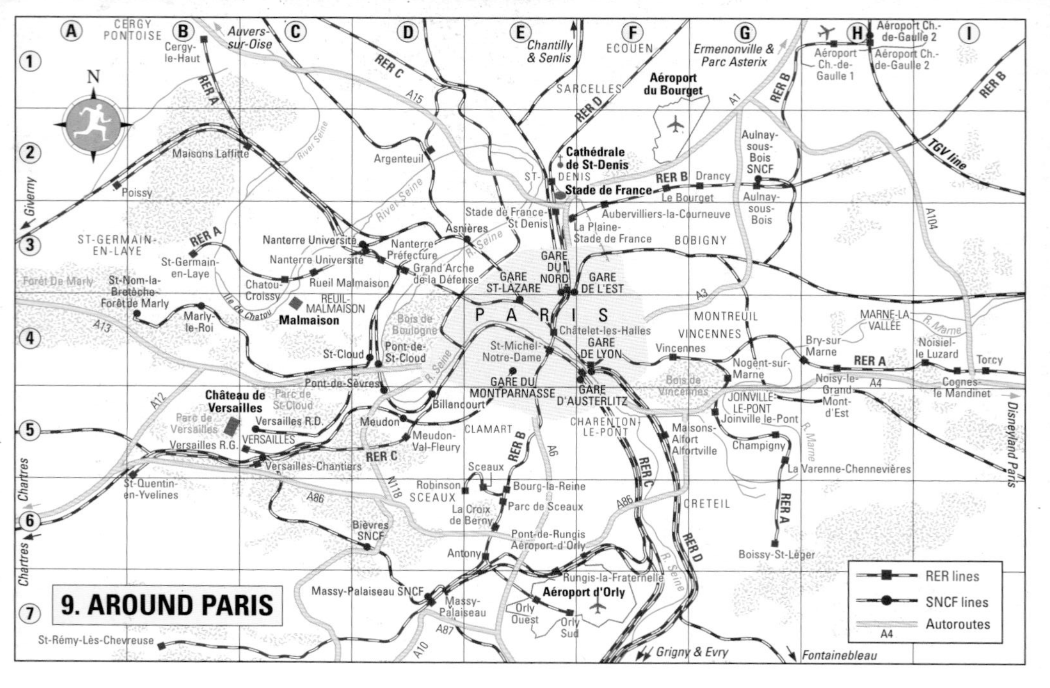
9. AROUND PARIS
RER lines
SNCF lines
Autoroutes
PARIS
Cergy-Pontoise
Cergy-le-Haut
Auvers-sur-Oise
Chantilly & Senlis
Ecouen
Ermenonville & Parc Asterix
Aéroport Ch.-de-Gaulle 1
Aéroport Ch.-de-Gaulle 2
Sarcelles
Aéroport du Bourget
Cathédrale de St-Denis
St-Denis
Stade de France
Maisons Laffitte
Poissy
Giverny
Argenteuil
Drancy
Le Bourget
Aulnay-sous-Bois SNCF
Aulnay-sous-Bois
TGV line
St-Germain-en-Laye
Nanterre Université
Nanterre Préfecture
Asnières
Stade de France-St Denis
La Plaine-Stade de France
Aubervilliers-la-Courneuve
Bobigny
Forêt De Marly
St-Nom-la-Bretèche-Forêt de Marly
Chatou-Croissy
Rueil Malmaison
Reuil-Malmaison
Malmaison
Ile de Chatou
Grand Arche de la Défense
Gare St-Lazare
Gare du Nord
Gare de l'Est
Marly-le-Roi
Bois de Boulogne
Châtelet-les-Halles
Montreuil
Vincennes
Marne-la-Vallée
R. Marne
St-Cloud
Pont-de-St-Cloud
St-Michel-Notre-Dame
Gare de Lyon
Bry-sur-Marne
Noisiel-le Luzard
Torcy
RER A
Nogent-sur-Marne
Noisy-le-Grand
Cognes-le Mandinet
Pont-de-Sèvres
Gare du Montparnasse
Gare d'Austerlitz
Bois de Vincennes
Joinville-le-Pont
Mont-d'Est
Disneyland Paris
Château de Versailles
Parc de St-Cloud
Parc de Versailles
Versailles R.D.
Versailles
Versailles R.G.
Versailles-Chantiers
Billancourt
Meudon
Meudon-Val-Fleury
Clamart
Charenton-le-Pont
Maisons-Alfort Alfortville
Champigny
La Varenne-Chennevières
RER B
RER C
RER D
Sceaux
Robinson
Bourg-la-Reine
Parc de Sceaux
La Croix de Berny
St-Quentin-en-Yvelines
Chartres
Bièvres SNCF
Pont-de-Rungis Aéroport-d'Orly
Antony
Creteil
Boissy-St-Léger
Massy-Palaiseau SNCF
Massy-Palaiseau
Rungis-la-Fraternelle
Aéroport d'Orly
Orly Ouest
Orly Sud
R. Seine
River Seine
St-Rémy-Lès-Chevreuse
Grigny & Evry
Fontainebleau
A1
A3
A4
A6
A10
A12
A13
A15
A86
A87
A104
N118